# CONTRACT AS ASSUMPTION

It has many times been said that contracts involve assumptions of obligation or liability, but what that means, and what it is that is assumed, have not often been discussed.

It is to further such discussion that some of the author's previously published writings around this subject have been brought together in this book. His basic premises are that contractual obligation and liability in this context are two sides to the same coin and that an assumption of one is an assumption of both. Parties are bound not because liability has been imposed upon them by law as a result of their having entered into a contract but because, in the act of assuming, they have imposed it upon themselves. Contract provides a facility the purpose of which is to enable this to be done within the limits prescribed by law.

The implication of these premises are much more significant than might be supposed when applied to such areas of contract as formation, consideration, intention to contract, exception clauses, privity and damages. The book concludes with a treatment of the role of assumption in tort.

Because of the importance of its subject matter and its wide-ranging treatment, this book should appeal not only to teachers and postgraduate students of contract but also to practitioners in the field and to anyone else with an interest in contract theory.

# Contract as Assumption

## Essays on a Theme

Brian Coote
Professor Emeritus of Law, The University of Auckland

edited and with a Preface
by

Rick Bigwood
Professor of Law, The University of Auckland

•HART•
PUBLISHING

OXFORD AND PORTLAND, OREGON
2010

Published in the United Kingdom by Hart Publishing Ltd
16C Worcester Place, Oxford, OX1 2JW
Telephone: +44 (0)1865 517530
Fax: +44 (0)1865 510710
E-mail: mail@hartpub.co.uk
Website: http://www.hartpub.co.uk

Published in North America (US and Canada) by
Hart Publishing
c/o International Specialized Book Services
920 NE 58th Avenue, Suite 300
Portland, OR 97213–3786
USA
Tel: +1 503 287 3093 or toll-free: (1) 800 944 6190
Fax: +1 503 280 8832
E-mail: orders@isbs.com
Website: http://www.isbs.com



British Library Cataloguing in Publication Data
Data Available

ISBN: 978-1-84946-029-3

Typeset by Columns Design Ltd, Reading
Printed and bound in Great Britain by
TJ International Ltd, Padstow, Cornwall

# Preface

I first approached Professor Emeritus Brian Coote in 2005, with a view to my preparing, in edited form, an anthology of some of his major writings in the field of contract law. The volume was to serve the dual purpose of recognising (and celebrating) Brian's long and distinguished career as a contract-law teacher-scholar in the Faculty of Law at the University of Auckland (1961–95), and of creating, for the benefit of fellow contract-law teachers and scholars, a compendious volume of Brian's writings on a theme for which he has become known not only in New Zealand but in the major jurisdictions of the Commonwealth as well: 'contract as assumption'.

Brian was at first, in typical fashion, modestly dismissive of the project. However, after some entreating on my part, he eventually came around and cooperated in selecting the pieces that now comprise the chapters of this—his—book. It has been a privilege for me to be involved in an instrumental and editorial way. Although I was never a student of Brian in the formal sense, despite my attending the Auckland Law School while he was Dean of Law and still teaching contract, I have from those early days been a dedicated pupil of his many and lucid writings in the field. I was initially directed to them by my own fine teacher of the subject, Francis Dawson, who was (and still is) a great admirer of Brian's work. Indeed, having read and re-read the pieces that now comprise the chapters of this book, I haven't stopped learning from Brian yet. His writing is elegant, coherent and precise without fuss.

As a matter of history, Brian was born in Cambridge, New Zealand, in 1929. He studied law at the (then) Auckland University College, graduating LLB in 1953. He qualified as a Solicitor of the Supreme (now High) Court of New Zealand in 1952, and as a Barrister of that Court in 1953, and graduated LLM in 1954 with First Class Honours. With the assistance of a University of New Zealand Travelling Scholarship in Law, he went to the University of Cambridge in 1956 to pursue a doctorate. His PhD was conferred in 1959, his thesis also being awarded the distinguished Yorke Prize. That thesis, a version of which was later to become his celebrated book *Exception Clauses* (London, Sweet & Maxwell, 1964), argued that, juristically, exception clauses function in a substantive and not merely procedural way: that instead of being mere shields to claims based on breach of accrued rights, exception clauses—a large class of them anyway—substantively help to define the rights (and correlative duties) themselves. The reader will see the core of that argument elaborated in chapter six of this book, but it is just one manifestation (or consequence) of Brian's theory of contract that is described and variously demonstrated in the other chapters as well. It was a view that was to prove influential in the House of Lords' rejection in 1966, and again in the late 1970s, of the so-called 'doctrine of fundamental breach'.

In 1961 Brian joined the Auckland Law Faculty as a Senior Lecturer and in 1966 was appointed to a Chair in Law, which he held until his retirement from the University at the end of January 1995. During his tenure as a Law Professor, he had several stints as Acting Dean of the Law Faculty (1969, 1977, 1983–4), and was the Dean of Law from 1984 to 1987. For 20 years he was an active member of the Contracts and Commercial Law Reform Committee, whose reports ultimately led to the legislative reform—indeed, sometimes radical reform—of many areas of contract and commercial law in New Zealand. Some of this legislation has served as a model for similar reforms in other legal systems, including Australia, Canada and the United Kingdom. Brian has continued, in his retirement, to write extensively in the domain of contract law, and some of the chapters in this book represent writings from his post-retirement era. (The reader will note an impressive and sustained consistency between his very early writings on contract, and his scholarly contributions to this very day, almost a half-century later!) He received a CBE in the 1995 New Year Honours list, and in 2007 was elected as an inaugural Fellow of the New Zealand Academy of the Humanities, for distinguished research achievement.

Just as I was never formally a student of Brian, I was never formally a colleague either (except that, technically, we overlapped by some 14 days after I took up my first academic position at the Auckland Law School and Brian retired from there). Still, he has always been generous toward me with his time and his advice (in both contract law and classical music), and I am grateful to have had an opportunity to repay him in a small way by lending my services to the production of this book. There can be no doubt, in my mind, that Brian is a leading figure in his academic discipline of contract law. He has helped to put New Zealand contract law and scholarship on the world map perhaps like no other New Zealand-based legal scholar in the twentieth century. Certainly, many fine legal scholars emanated from New Zealand during the same period, but virtually all of them earned their academic reputations as scholars in universities overseas. Brian, in contrast, managed to carve out his academic career from inside New Zealand's own borders, and his scholarship became internationally respected notwithstanding its author's relative geographic isolation. All this has advanced not only his personal reputation, but the Auckland Law Faculty's as well. Still, he remains unfailingly modest about the contributions he has made to his field and to the University of Auckland.

As to the content of this book, there is little that I need to say about it in this Preface. Brian has in chapter one, in prose much better than I could muster, compendiously summarised his theory and described its consequences, which are elaborated in detail through the successive chapters of this book.

Now, I am sure that Brian, who is essentially a positivist, worries that the theory on which he has based this book will be dismissed as 'formalist', which I take to be because his is a 'legalist' theory: while not mechanistic in its application, it is rooted, first and foremost, in formulations of positive law on the subject (and hence in the ancient craft-like traditions and benefits of the common-law legal method). This book presents a theory of contract *law* and does not purport to be a work of some other discipline such as art, economics, politics or philosophy. That, however, is surely not something to be concerned, and certainly not apologetic, about. A theory of contract law, if it is to stand any hope of general acceptance among academic lawyers and judges, must fit our experience of the existing legal concepts, principles, rules and practices of contract, and must of course be relatively stable. Formalism in this sense, it seems to me, while susceptible to incremental development and change, offers the virtue of stability that, so far at least, has not been forthcoming from alternative, 'realist' or instrumentalist accounts of contract. This is not to deny that a superior, non-formalist theory of contract might one day ascend to the throne, although I am myself sceptical that that will be any day soon. All of society's stable institutions, like the contract facility about which Brian writes in this book, reflect reasonable compromises that have had to be made at the political, ideological or moral level, given the insuperable circumstances of liberal constitutional democracies. That the 'classical' liberal conception of contract has proved so tenacious in the face of many years of critical assault by (mainly) critical-legal-scholar types is evidence that it might not be so easily dismissed, even as a mere place-holder pending the realisation of a more 'utopian' version of contract. In short, Brian has little to worry about if the worst feature of his theory is its formalism. Time may well ultimately disclose that to be its best feature.

Finally, in ending this Preface, it remains for me to thank two people—in addition, of course, to Brian himself, for his essential cooperation and assistance in seeing this book to fruition. First, Professor John Carter of the University of Sydney is to be acknowledged and thanked for his support of the project. Second, I am once again extremely grateful to Richard Hart of Hart Publishing for his generous spirit and open mind on the merits of a project that I have sent him.

Rick Bigwood
Auckland
1 August 2009

# Acknowledgements

Except for chapter one, the chapters in this book have been published elsewhere either in article or in book-chapter form. Each piece, however, has been edited and lightly modified for the purpose of their inclusion in this book. The author and editor wish to thank the publishers mentioned below for their permission to reproduce works in this book. Copyright in all of the reproduced works was retained by the author.

**Chapter two**: First published as Brian Coote, 'The Essence of Contract (Parts I and II)' (1988–89) 1 *Journal of Contract Law* 91–112 and 183–204. Reprinted with the permission of LexisNexis Australia.

**Chapter three**: First published as Brian Coote, 'Consideration and Benefit in Fact and in Law' (1990–91) 3 *Journal of Contract Law* 23–9. Reprinted with the permission of LexisNexis Australia.

**Chapter four**: First published as Brian Coote, 'Consideration and Variations: A Different Solution' (2004) 120 *Law Quarterly Review* 19–23. Reprinted with the permission of Sweet & Maxwell Ltd.

**Chapter five**: First published as Brian Coote, 'Consideration and the Joint Promisee' [1978] *Cambridge Law Journal* 301–12. Reprinted with the permission of Cambridge University Press.

**Chapter six**: First published as chapter one in Brian Coote, *Exception Clauses: Some Aspects of the Law Relating to Exception Clauses in Contracts for the Carriage, Bailment and Sale of Goods* (London, Sweet & Maxwell, 1964) 1–18. Reprinted with the permission of Sweet & Maxwell Ltd.

**Chapter seven**: First published as Brian Coote, 'The Second Rise and Fall of Fundamental Breach' (1981) 55 *Australian Law Journal* 788–803. Reprinted with the permission of Thomson Reuters.

**Chapter eight**: First published as Brian Coote, 'Contract Damages, *Ruxley*, and the Performance Interest' (1997) 56 *Cambridge Law Journal* 537–70. Reprinted with the permission of Cambridge University Press.

**Chapter nine**: First published as Brian Coote, 'The Performance Interest, *Panatown*, and the Problem of Loss' (2001) 117 *Law Quarterly Review* 81–95. Reprinted with the permission of Sweet & Maxwell Ltd.

**Chapter ten**: First published as Brian Coote, 'Contract Not Trust: Some Questions About the Contracts (Rights of Third Parties) Act From Another Perspective' (2006) 22 *Journal of Contract Law* 72–80. Reprinted with the permission of LexisNexis Australia.

**Chapter eleven**: First published as Brian Coote, 'Assumption of Responsibility and Pure Economic Loss in New Zealand' [2005] *New Zealand Law Review* 1–23. Reprinted with the permission of the Legal Research Foundation, New Zealand.

# Contents

*Preface* v
*Acknowledgements* ix
*Table of Cases* xv
*Table of Legislation* xxvii

**1. Introduction** 1

**2. The Essence of Contract** 7
Introduction 7
Textbook Definitions 10
Contract Theories 13
The Secret Paradox 24
The Failure of Traditional Contract Theories 28
The Reaction Against Classical Concepts of Contract 29
The Need for a More Inclusive Theory 37
A Suggested Solution to the 'Secret Paradox' 38
The Essence of a Contract 42
Some Consequences 42
The Contemporary Near-Contracts 47
Conclusion 50

**3. Consideration and Benefit in Fact and in Law** 53
The Facts 53
The Judgment 54
The Meaning of the Decision 56
An Explanation for the Decision 56
Bilateral Contracts 57
Unilateral Contracts 58
Conclusion 60

**4. Consideration and the Variation of Contracts: A Different Solution** 61

**5. Consideration and the Joint Promisee** 65
The Arguments for the Joint Promisee Principle 67
Two Fallacies 69
Joint Promisee as Promisor 74
Unilateral Contracts 75
Conclusion 76
Addendum 76

6. **The Function of Exception Clauses** 81
The Current Approach 81
Are Exception Clauses Substantive or Procedural In Their Effect? 83
Can the Parties to a Contract Create Rights Intended by Them to be Unenforceable? 84
A Different Approach Suggested 86
A Suggested Classification of Exception Clauses 88
The Interpretation of Exception Clauses In Relation to Their Function 90
Some Special Consequences of the Exception Form 92
Conclusions 95
Addendum 95

7. **The Second Rise and Fall of Fundamental Breach** 99
Discharge for Breach and Deviation Distinguished 100
The Function of Exception Clauses 105
The *Suisse Atlantique* Case 107
The Second Version of Fundamental Breach 109
The *Securicor* Case 115
The Significance of *Securicor* for the Future 119
Conclusion 125

8. **Contract Damages, *Ruxley*, and the Performance Interest** 127
The *Ruxley* case 128
A Basic Ambiguity in Contract Damages 130
Damages as Protection of the Performance Interest 130
Other Protections of the Performance Interest 132
Extending the Potential Inclusiveness of Performance Protection 133
The Compensation Principle 134
Reinstatement and Repair: Building Contracts 146
Difference in Value in Building Cases 147
Three Questions 149
The Place of General Damages 157
Summary and Conclusions 158
Addendum: Two Recent Cases 159

9. **The Performance Interest, *Panatown*, and the Problem of Loss** 165
The Arguments 166
The Problem of Characterisation 168
The Narrow Ground 169
The *Albazero* Exception 170
The Broad Ground 174
Who Suffered the Loss? 176
The Position Where Both Have Suffered Loss 178
Conclusion 179

**10. Contract not Trust: Some Questions About the Contracts (Rights of Third Parties) Act from Another Perspective** 181
Contract or Not? 182
A New Form of Contract? 184
The Availability of Equitable Remedies 186
Failure of Consideration 187
Defences Available to the Promisee 188
Conclusion 190

**11. Assumption of Responsibility and Pure Economic Loss in New Zealand** 191
Assumption of Legal Liability in Tort 193
Assumption of Non-Tort Obligation 203
Assumption of a Task 208
Conclusion 209

*Index* 211

# Table of Cases


A/S Awilco v Fulvia spA di Navigazione; The Chikuma [1981] 1 All ER 652 .............. 124
Addis v Gramophone Co Ltd [1909] AC 488 (HL) .............................................. 21
Aita v Silverstone Towers Ltd (1978) 86 DLR (3d) 439 ...................................... 112
AKAS Jamal v Moolla Dawood Sons & Co [1916] 1 AC 175 (PC) ........................ 139
Al-Kandari v JR Brown & Co [1987] QB 514 (CA) ............................................ 48
Albazero, The [1977] AC 744 (HL) ................................................ 142, 166, 169–173, 175
Albion, The [1953] 1 WLR 1026 (CA) .................................................... 85, 103
Alexander Stephen (Forth) Ltd v JJ Riley (UK) Ltd, 1976 SLT 269 .......................... 114
Alexander v Railway Executive [1951] 2 KB 882 (KBD) ...................................... 102
Alfred McAlpine Construction Ltd v Panatown Ltd [2000] 3 WLR 946 (HL) .............. 4, 165–179
Aliakmon, The [1986] AC 785 (HL) ................................................................ 9
Allied Finance & Investments Ltd v Haddow & Co [1983] NZLR 22 ........................ 199
Amalgamated Investment and Property Ltd v Texas Commerce International Bank Ltd [1982] QB 84 (CA) ................................................................ 10
Anglia Television Ltd v Reed [1972] 1 QB 60 (CA) ........................................ 157
Anglo-Continental Holidays Ltd v Typaldos Lines (London) Ltd [1967] 2 Lloyd's Rep 61 (CA) ................................................................ 109
Anns v Merton London Borough Council [1978] AC 728 (HL) ................ 9, 48, 191, 209
Antons Trawling Co Ltd v Smith [2003] 2 NZLR 23 (CA) ........................ 61–63, 184, 199
Appleby v Meyers (1867) LR 2 CP 651 ............................................................ 140
Applegate v Moss [1971] 1 QB 406 (CA) ........................................................ 148
Appleson v Littlewood [1939] 1 All ER 464 (CA) ............................................ 89
Arden v Tacker (1833) 4 B & Ad 815 ................................................................ 74
Arrow Transfer Co Ltd v Royal Bank of Canada (1971) 19 DLR (3d) 420; (1972) 27 DLR (3d) 420; (1972) 27 DLR (3d) 81 ................................................................ 107
Arthur White (Contractor) Ltd v Tarmac Civil Engineering Ltd [1967] 1 WLR 1508 (HL) ................................................................ 109
Ashby v Tolhurst [1937] 2 KB 242 (CA) .......................................................... 92
Ashington Piggeries Ltd v Christopher Hill Ltd [1972] AC 441 (HL) .................. 108, 134
Atkinson v Ritchie (1809) 10 East 530 ............................................................ 95
Atlantic Shipping & Trading Co Ltd v Louis Dreyfus & Co [1922] 2 AC 250 (HL) ..... 84, 103
Attica Sea Carriers Corp v Ferrostaal [1976] 1 Lloyd's Rep 250 (CA) .................. 156
Attorney-General for England and Wales v R [2002] 2 NZLR 91 (CA) .................. 62
Attorney-General of Hong Kong v Reid [1994] 1 NZLR 1; [1994] 1 AC 324 (PC) ..... 154
Attorney-General v Carter [2003] 2 NZLR 160 (CA) ...................................... 192–193
Attwood v Banks (1839) 2 Beav 192 ................................................................ 71
Auburn Municipal Council v Arc Engineering [1973] 1 NSWLR 513 ...................... 127
Auckland Gas Co v Farnsworth Galvanisers (1970) (unrep) ................................ 114
Auditor, The (1924) 18 Ll LR 464 (Ch) 468 ...................................................... 89

Australian Woollen Mills Pty Ltd v The Commonwealth (1954) 92 CLR 424 (High Court of Australia) .......... 41

Baltic Shipping Co v Dillon (1993) 176 CLR 344 .......... 154, 188
Banbury v Bank of Montreal [1918] AC 626 (HL) .......... 209
Bank of Montreal v Stuart [1911] AC 120 (PC) .......... 195
Barry v Davies [2000] 1 WLR 1962 (CA) .......... 76, 78
Basham, Re [1986] 1 WLR 1498 (Ch) .......... 10
Bata v City Parking Canada Ltd (1974) 13 DLR (3d) 190 .......... 107
Beach v Reed Corrugated Cases Ltd [1956] 1 WLR 807 (QBD) .......... 138
Beaufort Realties (1964) Inc and Belcourt Construction (Ottawa) Ltd v Chomedy Aluminium Co Ltd (1980) 116 DLR (3d) 193 .......... 36, 121
Beck v Szymanowski [1924] AC 43 (HL) .......... 92
Becker, Gray and Co v London Assurance Corp [1918] AC 101 (HL) .......... 40
Bellgrove v Eldridge (1954) 90 CLR 613 (High Court of Australia) ..... 147, 152, 154, 163
Belvoir Finance Co Ltd v Stapleton [1971] 1 QB 210 (CA) .......... 44
Beswick v Beswick [1968] AC 58 .......... 137
Bevan Investments Ltd v Blackhall & Struthers [1978] 2 NZLR 97 .......... 127
BG Linton Construction Ltd v Canadian National Railway Co (1974) 49 DLR (3d) 548 .......... 107, 112, 114
BG Transport Service Ltd v Marston Motor Co Ltd [1970] 1 Lloyd's Rep 371 (QBD) .......... 109
Blackwood v Andre 1947 SC 333 .......... 138
Blake v Galloway [2004] 1 WLR 2844 (CA) .......... 194
BP v Hunt (No 2) [1979] 1 WLR 783 (QBD .......... 140
Bremer Handels GmbH v Vanden-AvenneIzegem PVBA [1978] 2 Lloyd's Rep 109 (HL) .......... 119
British and Benningtons Ltd v NW Cachar Tea Co [1923] AC 48 (HL) .......... 61
British Crane Hire Contractors Ltd v Ipswich Plant Hire Ltd [1975] 1 QB 303 (CA) .......... 109
British Transport Commission v Gourley [1956] AC 185 (HL) .......... 133, 138–139
British Westinghouse v Underground Electric Railways [1912] AC 673 (HL) .......... 135
Brooke v Pickwick (1827) 4 Bing 219 .......... 89
Brown v Bristol & Exeter Railway Co (1861) 4 LT 830 .......... 85
Brownie Wills v Shrimpton [1998] 2 NZLR 320 .......... 191, 204, 208
Browning v Elmslie (1790) 7 TR 216 .......... 95
Brownlie v Campbell (1880) 5 App Cas 925 .......... 206
Buchanan v Parnshaw (1788) 2 Term Rep 745 .......... 89
Bunge Corporation v Tradax [1981] 1 WLR 711 (HL) .......... 133
Burrowes v Lock (1805) 10 Ves Jun 470; 32 ER 927 .......... 205
Bywater v Richardson (1834) 1 Ad & E 508 .......... 89

C Czarnikow Ltd v Koufos [1966] 2 QB 695 (CA) .......... 106–107, 112, 118, 131
Calico Printers v Barclays Bank (1930) 36 Com Cas 197 (CA) .......... 85
Canada Atlantic v Eilers (1929) 35 Com Cas 90 (KBD) .......... 95
Cann v Willson (1888) 39 Ch D 39 .......... 195
Caparo Industries plc v Dickman [1990] 2 AC 605 (HL) .......... 191, 202, 208–209
Captain v Far Eastern Steamship Co (1978) 97 DLR (3d) 250 .......... 114

Carlill v Carbolic Smoke Ball Co [1893] 1 QB 256 (CA) ........ 77–78
Carosella v Ginos (1981) 46 LGRA 51 ........ 136, 151
Central London Property Trust Ltd v High Trees House Ltd [1947] 1 KB 130 (KBD) ........ 48–49
Chandris v Isbrandtsen-Moller Co Inc [1951] 1 KB 240 (CA) ........ 102
Chappell & Co Ltd v Nestle Co Ltd [1960] AC 87 (HL) ........ 18
Charterhouse Credit Co Ltd v Tolly [1963] 2 QB 683 (CA) ........ 110, 117, 121
Chomedy Aluminium Co Ltd Ltd v Belcourt Construction (Ottawa) Ltd (1979) 97 DLR (3d) 170 ........ 36, 113
Clarke v Gray (1805) 6 East 564 ........ 89
Coggs v Bernard (1703) 2 Ld Raym 909; 92 ER 107 ........ 94, 102, 208
Colyear v Mulgrave (1836) 2 Keen 81 ........ 65
Commissioner of State Revenue (Victoria) v Royal Insurance Australia Ltd (1994) 182 CLR 51 (High Court of Australia) ........ 152
Commissioner of Taxation of the Commonwealth of Australia v Sara Lee Household and Body Care (Australia) Pty Ltd (2000) 201 CLR 520 ........ 61
Connell v Odlum [1993] 2 NZLR 257 ........ 191
Conquest v Ebbetts [1895] 2 Ch 377 (CA); [1896] AC 490 (HL) ........ 143–144
Cooke v Rowe [1950] NZLR 410 ........ 139
Cooper v Stuart (1889) 14 App Cas 289 (HL) ........ 95
Cornish v Midland Bank [1985] 3 All ER 513 (CA) ........ 208
Cotton v Wallis [1955] 1 WLR 1168 (CA) ........ 148
Coulls v Bagot's Executor and Trustee Co Ltd (1967) 119 CLR 460 (High Court of Australia) ........ 4, 46, 65, 68, 71–74, 76, 137, 141, 186
Council of the City of Sydney v West (1965) 114 CLR 481 (High Court of Australia) ........ 99, 107, 114
Coupar Transport v Smith's (Acton) Ltd [1959] 1 Lloyd's Rep 369 (QBD) ........ 87
CR Taylor (Wholesale) Ltd v Hepworths [1997] 1 WLR 659 (QBD) ........ 148, 150
Crabb v Arun District Council [1976] Ch 179 (CA) ........ 10
Craig v East Coast Bays City Council [1986] 1 NZLR 99 (CA) ........ 48
Cunningham v Insinger [1924] 2 DLR 433 ........ 135
Curran v Northern Ireland Co-ownership Housing Assn Ltd [1987] AC 718 (HL NI) .. 9
Currie v Misa (1875) LR 10 Exch 153 ........ 57
Czarnikow v Roth Schmidt [1922] 2 KB 478 (CA) ........ 89, 112, 118

Dann v Hamilton [1939] 1 KB 509 (KBD) ........ 87
Darlington BC v Wiltshire Northern Ltd [1995] 1 WLR 68 (CA) ........ 132, 141–142, 149, 152, 166
Daulia Ltd v Four Millbank Nominees Ltd [1978] Ch 231 (CA) ........ 77
Davidson v Three Spruces Realty Ltd (1977) 79 DLR (3d) 481 ........ 114
Davies v Collins [1945] 1 All ER 247 (CA) ........ 87
Davis v Commissioner for Main Roads (1968) 41 ALJR 322 (High Court of Australia) ........ 109
Davis v Garrett (1830) 6 Bing 716; 130 ER 1456 ........ 101
De Cesare v Deluxe Motors Pty Ltd (1996) 67 SASR 28 (FCSA) ........ 152
de Mattos v Gibson (1859) 4 De G & J 276 ........ 86
Deacon v Gridley (1854) 15 CB 295; 139 ER 436 ........ 45
Dean v Ainley [1987] 1 WLR 1729 (CA) ........ 152

Derry v Peek (1889) 14 App Cas 337 (HL) .... 206
Devonport Borough Council v Robins [1979] 1 NZLR 1 .... 114
Dickinson v Del Solar [1930] 1 KB 376 (KBD) .... 84
Dodd Property (Kent) Ltd v Canterbury CC [1980] 1 WLR 433 (CA) .... 136
Doe & Worcester School Trustees v Rowlands (1841) 9 C & P 734; 173 ER 1030 .... 144
Duff Development Co v Government of Kelantan [1924] AC 797 (HL) .... 84
Dunlop Pneumatic Tyre Co Ltd v Selfridge & Co Ltd [1915] AC 847 (HL) .... 57, 65, 68–70
Dunlop v Lambert (l839) 6 Cl & F 600; 7 ER 824 .... 142, 166–173, 176–179

E Clemens Horst v Norfolk & NASN Co (1906) 11 Com Cas 141 .... 81, 91
East Ham Corporation n v Bernard Sunley & Sons Ltd [1966] AC 406 (HL) .... 132–133, 148
East West Corp v DKBS A/S [2003] QB 1509 (CA) .... 209
Edgeworth Constructions Ltd v ND Lea & Associates Ltd (1993) 107 DLR (4th) 169 (SCC) .... 193, 198
Elder, Dempster v Paterson, Zochonis [1924] AC 522 (HL) .... 96
Elliott v Royal Exchange Assurance Co (1867) LR 2 Ex 237 .... 85
Ellis v Turner (1800) 5 TR 531; 101 ER 1529 .... 101
Esso Petroleum Co Ltd v Mardon [1976] QB 801 (CA) .... 9
Evans Products Ltd v Crest Warehousing Ltd (1979) 95 DLR (3d) 631 .... 114
Evans v Balog [1976] 1 NSWLR 36 .... 136, 147–148
Evans v Bicknell (1801) 6 Ves Jun 174; 31 ER 998 .... 205

Fairholme v Firth & Brown Ltd (1933) 149 LT 332 .... 138
Farnworth Finance Facilities Ltd v Attryde [1970] 1 WLR 1053 (CA) .... 112
Fibrosa Spolka Akcyjna v Fairbairn Lawson Combe Barbour Ltd [1943] AC 32 (HL) . 69
Firestone Tyre Co v Vokins [1951] 1 Lloyd's Rep 32 (KBD) .... 85, 92, 94
Fleming v Bank of New Zealand Ltd [1900] AC 577 (PC) .... 67, 69–71
Fletcher v Fletcher (1844) 4 Hare 67 .... 11
Foakes v Beer (1884) 9 App Cas 605 (HL) .... 54, 59
Ford v Beech (1848) 11 QB 852 .... 85
Foreman v Federal SN Co [1928] 2 KB 424 (KBD) .... 92
Forward v Pittard (1785) 1 TR 27 .... 94
Furnivall v Coombes (1843) 5 Man & G 736 .... 85

Gale v Gale (1877) 6 Ch D 144 (Ch) .... 187
Gallaher Ltd v British Road Services Ltd [1974] 2 Lloyd's Rep 440 (QBD) . 109, 114, 119
Garnham, Harris & Elton Ltd v Alfred W Ellis (Transport) Ltd [1967] 1 WLR 940 (QBD) .... 109
Gartside v Sheffield Young & Ellis [1983] NZLR 37 (CA) .... 9, 35, 48, 137
George Wimpey & Co Ltd v Territory Enterprises Pty Ltd (1970) 45 ALJR 38 (High Court of Australia) .... 107
Gillette Industries Ltd v WH Martin Ltd [1966] 1 Lloyd's Rep 57 (CA) .... 107
Glasbrook Brothers Ltd v Glamorgan County Council [1925] AC 270 (HL) .... 45
Gold v Essex County Council [1942] 2 KB 293 (CA) .... 195
Grand Trunk Railway Co of Canada v Robinson [1915] AC 740 (JC) .... 87
Great Northern Railway Co v LEP Transport and Depository [1922] 2 KB 742 (CA) .. 92

Green v Russell [1959] 2 QB 226 (CA) .......... 71
Grein v Imperial Airways [1937] 1 KB 50 (CA) 87 .......... 87, 89
Guarantee Trust of Jersey Ltd v Gardner (1973) 117 SJ 564 (CA) .......... 114
Gulbenkian's Settlements, In re [1970] AC 508 (HL) .......... 119
GW Atkins Ltd v Scott (1980) 7 Construction Law Journal 125 (CA) .......... 148, 156

H & B Van Der Sterren v Cibernetics (Holdings) Pty Ltd (1970) 44 ALJR 157 (High Court of Australia) .......... 109
H Dakin & Co Ltd v Lee [1916] 1 KB 566 (CA) .......... 133, 138, 146
Hadley v Baxendale (1854) 9 Exch 341; 156 ER 145 .......... 127, 130, 157, 160–161
Hadoplane Pty Ltd v Edward Rushton Pty Ltd [1996] 1 Qd R 156 .......... 137
Hain Steamship Co Ltd v Tate & Lyle Ltd [1936] 2 All ER 597 (HL) ... 100–103, 110, 121
Hall v Cazenove (1804) 4 East 477 .......... 74
Hall v Queensland Truck Centre [1970] Qd R 231 .......... 114
Hamlin v The Great Northern Railway Co (1856) 1 H & N 408, ER 1261 .......... 21
Hannah Blumenthal, The [1983] 1 AC 854 (HL) .......... 49
Harbutt's 'Plasticine' Ltd v Wayne Tank and Pump Co Ltd [1970] 1 QB 447 (CA) .... 99, 108–110, 112, 114, 116–118, 121–122, 127, 139, 147
Hardwick Game Farm v Suffolk Agricultural & Poultry Producers Association [1966] 1 WLR 287 (CA) .......... 106–107, 112, 118
Harris v Wyre Forest District Council [1988] 1 QB 835 (CA) .......... 193, 198
Hawkes Bay & East Coast Aero Club Inc v McLeod [1972] NZLR 289 .......... 109
Heaven v Pender (1883) 11 QBD 503 (CA) .......... 194
Hedley Byrne & Co Ltd v Heller & Partners Ltd [1964] AC 465 (HL) ...... 4, 9–10, 48, 91, 95, 136, 161, 191–192, 194–200, 202–209
Heffron v Imperial Parking Co (1974) 46 DLR (3d) 642 .......... 113
Henderson v Merrett Syndicates Ltd [1995] 2 AC 145 (HL) .......... 142, 191–192, 200
Henderson v Stevenson (1875) LR 2 Sc & Div 470 (HL) .......... 85
Henderson v Thorn [1893] 2 QB 164 (QB) .......... 150
Heyman v Darwins [1942] AC 356 (HL) .......... 83–84, 100–102, 117–118, 122–124
Hill v Van Erp (1997) 71 ALJR 487 (High Court of Australia) .......... 137, 195, 201
Hollebone v Midhurst & Fernhurst Builders Ltd [1968] 1 Lloyd's Rep 38 (QBD) ..... 136, 147
Hollier v Rambler Motors (AMC) Ltd [1972] 2 QB 71 (CA) .......... 119
Homburg Hout Import BV v Agrosin Private Ltd [2004] 1 AC 715 (HL) .......... 184–186
Honeybun v Harris [1995] 1 NZLR 64 .......... 153
Hong Kong Fir Shipping Co Ltd v Kawasaki Kisen Kaisha Ltd [1962] 2 QB 26 (CA) .......... 104, 121
Hood v Anchor Line [1918] AC 837 (HL Sc) .......... 87
Horsburgh v NZ Meat Processors Union [1988] 1 NZLR 698 .......... 133
Hotchkiss v National City Bank, 200 Fed 287, 293 (1911) .......... 20
Houghton Main Colliery Ltd, Re [1956] 1 WLR 1219 (Ch) .......... 138
Howard Marine & Dredging Co Ltd v A Ogden & Sons (Excavating) Ltd [1978] 1 QB 574 (CA) .......... 120
Hughes v Great Western Railway Co (1854) 14 CB 637 .......... 85
Hunt v Severs [1994] 2 AC 350 (HL) .......... 142
Hurst v Evans [1917] 1 KB 352 (KBD) .......... 94
Hyundai Heavy Industries Co Ltd v Papadopoulos [1980] 1 WLR 1129 (HL) .... 101, 124

Imodco Ltd v Wimpey Major Projects Ltd (1987) 40 BLR 1 (CA) .............................. 151
Inderwick v Leech (1885) 1 TLR 484 .............................................................................. 143
Insurance Commissioner v Joyce (1948) 77 CLR 39 (High Court of Australia) ........... 87
Istros v Dahlstroem [1931] 1 KB 247 (KBD) ...................................................... 81, 87, 91

J Dykes Ltd v Littlewoods Mail Order Stores Ltd, 1982 SC (HL) 157 ......................... 165
J Evans & Son (Portsmouth) Ltd v Andrea Merzario Ltd [1976] 1 WLR 1078 (CA) .. 114
Jackson v Horizon Holidays Ltd [1975] 1 WLR 1468 (CA) ................................. 155, 174
Jacob & Youngs v Kent 129 NE 889, 891 (1921) ........................................................... 149
Jaensch v Coffey (1984) 155 CLR 549 (High Court of Australia) ..................................... 9
James v Hutton and Cook Ltd [1950] 1 KB 9 (CA) .............................. 131, 135, 150–151
James v Thomas H Kent & Co [1951] 1 KB 551 (CA) ...................................................... 84
Jarvis v Swans Tours [1973] QB 233 (CA) ............................................................ 154–155
John Fox (a Firm) v Bannister, King & Rigbeys (Note) [1988] QB 925 (CA) ............. 199
Johnson v Agnew [1980] AC 367 (HL) .................................................................. 123, 133
Johnson v Ocean Accident and Guarantee Corporation Ltd (1915) 34 NZLR 358 ....... 71
Jones v Bright (1829) 5 Bing 533 ..................................................................................... 195
Jones v Stroud District Council [1986] 1 WLR 1141 (CA) .......................................... 151
Jones v Vernon's Pools ols [1938] 2 All ER 626 ................................................................ 89
Joseph v Knox (1813) 3 Camp 320 ................................................................................ 166
Joyner v Weeks [1891] 2 QB 31 (CA) ............................................ 132, 143–146, 151, 163
Jthell v Beane (1749) 1 Ves Sen 215 ............................................................................... 187
Junior Books Ltd v Veitchi Ltd [1983] 1 AC 520 (HL) .................................................. 9, 48

Kahan v Pakistan Federation [1951] 2 KB 1003 (CA) ..................................................... 84
Karsales v Wallis [1956] 1 WLR 936 (CA) .......................................... 81, 90, 103, 105
Kelner v Baxter (1866) LR 2 CP 174 .................................................................................. 85
Kelsall v Tyler (1856) 11 Ex 513 ........................................................................................ 85
Kenyon, Son & Craven Ltd v Baxter Hoare & Co Ltd [1971] 1 WLR 519 (QBD) ...... 107, 109, 111, 113
Kepong Prospecting Ltd v Schmidt [1968] AC 810 (PC) ................................................ 68
Keppel Bus Co Ltd v Sa'ad bin Ahman [1974] 1 WLR 1082 (JC) ................................ 115
Kirwan v Kirwan (1834) 2 C & M 617 ............................................................................. 72
Kleinwort Benson Ltd v Glasgow City Council [1996] QB 678 (CA) .......................... 131
Kondis v State Transport Authority (1984) 154 CLR 672 (High Court of Australia) .. 206
Koufos v C Czarnikow Ltd [1969] 1 AC 350 (HL) ................................................ 127, 160

Lane v Cotton (1701) 12 Mod 472 ...................................................................................... 94
Langley v Brown (1828) 1 Moo & P 583; 6 LJ (OS) CP 139 .......................................... 89
Lee v Shermans Pools [1951] WN 70 (CA) ........................................................................ 89
Leroux v Brown (1852) 12 CB 801 .................................................................................... 84
Levison v Patent Steam Carpet Cleaning Co Ltd [1978] QB 68 (CA) ................. 111, 120
Lilley v Doubleday (1881) LR 7 QBD 510 (QBD) .......................................................... 101
Linden Gardens Trust Ltd v Lenesta Sludge Disposals Ltd [1994] 1 AC 85 (HL) ...... 127, 132, 141–142, 151, 158, 166, 169–170, 172, 179
Livingstone v Rawyards Coal Co (1880) 5 App Cas 25 (HL) ....................... 134–135, 141
Lloyd (Doe d.) v Bennett (1837) 8 C & P 124 ................................................................... 11
Lockett v Charles [1938] 4 All ER 170 (KBD) ...................................................... 67–68, 70

Lockhart v Barnard (1845) 14 M & W 674 .......... 75
London Drugs Ltd v Kuehne & Nagel International Ltd [1992] 3 SCR 299 .. 63, 184, 198
London Graving Dock v Horton [1951] AC 737 (HL) .......... 87
Low v Bouverie (1891) 3 Ch 82 .......... 206
Lowns v Woods (1996) Aust Torts Reports 81–376 .......... 204
Lyth v Ault (1852) 7 Ex 669 .......... 72

McEvoy v Belfast Banking Co Ltd [1935] AC 24 (HL) .......... 67, 73
McFarlane v Tayside Health Board [2000] 2 AC 59 (HL) .......... 198, 207
McGarry v Richards, Ackroyd & Gall Ltd [1954] 2 DLR 367 .......... 135, 148, 150
Machirus Properties Ltd v Power Sports World (1987) Ltd (1999) 4 NZ Conv C 193,066 (High Court of New Zealand) .......... 79
McKinnon v Acadian Lines Ltd (1977) 81 DLR (3d) 480 .......... 114
McRae v Commonwealth Disposals Commission (1951) 84 CLR 377 (High Court of Australia) .......... 46, 74
McRobertson Miller Airline Services v Commissioner of State Taxation (Western Australia) (1975) 133 CLR 125 (High Court of Australia) .......... 107, 112
Maddison v Alderson (1883) 8 App Cas 467 (HL) .......... 84
Manchester, Sheffield, and Lincolnshire Railway v Brown (1883) 8 App Cas 703 (HL) .......... 87
Maori Trustee v Rogross Farms Ltd [1994] 3 NZLR 410 .......... 133, 145–146
Maratha Envoy, The [1978] AC 1 (HL) .......... 139
Mayfair Photographic Supplies s (London) Ltd v Baxter Hoare & Co Ltd [1972] 1 Lloyd's Rep 410 (QBD) .......... 116
Meates v Attorney-General [1983] NZLR 308 (CA) .......... 9, 48
Mendelssohn v Normand Ltd [1970] 1 QB 177 (CA) .......... 109
Mertens v Home Freeholds Co [1921] 2 KB 526 (CA) .......... 147
Mesnard v Aldridge (1801) 3 Esp 271 .......... 89
Metcalfe v London, Brighton & South Coast Railway Co (1858) 4 CBNS 307 .......... 67, 70
Metrotex Pty Ltd v Freight Investments Pty Ltd [1969] VR 9 .......... 112
Midland Bank Trust Co Ltd v Hett, Stubbs & Kemp [1979] Ch 384 (Ch) .......... 9
Midland Silicones v Scruttons [1962] AC 446 (HL) .......... 87, 96, 123, 140
Mihalis Angelos, The [1971] 1 QB 164 (CA) .......... 111
Mills v Fowkes (1839) 5 Bing NC 455 .......... 84
Ministry of Housing v Sharp [1970] 2 QB 223 (CA) .......... 205
Moon Trustee v Bolton [1971] NZLR 226 .......... 150
Morley v Attenborough (1849) 3 Ex 500; 154 ER 943 .......... 105
Morris v CW Martin & Sons Ltd [1966] 1 QB 716 (CA) .......... 115
Moschi v LEP Air Services Ltd [1973] AC 331 (HL) .......... 101, 106, 111, 117–118
Mulji v Cheong Yue Steamship Co Ltd [1926] AC 497 (PC) .......... 100
Mummelly v Calcon Ltd [1978] IR 387 .......... 132
Munro Brice & Co v War Risks Association [1918] 2 KB 78 (KBD); [1920] 3 KB 94 (CA) .......... 94
Murphy v Brentwood District Council [1991] AC 398 (HL) .......... 171, 177
Murray v Sperry Rand Corporation (1979) 96 DLR (3d) 113 .......... 114
Mutual Life & Citizens' Assurance Co Ltd v Evatt (1968) 122 CLR 556 (High Court of Australia); [1971] AC 793 (PC) .......... 197–198, 203, 208–209

New York Central Railroad v Lockwood (1873) 86 US (17 Wall) 357 .......... 34
Newton Abbot Development Ltd v Stockman Bros (1931) 47 TLR 616 .......... 148
Nocton v Lord Ashburton [1914] AC 932 (HL) .......... 195
Nu West Homes Ltd v Thunderbird Petroleums Ltd (1975) 59 DLR (3d) 292 ... 148–149
NZ Shipping Co Ltd v AM Satterthwaite & Co Ltd (The Eurymedon) [1975] AC 154 (PC); [1974] 1 NZLR 505 .......... 24, 45, 66, 70, 109, 122–124
NZ Wholesale Groceries v Hewin [1982] 2 NZLR 176 .......... 133

Olley v Marlborough Court Ltd [1949] 1 KB 532 (CA) .......... 67, 70, 92

Pacific Associates Inc v Baxter [1990] 1 QB 993 (CA) .......... 197
Pantalone v Alouie (1989) 18 NSWLR 119 .......... 132
Pao On v Lau Yiu Long [1980] AC 614 (PC) .......... 24, 45
Paramatta CC v Lutz (1988) 12 NSWLR 293 .......... 132, 136, 147
Parsons v BNM Laboratories Ltd [1964] 1 QB 95 (CA) .......... 138
Peabody Fund v Sir Lindsay Parkinson Ltd [1985] AC 210 (HL) .......... 9
Pearson-Burleigh Ltd v Pioneer Grain Co Ltd [1933] 1 WWR 179 .......... 146
Peek v Derry (1887) 37 Ch D 541 (CA) .......... 206
Peek v Gurney (1871) 13 LR Eq 79 .......... 206
Pell v Shearman (1855) 10 Ex 766; 156 ER 650 .......... 130
Perry v Sidney Phillips & Son [1982] 1 WLR 1297 (CA) .......... 136, 148
Phelps v Hillingdon London Borough Council [2001] 2 AC 619 (HL) .......... 205
Photo Production Ltd v Securicor (Transport) Ltd [1978] 1 WLR 856; [1978] 3 All ER 146 (CA); [1980] AC 827 (HL) . 99, 106–107, 109, 111, 113, 115–121, 123–124, 134
Pinnock v Lewis & Peat Ltd [1923] 1 KB 690 (KBD) .......... 103
Port Jackson Stevedoring Pty Ltd v Salmond & Spraggon (Australia) Pty Ltd (1980) 54 ALJR 552 (PC) .......... 122, 124
Power v Wells (1778) 2 Cowp 818 .......... 195
Price v Easton (1833) 4 B & Ad 433 .......... 65
Price Waterhouse v Kwan [2000] 3 NZLR 39 .......... 200–201

R (in Right of the Province of Ontario) v Jennings (1966) 57 DLR (2d) 644 .......... 133
R v Ward Ltd v Bignall [1967] 1 QB 534 (CA) .......... 118
Radford v De Froberville [1977] 1 WLR 1262 (Ch) ....... 133, 148, 150–151, 162–163, 174
Ramsay v Larsen (1964) 111 CLR 16 .......... 208
Rasbora Ltd v JC Marine Ltd [1977] 1 Lloyd's Rep 645 (QBD) .......... 114
Reeman v Department of Transport [1997] 2 Lloyd's Rep 648 (CA) .......... 198
Reid v Rush & Tompkins Group plc [1990] 1 WLR 212 (CA) .......... 208
Rendall v Arcos (1937) 43 Com Cas 1 (HL) .......... 89, 102
Renton v Palmyra [1956] 1 QB 462 (CA) .......... 82
Ribeiro v Canadian Imperial Bank of Commerce (1989) 67 OR (2d) 385 .......... 139
RM Turton & Co Ltd v Kerslake & Partners [2000] 3 NZLR 406 .......... 192
Robinson v Harman (1848) 1 Exch 850; 154 ER 363 .......... 130, 162
Rolls Royce NZ Ltd v Carter Holt Harvey Ltd CA 259/02, 23 June 2004 .......... 192, 198
Rose and Frank v Compton & Bros [1925] AC 445 (HL) .......... 85, 89, 105, 112
Rosin and Turpentine Export v Jacobs (1909) 14 Com Cas 247 (CA) .......... 85
Ross v Caunters [1980] Ch 297 (CA) .......... 9, 48, 137, 201
Rowling v Takaro Properties Ltd [1988] 2 WLR 418 (PC) .......... 9

Rozel, The [1994] 2 Lloyd's Rep 161 (QBD) .......... 131
Rust v Abbey Life Assurance Co Ltd [1979] 2 Lloyd's Rep 334 (CA) .......... 46
Ruxley Electronics and Construction Ltd v Forsyth [1994] 1 WLR 650 (CA); [1996] 1 AC 344 (HL) .......... 4, 127–134, 136, 138, 140–142, 144, 146–150, 152, 154–158, 160, 162–163, 167, 174
RW Green Ltd v Cade Bros Farms [1978] 1 Lloyd's Rep 602 (QBD) .......... 109, 113, 119
Ryons v Thomas [1986] IR 666 .......... 139

St Margaret's Rochester Burial Board v Thompson (1871) LR 6 CP 455 .......... 74
St Martin's Property Corporation v Sir Robert McAlpine Ltd *see* Linden Gardens Trust Ltd v Lenesta Sludge Disposals Ltd [1994] 1 AC 85 (HL)
Samson & Samson Ltd v Proctor [1975] 1 NZLR 655 .......... 153
Scarisbrick v Parkinson (1869) 20 LT 175 .......... 84
Scholtz v Thompson, 1996 (2) SA 409 .......... 129
Scott v Avery (1856) 8 Ex 487 .......... 85
Scott v Pattison [1923] 2 KB 723 (KBD) .......... 84
Sealace Shipping Co Ltd v Oceanvoice Ltd (The Alecos M) [1990] 1 Lloyd's Rep 82 (QBD); [1991] 1 Lloyd's Rep 120 (CA) .......... 152, 156
Seale v Perry [1982] VR 193 .......... 195, 201, 203
Semelhago v Paramadeven (1996) 136 DLR (4th) 1 .......... 132
Shaw v York & North Midland Railway Co (1849) 18 LJ (NS) QB 181 .......... 87
Shearson v Lehmann [1980] 1 Lloyd's Rep 441 .......... 151
Singh v Ali [1960] AC 167 (JC) .......... 44
Slim v Croucher (1860) 1 De GF & J 518; 45 ER 462 .......... 206
Smeaton Hanscomb v Sassoon I Setty [1953] 2 All ER 1471; [1953] 1 WLR 1468 (QBD) .......... 89, 102–103, 108, 122
Smiley v Townshend [1950] 2 KB 311 (CA) .......... 150
Smith v Baker [1891] AC 325 (HL) .......... 87
Smith v Bedouin SN Co [1896] AC 70 (HL Sc) .......... 93
Smith v Eric S Bush [1990] 1 AC 831 (HL) .......... 197–198, 200, 202, 205, 208
Smith v Littlewoods Organisation Ltd [1987] 2 WLR 480 (HL Sc) .......... 35
South Australia Asset Management Corporation v York Montague Ltd [1997] AC 191 (HL) .......... 135, 153, 159
Spears v Hartly (1800) 3 Esp 81 .......... 84
Spring v Guardian Assurance plc [1995] 2 AC 296 (HL) .......... 191, 198
Spurling v Bradshaw [1956] 1 WLR 461 (CA) .......... 81, 94
Standard Chartered Bank v Pakistan Shipping Corp [2003] 1 AC 959 (HL) .......... 198
State Government Insurance Office Queensland v Brisbane Stevedoring Pty Ltd (1969) 43 ALJR 456 (High Court of Australia) .......... 107, 112
Stevenson v Henderson, 1873 SC 215 .......... 85, 87
Stilk v Myrick (1809) 2 Camp 317 .......... 61–63
Stocznia Gdanska SA v Latvian Shipping Co [1998] 1 WLR 574 (CA) .......... 188
Strata Corp v Winkler (1987) 45 DLR (4th) 741 .......... 150
Strata v Winkler (1987) 45 DLR (4th) 741 .......... 148
Stuart v B & A Steam Navigation Co (1875) 2 Asp MC 497 .......... 92
Stuart v Wilkins (1778) 1 Doug 18 .......... 195
Suisse Atlantique Société d'Armement Maritime SA v NV Rotterdamsche Kolen Centrale [1967] 1 AC 361 (HL) .......... 99, 102, 107–114, 117, 119, 121–122, 125

Surrey County Council v Bredero Homes Ltd [1993] 1 WLR 1361 (CA) ... 127, 130, 137, 140, 154, 157
Sutherland Shire Council v Heyman (1985) 157 CLR 424 (High Court of Australia) .... 9
Suzuki v Benyon (1926) 42 TLR 269 (HL) .......... 85

Tabcorp Holdings Ltd v Bowen Investments Pty Ltd (2009) 236 CLR 272 (High Court of Australia) .......... 161
Tai Hing Cotton Mill Ltd v Lin Chong Hing Bank Ltd [1986] 1 AC 80 (PC) .......... 9
Tak & Co Inc v AEL Corporation Ltd (1995) NZBLC 103 .......... 139
Taylor Fashions Ltd v Liverpool Victoria Trustees Ltd [1982] 1 QB 133 (Ch) .......... 10
Taylor v Liverpool and Great Western Steam Co (1874) LR 9 QB 546 .......... 93
Thimbleby v Barron (1838) 3 M & W 210 .......... 85
Thomas National Transport (Melbourne) Pty Ltd v May & Baker (Australia) Pty Ltd (1966) 115 CLR 353 (High Court of Australia) .......... 107, 109, 114
Thomas v Quartermaine 1887) 18 QBD 685 (CA) .......... 87
Thomas v Thomas [1842] 2 QB 851; 114 ER 330 .......... 57, 65
Thompson v Charnock (1799) 8 Term Rep 139 .......... 89
Thompson v Percival (1834) 5 B & Ad 925 .......... 72
Thorman v Dowgate [1910] 1 KB 410 (KBD) .......... 92
Thornton v Place (1832) 1 Moo & R 218; 174 ER 74 .......... 146–147
Tito v Waddell (No 2) [1977] Ch 106 (Ch) .......... 140, 149–151, 153, 155–156
Torquay Hotel Co Ltd v Cousins [1969] 2 Ch 106 (CA) .......... 107
Trade and Transport Inc c v Iino Kaiun Kaisha Ltd (The Angelia) [1973] 2 All ER 144; [1973] 1 WLR 210 (QBD) .......... 107, 111, 116, 122
Trainor v Phoenix Fire Insurance Co (1892) 65 LT 825 .......... 85
Transfield Shipping Inc v Mercator Shipping Inc (The Achilleas) [2009] 1 AC 61 (HL) .......... 159, 161
Trident General Insurance Co Ltd v McNiece Bros Ltd (1988) 165 CLR 107; (1989) 62 ALJR 508 (High Court of Australia) .......... 60, 63, 184
Turner v Civil Service [1926] 1 KB 50 (KBD) .......... 92
Tweddle v Atkinson (1861) 1 B & S 393 .......... 65

Udall v Capri Lighting Ltd [1988] QB 907 (CA) .......... 199
UGS Finance v National Mortgage Bank of Greece & National Bank of Greece SA [1964] 1 Lloyd's Rep 446 (CA) .......... 107
United Dominion Corp (Jamaica) Ltd v Shoucair [1969] 1 AC 340 (PC) .......... 61
United Fresh Meat Co Ltd v Charterhouse Cold Storage Ltd [1974] 2 Lloyd's Rep 286 (QBD) .......... 114
United States Shipping Board v Bunge & Born Ltd, Buenos Aires (1925) 42 TLR 174 (HL) .......... 102
United States v Zara Contracting Co, 146 F 2d 606 (1944, US Circuit Court of Appeals, 2nd Cir) .......... 124

Van Dorne v North American Van Lines (Canada) Ltd (1979) 95 DLR (3d) 358 ....... 114
Vandepitte v Preferred Accident Insurance Corporation of New York [1933] AC 70 (PC) .......... 65, 71
VL Boots Pty Ltd v Booth (ERF) Pty Ltd [1968] 3 NSWR 519 .......... 114
Voulis v Kozary (1975) 5 ALJR 59 (High Court of Australia) .......... 67, 70

Wallis, Son & Walls v Pratt & Haynes [1910] 2 KB 1003 (CA); [1911] AC 394 (HL) .. 92, 105
Waltons Stores (Interstate) Ltd v Maher (1987) 62 ALJR 110 (High Court of Australia) .......... 10, 49
Warlow v Harrison (1858) 1 El & El 295; (1859) 1 EI & EI 309 .......... 79
Wathes, (Western) Ltd v Austins (Menswear) Ltd [1976] 1 Lloyd's Rep 14 (CA) .......... 110–113, 117
Westralian Farmers Co-operative Ltd v Southern Meat Packers Ltd [1981] WAR 241 .......... 186
White & Carter (Councils) v McGregor [1962] AC 413 (HL) .......... 154
White Arrow Express Ltd v Lamey's Distributors Ltd (CA, 21 July 1995) .......... 133
White v Jones [1995] 2 AC 207(HL) ....... 137, 142–143, 191, 193, 197, 200–201, 208–209
Whittaker v Ford Motor Co of Canada Ltd (1979) 98 DLR (3d) 162 .......... 114
Wickman Machine Tool Sales Ltd v L Schuler AG [1974] AC 235 (HL) .......... 119
Wigan v Edwards (1973) 47 ALJR 586 .......... 58
Wigsell Corporation v School for the Indigent Blind (1880) 43 LT 218 (Exch D); (1882) 8 QBD 357 (QBD) .......... 130, 150–151, 156
Wilkinson v Coverdale (1873) 1 Esp 75; 170 ER 284 .......... 208
Williams v Hathaway (1877) 6 Ch D 544 (Ch) .......... 85, 93
Williams v Natural Life Health Foods Ltd [1998] 1 WLR 830 (HL) .......... 192, 197–198, 200–201, 207
Williams v Roffey Bros and Nicholls (Contractors) Ltd [1991] 1 QB 1 (CA) .... 3, 53, 55, 58–64, 78, 140, 184
Williamson v Allison (1802) 2 East 446 .......... 195
Wilson v Darling Island Stevedoring Co [1956] 1 Lloyd's Rep 346 (High Court of Australia) .......... 87
WL Tinney & Co Ltd v John C Dougall Ltd 1977 SLT (Notes) 58 .......... 114
Woodar Investment Development Ltd v Wimpey Construction UK Ltd [1980] 1 WLR 277 (HL) .......... 47, 137, 141, 174
Woolf v Collis [1948] 1 KB 11 (CA) .......... 84
Woollatt Fuel & Lumber (London) Ltd v Matthews Group Ltd (1978) 83 DLR (3d) 137 .......... 114
Woollongong CC v Fregnan [1982] 1 NSWLR 244 .......... 136

Xenos v Wickham (1867) LR 2 HL 296 (HL) .......... 11

Yianni v Edwin Evans & Sons [1982] QB 438 (QBD) .......... 202
Young v BT Commn [1955] 2 QB 177 (QBD) .......... 92
Yuen Kun Yeu v Attorney-General of Hong Kong [1988] AC 175 (PC) .......... 9, 48

Zhu v Treasurer (NSW) (2004) 218 CLR 530 (High Court of Australia) .......... 161

# Table of Legislation

## Australia

Conveyancing Act 1919 (NSW), s 133A ........ 145

Property Law Act 1969 (Western Australia), s 11(2) ........ 140
Property Law Act 1974 (Queensland)
s 55 ........ 140
s 112 ........ 145

## Germany

Constitution ........ 16

## Imperial

Colonial Laws Validity Act 1865, s 4 ........ 185

## International

Hague Rules, art III r 8 ........ 185

Uniform Commercial Code, s 2–209(6) ........ 62

## New Zealand

Contracts (Privity) Act 1982 ........ 4, 44, 140, 181–190
s 4 ........ 44, 183, 187
s 7 ........ 183, 189
s 7(1) ........ 190
s 8 ........ 183, 185–186
s 9(2) ........ 188
s 14(1) ........ 190

Property Law Act 2007, s 9 ........ 184

## United Kingdom

Contracts (Rights of Third Parties) Act 1999 ........ 4, 140, 168, 174, 181–182, 184–190
s 1 ........ 182–183, 187
s 1(4) ........ 187
s 1(5) ........ 185
s 2 ........ 189–190

s 3(2) .................... 188
s 5 .................... 188

Limitation Act 1980, ss 5 and 8 .................... 183

Partnership Act, s 17(3) .................... 71

Unfair Contract Terms Act 1977 .................... 36, 119–120, 123, 153, 202
s 3(1) .................... 120
s 3(2)(b) .................... 36
s 3(2)(b)(i) .................... 120
s 11(3) .................... 120

**United States**

Constitution, Article I, s 10, cl 1 .................... 16

Restatement (Second) of Contracts .................... 8, 12–13, 18, 22, 30, 33, 49
§1 .................... 12
§2(2) .................... 13
§75 .................... 30
§90 .................... 8, 13, 22, 30, 49

# 1

# Introduction

DESPITE ITS SIMILAR title, this collection of writings is not an attempt to trespass on the ground covered by Charles Fried in his *Contract as Promise*.[1] It does, however, have this in common with that work: it accepts that contracts are made up of promises and that promises involve assumptions of obligation. Professor Fried's often-cited book contains an extended argument for, and defence of, the place of promises in contract theory, as the moral basis of contract and as declarations of the human will. By contrast, the pieces here collected concentrate on the role of the assumptions of which contractual promises are the expression. All are to some extent based on the proposition that a contractual promise is an assumption of legal obligations and their attendant liabilities, which are binding, not because they have been imposed by law *ab extra* upon fulfilment of the requirements for formation, but because the promisors, using means provided by law for that purpose, have themselves assumed them.

Of course, the obligations and liabilities thus assumed have to be as, and with the incidents, prescribed, implied, and circumscribed by law and it is the law which, self-help apart, supplies the remedies. But those remedies are to be seen, not as potential punishments for wrongdoing, but as going to determine the extent to which parties can by law bind themselves to their undertakings, either to performing them, or to the payment of damages or compensation for breach.

Once accepted, this proposition, that contracting parties assume rather than merely incur contractual liabilities, and that contract is a facility supplied by law to enable them to do so, has a number of implications. One is that it becomes no longer necessary to search for justifications for the existence of contracts and contract law. It is a sufficient that the facility is provided for the classic purposes of peace, order and good government. Suggested justifications such as, for example, upholding the institution of promising, or the sanctity of the human will, or protecting reasonable expectations, while they may undoubtedly have

[1] Charles Fried, *Contract as Promise: A Theory of Contractual Obligation* (Cambridge, Mass, Harvard University Press, 1981).

affected the way in which the law has been formulated, should also be characterised more accurately as motives for providing the facility. Then, too, intention to contract, its presence, of course, determined objectively, is seen to be a central requirement rather than peripheral or dispensable. The proposition that contractual liability is assumed also reveals the real consideration for a bilateral contract, as well as, as it happens, providing a test of the truth or otherwise of the view that contractual liability is imposed by law. This test takes the form of a problem posed by what Sir Frederick Pollock called 'the secret paradox', which was first identified by Sir William Anson in his 1879 book on contract.[2] Since then, a long succession of contract scholars,[3] on both sides of the Atlantic, has sought to find a convincing solution, it is submitted without success, very largely because of one particular reason.

The paradox, and solutions put forward over the years, are canvassed in some detail in chapter two ('The Essence of Contract'), which is the first of the pieces reproduced in this collection. The paradox arises from the fact that, in the great majority of cases at common law, consideration is required for the very existence of an executory bilateral simple contract. Unless and until there is consideration, there can be no contract. It follows, therefore, that the consideration each party provides has to be present and exchanged at the very point at which the contract is created, rather than something which results from formation.

It was obvious from the start that, at formation, there is an exchange of the parties' respective promises or undertakings. But it was also apparent that, until a contract is formed, promises and undertakings might well be binding in honour or in other similar ways but, if that were all the parties were bargaining for, there would be no need for a contract. The answer to that difficulty, it was suggested, was that the real considerations were the binding obligations to which the contract gave rise. The trouble with that as a solution was thought to be that contractual obligations are the result of formation and, hence, could not be present and exchanged at formation itself.

In a post-modern world, it would be all too easy to dismiss the paradox as trivial and the long list of distinguished contributors to its attempted solution as a group of misguided formalists and scholastics.[4] But the real reason for their interest was that they could see that what might be thought a puzzle of minimal import in fact raised quite fundamental questions about consideration in particular and contract in general, and was in consequence a challenge to received notions.

[2] Sir William R Anson, *Principles of the English Law of Contract* (Oxford, Clarendon Press, 1879).

[3] The list includes, besides Pollock and Anson, such luminaries, inter alios, as Langdell, Ames, Williston, Corbin, Llewellyn, Stone, Atiyah and Treitel.

[4] See, eg, S Hedley 'Keeping Contract in its Place—*Balfour v Balfour* and the Enforceability of Informal Agreements' (1985) 5 *Oxford Journal of Legal Studies* 391, 402, who describes those involved as 'High Priests', and the point they debated as 'not only simply trivial but utterly without practical import'.

For his part, Sir Frederick Pollock concluded that no answer was possible. Even so, those who originally identified the problem were surely right to suppose that what contracting parties bargain for is not just words, moral obligations, or hopeful expectations but, rather, obligations which will be binding and enforceable in law. They were right, too, to recognise that at formation there is an exchange of promises and undertakings. What, it is submitted, misled them and their successors was the perception that contractual obligation is imposed upon the parties as the *result* of formation rather than something the parties assume by, and therefore contemporaneously with, the act of exchanging their promises or undertakings with an intention (objectively determined) of being bound by them in law.

On the view adopted in this book, what really creates an executory bilateral simple contract is, thus, the exchange of effective *assumptions* of binding legal contractual obligation made in a manner recognised and provided by law for that purpose. It follows, too, that the respective assumptions thus exchanged must also be the consideration each provides for the other. In the case of unilateral contracts, the position is slightly different. The consideration on the one side is the assumption of obligation made by the promisor and, on the other, the performance of the stipulated act or acts by the promisee, on completion of which the promisor's assumption becomes binding upon him. In principle, the law could recognise other methods of contracting. After all, consideration is a feature peculiar to common law systems. The common law, itself, allows for inter partes contracts by deed without consideration and there could be no doctrinal objection to the creation or development of other forms.

Many of the consequences of adopting this view are summarised in chapter two. Several are considered in more detail elsewhere in the collection. As one such consequence, the treatment accorded to consideration in the textbooks is seen to be quite unnecessarily complicated. The only test for promissory consideration should be whether the purported assumptions were permitted by law and were not too vague, uncertain, or otherwise incapable of enforcement. In the case of unilateral contracts, the test for performative consideration would be whether it were of an act or acts within the law, known to have been stipulated for by the promisor.

There are consequences, too, for the variation of contracts and contracts to perform obligations already owed. These are canvassed in chapter three ('Consideration and Benefit in Fact and in Law') and in chapter four ('Consideration and the Variation of Contracts'), both of which necessarily question the validity of the concept of consideration which is enunciated in *Williams v Roffey Bros and Nicholls (Contractors) Ltd.*[5] Again, in chapter five ('Consideration and the Joint Promisee'), it is submitted that the principle adopted by the High Court of

[5] *Williams v Roffey Bros and Nicholls (Contractors) Ltd* [1991] 1 QB 1 (CA).

Australia in *Coulls v Bagot's Executor and Trustee Co Ltd*[6] stemmed from a confusion between consideration for, and the performance of, executory bilateral contracts.

Again, if it were once accepted that the primary purpose of the contract facility is to enable parties to assume legal contractual obligations, it ought to follow that the function of exception and limitation clauses is to help delineate the obligations thus assumed. This was the basic premise of *Exception Clauses.*[7] Its theoretical justification was discussed in chapter one of that book and the greater part of that chapter is reproduced in chapter six of this collection, under the title 'The Function of Exception Clauses'. The contrary view, that exception clauses are merely defences to rights of action which accrue independently of them, also led to the development of the substantive doctrine of fundamental breach, as well as of the notion that the termination of contracts at common law for a discharging breach is retrospective in its effect. Both these matters are discussed in chapter seven, 'The Second Rise and Fall of Fundamental Breach'.

Then, too, if the contract facility exists to enable the assumption of legal contractual obligation, the question arises whether the obligation thus undertaken is to perform or, otherwise, to pay the cost of performance, or, which might well be less, merely to compensate for the economic consequences of non-performance. In any individual case, the answer ought, so far as the law allows, to depend, in the first instance, on which of those sorts of obligation were undertaken. These questions are canvassed in the two chapters, 'Contract Damages, *Ruxley*, and the Performance Interest' (chapter eight) and 'The Performance Interest, *Panatown*, and the Problem of Loss' (chapter nine).

Another implication of the theme of this collection is that, in principle, and as already mentioned, law can (and in fact does) provide facilities by the use of which contractual undertakings can be assumed without the need for any reciprocal performance or undertaking by another party. Contracts by deed are only one such example. In some other jurisdictions, undertakings in the presence of a notary can have similar effect. More recent examples, it can be argued, have been provided in England and Wales by the Contracts (Rights of Third Parties) Act 1999 and, before that, in New Zealand, by the Contracts (Privity) Act 1982. This aspect of the two enactments is discussed in chapter ten, 'Contract not Trust: Some Questions About the Contracts (Rights of Third Parties) Act from Another Perspective'.

Finally, the suggestion is made, in chapter eleven, 'Assumption of Responsibility and Pure Economic Loss in New Zealand', that an 'assumption of responsibility' within the *Hedley Byrne* line of cases can, in at least some circumstances, be

[6] *Coulls v Bagot's Executor and Trustee Co Ltd* (1967) 119 CLR 460 (High Court of Australia).

[7] Brian Coote, *Exception Clauses: Some Aspects of the Law Relating to Exception Clauses in Contracts for the Carriage, Bailment and Sale of Goods* (London, Sweet & Maxwell, 1964).

an assumption of legal obligation and liability, just as in contract, with the difference that the obligation and liability assumed are in tort rather than contract.

The writings here collected may not all be up-to-date statements of the law as it is. Rather, the intention has been to use them to explore, in context, the implications of a basic theme, the correctness or otherwise of which ought not to be a matter of timing. A possible problem, however, is that most of these pieces, as published, included at least a summary statement of the overall theme. Retention of every such statement obviously carries the risk of tedium. On the other hand, lawyers, notoriously, tend not to read legal monographs from cover to cover. As it happens, the only full account is contained in chapter two, 'The Essence of Contract'. Since the others are relatively brief, it has been decided to retain them.

It remains to express the author's grateful thanks to Professor Rick Bigwood, without whose urgings, and his generosity in volunteering to act as editor, this collection would never have happened.

# 2

# The Essence of Contract

## Introduction

IT IS MORE than a quarter-century, now, since Professor Grant Gilmore published his book *The Death of Contract.*[1] Doubtless he would be the first to admit that his title (reminiscent of a magazine cover of the period which proclaimed that God was dead) was a mite premature. The law of contract is still taught as such in law schools, and books and articles on it keep appearing in at least as much profusion as ever.

Nevertheless, behind the exaggeration of the title lay a core of serious truth and intent. Though contract law has survived thus far, Professor Gilmore has not been alone in arguing[2] that it ought not to continue as a separate legal category but should instead be absorbed, or reabsorbed, into tort or into a single law of obligations encompassing contract, torts and restitution.[3] Outside the United States, similar arguments have been advanced, most notably by Professor PS Atiyah.[4] At a less extreme level, there has also been argument that much of the so-called 'classical' law of contract which emerged in the nineteenth century, and which is still the staple of leading textbooks throughout the common law world, should be modified in important respects if not abandoned altogether. Under attack have been such doctrines as offer and acceptance, intention to contract, consideration (including its associated doctrine of privity) and such notions as 'freedom of contract' and the characteristic classical emphasis on the 'intention of the parties'.[5]

[1] G Gilmore, *The Death of Contract* (Columbia, Ohio State University Press, 1974), based on lectures delivered at Ohio State University Law School in April 1970.

[2] ibid, especially, 87–8.

[3] eg LL Fuller and WR Perdue Jr in their famous article 'The Reliance Interest in Contract Damages' (1936) 46 *Yale Law Journal* 52, 373 and 419, argued that the boundaries of contract and tort should be erased.

[4] Especially in 'Contracts, Promises and the Law of Obligations' (1978) 94 *Law Quarterly Review* 193; *The Rise and Fall of Freedom of Contract* (Oxford, Clarendon Press, 1979). Compare H Collins, 'Contract and Legal Theory', in WL Twining (ed) *Legal Theory and Common Law* (Oxford, Blackwell, 1986) 136, 140–1.

[5] Below n 186.

To some extent, proposals of this kind are not new. If it is true, as has been suggested, that the classical common law of contract was a construct of the second half of the nineteenth century[6] (though there has, of course, been continuous development since then), the attack upon it began while it was still in its early stages. For example, ever since the 1880s, the doctrine of consideration has been the subject of a dispute which brought its rational justification into contention and which has successively engaged a fairly high proportion of the leading academic contract lawyers on both sides of the Atlantic.[7] Not long after that dispute developed, the American 'realists' began a reaction against the 'formalism' of classical contract law represented, for them, particularly by the teachings and writings of Professors Langdell and Williston of the Harvard Law School, the English equivalents of whom would have been Sir Frederick Pollock and Sir William Anson, and their successors amongst the English contract text writers of the twentieth century.[8] The notion of freedom of contract, closely associated with the classical law of contract, has also been the subject of adverse comment since the 1880s.[9]

As it happens, the dispute about consideration has never been satisfactorily resolved though, in the United States, its importance was diminished by a shift away from classical consideration doctrine, represented particularly by §90 of the *Restatement (Second) of Contracts*, which stated that promises that are not the subject of consideration should be enforceable wherever justice required.[10] For the most part, though, classical contract law has managed to survive the attacks upon it and formalism as such remains one of the chief targets of the Critical Legal Studies movement of more recent years.[11]

At least outside the United States, the reactions of the past against the classical common law of contract have tended to be rather more the concern of academic writers than of the courts and of the profession at large. As one recent commentator has put it, the latter 'have been able to sail on regardless, oblivious that the topic within which they are handling disputes has no clear identity and may even, on some views, not exist at all'.[12] But if this has been true in relation to the academic attacks of the past, at least outside the United States, the last quarter-century or so has seen developments in British and Commonwealth courts which have raised, not just for academic lawyers but for judges and practitioners as well,

[6] AWB Simpson, 'Innovations in Nineteenth Century Contract Law' (1975) 91 *Law Quarterly Review* 247.

[7] Below text at nn 137–63.

[8] Below text at nn 166–214.

[9] PS Atiyah, *The Rise and Fall of Freedom of Contract*, above n 4, 585ff and 613ff; BJ Reiter, 'The Control of Contract Power' (1981) 1 *Oxford Journal of Legal Studies* 347; R Pound, 'Liberty of Contract' (1909) 18 *Yale Law Journal* 454.

[10] eg above n 1, 61ff.

[11] RM Unger, 'The Critical Legal Studies Movement' (1983) 96 *Harvard Law Review* 561.

[12] FMB Reynolds, 'Contract, a Category Under Attack' [1987] *Malayan Law Journal* 246.

fundamental questions about the precise nature and limits of the law of contract. What is a contract? What is distinctive about it? How much of the present law of contract is inherent or essential?

One such line of development began with the decision of the House of Lords in *Hedley Byrne & Co Ltd v Heller & Partners Ltd*,[13] which pointed to the possibility of claims in tort for pure economic loss. When the House subsequently in *Anns v Merton London Borough Council*[14] seemed to have enlarged the potential scope of the tort of negligence, the way appeared open to claims in tort for loss caused by the breach of promises for which the plaintiff had not given consideration (*Junior Books Ltd v Veitchi Ltd*[15] being the prime example), damages for which might even cover expectation losses.[16] These cases also suggested ways seemingly of circumventing the doctrine of consideration while, at the other end of the spectrum, another group of cases showed that in general (though not always) it may be possible for actions to be brought in tort notwithstanding the existence of a contract between the parties.[17] Inevitably, these developments were perceived as blurring the differences between contract and tort and their respective obligations.[18] More recently, of course, the House of Lords,[19] the Privy Council[20] and the High Court of Australia[21] have all indicated that the *Anns* decision, and especially the famous two-stage test propounded by Lord Wilberforce,[22] have had too much read into them. As a result, developments

[13] *Hedley Byrne & Co Ltd v Heller & Partners Ltd* [1964] AC [HL], 465.

[14] *Anns v Merton London Borough Council* [1978] AC [HL],728.

[15] *Junior Books Ltd v Veitchi Ltd* [1983] 1 AC [HL], 520.

[16] eg *Ross v Caunters* [1980] Ch 297 (CA); *Gartside v Sheffield Young & Ellis* [1983] NZLR 37 (CA); *Meates v Attorney-General* [1983] NZLR 308 (CA). See the discussion in FMB Reynolds, 'Tort Actions in Contractual Situations' (1985) 11 *New Zealand Universities Law Review* 215; JC Smith and P Burns, '*Donoghue v Stevenson*—the Not So Golden Anniversary' (1983) 46 *Modern Law Review* 147; J Holyoak, 'Tort and Contract after *Junior Books*' (1983) 99 *Law Quarterly Review* 591; A Grubb, 'A Case for Recognising Economic Loss in Defective Building Cases' [1984] *Cambridge Law Journal* 111, 120; P Cane, 'Contract, Tort and Economic Loss', in MP Furmston (ed), *The The Law of Tort: Policies and Trends in Liability for Damage to Property and Economic Loss* (London, Duckworth, 1986) 113, 116ff; JC Smith, 'Economic Loss and the Common Law Marriage of Contracts and Torts' (1984) 18 *University of British Columbia Law Review* 95; BS Markesinis, 'An Expanding Tort Law' (1987) 103 *Law Quarterly Review* 354; B Feldthusen, 'Economic Loss: Where Are We Going after *Junior Books*?' (1987) 12 *Canadian Business Law Journal* 241; Atiyah, *The Rise and Fall of Freedom of Contract*, above n 4, 762–3.

[17] eg *Esso Petroleum Co Ltd v Mardon* [1976] QB 801 (CA); *Midland Bank Trust Co Ltd v Hett, Stubbs & Kemp* [1979] Ch 384 (Ch). Though see *Tai Hing Cotton Mill Ltd v Lin Chong Hing Bank Ltd* [1986] 1 AC 80 (PC).

[18] eg PS Atiyah, *Essays on Contract* (Oxford, Clarendon Press, 1986) 54–5. And see the articles cited above n 16.

[19] eg *Peabody Fund v Sir Lindsay Parkinson Ltd* [1985] AC 210 (HL); *The Aliakmon* [1986] AC 785 (HL); *Curran v Northern Ireland Co-ownership Housing Assn Ltd* [1987] AC 718 (HL NI).

[20] *Yuen Kun Yeu v Attorney-General of Hong Kong* [1988] AC 175 (PC); *Rowling v Takaro Properties Ltd* [1988] 2 WLR 418 (PC).

[21] *Sutherland Shire Council v Heyman* (1985) 157 CLR 424 (High Court of Australia); *Jaensch v Coffey* (1984) 155 CLR 549 (High Court of Australia). And see S Quinlan and D Gardiner, 'New Developments with Respect to the Duty of Care in Tort' (1988) 62 *Australian Law Journal* 347.

[22] [1978] AC 728, 751–2.

in the law of torts are likely, for the meantime at least, to proceed at a rather more measured pace and some of the cases which seemed to blur the distinction between contract and tort may be overruled. Others, though, like *Hedley Byrne* itself and *Junior Books*, will remain.

A further line of authority has seen developments of promissory and proprietary estoppel and estoppel *in pais* to the point where, in some cases at least, the most notable of which is *Waltons Stores (Interstate) Ltd v Maher*[23] in the High Court of Australia, a promise appears to have been held to give rise to a cause of action, notwithstanding the absence of any contract for consideration.[24]

If cases such as these raise questions about the nature of contracts, the limits within which contract law applies, and the extent to which classical contract law can still be regarded as valid, it ought to be possible to turn to legal theory for answers. But anyone who attempts to do so finds a vast literature seemingly full of differences and disagreement. Indeed, there may be less agreement now than there has ever been about the qualities essential to a contract and about the justifications for the existence of a separate contract law, even among those who concede that a separate contract category does exist, and should continue to do so. As Professor Atiyah has said, contract theory today 'is a mess'.[25]

It is the purpose of this chapter to suggest that, notwithstanding the 'mess' and despite the disagreements, and notwithstanding suggestions to the contrary, contract does, in an essential respect, differ from other forms of legal obligation. In the remainder of the first half of this chapter, it is proposed to look briefly at the traditional definitions and theories of contract, and at the unsolved problem of the consideration for an executory bilateral contract, which together form the background to the present uncertainties and which have in many respects contributed to them. In the second half of the chapter, there will be a brief review of the reactions both to the thinking contained in the traditional theories, and to classical contract law itself. A solution will be offered to the problem of consideration for an executory bilateral contract, based on what, it will in turn be argued, is also the distinguishing characteristic of a contract. The chapter will conclude with a discussion of some of the main implications for contract law of the recognition of that distinguishing characteristic.

## Textbook Definitions

Almost invariably, common law textbooks have defined contracts in terms of promise or agreement or of a combination of the two. And as we shall see,

23 *Waltons Stores (Interstate) Ltd v Maher* (1987) 62 ALJR 110 (High Court of Australia).

24 eg *Crabb v Arun District Council* [1976] Ch 179 (CA); *Taylor Fashions Ltd v Liverpool Victoria Trustees Ltd* [1982] 1 QB 133 (Ch); *Re Basham* [1986] 1 WLR 1498 (Ch); *Amalgamated Investment and Property Ltd v Texas Commerce International Bank Ltd* [1982] QB 84 (CA); GF Dawson, 'Making Representations Good' (1982) 1 *Canterbury Law Review* 329.

25 PS Atiyah, *Pragmatism and Theory in English Law* (London, Stevens, 1987) 173.

promise and agreement are in turn linked respectively to what have been, historically, the two main contract theories.

A third element in some definitions has been a statement that contracts create rights *in personam* rather than rights *in rem*, that being a distinction which descends from Roman law. For present purposes its significance is twofold.[26] It requires of a contract that, at its formation, at least some element should still need to be performed or fulfilled. It therefore also excludes from the category of contracts transactions, such as conveyances, which have the effect of granting or transferring rights *in rem* by the very fact of being executed.[27]

## In Terms of Agreement

Of the leading modern English contract texts, both *Treitel*[28] and *Cheshire and Fifoot*[29] define contract in terms of agreement. Definitions in those terms go back to *Doctor and Student* in the sixteenth century[30] and to such later works as *Blackstone*[31] and the earlier editions of *Chitty*.[32] The current edition of *Treitel* states that a contract is 'an agreement giving rise to obligations which are enforced or recognised by law'.[33] Such definitions have the advantage of being centred on an incident of the vast majority of contracts whether under common law or under the systems which derive from Roman law. In that sense, they correspond with popular perceptions of what contracts are about. Their disadvantage is that if they are confined to agreements they necessarily exclude contracts which are not agreements. Such contracts can be made at common law by the use of a deed[34] and they have their equivalents under the Scottish system,

[26] eg JW Salmond and J Williams, *Principles of the Law of Contracts* (2nd ed, London, Sweet & Maxwell, 1945) 2–7; A Berriedale Keith, *Elements of the Law of Contract* (London, Stevens & Sons, 1931) 1.

[27] eg *Sutton and Shannon on Contracts* (7th ed by AL Diamond et al, London, Butterworths, 1970) 3.

[28] GH Treitel, *The Law of Contract* (7th ed, London, Stevens & Sons, 1987) 1.

[29] MP Furmston (ed), *Law of Contract* (11th ed, London, Butterworths, 1986) 27.

[30] See also *Sutton and Shannon on Contracts*, above n 27, 3; E Jenks, *The Book of English Law* (6th ed by PB Fairest, Athens, Ohio University Press, 1967) 318; GW Paton and DP Derham, *Jurisprudence* (4th ed, Oxford, Clarendon Press, 1972). The history of the usage is traced in RM Jackson, 'The Scope of the Term "Contract"' (1937) 53 *Law Quarterly Review* 525.

[31] W Blackstone, *Commentaries* (Oxford, Clarendon Press, 1766) vol 2, 442.

[32] eg in J Chitty, *The Law of Contracts* (3rd ed by T Chitty, London, S Sweet, 1841) 2, it is stated that, in its more familiar sense, the word 'contract' applies to agreements not under seal and suggested that this is its more correct meaning.

[33] GH Treitel, *The Law of Contract* (12th ed, London, Sweet & Maxwell, 2007) 1.

[34] *Xenos v Wickham* (1867) LR 2 HL 296 (HL); *Lloyd (Doe d.) v Bennett* (1837) 8 C & P 124; *Fletcher v Fletcher* (1844) 4 Hare 67.

for example.[35] For this reason, if no other, a number of writers who include agreements in their definitions refer also to promises in the alternative.[36]

An alternative response would be to deny that arrangements made without agreement can be contracts at all. This is what *Cheshire and Fifoot* have done:

> [A party] is [by deed] bound, not because he has made a contract but because he has chosen to act within the limits of a prescribed formula. The idea of bargain, fundamental to the English conception of contract is absent. An Englishman is liable, not because he has made a promise but because he has made a bargain.[37]

By combining agreement with the notion of bargain in their definition of contract under English law, the learned authors have raised a second set of problems, to which reference will be made when the bargain theory comes to be considered.[38]

## In Terms of Promise

Of all English textbook definitions of contract, the most famous is probably that by Sir Frederick Pollock. A contract, he wrote, is 'a promise or set of promises which the law will enforce'.[39] The definition contained in the American *Restatement (Second) of Contracts* is not dissimilar: A contract is a promise or set of promises for the breach of which the law gives a remedy or the performance of which the law in some way recognises as a duty.[40]

Definitions in such terms have the advantage of being wide enough to cover contracts which are not the subject of agreements. Their disadvantage is that they may be too comprehensive. They are wide enough to include promises which the law enforces even though neither deed nor consideration is present. Amongst them would be those promises enforceable under the law of torts or by reason of

[35] Stair, *Institutions of the Law of Scotland* (2nd ed, 1693; tercentenary ed by DM Walker, Edinburgh, The Stair Society, 1981) 197.

[36] eg HG Beale, WD Bishop and MP Furmston, *Contract Cases and Materials* (London, Butterworths, 1985) 3; TG James, *Introduction to English Law* (11th ed, London, Butterworths, 1985) 267.

[37] Above n 29. At its appearance in the early editions of this work, Roscoe Pound in *Jurisprudence* (St Paul, Minn, West Publishing Co, 1959) vol 3, 218, characterised this passage as 'an example of the cult of local law for the sake of its localism which has been a feature of English institutional texts from the beginning'.

[38] Below at nn 78–83.

[39] F Pollock, *Principles of Contracts* (5th ed, London, Stevens, 1889) 1. In the four previous editions contract had been defined in terms of agreement. Definitions in terms of promises appear, for example, in OW Holmes, *The Common Law* (Boston, Macmillan, 1881) 227 and in 9 *Halsbury's Laws of England* (4th ed, 1974) 80.

[40] *Restatement (Second) of the Law of Contracts*, §1. The same wording appeared in the first *Restatement*. Similar definitions appear in *Williston on Contracts* (3rd ed by WHE Jaeger, New York, Baker, Voorhis & Co, 1957) vol 1, 1, and *Corbin on Contracts* (St Paul, Minn, West Publishing Co, 1963) vol 1, 6.

estoppel which have in recent times raised questions about the limits of contract.[41] They are promises of a kind which led to the inclusion of §90 in the *Restatement (Second) of Contracts*,[42] and they may frequently form part of courses on the law of contract. But whether they should now be classed as being themselves contracts is, in effect, what the present inquiry is about.[43] In classical common law contract theory, at least, it is clear that in the absence of either seal or consideration they could not be so considered.

Another supposed disadvantage of definitions in terms of promise has sometimes been thought to lie in the very nature of a promise. Some philosophers and others have assumed that promises must involve the doing (or refraining from doing) of some act in the future.[44] If promises were so limited, there could, prima facie, be no place in contract for a warranty, the essence of which is a statement of past or present fact rather than the promise of something to be done in the future. On this sort of reasoning, §2(2) of the *Restatement (Second) of Contracts* provided that warranties were to be treated as promises or undertakings to be answerable for damage caused by the non-happening of the event or the non-existence of the fact warranted.[45] The effect of that provision was to substitute the secondary for the primary obligation.[46] The better view is that past or present fact can be the subject of a promise.[47] To suppose otherwise, it will be suggested, is to misunderstand the distinguishing characteristic of a promise.

## Contract Theories

If some traditional definitions of contract have had their disadvantages, the position is rather worse with traditional theories of contract. All of them can be shown to have drawbacks of one sort or another.

[41] Above text at nn 23–4.

[42] JH Baker, 'From Sanctity of Contract to Reasonable Expectation?' [1979] *Current Legal Problems* 17.

[43] CJ Goetz and R Scott, 'Enforcing Promises' (1980) 89 *Yale Law Journal* 1261, appear to classify all enforceable promises as contracts.

[44] eg V Peetz, 'Promises and Threats' (1977) 86 *Mind (NS)* 579; J Searle, *Speech Acts: An Essay in the Philosophy of Language* (London, Cambridge University Press, 1969) 59–60; A Tettenborne, *Introduction to the Law of Obligations* (London: Butterworths, 1984) 125; S Stoljar, 'Promise, Expectation and Agreement' [1988] *Cambridge Law Journal* 193. Compare SM Waddams, *The Law of Contracts* (2nd ed, Toronto, Canada Law Book, 1984) 12.

[45] Compare AS Burrows, 'Contract, Tort and Restitution' (1983) 99 *Law Quarterly Review* 217, 251; RE Barnett, Review of *Farnsworth on Contracts* (1982) in (1984) 97 *Harvard Law Review* 1223 at 1242; *Williston on Contracts*, above n 40, vol 1, 4.

[46] Compare F Green, 'Is an Offer Always a Promise?' (1928) 23 *Illinois Law Review* 95, 98.

[47] PS Atiyah, 'Promises and the Law of Contract' (1979) 88 *Mind (NS)* 410; PS Ardal, 'Ought We to Keep Contracts Because They Are Promises?' (1983) 17 *Valparaiso University Law Review* 655, 657.

## The Purposes of Contract Theories

In evaluating contract theories it has to be appreciated that their purposes may vary.[48] Of some, the purpose may be to justify the legal recognition and enforcement of contracts. Of others, it may be to explain the role of contracts in society. A third purpose may be to provide a basis for predicting in a given situation whether a contract will arise or what the law of contract will be.

An illustration of this third type of purpose can be found in the search for a 'general' theory of contract. Before more modern times, what would now be recognised as contracts seem always to have been distinguished from other dealings by the use of special forms or ceremonies.[49] These could include hand clasps,[50] the taking of oaths or the pledging of faith, the use of writing or the recital of a formula,[51] the mingling of blood,[52] the exchange of tokens or weds,[53] or the exchange of hostages.[54] Later commentators saw the forms and ceremonies as being in themselves the source of legal contractual obligation.[55] It was assumed that the path to progress would lead away from form towards deriving obligations from the promise or agreement itself.[56] By the early seventeenth century, Grotius felt able to say that all contracts which proceeded from reasonable causes, whatever be the form of words used, gave a right of action.[57] The sort of general theory which passed into common currency on the Continent was that wherever there was a seriously intended agreement there was a contract, provided that the object the parties had in view was not illegal, immoral or contrary to public

[48] MD Bayles, 'The Purpose of Contract Law' (1983) 17 *Valparaiso University Law Review* 613–14.

[49] See, eg, MR Cohen, 'The Basis of Contract' (1933) 46 *Harvard Law Review* 553, 582; HS Maine, *Ancient Law* (F Pollock ed, London, John Murray, 1930) 339.

[50] As with the early Germans (GC Weeramantry, *The Law of Contracts* (Colombo, Cave & Co, 1967) 13), the Anglo-Saxons (HD Hazeltine, 'The Formal Contracts of Early English Law' (1910) 10 *Columbia Law Review* 608, 609) and the Church (JW Wessels, *The Law of Contract in South Africa* (2nd ed by AA Roberts, Durban, Butterworths, 1951) 83). In the case of the Hebrews, there was a striking of hands (Cohen, above n 49, 573).

[51] The Roman *stipulatio*, which involved the recital of a formula, apparently began as a form of oath-taking. The Roman literal contracts were made binding by book entries (see, eg, Maine, above n 49, 349).

[52] Adam Smith, *Lectures on Jurisprudence* (RL Meek, DD Raphael and PG Stein eds, Oxford, Oxford University Press, 1978) 97.

[53] HD Hazeltine, above n 50.

[54] OW Holmes, above n 39, 196.

[55] Compare HJ Berman and WR Greiner, *The Nature and Functions of Law* (Mineola, New York, Foundation Press, 1956) 378; Stair, above n 35, 202; P Collinet, 'The Evolution of Contract as Illustrating the General Evolution of Roman Law' (1932) 48 *Law Quarterly Review* 488.

[56] This seems to have been a quite early view of the Church. See TFT Plunknett, *A Concise History of the Common Law* (5th ed, London, Butterworths, 1956) 17. On the general point, see Maine, above n 49, 340; JP Dawson, *Gifts and Promises* (New Haven, Yale University Press, 1980) 113–14; Pound, above n 9, 455–6.

[57] H Grotius, *The Jurisprudence of Holland* (RW Lee trans, Oxford, Oxford University Press, 1926) 3.52.

policy.[58] A comparable common law version suggested by Professor Karl Llewellyn was that a bargain is enforceable unless reason appears to the contrary.[59]

General theories of this kind could say little, directly, about the justifications for enforcing contracts or about the place of contracts in society. They could, however, serve to predict the presence of a contract though, in practice, the extent to which they might do so could vary from one system to another. For present purposes, their importance lies in their tendency to support a search for theories which would base contract on general concepts like agreement, promise, will or bargain, rather than on the fulfillment of technical requirements.

The theories to be treated here are those justifications for the existence of contract liability which have some bearing on what constitutes a contract though they may, of course, at the same time serve other purposes as well. Indeed, their success or failure in the latter role may affect their validity in the former.

## The Theories Stated

### *The Will Theory*

Under the will theory, contracts are seen as expressions of the human will and, for that reason, as being inherently worthy of respect.[60] In that premise are found both the justification of contract law and the basis of many of its incidents. The theory asserts the liberal principle of individual self-determination and the value of individual judgment and volition. Both are thought to be enhanced when two or more wills meet in agreement.[61]

The idea of contract as an expression of will or intention can be traced back at least to classical Greece and Rome.[62] Later it was developed particularly by the Pandectists, the scholars who reintroduced the study of Roman law to Europe from the Renaissance onwards.[63] Through them the theory influenced provisions

[58] FH Lawson, *A Common Lawyer Looks at the Civil Law* (Ann Arbor, University of Michigan Law School, 1953) 149, and compare RH Christie, *Law of Contract in South Africa* (Durban, Butterworths, 1983) 6 (Roman Dutch Law).

[59] KN Llewellyn, 'What Price Contract?' (1931) 40 *Yale Law Journal* 704 at 710. Similar views are found in J Swan, 'Consideration and the Reasons for Enforcing Contracts', in BJ Reiter and J Swan (eds), *Studies in Contract Law* (Toronto, Butterworths, 1980) 24ff, especially 40.

[60] Cohen, above n 49, 575; D Hughes Parry, *The Sanctity of Contracts* (London, Sweet & Maxwell, 1959) 16.

[61] WA Watt, *The Theory of Contract* (Edinburgh, T & T Clark, 1896) 11; B Nicholas, *The French Law of Contract* (London, Butterworths, 1982) 31; R Demogue, *Treatise on Obligations* (Paris, Rousseau, 1923) 130–1, cited by MA Eisenberg, 'Donative Promises' (1979) 47 *University Chicago Law Review* 1, 51.

[62] Weeramantry, above n 50, 10; AJ Kerr, *Principles of the Law of Contract* (Durban, Butterworths, 1980) 1.

[63] B Nicholas, above n 61, 31; R Pound, 'The Role of Will in the Law' (1954) 68 *Harvard Law Review* 1.

of the French and German Civil Codes[64] as well as of Scottish law.[65] In turn, it influenced the development of the common law in the nineteenth century, through the writings of such European theorists as Pothier and Savigny.[66]

Associated with the will theory, or derived from it, have been the concepts of contract as agreement, of consensus ad idem,[67] offer and acceptance,[68] intention to contract,[69] privity and the *vinculum juris*, and construction and interpretation by reference to the intention of the parties. The theory has also lent support to defences such as mistake, misrepresentation, duress and undue influence and hence to the idea that consent to a contract should be full, free and true.[70] In the common law of the classical period, perhaps its best-known manifestation was freedom of contract, a doctrine which both reinforced, and was itself reinforced by, the then prevailing philosophy of laissez-faire. So pervading did that doctrine become that it found its way into the constitutions of both the United States[71] and Germany.[72]

Subject to a limited number of restrictions, the law of contract could be seen to have delegated to individual citizens a form of legislative authority.[73] While this could mean that one party could place him- or herself to some degree under the control of another, the power to do so was itself an expression of individual autonomy and an incident of freedom.[74] The most often-quoted judicial statement of the freedom of contract doctrine was that of Sir George Jessel in the 1875 case of *Printing and Numerical Registering Co v Sampson*[75] where he said:

64 B Nicholas, *ibid*, 31; A de Moor, 'Contract and Agreement in English and French Law' (1986) 6 *Oxford Journal of Legal Studies* 275, 285; N Horn, H Kotz and HG Leser, *An Introduction to German Private Commercial Law* (T Weir transl, Oxford, Clarendon Press, 1982) 74ff.

65 Stair, above n 35, 195ff.

66 WS Holdsworth, *History of English Law* (2nd ed, London, Methuen, Sweet and Maxwell, 1937) vol 8, 1, suggested that the will theory was recognised by English lawyers as early as the sixteenth century. He cited *Browning v Beston* (1555) Plowden 140–1: 'the agreement of the minds of the parties is the only thing the law respects in contracts'.

67 DM Walker, *The Law of Contracts and Related Obligations in Scotland* (2nd ed, London, Butterworths, 1985) 8–9; Lawson, above n 58, 149.

68 Stair, above n 35, 196.

69 Savigny saw mutual communication of agreement and intention as being two of the four elements of a contract.

70 GHL Fridman, 'On the Nature of Contract' (1983) 17 *Valparaiso University Law Review* 627 at 631–2; F Pollock, *Principles of Contract* (London, Stevens & Sons, 1876) 356. In the twenty-first and later editions of *Anson's Law of Contract*, AG Guest, citing HLA Hart (1949) 49 *Proc Aristotelian Soc* 179, has pointed out that the existence of defences such as mistake does not mean that the psychological elements they represent need form part of the definition of contract.

71 Article I, s 10, cl 1.

72 Horn et al, above n 64, 84.

73 J Stone, *The Province and Function of Law* (London, Stevens, 1946) 101; Cohen, above n 49, 585ff; LL Fuller, 'Consideration and Form' (1941) 41 *Columbia Law Review* 799 at 806ff; B Nicholas, above n 61, 31. For the contrary view, see Paton and Derham, above n 30, 454.

74 J Stone, above n 73, 251; C Fried, *Contract as Promise: A Theory of Contractual Obligation* (Cambridge Mass, Harvard University Press, 1981) 13–14.

75 *Printing and Numerical Registering Co v Sampson* (1875) LR 19 Eq 462, 465.

> If there is one thing which more than another public policy requires it is that men of full age and competent understanding shall have the utmost liberty of contracting, and that their contracts when entered into freely and voluntarily shall be held sacred and shall be enforced by Courts of Justice.

In the common law context, however, the will theory has its weaknesses, both as a justification for the enforcement of contracts and as a basis for prediction. Under the postal rule, for example, it is clear that an offeror could be bound to an offer he had already attempted to withdraw. The theory is also prima facie incompatible with the existence of implied-by-law terms. The most obvious weakness is the impossibility in practice of determining what the will of the parties might be, even supposing an exact concurrence of wills could ever exist about all aspects of any particular contract. The common law response has, of course, been to apply objective tests of will and intention.[76] The parties are bound, not by what they actually intended, but by the inferences to be drawn from what they said and did. This objective approach has meant that a search for the apparent intention of the parties has been a practical possibility. But it also means that the existence of contract law can hardly be justified by reference to some mystical need to give effect to the human will, since it is not necessarily the actual will which is the determinant.

The use of standard forms, which gained momentum in the nineteenth century and which has accelerated since, has also undermined the idea of consensus ad idem. There has, too, been a retreat from the notion of freedom of contract, coinciding with a retreat from laissez-faire economics which has only recently been reversed. These matters will be adverted to again in due course.[77]

## *The Bargain Theory*

The bargain theory is a common law development from the notion of contract as agreement. It incorporates what has been called the bargain theory of consideration, attributed in the United States to OW Holmes, which sees consideration in terms of reciprocal conventional inducement.[78] The distinguishing feature of a contract at common law is said to be a bargain or exchange between the parties. As a theory it is necessarily confined to the common law system, which is the only one to contain, through the doctrine of consideration, any requirement of reciprocity between the parties.

As we have seen, *Cheshire and Fifoot* subscribe to this theory.[79] They are seemingly not alone. Professor CJ Hamson, for example, has suggested that 'consideration, offer and acceptance are an indissoluble trinity, facets of one

[76] French law has not taken objectivity as far as has the common law: A de Moor, 'Contract and Agreement in English and French Law' (1986) 6 *Oxford Journal of Legal Studies* 275, 279.

[77] Below text at nn 159–214.

[78] Holmes, *The Common Law*, above n 39, 230.

[79] Above text at n 37.

identical notion which is that of bargain'.[80] The requirement of reciprocal consideration ensures that the parties make their undertakings to each other and that, since each makes a 'payment', each desires those undertakings to be made.[81] The bargain theory, therefore, reinforces the ideas of privity, request and mutuality.

An obvious drawback to the theory is its exclusiveness. Not only has it to be confined to contracts at common law. Within the common law it fails to include contracts by deed made without consideration. On the other hand, it can also be argued in its favour that it does not exclude the possibility of gratuitous contracts.[82] Even if simple contracts must be bargains, the common law does not require any equivalence of exchange. If the promise of a peppercorn[83] can be a sufficient consideration, the bargain theory could be said to include the possibility of a contract being made by way of gift, otherwise than by use of a deed.

### *The Promise Theory*

The promise theory says in effect that contracts are promises, that promises should be kept, and that it is therefore appropriate that the law should enforce them.[84]

The idea of a promise as something to be kept is an ancient one and has drawn support from the Jewish,[85] Christian and Muslim[86] religions. The nearest Roman law came to a general type of contract took the form of a ritual promise.[87] In Roman times and since, the bindingness of promises has been seen to be required by natural law.[88] In England, promises were important to the Anglo-Saxons.[89] For centuries they were also enforced by the ecclesiastical courts.[90] In the King's courts, the writ of assumpsit was, in form, an action on the case for damage caused by breach of promise. In more recent times, as we have already seen, textbook definitions of contract have frequently been cast in terms of promise, as was the definition in the *Restatement (Second) of Contracts.*[91]

The promise theory, then, has the advantages of reflecting a practice of some antiquity and of giving legal expression to widely held intuitions of what is fair

[80] CJ Hamson, 'The Reform of Consideration' (1938) 54 *Law Quarterly Review* 233, 234.
[81] Fried, above note 74, 19; A de Moor, above n 76, 283.
[82] Compare: Simpson, above n 6, 263; AG Chloros, 'The Doctrine of Consideration and the Reform of the Law of Contract' (1968) 17 *International & Comparative Law Quarterly* 137, 155.
[83] *Chappell & Co Ltd v Nestle Co Ltd* [1960] AC 87 (HL), 114 per Lord Somervell.
[84] eg Cohen, above n 49, 553 and 572–3; Stair, above n 35, 200.
[85] Cohen, above n 49, 574.
[86] Weeramantry, above n 50, 20.
[87] That is, the *stipulatio.*
[88] Atiyah, *The Rise and Fall of Freedom of Contract*, above n 4, 140; CG Addison, *Treatise on Contracts* (London, Benning & Co, 1847); Walker, above n 67, 8–9.
[89] Above n 50.
[90] RH Helmholz, 'Assumpsit and *Fidei Laesio*' (1975) 91 *Law Quarterly Review* 406.
[91] Above n 50.

and right. It is not confined to agreements. But as a theory of contract it, too, has its drawbacks. It assumes that contracts are enforced because they are promises but, in practice, no legal system has ever enforced every promise and life would be intolerable under any system which did so, human nature being what it is.[92] On the other hand, as has already been pointed out, some promises are nowadays enforceable which would not have been recognised as contracts under classical common law.[93] There are problems too about what comprises a promise, why promises should be kept, and why the law should intervene to enforce them.

It seems generally to be agreed that promisors place themselves under an obligation to their promisees and in that sense surrender a measure of autonomy to them. Promises are seen as voluntary acts and the resultant obligation as being in some sense or another voluntarily incurred by the promisor.[94] There is less agreement as to what constitutes a promise. Some regard it as merely an emphatic expression of intent, a statement of resolve or commitment, or a prediction.[95] For others, it depends on an intention by the promisor to accept an obligation in respect of whatever he or she has undertaken.[96] The problem of futurity has already been mentioned.

As to why promises should be kept and, in particular, why the law should intervene to enforce them, there is again an absence of agreement. In the past, morality and religion have been accepted reasons. Professor Roscoe Pound argued that the extensive modern use of common forms had, in itself, 'relaxed' the claims of morality for the enforcement of contracts.[97] Even so, Professor Fried has recently argued the moral basis of contracts.[98] More widely acceptable nowadays might be claims of utility and convenience. Promising can be regarded as a socially useful practice which it is in the interests of society to foster and protect.[99] It could be said to provide facilities for its members in the form of systems of rules which give them the power, at their choice, to place themselves under obligation.[100]

92 Cohen, above n 49, 573.

93 Above text at nn 13–24.

94 eg Walker, above n 67, 4; J Raz, 'Voluntary Obligations and Normative Powers' (1972) 46 *Aristotelian Society, Suppl Vol* 79, 100–1; Searle, above n 44, 60; GK Gardner, 'An Inquiry into the Principles of the Law of Contracts' (1932) 46 *Harvard Law Review* 1, 5; Fried, above note 74, 13; Burrows, above n 45, 244; J Rawls, *A Theory of Justice* (Cambridge, Mass, Belknap Press, 1971) 342–7; Atiyah, 'Contracts, Promises and the Law of Obligation', above n 4, 210.

95 eg N MacCormick 'Voluntary Obligations and Normative Powers' (1972) 46 *Aristotelian Society, Suppl Vol* 59, 63 and 72; Ardal, above n 47, 659–61; BJ Reiter, 'Good Faith in Contracts' (1983) 17 *Valparaiso University Law Review* 705 at 721; Goetz and Scott, above n 43, 1267.

96 Above n 94.

97 Pound, above n 63, 16.

98 Above n 94, 17 and 41. In 9 *Halsbury's Laws of England* (4th ed, 1974) [202], morality is given as one of two justifications for the enforcement of contractual obligation.

99 Raz, above n 94, 87 and 101; J Raz, Review of P S Atiyah, *Promises, Morals and Law* (1982) 95 *Harvard Law Review* 916, 933–4; Pound, above note 37, vol 3, 175.

100 HLA Hart, *The Concept of Law* (Oxford, Clarendon Press, 1961) 27; N MacCormick, 'Law as Institutional Fact' (1974) 90 *Law Quarterly Review* 102, 116; Raz, above n 94, 101; Atiyah, 'Contracts, Promises and the Law of Obligation', above n 4, 195.

This latter view of promises, too, has its detractors, principally on the ground that it presupposes an intention to be bound on the part of the promisor. If promises depend on intention, argued Adam Smith, a promise made without an intention to perform it would never be binding.[101] Other commentators would claim that the search for intention is an unnecessary fiction.[102] In practice, of course, the common law derives intention objectively, on the basis of the appearance of what the promisor has said and done.

For himself, Adam Smith preferred to found obligation on the reasonable expectations induced in the promisee.[103] Some later commentators have taken the argument a step further by basing obligation on reliance by the promisee in pursuance of his or her reasonable expectations. These approaches have both been sufficiently important in contract theory to justify separate treatment here.

### *The Reasonable Expectations Theory*

Adam Smith's theory of the foundation of contract law has come down to us in transcripts made by his students of his lectures in Jurisprudence. He based the obligation to perform a contract on the reasonable expectations induced by a promise and the disappointment of those obligations occasioned by breach.[104]

In the classical period and since, views similar to those seem to have been shared very widely. In England, for example, they have appeared in such textbooks as *Pollock*,[105] *Holland*,[106] *Salmond*,[107] *Anson*[108] and *Cheshire and Fifoot*,[109] and to have had the endorsement of Austin[110] and Goodhart.[111] In the United States, they were supported by *Corbin*[112] and were incorporated by Roscoe Pound

[101] Above n 52, 93.

[102] *Williston on Contracts*, above n 40, vol 1, s 21; R Tuck, 'Intent to Contract and Mutuality of Assent' (1943) 21 *Canadian Bar Review* 123; KO Shatwell, 'The Doctrine of Consideration in the Modern Law' (1954) 1 *Sydney Law Review* 289; J Unger, 'Intention to Create Legal Relations, Mutuality and Consideration' (1956) 19 *Modern Law Review* 96; BA Hepple, 'Intention to Create Legal Relations' [1970] *Cambridge Law Journal* 122; *Hotchkiss v National City Bank*, 200 Fed 287, 293 (1911) per Learned Hand J.

[103] Above n 52.

[104] ibid, 87 and 92.

[105] Above n 70, 1.

[106] TE Holland, *The Elements of Jurisprudence* (13th ed, Oxford, Clarendon Press, 1924) 262.

[107] JW Salmond, *Jurisprudence* (12th ed by PJ Fitzgerald, London, Sweet & Maxwell, 1966) 337.

[108] *Anson's Law of Contract* (26th ed by AG Guest, Oxford, Clarendon Press, 1984) 2.

[109] Above n 29, 28.

[110] J Austin, *Lectures on Jurisprudence* (5th ed, revised and edited by R Campbell, London, J Murray, 1885) vol 2, 906.

[111] AL Goodhart, *English Law and the Moral Law* (London, Stevens & Sons, 1953) 10. See also Burrows, above n 45.

[112] *Corbin on Contracts*, above n 40, vol 1, 2.

into one of his jural postulates.[113] In Canada they have the support of contributors to *Studies in Contract Law*[114] and are endorsed, for example, in Professor Waddams' *Contract* text.[115] So widespread has been their acceptance that they have been described by Professor Atiyah as being now traditional.[116]

It is not immediately obvious why the reasonable expectations theory should have held so much appeal, for so long. No doubt, promises and contracts do usually raise expectations and in most cases are intended to do so. But in practice, the raising of reasonable expectations is neither sufficient nor necessary for the existence of a promise or contract.[117] A statement that I am likely to call at your home on Saturday afternoon may well raise expectations of a visit but it would not be a promise. On the other hand a statement would not be any less a promise merely because the promisee did not believe it could or would be performed. And a promise made by deed can be a binding contract even though the beneficiary is unaware of its existence.[118] Then, too, there is a certain circularity in the theory. What marks it as especially reasonable to base expectations on a promise or contract if not that it is regarded as binding?[119]

There is a further problem in the nature of expectation itself. Life is full of disappointments but we do not ordinarily expect the law to make provision for them to be compensated, even when the expectations themselves are reasonable.[120] And if contract law exists to protect reasonable expectations, how are we to explain the decision of the House of Lords in *Addis v Gramophone Co Ltd*,[121] the effect of which in most cases is to deny compensation for the 'disappointment of mind' caused by breach of contract?

It was doubtless reasons of this kind, at least in part, which led to the development of the reliance theory.

### The Reliance Theory

This theory, in its strongest form, is that a contract arises (or should arise) whenever a promisee has relied upon a promise in a way which would cause detriment if it were not kept. Writing in 1933 about justifications for contract

[113] Pound, *Jurisprudence*, above n 37, vol 3, 175. See also his 'Consideration in Equity' (1919) 13 *Illinois University Law Review* 435, 459.

[114] BJ Reiter and J Swan (eds), *Studies in Contract Law* (Toronto, Butterworths, 1980), especially at 6. See also Reiter, above n 95, 705.

[115] Above n 44, 11–12.

[116] Atiyah, 'Contracts, Promises and the Law of Obligation', above n 4, 214.

[117] Raz, above n 94, 101. For a contrary view, see AS Burrows, 'The Will Theory of Contract Revived' [1985] *Current Legal Problems* 141, 149.

[118] Salmond and Williams, above n 26, 16.

[119] Atiyah, above n 16; BJ Reiter and J Swan, 'Contracts and the Protection of Reasonable Expectations', in Reiter and Swan, above n 114, 6.

[120] Eisenberg, above n 61, 3; Baker, above n 42, 23–4; Atiyah, 'Contracts, Promises and the Law of Obligation', above n 4, 215.

[121] *Addis v Gramophone Co Ltd* [1909] AC 488 (HL); *Hamlin v The Great Northern Railway Co* (1856) 1 H & N 408, 410–11, 156 ER 1261, 1262 per Pollock CB.

liability, Professor MR Cohen described it as 'the favourite theory today'.[122] Since then, it has attracted strong support from Fuller and Perdue in their famous 1937 article on 'The Reliance Interest in Damages'[123] and, in more recent times, from Professors Horwitz and Atiyah in particular.[124]

Since it is based on loss or injury to the promisee, the theory has the advantage of appearing both objective (in not depending upon the intentions of the promisor) and fair (in visiting liability on the one who by inviting reliance has caused the loss or injury). It appears, too, to draw some historical justification from the earliest actions in assumpsit, which could be said to have been based on loss or damage suffered as the result of reliance on the defendant's promise.[125] Professor Cohen recognised that in basing liability on loss or damage the theory would appeal to those who wished to see contract integrated with other forms of obligation and particularly with tort.[126]

Nevertheless, as a theory of contract it has serious limitations. For example, damages in contract characteristically are measured not by the loss suffered by the promisee in reliance on the promise but by the loss resulting from the promisor's failure to perform. The promisee is entitled in general to be put in the position he or she would have occupied had the contract been performed, the so-called 'expectation' measure. Fuller and Perdue's answer to this objection was to extend their concept of 'reliance' to include failure by the promisee to make alternative contractual arrangements in reliance on the promise (lost opportunity costs). On that basis, they suggested, the expectation measure was essentially a rule-of-thumb means of assessing reliance loss, followed by the courts for the sake of efficiency and convenience.[127]

The reliance theory also seemingly fails to explain why, as is the case, executory contracts are binding from the moment of their formation and are enforceable independently of whether either party has acted to his or her detriment. Professor Atiyah would answer that the law has been wrong in this respect.[128] A

[122] Above n 49, 578.

[123] Above n 3, 60–2.

[124] Atiyah, 'Contracts, Promises and the Law of Obligation', above n 4, 193; MJ Horwitz, 'The Historical Foundations of Modern Contract Law' (1974) 87 *Harvard Law Review* 917. The claim that before the nineteenth century damages in contract law were based on reliance has been rejected by AWB Simpson, 'The Horwitz Thesis and the History of Contracts' (1979) 46 *University Chicago Law Review* 533. See also Baker, above n 42, 24.

[125] Compare comment to §90 in the *Restatement (Second) of Contracts* (1981) vol 1, 242.

[126] Above n 49, 578. See also Fried, above note 74, 4; Fuller and Perdue, above n 3, 419; Gilmore, above n 1, 87–8; Bayles, above n 48, 622–3; JG Murphy and JL Coleman, *The Philosophy of Law* (Boulder, Westview Press, 1984) 206; BJ Reiter, 'Contracts, Torts, Relations and Reliance', in Reiter and Swan, above n 114, 236.

[127] Fuller and Perdue, above note 3, 61–2. RN Bronaugh, 'Lost Opportunities in Contract Damages' (1983) 17 *Valparaiso University Law Review* 735, especially 749, criticises their reasoning on the basis that there is no promise upon which the promisee could rely until after the formation of the contract, a criticism which looks rather like the 'secret paradox' considered below, text at nn 137–63.

[128] eg Atiyah, 'Contracts, Promises and the Law of Obligation', above n 4, 220–1. Compare the comment to §90 in *Restatement (Second) of Contracts* (1981) 242.

less drastic answer might be to say that, in enforcing wholly executory contracts, the object of the law is to protect not only particular acts of reliance but also the practice of relying on contracts generally.[129]

A third difficulty is that neither reliance nor a tendency to induce reliance is either sufficient or necessary for the existence of a contract.[130] Promises made in a social context, such as an invitation to dinner, may induce reliance but are not contracts. The same can be true of invitations to treat, such as advertisements for the holding of an auction, or offers such as tenders, which may induce reliance before being withdrawn. On the other hand, a contract by deed can bind even though it has not been communicated to, let alone been relied upon by, the promisee. Like the reasonable expectations theory, the reliance theory also contains an element of circularity.[131]

Finally, the reliance theory bases contractual obligation, not on what a promisor said or did, but on the reactions of another to those things. As such it would be a potential instrument for the imposition of obligations for which the promisor had not contracted.[132]

### *Miscellaneous*

In his 1933 article on the basis of contract,[133] Professor Cohen identified three theories in justification of contract liability apart from those already mentioned.

One was a theory of OW Holmes that the parties to a contract had in effect an option to perform it or pay damages.[134] In respect of matters outside the control of a promisor, the theory contains an element of truth. The same could be true of cases where the law does not allow for specific enforcement. But as a theory of contract generally, it is inconsistent with the availability of specific performance and of actions in debt for the recovery of contract sums.

A second theory was that the formalities associated with contracts in different cultures and at different times were not only designed to make evidence secure but were also, in large part, expressions of a fundamental human need for formality and ceremony.[135] This theory draws attention to what may well be an important feature of formation but it does not, for example, supply any very obvious explanation of or justification for contract liability, let alone indicate what constitutes a contract.

[129] AJ Kronman, Review of Fried, *Contract as Promise* (1981) 91 *Yale Law Journal* 404, 411; Fuller and Perdue, above note 3, especially 57–66.

[130] Cohen, above n 49, 575.

[131] Goetz and Scott, above n 43, 1264 (fn).

[132] Compare Fridman, above n 70, 636.

[133] Above n 30.

[134] *The Common Law*, above n 39, 237 and his 'The Path of the Law' (1897) in *Collected Legal Papers* (New York, Harcourt, Brace & Co, 1920) 167, 174–5. There is a discussion of the theory in Atiyah, above n 18, 57ff.

[135] Cohen, above n 49, 582.

The third theory, which Cohen put forward as his own, was that the role played by the State in contract enforcement made the law of contract part of public law.[136] The law was justified in placing limitations on the extent of the parties' freedom to invoke the power of the State. Again, the emphasis of the theory is on just one feature of the law of contract, albeit an important one.

## The Secret Paradox

The fact that the traditional theories of contract could all be shown to be flawed inevitably invited scepticism, not only about the theories themselves but also about contract doctrines generally. Contributing to the same tendency were doubts raised by a conceptual problem described by Sir Frederick Pollock as 'the secret paradox of the common law'.[137]

### The Paradox Stated

The 'secret paradox' was first identified by Sir William Anson in 1879 in the first edition of his book on contract.[138] It arose in the specific context of a purported contract to perform something which was already the subject of a contract between the promisor and a third party. Some English decisions had suggested that the second contract would be valid. But since the promisor had offered no more than he or she was already bound to perform, where was the detriment which would constitute the consideration? The solution proposed by both Pollock[139] and Dean Langdell of Harvard[140] was that consideration lay in the obligations owed by the promisor under the second contract. In more recent years the Privy Council also adopted a similar view.[141] But, as Anson pointed out, that argument was circular.[142] Obligation was the product of the contract when formed. Consideration was something which had to be brought to its formation. A consequence of a contract could not be a prerequisite to its existence.

While this problem had been raised in the specific context of an existing duty, it was soon apparent that it applied to the formation of executory bilateral contracts in general. The law was clear that a contract could be formed by an

[136] ibid, 585ff. Compare n 73, above.

[137] In an anonymous review of Pease and Latter, *The Students' Summary of the Law of Contract* (London, Butterworth & Co, 1913) in (1914) 30 *Law Quarterly Review* 128, 129. For a treatment of this topic, see RN Bronaugh, 'A Secret Paradox of the Common Law' (1983) 2 *Law and Philosophy* 193.

[138] WR Anson, *Principles of the English Law of Contract* (Oxford, Clarendon Press, 1879) 81.

[139] Above n 70.

[140] CC Langdell, *Summary of the Law of Contract* (Boston, Little, Brown & Co, 1880) 105. Compare *Green's Encyclopaedia of Scots Law* (Edinburgh, William Green & Son Ltd, 1896) vol 5, 266.

[141] *NZ Shipping Co Ltd v A M Satterthwaite & Co Ltd* [1975] AC 154 (PC), 168; *Pao On v Lau Yiu Long* [1980] AC 614 (PC), 632.

[142] Above n 138, 8l.

exchange of promises, provided of course that what was promised was itself capable of being consideration. (A promise to accept a gift, for example, would not qualify.) There would be few cases in which the parties had bargained for a mere mouthing of words. Yet neither performance itself, nor the obligation to perform, could be consideration, since the one lay in the future and the other presupposed that the contract had already been formed.

To the controversy thus begun, no satisfactory solution has so far been found. It remains, in the words of Professor Atiyah, 'one of the puzzles of the Common Law'.[143]

## The Suggested Solutions

The many attempts to suggest a solution tend to fall into one or other of three groups.

### The Promise

The first group of solutions accepted that the resulting obligation could not be the consideration and concluded therefore that, in one way or another, consideration must come from within the pre-contractual promise. Various suggestions were made as to how this could be. Professor Ames, for example, regarded a promise as good consideration if it were made with the intention of contracting (*animo contrahendi*). Each promisor, he thought, was thereby brought within the rule of law which imposed an obligation upon anyone who had received what he bargained for.[144] Later commentators took Ames to mean that consideration lay in the action of promising and that, in effect, he was treating bilateral contracts as if they were unilateral.[145] Professor Williston's solution was to deny that consideration had to be a present detriment at the time the contract was made. It was sufficient if the promise had present value. Words of promise inherently had such a value and could therefore be consideration. Moreover, thought Williston, it was for the promises rather than the resulting obligations that parties actually bargained.[146] Professor Corbin's view, by contrast, was that an offeror bargained not for mere words of promise but for both the words and the performance which they promised. Mutual promises created a legal obligation because customary notions of honour and wellbeing caused promisors to perform as they had promised.[147]

[143] Atiyah, 'Contracts, Promises and the Law of Obligation', above n 4, 195.

[144] JB Ames 'Two Theories of Consideration II' (1899) 13 *Harvard Law Review* 13, 31–2.

[145] RN Bronaugh, above n 137, 200.

[146] *Williston on Contracts*, above n 40, vol 1, 330, [103], and 'Consideration in Bilateral Contracts' (1914) 27 *Harvard Law Review* 503, 506ff and 518ff.

[147] *Corbin on Contracts*, above n 40, [142], and AL Corbin, 'Does a Pre-existing Duty Defeat Consideration? Recent Noteworthy Decisions' (1918) 27 *Yale Law Journal* 362, 375ff.

Several other commentators found consideration in the inferences to be derived from a promise. For Professor Gardiner, the value of a promise resulted from the promisee's belief that the promisor would be both able and willing to perform it.[148] Professor Ballantine thought a promise furnished present potential value in exchange because it would have actual value when it became binding.[149] For Professor Karl Llewellyn, what businessmen offered each other was not words but 'a continuing expectation and sense of security', 'an assurance in the result'. Value existed in 'the ultimate actual performance' and legal obligation played 'third fiddle' to those elements.[150] Writing at about the same period, Professor F Green found consideration not in the act of speaking but in the pledge of faith manifested by the speaking.[151] More recently, Professor Treitel has adopted what seems to be a not dissimilar approach. Businessmen who make and receive promises expect them to be kept. In his view, these expectations, based on commercial morality, can be called a detriment and a benefit and therefore satisfy the requirements of consideration.[152] For his part Professor Atiyah has attributed the problem to historical causes. In the days when actions in contract were brought in assumpsit, each party had an independent claim against the other. To obtain enforcement, each had to show performance of his or her own promises. The promises each made to the other therefore presupposed that performance would follow.[153]

## *The Obligation*

In the second group of solutions, consideration has been found in the legal obligations of the promisor. To this group, of course, belong the suggestions originally made by Pollock and Langdell, but a third came later from Professor Ferson. For him, the exchange of promises was an exchange of juristic acts by which the parties could subject themselves to obligations.[154] There was a synchronous creation of mutual detriment and mutual rights. Both were created by law, being merely incurred by the acts of the parties. He gave the analogy of the simultaneous exchange which occurs in barter.[155]

[148] GK Gardiner 'Inquiry into the Principles of Contracts' (1932) 46 *Harvard Law Review* 1, 8.

[149] HW Ballantine, 'Mutuality and Consideration' (1914) 28 *Harvard Law Review* 121, 125.

[150] KN Llewellyn, 'Our Case-Law of Contract (Parts I and II)' (1938) 48 *Yale Law Journal* 1 and 779, 789–90.

[151] Above n 46, 96.

[152] Above n 28, 55.

[153] Atiyah, 'Contracts, Promises and the Law of Obligation', above n 4, 211.

[154] ML Ferson, 'The Formation of Simple Contracts' (1924) 9 *Cornell Law Quarterly* 402, 405. Compare Salmond and Williams, above n 26, 4.

[155] ibid, 415.

### *No Logical Justification*

The third group of solutions, while recognising the de facto existence of executory bilateral contracts, accepted that there could be no justification in logic for them. This was the view eventually adopted by Pollock.[156] Professor Julius Stone used the paradox as an example of the difficulties caused when syllogistic logic was applied to legal problems.[157] Professor KCT Sutton thought that since no logical justification existed, the attempt to find a detriment by invoking the logic of schoolmen was misplaced. A bilateral contract was valid simply because it accorded with common sense and practical convenience.[158]

## The Need for a Different Solution

In a more recent full-scale discussion of the paradox, Professor Bronaugh has suggested that consideration can be seen either in normative terms, that is, as involving a change in the promisor's position of entitlement power, or in value terms, that is, as some immediate reduction in welfare (though not necessarily so on balance). In his view, both Ames and Corbin saw the value of promises exchanged in a bilateral contract as normative in this sense. Each promise, by placing the maker under a moral obligation, changed his or her position of non-legal entitlement or power as a kind of normative detriment. Since that normative detriment did not depend upon any legal obligation arising from the contract being created, no circularity was involved.[159]

While this suggestion was a useful contribution to the debate, it cannot be a full solution. Like its predecessors based on the non-legal implications of a promise, it presupposes that contracting parties bargain for less than a legal obligation. If that were true, the bargain would be complete without the need for any contract to eventuate. The law would be an intruder, imposing legal consequences where none had been sought. What distinguishes contract from most other voluntary relationships is its bindingness in law. The result of a contractual exchange of promises is that, in the normal case, each party is bound in law by the whole of his or her promises. To treat consideration as a matter of aspiration, moral obligation, or as otherwise dissociated from legal obligation is to trivialise

[156] F Pollock, Review of Ashley, *The Law of Contracts* (1912) 28 *Law Quarterly Review* 100, 101, and in his *Principles of the Law of Contract* (9th ed, London, Stevens, 1921) x–xi. Compare Lord Wright, 'In Memoriam: Sir Frederick Pollock' (1937) 53 *Law Quarterly Review* 151, 159.

[157] Above n 73, 198 and 544.

[158] KCT Sutton, *Consideration Reconsidered: Studies on the Doctrine of Consideration of the Law of Contract* (St Lucia, Queensland, University of Queensland Press, 1974) 28. Compare Cohen, above n 49, who concluded at 581–2 that since an exchange of promises, themselves being without value, can create a contract, consideration must in effect be a formality, like the affixing of a seal. The whole controversy is dismissed by S Hedley, 'Keeping Contract in its Place' (1985) 5 *Oxford Journal of Legal Studies* 391, 402 as 'not simply trivial but utterly without practical import'.

[159] Bronaugh, above n 137, 222–3 and 227.

its role in the common law of contract. The other objection is that, ultimately, such approaches find justification for the enforcement of contracts in the desirability of enforcing promises as such. They are therefore subject to the same objections as the promissory theory of contract.[160]

It is proposed, later in this chapter, to offer a solution to the exchange of promises paradox.[161] In the meantime, though, it is not difficult to see how it might be concluded, on the basis of the controversy, that there was something illogical at the heart of the doctrine of consideration and, therefore, at the heart of the classical contract law itself or, alternatively, that consideration was either valueless or unnecessary.[162]

Interestingly enough, a very similar paradox has been identified in the French law of contract, which requires that an enforceable contractual promise should have a 'cause' (that is, a reason or purpose for its existence). In the case of bilateral (or synallagmatic) contracts, the cause of each party's obligation was believed to be the obligation owed by the other. Anti-causalist commentators objected that this reasoning was circular. In response it was suggested that the cause of each party's obligation was the expectation that the other would be obliged.[163]

## The Failure of Traditional Contract Theories

None of the traditional theories can be said to indicate precisely what a contract is. All of them are wide enough to include relationships which have not been regarded as contracts. Equally, all of them (unless the will theory is dissociated from agreement) exclude relationships which have been so regarded. In every case the problem has been the result of generalising from too narrow a base. The will theory has seized upon the element of individual choice. Theories based on agreement and bargain have generalised from a single kind of contract and, in the case of bargain, from a characteristic (consideration) found in one type of legal system only. The expectation and reliance theories have generalised from the reactions of one party, the promisee.

The failings of traditional contract theories, coupled with the unresolved problem of consideration for an executory bilateral contract, have meant an absence of adequate theoretical support for classical notions of a contract and have left those notions exposed and vulnerable to attack. More than that, they have provided potential ammunition for such attack. The notion of a general theory, for example, reinforces trends towards generalisation and away from the 'technical' requirements of classical contract law. The will theory has been so

[160] Above text at nn 84–103.

[161] Below text at nn 216–32.

[162] Compare Atiyah, *The Rise and Fall of Freedom of Contract*, above n 4, 688, and his *Essays on Contract*, above n 18, 180; Cohen, above n 49, 581.

[163] Nicholas, above n 61, 113–14.

closely associated with laissez-faire politics and economics that rejection of the latter seemingly leaves such aspects of autonomy as intention, privity, and offer and acceptance without support. The bargain theory, as an alternative to the will theory, seems to point towards a requirement of equivalence of exchange, something which is absent from classical contract law. The promissory theory, in appearing to justify the enforcement of all promises, undermines the requirements of form and consideration as, in the case of consideration, does the 'secret paradox' itself. The reasonable expectation theory seemingly invites the resolution of contract disputes by reference to external standards of reasonableness rather than to the provisions of the contract itself. The reliance theory, in seeking to base contracts on injury suffered, points towards torts and restitution and away from personal choice.

Perhaps most damaging of all is the inference left open that for classical conceptions of contract no theoretical justification is possible and that they are the quite arbitrary and accidental products of their history.[164] Indeed, some commentators have asked whether, having regard to the way in which judge-made law develops, any theory of contract could ever be entirely consistent with the common law as it is.[165]

## The Reaction Against Classical Concepts of Contract

The reaction against nineteenth-century classical notions of contract began even before that century was over and before the classical law had fully evolved. For the most part, it has involved movement away from the doctrine of freedom of contract and from what has been called 'formalism'. Again, for the most part, it has tended to emanate from the United States of America and to have had its strongest effects there.

### Against Formalism

There has been reaction against two kinds of formalism. Historically, formalism meant dependence on the use of oaths, writings, seals and other forms and ceremonies for creating contracts or marking their existence. More recently there has also been a reaction against the concept of contract law as an internally consistent system constructed, by the use of deductive reasoning, from basic principles or premises. That concept, too, has been labelled 'formalism'.

[164] Compare Fried, above note 74, 3; Gilmore, above n 1, 59.

[165] Bayles, above n 48; Paton and Derham, above note 30, 447; RM Unger, *The Critical Legal Studies Movement* (Cambridge, Mass, Harvard University Press, 1986) 9. Compare also Reynolds, above n 12; Fried, above note 74, 3; M Krygier, 'Critical Legal Studies and Social Theory' (1987) 7 *Oxford Journal of Legal Studies* 26, 34–7.

## Form

The reaction against the first kind of formalism has seen a continuation into modern times of the search for a general theory of contract, independent of form. Since, under the common law, the forms commonly recognised as marking the existence of a contract are seal (or deed) and consideration, it is not surprising to find that, in half the States of America, contract by seal has been abolished.[166] As to consideration, §90 of the *Restatement (Second) of Contracts* can be interpreted as a step towards the replacement of consideration in the United States by a general right of compensation for loss incurred on the faith of a promise.[167] The movement to displace consideration can also draw support from the theory that a contract is a promise which the law will enforce. Similar support can be drawn from the injurious reliance theory. Despite the relative conservatism of his position overall, Professor Fried, in his book *Contract as Promise*, has denounced the doctrine of consideration as 'artificial and unfortunate'.[168] The English Law Revision Committee recommended as long ago as 1937 that the doctrine of consideration be abolished, though its recommendations have never been adopted.[169]

## Internal Consistency

Formalism, in its other sense of an internally consistent body of doctrine, had a natural appeal for nineteenth-century academic lawyers.[170] Such notions of law had existed in Roman times and had influenced the Continental writers whose efforts led to the codes of France and Germany.[171] In one of the very first common law treatises in modern form, Jones on *Bailments* (which drew in part on Roman Law), the author declared that if law be a science it must be founded on principle.[172] Bentham subsequently argued for codification of the law, and Maine saw the evolution of law to be from the individual decisions of the king, through the application of custom, to the achievement of codification.[173] For Langdell in the United States, as for Jones 100 years before him, law was a science

166 Fried, above note 74, 28, fn 2.

167 Gilmore, above n 1, 61, see §75 (consideration) and §90 of the *Restatement (Second) of Contracts* as contradictory propositions.

168 Above n 74, 25. And see HG Collins, 'Contract and Legal Theory', in Twining, above n 4, 136, 142–4.

169 *Sixth Interim Report* (1937, Cmd 5449).

170 See especially Atiyah, *The Rise and Fall of Freedom of Contract*, above n 4, 345ff. There, and in his *From Principles to Pragmatism* (Oxford, Clarendon Press, 1978) 17, he describes the period 1770–1870 as an 'Age of Principles'.

171 Horn et al, above n 64, 11–12.

172 W Jones, *An Essay on the Law of Bailments* (London, Charles Dilly, 1781) 123.

173 *Ancient Law*, above n 49, ch 1, as summarised by WA Robson, 'Sir Henry Maine Today', in WI Jennings (ed), *Modern Theories of Law* (Oxford, Oxford University Press, 1933) 160, 162–3. MJ

based on principles and doctrines.[174] What writers like Langdell and his English contemporaries, Anson and Pollock, were doing was in effect to evolve a systematisation of contract law which could serve purposes similar to those of formal codification.

As a matter of aspiration, internal self-consistency can have its attractions. But it would be unrealistic to expect that it could ever be fully achieved in a system of judge-made law.[175] One has only to look at the summaries of 'classical contract law' produced by some of the modern critics, to see how difficult it is to say, definitively, just what the common law is, even on basic questions within a single system.[176] There is no definitive text. Although, in the longer term, the tendency may be towards consistency,[177] inconsistencies are very likely to exist at any given time, since development and change are continuous. Nevertheless, the difficulties ought not to be exaggerated. At least in unitary systems it is still possible to view the common law of contract as a broadly coherent body of doctrine, if perhaps as a little more flexible and a little less certain than its critics might allow.

In the event, the reaction in America to Langdell's efforts was fairly prompt. For OW Holmes, law was not a self-consistent doctrinal system. It was more a matter of prediction. What was important was what the judges actually did.[178] The life of the law was not logic but experience.[179] He characterised Langdell as 'perhaps the greatest living theologian … less concerned with his postulates than to show that the conclusions from them hang together'.[180] Coincidentally, at about the same period in Germany, Jhering was criticising the Pandectists for their conceptualistic and systematic way of thinking. He insisted that rules could be understood only in the light of their purpose and the interests they were designed to protect.[181]

Views of this kind met a ready response in the United States and before long found expression in the emerging realist movement. There were several reasons

Horwitz, *The Transformation of American Law 1780–1860* (Cambridge Mass, Harvard University Press, 1977) 257ff sees formalism as in part a response to the possibility of codification, perceived as a threat.

[174] See his preface to CC Langdell, *A Selection of Cases in the Law of Contracts* (Boston, Little, Brown & Co, 1871) viii, reproduced by WL Twining in *Karl Llewellyn and the Realist Movement* (Norman, University of Oklahoma Press, 1985 reprint) 11. See also MA Eisenberg, 'The Responsive Model of Contract Law' (1984) 36 *Stanford Law Review* 1107, 1108–9.

[175] See, eg, Krygier, above n 165, 34–7.

[176] As, eg, by Reiter and Swan, above n 119, 3 and HG Collins, *The Law of Contract* (London, Butterworths, 1986). See the review of the latter book by FMB Reynolds (1986) 102 *Law Quarterly Review* 628, 632–3.

[177] Examples are the eventual rejection of the substantive doctrine of fundamental breach and the eventual extension to contracts for the sale of land of the common law rules relating to discharge for breach and damages.

[178] Above n 134, 173 ('The prophecies of what the courts will do in fact and nothing more pretentious are what I mean by law').

[179] Holmes, *The Common Law*, above n 39, 1.

[180] Review of Langdell's casebook in (1880) 14 *American Law School Review* 233, cited by WL Twining, above n 174, 15.

[181] Horn et al, above n 64, 11, citing *Kampf ums Recht* (1872) and *Zweck in Recht* (1877–1884).

special to that country why this should have been so. In the first place, the United States does not have a unitary system. There is no common law of the country as a whole, each State having a common law of its own. Inevitably, the quality of the judiciary varied widely, as did the conditions under which they had to work during the expansionist years of the nineteenth century. It was a system where, somewhere across the continent, decisions could be found both for and against many of the more important propositions of law.[182] Such a situation could be expected to induce a degree of scepticism about the status of legal principles and doctrines, and particularly about the role they played in the actual decisions of the judges.

A second reason was a tendency within the United States system to emphasise the law-making role of the judiciary. Professor Goodhart has ascribed this to four factors: the absence of a single legislative sovereign, the power of the courts to declare legislation invalid, the need in a frontier society for the judges to make new law and adapt the old, and the existence of so many different jurisdictions.[183]

A third reason was the need in the national law schools to teach students independently of the particular jurisdictions in which they would eventually practice. Langdell's response, in the absence of a native unitary system, was to use mainly English cases in his contract casebook and commentary. It was inevitable that at least some teachers in national law schools would see that as a hopelessly artificial solution and should instead seek bases other than strict legal doctrine for predicting the results of litigation. To this task they brought a mistrust of traditional legal rules and concepts as a description of what the courts actually do or as operative factors in producing court decisions. That mistrust was in part expressed by the theory of 'rationalisation' (or ex post facto reasoning) which assumes that the reasons given for a judgment may be no more than formal justification for conclusions reached on other grounds.[184] One consequence of this approach for law teaching could be a shift in classroom emphasis from obligations to remedies.

From this background has come a movement towards a general law of contract, freed from the constraints of doctrines and distinctions thought to be unnecessary.[185] Since they limited the application of contract law and, hence, the availability of contract remedies, doctrines such as offer and acceptance, intention to contract, privity and request, as well as consideration, came under attack.[186] To that approach, the ultimate expression would, of course, be the

[182] Compare KN Llewellyn, *The Common Law Tradition* (Boston, Little, Brown & Co, 1960) 521–35; PS Atiyah, 'American Tort Law in Crisis' (1987) 70 *Journal Legal Studies* 279, 280.

[183] AL Goodhart, 'Some American Interpretations of Law', in Jennings, above n 173, 1, 2ff.

[184] KN Llewellyn, 'Some Realism about Realism' (1931) 44 *Harvard Law Review* 1223, 1236–9. Compare Unger, above n 165, 8.

[185] Compare Pound, above n 9, 455–6.

[186] eg HW Ballantine, 'Mutuality and Consideration' (1914) 28 *Harvard Law Review* 121 (mutuality); *Corbin on Contracts*, above note 40, vol 1A, s 152 (mutuality); KN Llewellyn, 'Our Case-Law of Contract (Part II)' (1938) 48 *Yale Law Journal* 779 (offer and acceptance); Dawson, above n 56, 221

abolition of many if not all the distinguishing features of contract and its absorption, with tort and restitution, into a single law of obligations. That, effectively, is what Professors Gilmore and Atiyah in more recent years seem to have been suggesting. The executory bilateral contract would be replaced by remedies for injurious reliance.

There is, though, another side to the story. Largely through the influence of Professor Williston,[187] much of the classical law of contract found its way into the *Restatement (Second) of Contracts.* Classical contract law continues to form the basis of contract courses in law schools of the United States, as it does of other common law countries. It continues, also, to form the basis of judicial decisions even in the United States, as any random search of the Reporter system will show. And so resilient has formalism proved to be that, as has already been pointed out, it is still seen as a primary target by adherents to the Critical Legal Studies movement.[188]

## Against Freedom of Contract

According to Roscoe Pound, freedom of contract began with the Romans as an appeal to reason against the primacy of form and developed in more recent times into an appeal to reason against authority.[189] It encompassed freedom to choose whether to enter into a contract, freedom to determine what the terms of the contract should be, and freedom to delimit the obligations to arise from the contractual relationship. In that guise, it coincided neatly with laissez-faire political and economic theories. Individuals were the best judges of their own interests, and freedom to further those interests was to the benefit of all. However, the freedom envisaged by the doctrine was freedom from authority, that is, freedom from state interference and in practice could be no guarantee of the freedoms of particular individuals. It could ensure a proper balancing of interests only if the parties were of reasonably equal bargaining power or if the stronger of them were prepared to exercise self-restraint. Short of that, freedom of contract could be an instrument of oppression of a weaker by a stronger party.[190] Thus in a field such as master and servant, it was absurd, as Dean Pound pointed out, for American courts to hold legislation, which was designed to

(consideration); J Swan, 'Consideration and the Reasons for Enforcing Contracts', in Reiter and Swan, above n 114, 24ff (consideration) and 56–8 (intention to contract); HG Collins, 'Contract and Legal Theory', in Twining, above n 4, 136, 140 (privity); AL Harding, 'Williston's Fundamental Conceptions' (1938) 3 *Modern Law Review* 219, 241; Atiyah, *The Rise and Fall of Freedom of Contract*, above n 4, 688.

[187] He was Reporter of the Committee on Contracts which produced the *Restatement,* AL Corbin being his principal assistant. See Gilmore, above n 1, 58ff.

[188] Above n 11. Compare, too, RB Ferguson, 'The Horwitz Thesis and Common Law Discourse in England' (1983) 3 *Oxford Journal of Legal Studies* 34.

[189] R Pound, 'Liberty of Contract' (1909) 18 *Yale Law Journal* 459, 464.

[190] For example, Cohen, above n 49, 560ff. What constitutes 'inequality' is explored in HG Beale, 'Inequality of Bargaining Power' (1986) 6 *Oxford Journal of Legal Studies* 123.

protect employees, to be unconstitutional on the ground that it interfered with freedom of contract. Social justice he saw as the last form of justice to develop.[191]

## *Classical Controls*

The inevitable reaction against freedom of contract has been directed not at the notion of freedom *to* contract (though some few disqualifications exist, as do some instances of contracts by compulsion) but at the control exercised by the parties over the contents of their contracts and over the nature and limits of the obligations assumed.

Even under classical contract law, freedom of contract was not a complete licence for laissez-faire.[192] Victims could be released from their contracts in cases of duress, undue influence and, under the rubric of unconscionability, in the more extreme instances of the strong taking advantage of the weak. Exception clauses were interpreted contra preferentem, which in practice could mean that a promisor might be impressed with an obligation he or she had bargained not to undertake.[193] Another classical device was 'public policy' which enabled 'slavery'-type contracts to be set aside.[194] In the United States, common carriers' exceptions of liability for negligence were eventually held void under the head of public policy.[195] Again, freedom of contract did not mean that the courts could not fill out gaps left by the parties in their contracts. What it did mean was that if those gaps were to be filled it should be by reference to what the parties did intend or would have intended.

By and large, the function of the classical controls on freedom of contract was to relieve from the effects of contracts. But the main thrust of the reaction against freedom of contract has been towards the use of contract for the achievement of positive policy objectives and for such a role classical contract law has, prima facie, not been well suited. Thus, if distributive justice were the aim, classical contract law knew no requirement of equality of exchange. If the objective were the imposition of obligation *ab extra* for ulterior ends, the requirements of the will and promissory theories, that the intention of the parties should be the test for the interpretation and construction of contracts and the implication of terms, were a barrier, at least in theory. In practice, of course, interpretation, construction and implication have all been used at times for the achievement of policy objectives.

[191] Above n 189, 450.

[192] See, eg: Atiyah, *The Rise and Fall of Freedom of Contract*, above n 4, 148–9, 476–9 (equity), 335ff (legislative restriction), 464ff (implied terms); Reiter, above n 9, 353ff.

[193] The contra proferentem rule antedates the emergence of exception clauses. 'All the words of a deed shall be taken most strongly against him that doth speak them, and most in advantage of the other party': *Shep Touch*, 87.

[194] eg *Horwood v Millar's Timber and Trading Co* [1917] 3 KB 305 (CA).

[195] *New York Central Railroad v Lockwood* (1873) 86 US (17 Wall) 357; S Todd, 'The Negligence Liability of Public Authorities' (1986) 102 *Law Quarterly Review* 370, 383–4.

## *Contract for Ulterior Ends*

Nevertheless, for those seeking to pursue ulterior ends, the most desirable outcome might seem to be the displacement altogether of the special characteristics of contract law and the substitution of tort and restitution. That would, however, be at a price. Tort law imposes obligations but ordinarily penalises misconduct rather than (as does contract) mere nonfeasance.[196] Contract liability is strict but in general tort liability is not. And, of course, the expectation measure of damages in contract can place a higher burden on a defendant than would the normal restorative measure in tort. In other words, to impose obligation in contract may be to deal more severely with a party than has so far been possible in tort.

A number of modern theories seek the use of contract law for the attainment of policy ends, particularly in the economic field.[197] Professors Horwitz[198] and Atiyah[199] have, for example, argued for a return to concerns for fairness and equality of exchange which they discern in the law of contract prior to the classical period. Claims for the existence of such a golden age have been denied by Professor Simpson.[200] Then there is the economic efficiency theory advanced by Professor Posner, which requires that the judges try to promote the efficient allocation of resources. For him, economics is not just a useful tool for measuring the practical consequences of the law but provides norms by which the law of contract should be shaped and terms implied.[201] Another normative economic theory, the neo-institutionalist, recognises that not all contracts are single, stand-alone transactions. Many, particularly in the commercial field, involve continuing relationships. To enable such relationships to be maintained, the law needs to fill in any gaps which may appear in the contract and provide processes by which adjustments can be effected.[202]

A more general theory has been advanced by Professor BJ Reiter. He sees 'good faith' as the primary basis of contractual liability and defines it as 'what the makers of "right conduct" … accept as being properly done in this sort of case.

[196] Baker, above n 42, 18; *Smith v Littlewoods Organisation Ltd* [1987] 2 WLR 480 (HL Sc), 503 per Lord Goff. An exception is *Gartside v Sheffield Young & Ellis* [1983] NZLR 37 (CA).

[197] Summaries of a number of modern theories are contained in JN Adams and R Brownsword, *Understanding Contract Law* (London, Sweet & Maxwell, 1987), and R Flannigan, 'Privity, the End of an Era (Error)' (1987) 103 *Law Quarterly Review* 564, 587–92.

[198] Horwitz, above n 124.

[199] Atiyah, *The Rise and Fall of Freedom of Contract*, above n 4, 146ff.

[200] Simpson, above n 124. See also JL Barton, 'The Enforcement of Hard Bargains' (1987) 103 *Law Quarterly Review* 118. A plea for the basing of contract principles on considerations of fairness independently of contract history is contained in Eisenberg, above n 174, especially 1111–12.

[201] First advanced by him in R Posner, 'A Theory of Negligence' (1972) 1 *Journal of Law and Society* 28.

[202] IR Macneil, 'Contracts: Adjustment of Long-Term Economic Relations' (1978) 72 *Northwestern University Law Review* 854; P Burrows and CG Veljanovski (eds), *The Economic Approach to Law* (London, Butterworths, 1981) 22–4.

What good faith requires must differ industry by industry, depending on customary practice and expectations.'[203] He sees traditional contract values as 'only included along with such others as role integrity, solidarity, power and harmonisation with the social matrix'. For him 'social control of contract is pervasive'.[204]

Writing as a proponent of Critical Legal Studies, Professor RM Unger has urged that obligations explicit in bargains on the one hand and duties imposed by government on the other are only the extremes of a spectrum. Contractual obligations arise primarily from relationships of mutual dependence. Between the extremes of agreement and government imposition, boundaries are to be drawn and redrawn in contract according to the judgments of both the expectations generated by interdependence and the impact that a particular exercise of right might have upon the relation itself.[205]

In another theory, Professor Reiter has sought to base the imposition of 'relational liability', whether in contract or tort, on the reasonable expectations of the parties, tempered by judicial discretion in the choice of appropriate remedies. He detects a trend among courts deciding contract cases to recognise the responsibility they have in defining the duties of parties to contracts.[206] Obviously enough, the notion of reasonable expectations might be perceived as an instrument for the imposition of objective standards of reasonableness on the parties, independently of their particular intentions.[207] A statutory illustration of this approach is contained in s 3(2)(b) of the Unfair Contract Terms Act 1977 (UK) which prevents a contracting party claiming to be entitled, by reference to any contract, 'to render a contractual performance substantially different from that which was reasonably expected of him'. Another theory of rather similar effect, associated particularly with Lord Denning, seeks to determine contract questions by reference to the appearance a contract would have, not to the parties, but to an outside observer, sometimes known as the 'fly on the wall' theory.[208] This approach, too, could be used as an instrument for the imposition of liabilities on the basis of criteria external to the parties.[209]

Yet another device for those seeking to use contract law for ulterior purposes might start with the 'purposive' view of law proposed by Jhering[210] and associated

[203] Reiter, above n 95, 714.
[204] ibid, 726 and 729.
[205] Unger, above n 165, 81.
[206] Above n 126, especially 247 and 256.
[207] *cf* Baker, above n 42.
[208] See JR Spencer, 'Signature, Consent and the Rule in *L'Estrange v Graucob*' [1973] *Cambridge Law Journal* 104; IW Howarth, 'The Meaning of Objectivity in Contract' (1984) 100 *Law Quarterly Review* 265 and his note at (1987) 103 *Law Quarterly Review* 527; JP Vorster, 'A Comment on the Meaning of Objectivity in Contract' (1987) 103 *Law Quarterly Review* 275; Atiyah, above n 18, 109–10.
[209] *cf* TA Downes, *Textbook on Contract* (London, Blackstone Press, 1987) 51. For what comes close to an application of this approach, see *Chomedy Aluminium Co Ltd v Belcourt Construction (Ottawa) Ltd* (1979) 97 DLR (3d) 170, 178 and 180 (aff'd *sub nom Beaufort Realties (1964) Inc and Belcourt Construction (Ottawa) Ltd v Chomedy Aluminium Co Ltd* (1980) 116 DLR (3d) 193).
[210] Above n 181.

in the United States particularly with Professors Llewellyn and Fuller.[211] If rules are best understood in the light of their purposes, it might be argued, the purposes and justifications of contract rules should dictate what those rules should be.[212] By this means, policy objectives could be used to bring about changes in the law of contract.

On the other hand, not all contemporary theorists have argued for the rejection of the traditional concept of contract as a matter of voluntary obligation. Professor Fried has come down unequivocally on the side of contract as promise[213] and, more recently still, Professor Barnett has put forward a 'consent' theory which bases obligation on its having been freely assumed.[214]

## The Need for a More Inclusive Theory

On the evidence of the theories treated thus far, seemingly no consensus exists about what distinguishes contract from other forms of obligation, beyond the notion that entry into a contract requires some act of submission by the parties.

In linking contract with agreement, the will theory proves to have been too narrow. The common law is not the only system under which agreement is not essential. On the other hand, the promissory theory has been too wide, since not all promises are contracts. The bargain theory is too exclusive, since it is necessarily confined to contracts at common law and even within the common law excludes contracts by deed. The reasonable expectations and injurious reliance theories are too wide and too narrow respectively, since not all reasonable expectations are protected by contract and a contract can be binding notwithstanding the absence of reliance. As to the more modern theories, where they have not been directed to minimising or eliminating the distinctiveness of contract or limiting its technical requirements, they have been concerned not so much with what a contract is as with how contract law can be used for particular ulterior purposes.

Clearly, the traditional theories of contract must contain much of the truth or they would not have drawn the support they have. Under any more inclusive theory, entry into a contract would still have to be willed by the parties even if that will were the subject of external pressures and constraints and even if some of the incidents of a contract once entered into were imposed on the parties *ab extra*. While not requiring the presence of an agreement, a more inclusive theory would have to be flexible enough to allow for the fact that most contracts are agreements. Similarly, while not requiring the presence of consideration or cause,

211 eg 'Some Realism about Realism' (1931) 44 *Harvard Law Review* 1222, 1236.

212 Compare in Reiter and Swan, above n 119, 2.

213 Fried, *Contract as Promise*, above n 74.

214 RE Barnett, 'A Consent Theory of Contract' (1986) 86 *Columbia Law Review* 269, especially 300.

it would need to allow the possibility that either might be a requirement in a particular jurisdiction. Such a theory would have to be consistent with the fact that contracts raise expectations and induce reliance. It must allow for the variety of forms which contracts have taken at different times and in different societies. It would be a basic premise that the obligations which flow from a contract are legal obligations.[215] A more inclusive theory should also be consistent with the existence of executory bilateral contracts and should preferably offer a solution to the problem of how they are able to bind by an exchange of promises. And it should also leave room for the use of contract law for a variety of policy objectives.

A theory which met these criteria could not be a generalisation from any one type of contract, such as an agreement, or from the contracts of a single legal system, such as the common law. In other words it must be directed to the essence of contract rather than to developments from, or elaborations of, it. It is believed that the key to such a theory lies in the resolution of the 'secret paradox' of the executory bilateral contract.

## A Suggested Solution to the 'Secret Paradox'

The secret paradox, it will be recalled, arises because while an executory bilateral contract can be formed by an exchange of promises, the consideration (or, in some Continental systems, the cause) cannot be found in the obligations created by it. Nor does it seem sensible to say that mere words of promise are a sufficient consideration. Almost all proposed solutions have purported to find consideration in some non-contractual aspect of the promise and, in so doing, have tended to trivialise the consideration requirement. What is needed is a resolution which reflects the fact that obligation is involved in what is being bargained for but which is nevertheless composed of something which the parties bring to the point of formation. It is submitted that there is one, and only one, positive, creative action of the parties, occurring at the point of formation and involving reciprocal benefit and detriment, which could meet those criteria.

### The Nature of a Promise

The answer to the paradox begins with the inherent nature of a promise. While, as we have seen, a few commentators have regarded a promise as no more than an emphatic statement of intention to do, or refrain from doing, something in the future, most have seen its distinguishing feature to be the promisor's acceptance

[215] Amongst anthropologists, there would seem to be no agreement about whether the criteria for a contract include the creation of legal obligation; see G MacCormack, 'Gift Exchange and Contract' in AR Blackshield (ed), *Legal Change* (Sydney, Butterworths, 1983) 68, 77.

or (to use an expression with long associations in the history of the common law) 'assumption' of an obligation.[216] The fact that that is so explains, for example, why promises do not have to be confined to future acts or abstentions from acting. The promise of an existing or past fact is simply the assumption of an obligation in respect of that fact.

In the ordinary case, a promise is morally or socially binding and the obligation the promisor undertakes is a moral or a social one. In the institution of promising, society has afforded a 'facility' through which such obligations may be undertaken.[217] There can, however, be situations where to take upon oneself a moral or a social obligation may not be enough. The promise needs to be at a higher level of obligation. Historically, religion has provided one such means. To promise under oath, to swear to whatever is being promised, has been seen as the assumption of an obligation which was distinctively religious.[218]

If it is once accepted that a promisor may assume differing types or degrees of obligation, it is a very short step to appreciating that legal contractual obligation might as such also be assumed;[219] to accepting, in other words, that a contractual promise involves an assumption of legal contractual obligation and that the institution of contract, itself, is a facility afforded by society or the state by which such an assumption is made possible. And if that is so, it is not difficult to see how the consideration for an executory bilateral contract could involve legal obligation, not as a mere result, but as part of the very process of formation. The attachment of a legal contractual obligation and its assumption are not separate, consecutive events but rather two aspects of a single act, the one being inherent in the other. It is the reciprocal exchange of the assumptions of legal contractual obligation, occurring simultaneously at the point of formation, which brings an executory bilateral contract into being. What each party is seen to have bargained for is the assumption, by the other, of reciprocal legal obligation to him or her. Those assumptions are the consideration each provides for the other. No circularity of reasoning is involved.

Obviously enough, this process of assumption does not require that the parties necessarily advert to the concept of assumption, as such, in contract any more than it does in respect of other kinds of promise. What is required is no more than classical contract law already requires, namely, an exchange of promises made with intention to contract.[220] These take effect as reciprocal assumptions at the point of exchange. Nor does assumption require that the parties be aware of, let

[216] Above text at nn 94–6.

[217] Above text at nn 99–100.

[218] Thus, the ecclesiastical courts were apparently more concerned with the enforcement of promises under oath than with promises generally. See Helmholz, above n 90.

[219] *cf* Holmes, *The Common Law*, above n 39, 234; Hamson, above n 80, 243 and 254.

[220] *cf* Ames, above n 144.

alone advert to, every potential legal consequence of their acts[221] any more than is the case with the parties to a marriage when they exchange their wedding vows.

## Why Should the Solution be Novel?

The question which then arises is why, if that is the solution and it is so simple and (dare it be suggested?) so obvious, should it not have been put forward before now? As it happens, some of the protagonists in the debate did come some distance towards the same solution. Pollock and Langdell (and, for that matter, the Privy Council) can be seen to have been right in thinking that consideration was in some way associated with obligation.[222] Ames was right to perceive a connection with the parties promising *animo contrahendi*.[223] Bronaugh wrote of the importance of seeing consideration in normative rather than value terms.[224] Closer still, Ferson saw a contractual promise as a juristic act directed by the actor to producing its legal result. Each obligor he saw as assuming the burden of his obligation.[225] Professor Green saw not the act of speaking but the pledge of faith, manifested by that speaking, as the consideration.[226] In the legal sphere, these last two suggestions come close to the modern conception of a promise as an 'illocutionary' speech act, that is, one involving performance of an act in saying something (as opposed to performance of an act of saying something or of an act the effect of which consists in persuading or convincing by saying something).[227]

There would seem to have been two main reasons why contractual promises were not seen as assumptions of specifically legal contractual obligations. The first was that though the protagonists saw the actual exchange of promises as voluntary, many of them seem to have thought that contractual (as distinct from moral or social) obligation was incurred rather than assumed.[228] It was something imposed *ab extra* on parties who had first gone through the appropriate motions almost as though contract were a punishment, or at least a disadvantage, rather than a power and a privilege, and as though the only assumption involved were of merely moral or social obligation (a view by no means confined to the protagonists[229]). Of course it is true that it is the law which gives contracts their legal force, and many of the incidents of contracts are prescribed by law for the

[221] *cf Becker, Gray and Co v London Assurance Corp* [1918] AC 101 (HL), 112–13 per Lord Sumner ('what they intend contractually does not depend on what they understand individually').

[222] Above nn 139–41.

[223] Above n 220.

[224] Above text at n 159.

[225] Above nn 154–5.

[226] Above n 151.

[227] Searle, above n 44, 99.

[228] Evidence for this can be found in many of the published contributions to the controversy and particularly in those from North America.

[229] A recent example of this sort of approach occurs in Atiyah, *Essays on Contract*, above n 18. At p 280 he accepts the 'dogma' that contractual liability rests on voluntary assumption but then on pp 282–3 takes it as self-evident that such liability is *imposed* by law on the ground that it is the law which

parties and are in that sense imposed upon them. But neither of those facts is in any way inconsistent with their depending on an initial active assumption by the parties of legal contractual responsibility for their respective promises to the extent and under the conditions which the law allows. The very point of contract as a facility, it is submitted, is that it gives parties the power to make such an assumption.[230]

The second reason, less often occurring, has been a rejection of the relevance of contractual intention to the formation of contracts. In a sense, that would follow as a corollary to the first reason. There are also commentators who, in any event, regard the search for intention in contracts as illusory and for them it would no doubt be inconceivable that the formation of a contract should depend on whether the parties intended a contract rather than some other form of relationship.[231] But even if it be assumed that nowadays parties enter into executory contracts ignorant of what they are doing, that must be a relatively modern phenomenon. In times past, societies ensured that entry into such a contract was marked off from other actions by the use of distinctive forms or ceremonies.[232] It has too easily been assumed that these forms or ceremonies made the promises or agreements they attested somehow the less contracts. The reality was that society provided such forms and ceremonies as the specific means by which contractual obligations in respect of those promises or agreements could be assumed or undertaken. That such forms and ceremonies (apart from the execution of deeds) have disappeared from our law may even be a matter for regret. At common law consideration now in most cases substitutes for form. The parties may meet any need for ceremony with inventions of their own, the shaking of hands being a common example. For present purposes the important point is that, whatever the actual intentions of the parties might be, the law has long since chosen to deduce those intentions objectively. In that light, it has also realistically been able to maintain the need for an intention to contract. After all, even the action on the case in contract required an *assumpsit super se* as well as words of promise.

creates legal rights and duties. Compare MR Cohen and FS Cohen, *Readings in Jurisprudence and Legal Philosophy* (New York, Prentice-Hall, 1953) 102 ('One contracts an obligation as one contracts pneumonia').

[230] *cf* Fried, above note 74, 19 ('the obligation I chose to undertake'); Hart, above n 100, 27; Barnett, above n 214, 300; *Australian Woollen Mills Pty Ltd v The Commonwealth* (1954) 92 CLR 424 (High Court of Australia), 457.

[231] An example is S Williston, 'Consideration in Bilateral Contracts' (1914) 27 *Harvard Law Review* 503, 506. Compare MacCormick, above n 95, 72. In *The Rise and Fall of Freedom of Contract*, above n 4, 690. Atiyah asserts that intention to contract was largely unknown in the nineteenth century and in his *Pragmatism and Theory in English Law*, above n 25, 172, ascribes its invention to Pollock, borrowing from Savigny. See also Kronman, above n 129, 416.

[232] AG Chloros, 'Comparative Aspects of the Intention to Create Legal Relations in Contract' (1959) 33 *Tulane Law Review* 607; Hamson, above n 80, 241–2 and 246–57; MacCormick, above n 95, 75–6. Compare Fuller, above n 73, 803.

## The Essence of a Contract

The secret paradox arose in the specific context of bilateral contracts and in connection with the peculiarly common law requirement of consideration (though, as we have seen, a similar paradox arose in France through the corresponding, though not equivalent, requirement of cause). Even so, it is believed that the solution to the paradox also indicates the essential nature of contracts, whether or not they are bilateral and whether or not they require consideration or cause.

In essence, a contract is a promise or undertaking in respect of which legal contractual obligation has been assumed by means which the law recognises as effective for that purpose. A unilateral contract is a contract of this kind once performance of the stipulated act has reached the point where the law treats the promise as binding on the promisor, at which stage the assumption takes effect. Bilateral and synallagmatic contracts are in effect reciprocal multiples of the basic type. The means recognised as effective by law can vary from one legal system to another and from time to time. To seek to incorporate in the definition of contract such specific requirements as consideration, cause, seal or agreement is to confuse the objective of forming a contract with the means by which it can be achieved.

## Some Consequences

Once it is accepted that a contract is an assumption of legal contractual obligation by a means which the law recognises as effective for that purpose, a number of consequences follow.

(i) In the first place, the search for a justification for the existence of contract law changes. Instead of being 'why should the law impose contractual obligation *ab extra* upon a promisor or the parties to an agreement?' the question becomes in the first instance 'why should the law enable those persons to take legal contractual obligations upon themselves?' and only secondarily 'why should the law attach conditions and limitations to the facility thus provided?' In that light it becomes obvious that the enforcement of contracts does not have to depend on any one particular justification. It may be that in most societies the real reasons for enforcement are the classic ones of peace, order and good government. But equally, contracts could be enforced, and limitations and conditions be attached, for any number of reasons and purposes whether political, social or economic, which could vary from one society to another and from time to time, without the adoption of any one or more of them necessarily having to effect the essential nature of a contract as such.

(ii) If that is accepted, many of the difficulties posed by the traditional theories disappear. Since contracts no longer have to be enforced just because they are promises or just because they are expressions of the human will, it is no longer an embarrassment that the law does not recognise all promises or agreements to be contracts. Contracts are instead seen to be promises or agreements of a special, limited kind.

Again, because contracts do not have to be justified as the concurrence of the wills of the parties or depend upon the sanctity of promises as such, it need not be thought inconsistent for society to fill in the gaps in any contract or to circumscribe or limit the extent to which it provides enforcement, or even to impose obligations upon the parties as the price of the facility which it provides for them.[233] Even 'compulsory contracts' would be possible, since an assumption could be 'compelled' like any other action.[234] Freedom of contract, in the full sense of that expression, no longer has to be seen as an essential requirement of any contract system. To that assertion, however, three qualifications must be made. In the first place, any interference with the freedom or the sanctity of contract is an interference with the contract facility. Secondly, if contract is to remain a voluntary facility, society cannot move so far from freedom and sanctity of contract as to remove altogether the utility and attractiveness of the institution itself.[235] On the other hand, of course, a movement in some respects away from freedom and sanctity of contract might conceivably enhance those qualities.[236] Thirdly, the fact that in theory the law of contract could, within those limits, be used by society for collective or other ulterior purposes, does not determine the quite separate question; namely whether, and to what extent, in any particular legal system and, at any particular time, the law does in fact either require or allow the use of contract for such collective or ulterior ends. In actual practice, the notion of freedom of contract still retains some force within the common law.[237]

(iii) Contracts by deed are seen to be genuine contracts and consideration to be no more fundamental to the concept of a contract than any form or ceremony prescribed for the assumption of legal contractual obligation. Contracts would be nonetheless contracts at common law if new forms or ceremonies were to be invented and the present requirements of a deed or consideration abolished,

[233] *cf* CD Johnson, 'The Idea of Autonomy and the Foundations of Contractual Liability' (1983) 2 *Law and Philosophy* 271, 285ff, especially 294; M Radin, 'Contract Obligation and the Human Will' (1943) 43 *Columbia Law Review* 575, 585.

[234] A Lenhoff, 'The Scope of Compulsory Contracts Proper' (1943) 43 *Columbia Law Review* 586. The contrary view is expressed in Treitel, above n 28, ch 2. Imputed contracts would be a different case again.

[235] In Japan, it seems, the contract law contained in the Codes has proved so unsuitable that the commercial community tends to operate outside the legal system: DE Allan (ed), *Asian Contract Law* (Melbourne, Melbourne University Press, 1969) 99.

[236] In 'The New Lex Mercatoria: The First Twenty-five Years', M Bos and I Brownlie (eds), *Liber Amicorum for Lord Wilberforce* (Oxford, Clarendon Press, 1987) 149, 174ff, MJ Mustill places first, as a reflection of contractual obligations, the general principle *pacta sunt servanda*, but proceeds to list a number of qualifications (presumably thought desirable) to that principle within mercantile law and practice, including several not yet incorporated into the common law.

[237] *cf* Burrows, above n 45, 265.

provided always that the new inventions remained means by which legal contractual obligation could effectively be assumed. It follows also that there is nothing inherently objectionable in the fact that the common law already recognises as contracts some dealings in respect of which neither consideration nor a deed is required. Negotiable instruments and letters of credit, for example, rather than being anomalous simple contracts, are better regarded as additional kinds of formal contract.[238] They can correctly be regarded as contracts because they are means by which, notwithstanding the want of a deed or consideration, legal contractual obligation can be assumed, and are recognised by law as effective for that purpose. By the same token, the fact that at one time in the history of the common law a tort remedy was used for claims in respect of what we now know as simple contracts does not mean that during that period the common law knew no simple contract, still less that contract was a mere aspect of the law of tort. The concern of the time was to find a remedy for breach of contract which was not subject to the limitations of covenant or debt. That a remedy in tort could be adapted to serve those ends dictated the form the action took but without affecting the underlying purpose for which it was brought.[239]

(iv) Again, if the mark of a contract is an assumption of legal obligation, equity can be seen, in declarations of trust, to have come very close to developing its own form of contract, a point which has not gone entirely unnoticed in the past.[240] Indeed, it might be suggested that equity has done for contracts other than bargains what the common law did for bargains themselves, namely to free them from the constraints of a deed under seal. While it is true that in equity the assumption must take the special form of an acceptance of a trust, that is in a sense no more special than the requirements of consideration, coupled with intention to contract, for a simple contract at common law.

(v) If consideration for a bilateral contract is found in the assumption of obligation, the factor which will make a contract fail for want of consideration will be not an absence of economic value but the fact that a purported assumption was ineffective. Examples would be promises which are too uncertain to be enforced or which reserve an absolute discretion to the promisor, or which are known by both parties at the time of formation to be impossible to perform. Whether contracts will fail for want of consideration because the obligation assumed is illegal is still uncertain on the cases.[241]

[238] *cf* Harding, above n 186, 221. Statutory reforms of the privity rule may, if they require an intention by the promisor to confer a legally enforceable benefit on the third-party beneficiary, also create a new form of contract. Compare Contracts (Privity) Act 1982 (NZ), s 4. See also ch 10 of this book.

[239] JH Baker, *The Legal Profession and the Common Law* (London, Hambledon Press, 1986) 389.

[240] eg FW Maitland, *Equity* (2nd ed by J Brunyate, Cambridge, Cambridge University Press, 1936) 54; Salmond and Williams, above n 26, 24.

[241] The answer would depend upon the explanation for the transfer of title recognised in *Singh v Ali* [1960] AC 167 (JC) and *Belvoir Finance Co Ltd v Stapleton* [1971] 1 QB 210 (CA).

(vi) The concept of assumption of obligation provides clear answers in the 'existing duty' cases where bilateral contracts are involved. There would be no consideration and no contract where the promise was to perform an existing duty owed to the same promisee under a contract between the same parties. Such a promise would be a tautology and no new obligation would be assumed.[242] That objection would disappear in the case of a promise to perform a duty already owed to a third person. It would follow, too, that a promise to perform something which was already the subject of a public duty could be good consideration, except in those cases where public policy required otherwise as, for example, in the case of a promise by a private citizen to reward the police for performing their ordinary duties.[243] A different rationale has to be found in the case of unilateral contracts where different persons have promised to reward a single act. As it happens, the Privy Council has drawn no distinction between unilateral and bilateral contracts in this connection[244] and it would be inconvenient, if not absurd, if, for example, a participant in a sponsored walk should be able to claim only against the first of his or her sponsors. There is no difficulty in such cases if it is accepted that consideration does not have to be a detriment to the promisee if it is a benefit to the promisor. An alternative would be to accept that performance of a required act may be no less a detriment to a promisee because it stands to be rewarded from more than one source.

(vii) If contracts depend upon an assumption of legal obligation, it follows that, far from being a peripheral requirement, intention to contract is central to formation.[245] Nor should that requirement be regarded as a purely modern invention. In earlier legal systems the use of special ceremonies, such as the Roman stipulation or the Anglo-Saxon wed, would have ensured that intention to contract was present rather as the taking of an oath would, in the mind of the promisor, distinguish a promise incurring special religious consequences from the ordinary run of promises. And even though the action *in assumpsit* did not require a ceremonial promise, it clearly presupposed some kind of taking upon oneself by the promisor. Intention to contract does not, of course, require that the parties turn their minds beforehand to every incident of the intended relationship. It is quite possible to intend an act the consequences of which are unknown and even, by a leap of faith, to take the risk of accepting responsibility for a promise or statement the terms of which are at the time unknown. Accordingly, once it is accepted that the justification for the enforcement of contracts is not the primacy of the human will or the sacredness of promises,

[242] *Deacon v Gridley* (1854) 15 CB 295, 308 and 309; 139 ER 436, 442. See, further, chs 3 and 4 of this book.

[243] *Glasbrook Brothers Ltd v Glamorgan County Council* [1925] AC 270 (HL), especially 277–8, 286 and 290.

[244] [1975] AC 154 (PC), 168; [1980] AC 614 (PC), 632.

[245] Chloros, above n 232, claims that all systems of law have required an intention to create legal relations. See also his 'The Doctrine of Consideration and the Reform of the Law of Contract', above n 82, 147–9. The presence of the intention may, of course, be ascertained objectively.

there can be no conceptual objection to parties being bound by the common practice of assuming obligation in ignorance of its full extent as, for example, by a contract the terms of which are contained in an unread ticket or other common form.[246]

(viii) If contracts indeed depend on an assumption of legal obligation, the enquiry for courts called upon to interpret or construe them should prima facie not depend upon the expectations aroused in the promisee, any more than a will is to be interpreted by reference to the expectations aroused in the legatees. The enquiry should be what obligations were undertaken by the promisor[247] as that undertaking should have been understood by a reasonable person in the position of the promisee. The problem of circularity raised by the 'expectations' approach would be altogether avoided. At the same time, as has already been pointed out, this does not in itself mean that the courts cannot, where the law so requires or allows, prescribe additional obligations for the promisor or decline to enforce all or any part of those purportedly undertaken.

(ix) The concept of contract as an assumption sheds light on some other problems connected with contract formation. For example, it becomes rather clearer that the primary function of exception clauses is to help determine what obligations were assumed by the promisor rather than to serve as mere defences to breaches of obligations which accrued independently of such clauses.[248] Similarly, it becomes clearer that the 'joint promisee' doctrine propounded in *Coulls v Bagot's Executor and Trustee Co Ltd*,[249] which postulates that consideration for two or more joint promisees can be provided by only one of them, confuses performance of a contract with its formation. It also becomes clearer why it should be possible, as in *McRae v Commonwealth Disposals Commission*,[250] to be bound by a contract to perform the impossible or under which liability can turn on facts or events beyond the control of the promisor. There is nothing conceptually impossible about assuming legal responsibility for something beyond one's power to perform.[251]

(x) Another set of consequences follows in the law of damages. To the extent that contractual obligation is something assumed rather than imposed, the remedies for failure to perform ought prima facie to be no less than the

[246] eg insurance policies: *Rust v Abbey Life Assurance Co Ltd* [1979] 2 Lloyd's Rep 334 (CA), 339 and cases there cited; *MacGillivray and Parkington on Insurance Law* (7th ed by M Parkington and A Dowd, London, Sweet & Maxwell, 1981) [285]–[289].

[247] *cf McRae v Commonwealth Disposals Commission* (1951) 84 CLR 377 (High Court of Australia), 407 per Dixon CJ ('What did the promisor really promise?'); Fridman, above n 70, 636.

[248] Brian Coote, *Exception Clauses: Some Aspects of the Law Relating to Exception Clauses in Contracts for the Carriage, Bailment and Sale of Goods* (London, Sweet & Maxwell, 1964) ch 1; D Yates, *Exclusion Clauses* (2nd ed, London, Sweet & Maxwell, 1982) ch 4. See ch 6 of this book.

[249] *Coulls v Bagot's Executor and Trustee Co Ltd* (1967) 119 CLR 460 (High Court of Australia). See ch 5 of this book.

[250] (1951) 84 CLR 377 (High Court of Australia). Contrast the discussion of this case in Furmston, above n 29, 221–3.

[251] *cf* Holmes, *The Common Law*, above n 39, 234.

equivalent of the obligations assumed. Anything less would mean that the facility to assume obligation given by the law of contract was to that extent a partial facility only.[252] In the normal case, if specific performance were not available damages should be not less than the cost of alternative performance. The position would of course be different if the object of the contract, and the obligation undertaken, were not performance as such but an economic end result.[253] Once it were accepted that the normal measure of damages were the cost of alternative performance rather than an economic end result, there would be a ready solution to the problem of damages under a contract for the benefit of a person not a party to it.[254] The damages recoverable by the promisee from the promisor would be what it would cost to obtain substitute performance of the promise for the benefit of the third-party beneficiary.[255]

Where the remedy is damages, the mitigation principle might be seen as a limitation on the extent to which obligation can be assumed. However, in that the essential justification for the principle is that claimants should be unable to recover losses they have brought upon themselves, the limiting effect can be regarded as relatively minor and certainly as not affecting the general proposition that contracts come into being as the result of an assumption of liability.

Contract as assumption may also shed light on questions such as damages in respect of pre-contractual expenditure. It may even help to explain why the test for remoteness in contract should be different from that in tort.

## The Contemporary Near-Contracts

Contract remains alive at common law and its retention can be justified for as long as the balance of advantage to society remains with providing a facility by which parties are able to take legal contractual obligations upon themselves. It is the power thus given to the parties which distinguishes contract from other kinds of obligation. It also justifies the generally strict form taken by contractual obligation and the application of the expectation measure of damages.

[252] Fried, above note 74, 19; Horn et al, above n 64, 95; *The Common Law*, above n 39, 244; Gardner, above n 94, 17. Compare Smith, above n 52, 99; DM Walker, *Civil Remedies in Scotland* (Edinburgh, Green & Son Ltd, 1974) 283; Eisenberg, above n 174, 1127–8; FMB Reynolds, 'Discharge by Breach as a Remedy', in Finn (ed), *Essays on Contract* (Sydney, Law Book Company, 1983) 184 makes the point that the rules governing breach at common law are 'hostile to the notion that the plaintiff is entitled to the performance promised'.

[253] *cf* Unger, above n 165, 69; Eisenberg, above n 174, 1155–65. For arguments against awarding the cost of alternative performance, see Waddams, above n 44, especially 146–8. See also DR Harris, A Ogus and J Phillips, 'Contract Remedies and the Consumer Surplus' (1979) 95 *Law Quarterly Review* 581. See, further, chs 8 and 9 of this book.

[254] *Woodar Investment Development Ltd v Wimpey Construction UK Ltd* [1980] 1 WLR 277 (HL), 300–1. Other solutions are discussed in Waddams, above n 44, 316–18.

[255] Compare EJ Jacobs, 'Judicial Reform of Privity and Consideration' [1986] *Journal of Business Law* 466, 469–70.

None of this means that no new forms of contract should be invented but, to be genuine contracts, they would have to be methods by which the party or parties took upon themselves legal obligation. It is the absence of this quality which marks off contemporary near-contracts (to the extent that they survive reassessment of *Anns)* from contracts properly so-called.[256]

That is true, for example, of the *Hedley Byrne* tort and its derivatives, whatever the superficial appearances to the contrary. In the *Hedley Byrne* case itself, there are certainly suggestions that responsibility for the representation must have been accepted by the representor.[257] And the Privy Council has explained *Junior Books Ltd v Veitchi Ltd*[258] as depending on a similar assumption.[259] Acceptance or assumption of responsibility implies that the representation must be in the nature of a promise so that it need come as no surprise that the tort has been extended to cover promises as to future action.[260] But the responsibility which the representor is required to have assumed must *ex hypothesi* be something other than legal *contractual* obligation. Otherwise it would have been unnecessary to invent the tort in the first place.[261] Moreover, liability under *Hedley Byrne* and its successors requires some form of detrimental reliance which a contract, at least for the present, does not, and, for the most part, expectation damages have not been thought appropriate.[262]

In the case of claims in tort for economic loss arising from the misperformance (or in some few instances, the non-performance) of a contract to which the claimant is not a party, it seems that reliance is unnecessary and that expectation damages can be awarded.[263] But even that does not mean that the privity rule has entirely been circumvented. There still has to have been negligence before liability can arise. Nor is any assumption of liability required.

Promises are also enforced in equity under various forms of estoppel. With those falling under the *High Trees* doctrine, estoppel has for the most part operated as a defence, though the end result has been to give them an effect not unlike that of a variation of contract for consideration. In other cases, the promise has been held by reason of the estoppel to give rise to a cause of action with, again, end results which can be substantially like those of contracts. At least

256 Compare Burrows, above n 45.

257 [1964] AC 465 (HL), 486, 495, 504 and 529 (and compare at 511). See, further, ch 11 of this book.

258 [1983] 1 AC 520 (HL).

259 *Yuen Kun Yeu v Attorney-General of Hong Kong* [1988] AC 175 (PC).

260 *cf Meates v Attorney-General* [1983] NZLR 308 (CA), especially 335–6 and 379–80; *Al-Kandari v JR Brown & Co* [1987] QB 514 (CA). Compare *Craig v East Coast Bays City Council* [1986] 1 NZLR 99 (CA), 107.

261 *cf* DW McLauchlan, 'Pre-contract Negligent Misrepresentation' (1977) 4 *Otago Law Review* 23 at 47–51.

262 In *Meates v Attorney-General* [1983] NZLR 308 (CA), for example, the reliance measure was adopted. The assumption involved is discussed in ch 11.

263 *Junior Books v Veitchi Co Ltd* [1983] 1 AC 520 (HL); *Ross v Caunters* [1980] Ch 297 (Ch); *Gartside v Sheffield Young & Ellis* [1983] NZLR 37 (CA).

in the past, remedies have been given in these cases not because of a legal contractual obligation assumed by the promisor[264] but because the circumstances, including reliance by the promisee,[265] were such that, in equity, it was seen as unconscientious for the promisor to act as though the promise had not been made. Moreover, the remedies themselves have proceeded on a different basis. As was said by Brennan J in *Waltons Stores (Interstate) Ltd v Maher*:

> The measure of a contractual obligation depends on the terms of the contract and the circumstances in which it applies; the measure of an equity created by estoppel varies according to what is necessary to prevent detriment resulting from unconscionable conduct.[266]

Notwithstanding those differences, there has been a suggestion by Lord Diplock in *The Hannah Blumenthal*[267] that promissory estoppel is a means by which legally enforceable obligations can be assumed when coupled with injurious reliance. As Professor Atiyah has pointed out, this was the first (and, so far, the only) judicial statement of its kind.[268] On the other hand, references can be found in the cases on promissory estoppel to a requirement of intention to effect legal relations.[269] Presumably what would be involved would be a promise to vary existing legal relations which would become a contract to that effect once the promisee had acted upon it, but it would be going rather far to suggest on the basis of one obiter dictum by a single judge, however distinguished, that that stage in the law has already been reached. Of course, if new types of contract are to be introduced at some time in the future, one of them might well take the form of a promise made with intention to create legal relations which would ripen into a contract if and when the promisee should act to his or her detriment upon it. The analogy with unilateral contracts would be quite strong.

Recent setbacks notwithstanding, it is not improbable that the law will continue to develop remedies for those who, in the absence of contract, have relied upon promises to their detriment though, in fairness to the promisor, damages or compensation ought usually to be based on reliance rather than expectation.[270] Similarly, new forms of contract may be devised. But there is no good reason why those separate processes should be confused. To do so would be

[264] Raz, above n 94, 101.

[265] Murphy and Coleman, above n 126, 19.

[266] *Waltons Stores (Interstate) Ltd v Maher* (1988) 62 ALJR 110 (CA), 125.

[267] *The Hannah Blumenthal* [1983] 1 AC 854 (HL), 916.

[268] PS Atiyah, '*The Hannah Blumenthal* and Classical Contract Law' (1986) 102 *Law Quarterly Review* 363, 369.

[269] An obvious example is the *High Trees* case itself: *Central London Property Trust Ltd v High Trees House Ltd* [1947] 1 KB 130 (KBD), 134.

[270] Raz, above n 99, 937; Reiter, above n 126, 280ff; Waddams, above n 44, 138–41; MP Thompson, 'From Representation to Expectation' [1983] *Cambridge Law Journal* 257, 276–7; W Howarth, 'Contract Reliance and Business Transactions' [1987] *Journal of Business Law* 122, 125. Burrows, above n 45, 243–4 and 262, argues for expectation damages in estoppel cases. In the *Restatement (Second) of Contracts*, the principal change made in respect of §90 (which is based on reliance) is recognition of the possibility of enforcement at other than the expectation level.

to limit the potential for development and at the same time, by obscuring the rationale of contract, would be to weaken a useful and historic institution. By the same token, there is no good reason, either, why this should be the first generation for centuries to be without the facility which contract provides.

Once the true nature of a contract is grasped, it can be seen to be a very much more flexible concept than traditional theories have allowed, giving considerable scope for modification and development for a potentially wide range of purposes and objectives. In that sense, contract as assumption allows to many modern theories a potential legitimacy which the traditional contract theories would deny them.

## Conclusion

In essence, the institution of contract is a quite simple one. Perhaps for that very reason it has proved to be the kind of institution about which variations in perception and emphasis can occur from one society to another and from time to time, and these variations have in turn found reflection in differences in the rules and doctrines which make up the laws of contract which prevail at any given time or place, in the theories which underpin them, and in the justifications given for enforcement. But these differences should not be allowed to obscure the truth that lies behind them. The one characteristic essential to a contract is that it should be a means by which legal contractual liability can effectively be assumed by the party or parties to it.

But where this concept has been lost sight of and all contract liability has been regarded as something imposed *ab extra*, it is easy to imagine, on the one hand, how primary features like assumption and intention to contract could come to be treated as secondary or of no account and, on the other, how whole theories of contract could have been based on partial primary features like promise and will. It is also easy to imagine how a secondary feature such as consideration could, at the one extreme, be treated as though it were primary and, at the other, be dismissed as a mere anachronism and, equally, how agreement, which is only one kind of contract, should have come to be thought of as the only one possible. Nor is it difficult to imagine how contract could come to be regarded as being at least substantially on a par with tort. With the essential character of its subject matter thus unrecognised, it is no wonder that contract theory should, in Professor Atiyah's words, be 'in a mess'.

Once the essential characteristic of a contract is grasped, the classical common law of contract can be regarded as having no less conceptual validity than other developed systems. By the same token, it could be subjected to a great many quite radical alterations and still remain a conceptually valid contract system. The only limitation would be that relationships which did not depend upon, or allow, an assumption of legal contractual responsibility could not be contracts, whatever else they might be. But that would be no reason in itself why those other relationships should not be the subject of continuing legal development.

On the other hand, while the classical common law of contract could undergo extensive change and still remain a conceptually valid contractual system, it does not necessarily follow that it will or should so change. That will depend in part on value judgments about such questions as whether and to what extent the law of contract should be used as an instrument for social or economic control and within what limits paternalism should apply. In at least some common law jurisdictions, it will also depend in part on the degree to which the stare decisis principle prevails and the extent to which the legislature is prepared to intervene.

# 3

# Consideration and Benefit in Fact and in Law

CONTRACT LAWYERS WILL be watching with interest to see what the House of Lords makes of *Williams v Roffey Bros & Nicholls (Contractors) Ltd.*[1] The decision of the Court of Appeal in that case is of a kind likely to polarise academic opinion. Some will welcome it because it appears to circumvent what they see as a defect in the law.[2] Others will reject it because the judgments follow a line of reasoning which even the most avid realist might find hard to justify.

## The Facts

The defendants had contracted to refurbish a block of 27 flats and had subcontracted the carpentry work to the plaintiff for £20,000. On the evidence, that figure was by £3,783 too low to be economically feasible. By the time the plaintiff had finished the 'first fix' of all 27 flats and the 'second fix' of nine of them he was in financial difficulty, partly because of the lowness of the price, but mainly, it seems, because of his poor supervision of his workforce. The defendants were keen to complete the head contract on time, since they would otherwise have to pay penalties for lateness under their head contract with the building owner. With that in view, they approached the plaintiff and offered to increase the subcontract price by £10,300. The plaintiff accepted that proposal and had substantially completed the second fix of a further eight flats when he ceased work altogether. The defendants thereupon engaged other carpenters and, in the end, incurred a one-week penalty under the head contract. They declined to pay for the work the plaintiff had done subsequent to the promise of additional remuneration.

The plaintiff having sued to recover the outstanding amounts, the defendants argued, inter alia, that since the plaintiff had undertaken to do no more in return

1 *Williams v Roffey Bros & Nicholls (Contractors) Ltd* [1991] 1 QB 1 (CA).
2 See, eg, Roger Halson's note at (1990) 106 *Law Quarterly Review* 183.

for the additional payment than he was already obliged to do under the subcontract, the defendants' promise to make that payment was without consideration and, therefore, unenforceable. At the first instance, judgment was given for the plaintiff for £3,500 damages with £1,400 interest and costs. The defendants' subsequent appeal was dismissed in a reserved decision by a unanimous Court of Appeal (Purchas, Glidewell and Russell LJJ). On the issue with which this chapter is concerned, none of their Lordships questioned the need for the plaintiff to show consideration for the defendants' promise of additional payment but all were agreed that sufficient additional consideration had been provided. That additional consideration, they held, was to be found, not in any undertaking or work additional to what was provided for in the original contract, for there was none, but in the potential benefits to the defendants of the plaintiff's completing his carpenter's work on time, in particular by making it possible for the defendants to avoid having to pay the already-mentioned penalties under their head contract.

It is not proposed at this point to enter into a full discussion of the law governing promises to perform existing duties. On the other hand, over the years there have been many expressions of regret, amongst them some from the House of Lords,[3] that consideration should be necessary for the variation of a contract.[4] The actual result reached by the Court of Appeal would therefore not be without its attractions. As against that, the Lord Justices' views of what can constitute fresh consideration are so remote from received learning that it may be instructive to consider briefly by what reasoning they came to reach the conclusions they did.

## The Judgment

The leading judgment was given by Glidewell LJ, whose reasoning is encapsulated in the following passage:

> The present state of the law on this subject can be expressed in the following proposition: (i) if A has entered into a contract with B to do work for, or to supply goods or services to, B in return for payment by B and (ii) at some stage before A has completely performed his obligations under the contract B has reason to doubt whether A will, or will be able to, complete his side of the bargain and (iii) B thereupon promises A an additional payment in return for A's promise to perform his contractual obligations on time and (iv) as a result of giving his promise B obtains in practice a benefit, or

[3] *Foakes v Beer* (1884) 9 App Cas 605 (HL).

[4] See, eg, FMB Reynolds and GH Treitel, 'Consideration for the Modification of Contracts' (1965) 7 *Malaya Law Review* 1; JB Ames, 'Two Theories of Consideration' (1899) 12 *Harvard Law Review* 515; DW Greig and JLR Davis, *The Law of Contract* (Sydney, Law Book Company, 1987) 108; Cheshire, Fifoot and Furmston, *The Law of Contract* (11th ed, London, Butterworths, 1986) 90. The English Law Revision Committee in its *Sixth Interim Report* (1937) proposed that a promise to perform an existing duty be deemed to be made for consideration.

> obviates a disbenefit, and (v) B's promise is not given as a result of economic duress or fraud on the part of A, then (vi) the benefit to B is capable of being consideration for B's promise, so that the promise will be legally binding.[5]

According to the Lord Justice, counsel for the defendants had acknowledged that, in promising additional payment, his clients had sought (i) to ensure the plaintiff did not stop work in breach of the subcontract, (ii) to avoid having to pay the penalty for the delay, and (iii) to avoid the trouble and expense of engaging others to complete the subcontract. Counsel accepted that the achievement of these objectives could be benefits in practice but denied that they could be benefits in law sufficient to constitute consideration. As the above-quoted passage shows, Glidewell LJ declined to make this distinction. In his view, practical benefits in fact did constitute consideration unless vitiated by fraud or duress, and neither of those had been suggested in this case.[6]

The approach of Russell LJ was very similar except that, to the benefits to be received by the defendants, he added replacement of hitherto haphazard methods of payment by a more formalised scheme involving the payment of a specified sum on completion of each flat.[7] Arguably, as it entailed the surrender by the plaintiff of any of his existing rights under the subcontract, that alteration would have provided a sufficient consideration. But at least according to Purchas LJ, the payment 'per flat' was restricted to disbursement of the additional remuneration and in respect of that, *ex hypothesi*, the plaintiff had no existing rights.[8] Russell LJ concluded that the defendants' promise of the additional sum was supported by consideration 'which a pragmatic approach to the true relationship between the parties readily demonstrates'.[9] His use of the word 'pragmatic' tends to confirm that, like Glidewell LJ, he considered that a practical benefit would be a sufficient consideration.

For Purchas LJ, the arrangement to pay the extra £10,300 appeared beneficial to both sides for the added reason that payment of that sum was to be made at the rate of £575 on the completion of each flat. This meant that 'by completing one flat at a time rather than half completing all the flats, the plaintiff was able to receive moneys on account and the defendants were able to direct their other trades to do work in the completed flats which otherwise would have been held up until the plaintiff had completed his work'.[10] Here again, if the altered arrangements between the parties had meant that the plaintiff surrendered existing rights to payment, or accepted a new obligation to complete the flats one at a time, there would have been sufficient fresh consideration. But neither Purchas LJ nor the other two members of the Court said as much and, at first

5 [1991] 1 QB 1, 15–16.
6 ibid, 16.
7 ibid, 19.
8 ibid, 20.
9 ibid, 19.
10 ibid, 20.

instance, the finding of consideration was apparently justified by the learned judge simply on the basis that where an original contract price is too low it is in the interests of both parties to increase it.[11] As it was, Purchas LJ went on to deny that the plaintiff had accepted any additional obligation. He found consideration for the arrangement in its commercial advantage to both sides 'from a pragmatic point of view'.[12] Again the use of the word 'pragmatic' suggests that, like his brethren, he was rejecting any distinction between benefits in practice and benefits in law.

## The Meaning of the Decision

It follows that central to the results reached by all three members of the Court was the premise that should a contracting party actually perform his or her side of an existing bargain, or re-promise such performance, there would be good consideration for a promise by the other party to pay additional remuneration provided actual performance would provide more benefits to the promisor than would non-performance (or, for that matter, fewer harms than would breach). If that were correct, of course, it would also have to follow that consideration for promises of additional remuneration would be absent only in cases where the promisor had stood to obtain no advantage from performance of the contract when it was first made, or where the circumstances had so changed since the contract was made that all chance of the promisor's obtaining an advantage from performance had been lost. Since in neither of those cases would a rational party be likely to offer increased remuneration for completion (which would be to throw good money after irretrievably bad) it would be rare indeed for promises of extra payment to fail for lack of consideration.

That so comprehensive a solution to a perceived problem had hitherto remained unrecognised by the courts might have been expected to put their Lordships on enquiry. How did they come to suppose that such a solution could be plausible?

## An Explanation for the Decision

The clue to that, it is believed, lies in their rejection of counsel's distinction between a benefit in fact (or in practice) and a benefit in law—a rejection which presupposed a particular view of what constitutes the consideration for a contract. In their search for consideration, what each member of the Court fastened upon were the benefits or advantages the promisee stood to gain from

[11] ibid, 10.
[12] ibid, 22.

actual performance by the promisor. The impression derived from the judgments is that it was the benefits or advantages themselves which were thought to constitute the consideration. If so, some support for such a view might be drawn from some nineteenth-century cases, which do define consideration in terms of benefit and detriment, the best-known being *Currie v Misa*[13] where the formula used was:

> A valuable consideration, in the sense of the law, may consist either in some right, interest, profit, or benefit accruing to one party, or some forbearance, detriment, loss or responsibility given, suffered or undertaken by the other.[14]

In the application of a formula such as that, the crucial question, of course, is what was meant by a 'benefit'.

## Bilateral Contracts

If not before, then at least by the 1880s,[15] it became clear that in the case of an executory bilateral contract, consideration could not be an advantage gained as the result of performance. The reason why that should be so is that consideration is required for the formation of a contract. Performance, *ex hypothesi*, comes too late to qualify. Since executory bilateral contracts are formed by an exchange of promises with intention to contract, consideration for them must lie not in performance or its consequences but in some aspect of the exchange of promises. The only situation where performance is also the consideration is in the case of a unilateral contract—of a promise to reward the performance of an act.

All of this was very apparent to such late nineteenth-century writers as Sir William Anson[16] and Sir Frederick Pollock,[17] and it explains why the latter's famous definition of consideration, adopted by Lord Dunedin in *Dunlop Pneumatic Tyre Co Ltd v Selfridge & Co Ltd*,[18] took the form:

> An act or forbearance of one party, or the promise thereof, is the price for which the promise of the other is bought, and the promise thus given for value is enforceable.[19]

It was in this sort of context that a distinction had to be drawn between a benefit in fact or in practice (which could not itself be consideration, but was the hoped-for end result of performance) and a benefit in law (which referred to what the parties gave in exchange at the moment of formation).

13 *Currie v Misa* (1875) LR 10 Exch 153.

14 ibid, 162. See also *Thomas v Thomas* [1842] 2 QB 851 at 859; 114 ER 330 at 333–4. In Lindgren, Carter and Harland, *Contract Law in Australia* (Sydney, Butterworths, 1986) 80, 10 definitions of consideration are reproduced.

15 See below at nn 15–18 and accompanying text.

16 WR Anson, *Principles of the English Law of Contract* (Oxford, Clarendon Press, 1879) 81.

17 F Pollock, *Principles of the Law of Contract* (8th ed, London, Stevens & Sons, 1911) 175.

18 *Dunlop Pneumatic Tyre Co Ltd v Selfridge & Co Ltd* [1915] AC 847 (HL), 855.

19 Above n 17, 175.

Just what aspect of the exchange constituted the actual consideration in its turn gave rise to conceptual difficulties to which Anson drew attention in the first edition of his textbook on contract.[20] It was thought that the promises themselves could not be consideration because until the contract was formed they were no more than words. On the other hand, neither could the resulting contractual obligations qualify because, while consideration was a prerequisite to formation, the obligations resulted from it. The present writer has earlier[21] suggested that a solution to this apparent difficulty (what Sir Frederick Pollock called 'the secret paradox'[22]) could be found in the notion that a contract is an assumption of legal contractual obligation by a means which the law recognises as effective for that purpose. If that is so, the considerations the parties offer each other in a bilateral contract are their reciprocal assumptions of obligation.

Whether one accepts that analysis or prefers to regard consideration as the promise or as the resulting obligation, makes little difference in the present existing-duty context. The crucial point is that the considerations for the new bilateral arrangement have to be exchanged at the time the arrangement is made and they therefore have to stem from the promises exchanged at that point. But if a promise or undertaking relied on is the mere repetition of a promise or undertaking already made or given to the other party, it cannot constitute a new and additional consideration because nothing new or additional has been promised or undertaken. The newly repeated promise or undertaking is no more than a tautology.[23]

## Unilateral Contracts

In the *Roffey Bros* case, Glidewell LJ treated the plaintiff as a promisor within the new arrangement, which means that he saw the arrangement as a bilateral one.[24] That was the basis on which counsel for the defendants had framed his argument[25] and, while neither of the other two members of the Court mentioned the issue, it can be assumed that they did not dissent from that analysis. That notwithstanding, it would perhaps be as well to consider what would have been the position had the new arrangement been a unilateral one, under which the defendants had promised to reward the plaintiff for actual completion, without requiring in return any fresh promise by the plaintiff to perform his existing obligations. Since completion of the act required to earn the reward is both

[20] Above, n 16, 191–3.

[21] Brian Coote, 'The Essence of Contract (Parts I and II)' (1988–89) 1 *Journal of Contract Law* 91 and 183, 191–3. The article now forms ch 2 of this book. See ch 2 text around n 215ff.

[22] In an anonymous book review in (1914) 30 *Law Quarterly Review* 128, 129.

[23] *cf Wigan v Edwards* (1973) 47 ALJR 586, 594 per Mason J ('the new promise … is an illusory consideration').

[24] [1991] 1 QB 1(CA), 15–16.

[25] ibid, 11.

performance and consideration, this is a situation where benefit in fact (or practice) and benefit in law are more closely linked. That being so, it may in such a case appear rather more plausible to suggest that an actual performance or its results can amount to a fresh consideration. No longer is the concern with the mere repetition of the earlier promise. Performance and its results, and the promise of performance, it might be suggested, are distinct both conceptually and in fact. As it happens, in the context of an existing duty owed to a third person, such a distinction was drawn by Professor AG Davis in an article[26] which has found favour in successive editions of *Cheshire and Fifoot.*

Nevertheless, and with respect, it is submitted that that argument has to fail. Actual performance of an obligation that the actor already owes to the promisor provides nothing that is not already the promisor's right. It could constitute fresh consideration only if the law were to recognise some break in that link between a contract and its performance which is inherent in the concept of enforceable legal obligation.

Historically, two relevant suggestions have gained some currency. One is the well-known thesis of Oliver Wendell Holmes Jr,[27] echoed by Purchas LJ in the *Roffey Bros* case,[28] that a contract is a form of option under which a contracting party has a choice whether to perform or pay damages. Neither at the time it was propounded, nor since, has that thesis found much support. The other is a variant of the 'bird in the hand' argument, that actual performance of an existing obligation can be good consideration because it is to the claimant's advantage not to have to bring action to enforce the claim. In an article published at the turn of the twentieth century, Professor JB Ames listed several sixteenth- and seventeenth-century cases where that argument succeeded.[29] Some might find it mildly surprising that the courts should once have accepted as a legal principle that it was a detriment to bring actions before them. But in any event, whatever weight those cases may have had has long since been displaced by the House of Lords in *Foakes v Beer.*[30] It is noteworthy that in his famous near-dissent in that case, Lord Blackburn, while expressly recognising the advantages of having a bird in the hand,[31] did not assert that those advantages constituted fresh consideration. On the contrary, his argument was that, historically, consideration was irrelevant to and unnecessary for the satisfaction of a debt,[32] an argument made also by Professor Ames in his article.

[26] AG Davis, 'Promises to Perform an Existing Duty' (1938) 6 *Cambridge Law Journal* 202.

[27] OW Holmes, *The Common Law* (Boston, Macmillan, 1881) 298.

[28] [1991] 1 QB 1 (CA), 23.

[29] Above n 4, 523ff.

[30] (1884) 9 App Cas 605 (HL).

[31] ibid, 622.

[32] ibid, 616ff.

## Conclusion

Theoretically, it may still be open to a court of final resort in a common law country to decide that consideration should not be necessary for the variation of a contract.[33] After all, the High Court of Australia did something not too dissimilar in *Trident v McNiece*,[34] though the chances of the present House of Lords acting in such a way seem remote. But what, it is submitted, no court of final resort could do without hopelessly compromising the doctrine of consideration would be to hold, as the Court of Appeal did in *Roffey Bros*, that additional consideration is to be found in the benefits flowing from the mere performance of a duty already owed to the promisee under a contract between the same parties. By the same token, neither could additional consideration be found in the performance itself.[35]

[33] A decision to that effect by the New Zealand Court of Appeal is discussed in ch 4 below.

[34] *Trident General Insurance Co Ltd v McNiece Bros Ltd* (1989) 62 ALJR 508 (High Court of Australia).

[35] For the position where the existing duty arises under a contract with a third party or is publicly owed, see the text at nn 242–4 of ch 2 of this book.

# 4

# Consideration and Variations: A Different Solution

UNLESS THE CONDITIONS for waiver or estoppel are present, the variation of a contract has also to be by contract.[1] A simple contract to vary therefore needs to conform to the requirements for formation, namely agreement, consideration and an intention to effect legal relations. Notoriously, though, when one of the parties promises no more than he undertook under the contract being varied, this need for consideration raises special problems. If the contract to vary is an executory bilateral one, neither the promise, nor the benefits promised, can count as consideration because they are already owed by the promisor to the promisee.[2] Nevertheless, on the 'bird in the hand' principle, it may well be to the advantage of a promisee in some cases to undertake new obligations without additional return, rather than simply to stand on his rights.

In *Williams v Roffey Bros & Nicholls (Contractors) Ltd*[3] (hereinafter '*Roffey Bros*') the Court of Appeal sought to solve this problem by extending the concept of consideration to encompass incidental benefits, additional to those contracted for, which the promisee might hope or expect to flow from the promisor's continued performance of his existing obligations. Inevitably, there are those who, whatever the context, find it difficult to accept that the consideration required for the formation of a contract can consist of no more than the hopes and expectations of benefit entertained by a promisee. Such persons (and always assuming that a solution to the perceived problem does need to be found) may be interested to learn that, in *Antons Trawling Co Ltd v Smith*,[4] the Court of Appeal of New Zealand has preferred to dispense altogether with the need for consideration in variation contracts.

[1] eg *British and Benningtons Ltd v NW Cachar Tea Co* [1923] AC 48 (HL), 62 and 69; *United Dominion Corp (Jamaica) Ltd v Shoucair* [1969] 1 AC 340 (PC), 347; *Commissioner of Taxation of the Commonwealth of Australia v Sara Lee Household and Body Care (Australia) Pty Ltd* (2000) 201 CLR 520, 526–7 and 533.

[2] *Stilk v Myrick* (1809) 2 Camp 317.

[3] *Williams v Roffey Bros & Nicholls (Contractors) Ltd* [1991] 1 QB 1 (CA).

[4] *Antons Trawling Co Ltd v Smith* [2003] 2 NZLR 23 (CA).

Under New Zealand law, the extraction of many species of fish from within the country's exclusive economic zone is controlled by the issue of transferable quotas. Once issued, they confer valuable property rights in respect of the species to which they relate. Antons owned fishing vessels and wished to obtain additional quota by proving the existence of a new commercial fishery in an area and for a species in respect of which no quota had yet been issued. To this end, they engaged the plaintiff Smith as master of one of their vessels on the terms of a standard form of agreement under which he could be required to undertake exploratory fishing and under which he and his crew would be paid a percentage of the net value of any fish they were able to catch. Since the fishing would be exploratory, the uncertainty involved put the plaintiff's income at some risk. He therefore, before the first voyage started, asked Antons to pay a daily rate under the terms of another clause in the agreement which referred to 'experimental or exploratory fishing' and which made provision for a daily rate to 'be agreed upon from time to time'. Antons declined so to agree but undertook instead that, if the plaintiff could prove a commercial fishery, he could have 10 per cent of any additional quota issued as a result. A commercial fishery was in fact proved and a relatively small additional quota was issued to Antons. A dispute having arisen between Smith and his employers, he commenced the action which in due course came before the Court of Appeal.

A key issue for determination was whether, since the plaintiff was to do no more than the standard form of agreement already required of him, Antons had received consideration for their undertaking to reward him with 10 per cent of the quota. The Court of Appeal held that there had indeed been a binding unilateral contract of variation.

Delivering the judgment of the Court, Baragwanath J noted that, while *Roffey Bros* had been followed at first instance in New Zealand and had received favourable (obiter) comment from a Judge of the Court of Appeal in *Attorney-General for England and Wales v R*,[5] it had also been 'trenchantly' criticised. He referred to material such as the Uniform Commercial Code, s 2–209(6), and to academic comment which supported the alternative solution of ceasing to require consideration for variations[6] and continued:

> We are satisfied that *Stilk v Myrick* can no longer be taken to control such cases as *Roffey Bros*, *Attorney-General for England and Wales* and the present case where there is no element of duress or other policy factor suggesting that an agreement, duly performed, should not attract the legal consequences that each party must reasonably be taken to have expected. On the contrary, a result that deprived Mr Smith of the benefit of what Antons promised he should receive would be inconsistent with the essential principle underlying the law of contract, that the law will seek or give effect to freely accepted reciprocal undertakings. The importance of consideration is as a valuable signal that the parties intend to be bound by their agreement, rather than an end in itself. Where

[5] *Attorney-General for England and Wales v R* [2002] 2 NZLR 91 (CA).

[6] Including the article which now forms ch 3 of this book.

> the parties who have already made such intention clear by entering legal relations have acted upon an agreement to a variation, in the absence of policy reasons to the contrary they should be bound by their agreement. Whichever option is adopted, whether that of *Roffey Bros* or that [of dispensing with the need for consideration] the result is in this case the same.[7]

The concept thus stated will no doubt in due course be further developed by the New Zealand courts. In the meantime, it prompts the following comments:

1. Of the two options last mentioned in the judgment, the second seems the more likely to emerge as the ratio. Not only are the options mutually exclusive, but the first is also hard to reconcile with what is said in the judgment about *Stilk v Myrick*.
2. The second option seems to recognise that for the variation of a contract a further contract is still required, the novelty being that consideration need no longer be supplied by the party under the existing duty. There can be no objection in theory to the notion of a contract, as such, without consideration, consideration being peculiar to the common law system. That system, anyway, already allows such exceptions as contracts by deed and letters of credit. The actions of the High Court of Australia and the Supreme Court of Canada, in *Trident General Insurance Co Ltd v McNiece Brothers Pty Ltd*[8] and *London Drugs Ltd v Kuehne & Nagel International Ltd*[9] respectively, in dispensing, as against a third party, with the requirement that consideration pass from the promisee, is not too far removed, nor are the statutory reforms of the privity rule in countries such as England, Wales and Northern Ireland, Australia and New Zealand.[10]
3. What *is* essential to the formation of a contract is that the parties employ a means which courts of the jurisdiction recognise as effective for the purpose. Depending on the system of law, this characteristically involves the use of external signs or symbols, such as an action, ritual or formula, which mark the transaction as different from other forms of undertaking or agreement. Such use must also be made with intention to effect legal relations. In *Antons*, the Court of Appeal dispensed with the need for external signs, unless the requirement that the variation be acted upon was intended to serve that purpose and was not prompted simply by the fact that the contract before the Court was a unilateral one. The resulting variation acts rather like a deed under which one party, only, has to undertake a fresh contractual obligation.
4. As was recognised in *Roffey Bros*, some other method would be needed by which to limit or control the circumstances in which a variation would still

[7] ibid, 45–6.

[8] *Trident General Insurance Co Ltd v McNiece Brothers Pty Ltd* (1988) 165 CLR 107 (High Court of Australia).

[9] *London Drugs Ltd v Kuehne & Nagel International Ltd* [1992] 3 SCR 299.

[10] See ch 10 of this book.

> be binding. It would defeat a principal object of the law of contract if a party, having secured a contract (quite possibly in competition with others) and having embarked upon performance, were free to refuse to proceed and demand extra payment *merely* on the ground that he had under-quoted for the job or that it had proved to be more difficult than he had expected, let alone just because he wished to extract a larger profit. Fraud and duress are obvious possible controls but the New Zealand court has gone further and referred more generally to 'policy reasons' why the parties should not be bound by the variation. Applied flexibly, that formula could be used to discourage behaviour by contractors which, although short of fraud or duress, took unfair advantage of the other party and so was contrary to good faith, or which otherwise was an abuse of a dominant bargaining position. The security of the original contract would thus receive greater protection, albeit at some cost to certainty.

Dispensing with the need for consideration in variations has been proposed for many years.[11] Its adoption means that the *Roffey Bros* type of 'consideration' can be discarded while making it still possible to secure results of the sort *Roffey Bros* was intended to achieve.

[11] See, eg, FMB Reynolds and GH Treitel, 'Consideration for the Modification of Contracts' (1965) 7 *Malaya Law Review* 1.

# 5

# Consideration and the Joint Promisee

IT IS ONE of the best-known axioms of the common law of contract that consideration must move from the promisee.[1] Expanded, this means that no person can in contract enforce a promise for which he has not provided consideration. As a principle, it has on its side the highest authority[2] and a reasonable degree of antiquity.[3]

However, in *Coulls v Bagot's Executor and Trustee Co Ltd*,[4] the High Court of Australia came up with a formula which, while purporting to respect the principle, would, if accepted, have the effect of reducing its impact in a potentially important group of cases. Four of the five High Court judges expressed the view that a joint promisee, if she were party to a contract, could sue to enforce it notwithstanding that she had not herself furnished any part of the consideration. The case concerned a widow whose late husband had contracted to grant a licence to a quarrying company for the extraction of metal from a quarry which the husband owned. Under the contract, royalties were to be paid to the husband and wife jointly while they both lived, and thereafter to the survivor of them. The wife's only part in the proceedings had been to append her signature to the contract document. Barwick CJ and Windeyer J (dissenting) held that the plaintiff was a party to the contract and, as a joint promisee, could enforce it notwithstanding that her husband alone had provided the consideration.[5] McTiernan, Taylor and Owen JJ held that the wife was not a party,[6] but Taylor

[1] See, eg: GC Cheshire and CHS Fifoot, *The Law of Contract* (9th ed by MP Furmston, London, Butterworths, 1976) 69; *Anson's Law of Contract* (24th ed by AG Guest, Oxford, Clarendon Press, 1975) 97; GH Treitel, *The Law of Contract* (4th ed, London, Stevens & Sons, 1975) 55; *Chitty on Contract* (24th ed by HG Beale, London, Sweet & Maxwell, 1977) vol 1, 77; *Sutton and Shannon on Contracts* (7th ed by AL Diamond et al, London, Butterworths, 1970) 76–7; JW Salmond and J Williams, *Principles of the Law of Contracts* (2nd ed, London, Sweet & Maxwell, 1945) 99; 9 *Halsbury's Laws of England* (4th ed) 188. A different view appears to obtain in the United States: see *Corbin on Contracts* (St Paul, Minn, West Publishing Co, 1963) vol 1, 532; *Restatement of Contracts*, §75(2).

[2] *Dunlop Pneumatic Tyre Co Ltd v Selfridge & Co Ltd* [1915] AC 847 (HL); *Vandepitte v Preferred Accident Insurance Corporation of New York* [1933] AC 70 (PC).

[3] eg *Tweddle v Atkinson* (1861) 1 B & S 393; *Price v Easton* (1833) 4 B & Ad 433; *Colyear v Mulgrave* (1836) 2 Keen 81; *Thomas v Thomas* (1842) 2 QB 851.

[4] *Coulls v Bagot's Executor and Trustee Co Ltd* (1967) 119 CLR 460 (High Court of Australia)

[5] ibid, 478–80 and 492–3.

[6] ibid, 483 and 486.

and Owen JJ agreed that if she had been a party the fact that it was her husband who had provided the consideration would not have been an impediment to her.[7]

In the course of his judgment, Windeyer J said of a promise made to joint promisees:

> It must, of course, be supported by consideration, but that does not mean by consideration furnished by them separately. It means a consideration given on behalf of them both and therefore moving from both of them. In such a case the promise of the promisor is not gratuitous; and, as between him and the joint promisees, it matters not how they were able to provide the price of his promise to them.[8]

Thus, the joint promisee principle was justified as being consistent with the ordinary law. Its practical consequence, though, does appear to be a negation of the requirement that consideration move from the promisee.[9] Even if consideration has been supplied on behalf of both joint promisees, the reality remains that one of them has himself provided nothing.

In the years since 1967, this apparent contradiction has not prevented an accumulation of support for the joint promisee principle. In *NZ Shipping Co Ltd v AM Satterthwaite & Co Ltd*[10] Lord Simon of Glaisdale saw it as 'an attractive proposition'. Text writers, too, have accepted it in varying degrees. Cheshire and Fifoot,[11] for example, have expressed the hope that the English courts may find themselves able to adopt it. Smith and Thomas[12] have altered their treatment of privity and consideration to take account of it. So, too, has the fourth edition of *Halsbury*.[13] After some initial hesitation, Treitel[14] seems now to treat it as accurately stating the law, while Professor Atiyah sees it as incidental support for his more general attack on the doctrine of consideration.[15] In the United States, it can be inferred that it would have had the support of the late Professors Williston and Corbin.[16] In Canada, it has the support of Professor Waddams in his textbook on contracts.[17]

[7] ibid, 486.

[8] ibid, 493.

[9] *cf* MC Cullity, 'Joint Bank Accounts with Volunteers' (1969) 85 *Law Quarterly Review* 530, 534; SM Waddams, *The Law of Contracts* (Toronto, Canada Law Book, 1977) 164–5.

[10] *NZ Shipping Co Ltd v AM Satterthwaite & Co Ltd* [1975] AC 154 (PC), 180; [1974] 1 NZLR 505, 522.

[11] Cheshire and Fifoot, above n 1, 72.

[12] JC Smith and JAC Thomas, *A Casebook on Contract* (6th ed, London, Sweet & Maxwell, 1977) 221–3.

[13] 9 *Halsbury's Laws of England* (4th ed) 188 and 202–5.

[14] Treitel, above n 1, 414–15. In the third edition (1970), 530 and 543, the *Coulls* case was treated as one of mandate rather than of promise. See also GH Treitel, 'Consideration: A Critical Analysis of Professor Atiyah's Fundamental Restatement' (1976) 50 *Australian Law Journal* 439, 445–46.

[15] PS Atiyah, *Consideration in Contracts: A Fundamental Restatement* (Canberra, ANU Press, 1971) 41–2.

[16] Both denied that consideration need move from the promisee: *Williston on Contracts* (3rd ed by WHE Jaeger, New York, Baker, Voorhis & Co, 1957) vol 2 at 819–20; *Corbin on Contracts*, above n 1, 532.

[17] Waddams, above n 9, 164.

We have, then, a statement of principle which needs to be taken seriously, and not only so in the antipodes. The problem remains whether it really can stand in the face of classical notions of consideration.

## The Arguments for the Joint Promisee Principle

As it happens, it is not too difficult to find decided cases in which one of two or more joint promisees was held able to enforce a contract notwithstanding that the consideration was apparently provided by the other or others of them. Thus, for example, in *Metcalfe v London, Brighton & South Coast Railway Co*[18] a box which contained the goods of two persons had been consigned 'freight on delivery'. The freight had been paid on arrival by one of these persons. Even so, there was held to have been a bailment contract with both jointly. In *Lockett v Charles*[19] a wife was held to have a contract with a restaurant notwithstanding that it was her husband who had paid for the meal. In *Olley v Marlborough Court Ltd*[20] another wife was held to have a contract with a hotel even though it was her husband who had booked her in in the first place, and had paid for her accommodation thereafter. In a more recent case[21] before the High Court of Australia it was said that a member of a small syndicate could be party to a contract to take a lottery ticket, even if he had not in fact contributed to its purchase.

Then there is the judgment of Lord Atkin in *McEvoy v Belfast Banking Co Ltd*,[22] referred to by Cheshire and Fifoot,[23] Treitel[24] and Professor Atiyah.[25] In that case a father had deposited a sum of his own money with the Belfast Bank, in the names of himself and his infant son. Lord Atkin thought the father and son had a contract with the bank jointly and severally.[26] Perhaps the strongest case of all, because the relevant parties were strictly not even joint promisees, is *Fleming v Bank of New Zealand Ltd*,[27] a decision of the Privy Council. There it was held that the respondent Bank had contracted with a customer to honour his cheque notwithstanding that it was a third party, his agent, who had provided the security against which the cheque was to be honoured.

As further support, another writer, Mr Dawson,[28] has drawn upon the cases which establish that a creditor can lose his right to proceed against a retiring

[18] *Metcalfe v London, Brighton & South Coast Railway Co* (1858) 4 CBNS 307.
[19] *Lockett v Charles* [1938] 4 All ER 170 (KBD).
[20] *Olley v Marlborough Court Ltd* [1949] 1 KB 532 (CA).
[21] *Voulis v Kozary* (1975) 5 ALJR 59 (High Court of Australia), 67 per Jacobs J, 68 per Murphy J
[22] *McEvoy v Belfast Banking Co Ltd* [1935] AC 24 (HL).
[23] Above n 1, 72.
[24] ibid, 415.
[25] Above n 15, 41.
[26] [1935] AC 24 (HL), 43.
[27] *Fleming v Bank of New Zealand Ltd* [1900] AC 577 (PC).
[28] F Dawson, 'Himalaya Clauses: Consideration, and Privity in Contract' (1974) 6 *New Zealand Universities Law Review* 161, 169.

partner if he has accepted a novation of a partnership debt with the remaining partners. In such cases, Mr Dawson suggests, it is the remaining partners who supply the consideration.[29] For his part Dr Treitel[30] argues that it is a matter of necessity that a promise to A and B jointly should be enforceable by them both, even if only one of them should have provided the consideration. If the position were otherwise, he claims, the promise would not be enforceable at all. The reason for this is that if the party who had provided the consideration were to sue alone, he would be defeated by the rule that all promisees under a joint promise must be parties to the action. Moreover, he continues, it follows from the doctrine of survivorship that the non-contributing party should be entitled to the entire benefit of the promise after the death of the other of them. As Dr Treitel has pointed out,[31] his reasoning receives support from passages in the judgments in *Coulls v Bagot's Executor and Trustee Co Ltd*.[32]

It can be claimed, therefore, that there are quite weighty arguments to support the joint promisee principle. Nevertheless, it still has to be reconciled with basic notions of privity and consideration. According to the classic case of *Dunlop v Selfridge*,[33] before he can enforce a promise in contract, a promisee must be a party and he must also provide consideration.

The answer to this problem, it might be suggested, is that the requirements of privity and consideration are separate and distinct.[34] As a requirement, privity can stand on its own and would remain a requirement even if the doctrine of consideration were to be abolished.[35] Under the privity rule the promisee must be a party to the contract. But the consideration rule does not require that a party should himself provide the consideration. So long as consideration is provided by someone on the party-promisee's behalf, the promise is not gratuitous.[36] Accordingly, if the promisor is paid his price, it is no concern of his how, as between parties who are joint promisees, the price has been found.[37] This, the argument might presumably be, would be the real meaning of cases like *Lockett v Charles*[38]

[29] A similar view is expressed in *Williston on Contracts*, above n 16, 453. As a further example of consideration moving from someone other than the promisee, Williston cites (at 452) the right of a mortgagee to recover under the mortgagee clause of a fire insurance policy even though it is the mortgagor who has paid the premiums. *Corbin on Contracts*, above n 1, 532, gives the case of a mortgagee whose rights as such are unaffected by the fact that the money for the advance has been supplied by a third person.

[30] Above n 1, 414–15. The same argument is advanced in Treitel, 'Consideration: A Critical Analysis of Professor Atiyah's Fundamental Restatement', above n 14, 445.

[31] Treitel, 'Consideration: A Critical Analysis of Professor Atiyah's Fundamental Restatement', above n 14, 445.

[32] (1967) 119 CLR 460 (High Court of Australia), 479, 486 and 493.

[33] [1915] AC 847 (HL).

[34] eg (1967) 119 CLR 460 (High Court of Australia), 478 per Barwick CJ; Treitel, above n 1, 420; Cullity, above n 9, 582; Waddams, above n 9, 164.

[35] *Kepong Prospecting Ltd v Schmidt* [1968] AC 810 (PC).

[36] eg *Coulls v Bagot's Executor and Trustee Co Ltd* (1967) 119 CLR 460 (High Court of Australia), 478–9 per Barwick CJ, 493 per Windeyer J.

[37] *cf Williston on Contracts*, above n 16, 451.

[38] *Lockett v Charles* [1938] 4 All ER 170 (KBD).

where a husband paid for his wife's meal, and of the cases according immunity to a retiring partner. All that would be required of a wife or of a retiring partner would be that she or he be a party to the contract. The consideration could be supplied on her or his behalf by an agent or joint promisee. *Fleming v Bank of New Zealand*,[39] where the security was provided by an agent of the Bank's customer, could be seen as another illustration of this truth.

The trouble with these arguments, however attractive they may seem, is that they run directly counter to what was actually said in *Dunlop v Selfridge*.[40] It is clear from the judgments in that case that their Lordships saw as essential to a promisee's right to enforce a contract not only that he be a party but also that consideration should move from him.[41] The two requirements were seen as cumulative.[42] Indeed, some commentators would go even further and say that the two requirements are really one.[43] Where, then, does the truth lie?

## Two Fallacies

It is submitted that the joint promisee principle is based on, and owes its attractiveness to, two fallacies, each of a kind which can all too easily occur in the common law.

### Consideration and Performance

The first of these fallacies arises from a confusion between the formation of a contract on the one hand and its performance on the other. It is not only laymen who incline to think of consideration in terms of the actual payment of a price.[44] Conveyancing practice itself tends to give support to such usage. But the actual payment of a price, in the case of bilateral (or synallagmatic) contracts, is a matter not of consideration but of performance. In the case of such contracts, the consideration is not payment by the promisee, but his initial promise to pay[45] or,

39 [1900] AC 577 (PC).

40 [1915] AC 847 (HL).

41 ibid, 853 per Viscount Haldane LC, 855 per Lord Dunedin; *cf* SJB (1935) 51 *Law Quarterly Review* 419.

42 ibid, 854 per Viscount Haldane LC, 855 per Lord Dunedin, 858 per Lord Atkinson, 859 per Lord Parker of Waddington, 862–3 per Lord Sumner, 864 per Lord Parmoor.

43 Smith and Thomas, above n 12, 21; Cheshire and Fifoot, above n 1, 69; Salmond and Williams, above n 1, 100; MP Furmston, 'Return to *Dunlop v Selfridge*?' (1960) 23 *Modern Law Review* 393, 382–4; G Samuels, 'Contracts for the Benefit of Third Parties' (1968) 8 *Western Australia Law Review* 378, 383.

44 *Fibrosa Spolka Akcyjna v Fairbairn Lawson Combe Barbour Ltd* [1943] AC 32 (HL), 56 per Lord Russell of Killowen. The expression 'failure of consideration', referring as it does to a failure in performance, only adds to the difficulty.

45 ibid, 48 per Viscount Simon LC, 53 per Lord Atkin, 72 per Lord Wright.

as the present writer would prefer, his initial acceptance of an obligation to pay.[46] Thus, for example, if a young man enters into an agreement for the purchase of a house property, the consideration he provides is his promise to pay the purchase price. He will be bound by his contract even though all parties realise that the actual source of funds is going to be a building society, or his father-in-law, or both.[47] It is possible to go further and say that the only cases where a party to a synallagmatic contract must himself execute the promised performance are those where personal performance is an express or implied requirement of the contract. If this is once accepted, it is easy to see how there can exist a series of cases in which a person was held able to enforce a contract even though the contract price had been paid or found by someone else.

Thus, in the case where goods were consigned to A and B but A paid the freight on arrival, B had a contract because he had expressly or impliedly undertaken to pay.[48] The other merely performed that obligation for him. And the wives whose husbands paid for their meal[49] or their accommodation[50] had contracts because they, too, had impliedly accepted an obligation to pay. The husbands' payment of the accounts was no more than performance of their wives' obligations. So, too, the syndicate member undertook an obligation to pay his share of the price of the lottery ticket and hence would have provided consideration, even if, in the event, no one had ever got around to collecting the money from him.[51]

Approached in this manner, the result of *Fleming v Bank of New Zealand*[52] could have been reached in a way which would no longer appear, as Lord Simon of Glaisdale in the *Satterthwaite* case[53] thought it did, inconsistent with *Dunlop v Selfridge*.[54] According to the Privy Council,[55] the Bank's manager had been told

[46] While it is indisputable that an exchange of promises can create a bilateral contract, to say that a promise per se constitutes consideration is to invite the logical difficulties noted by Corbin (above n 1, 611–14) and Williston (above n 16, 385–96) and which led Corbin to conclude (at 612) that consideration was a combination of promise and performance. However, even if these writers were correct in their objections it does not follow that they were right in their conclusions. To say that a promise constitutes consideration in most cases involves an ellipsis. The consideration is neither the promise per se nor its performance. It is the promisor's acceptance or assumption, at the time the contract is formed, of an obligation intended to be binding in law. It is hoped to develop that theme on a later occasion. (See now the article forming ch 2 of this book.) In the meantime, since the concept of an executory bilateral contract presupposes that formation of a contract will antedate performance, the consideration for such contracts has to be something other than the actual performance.

[47] Likewise, in the case cited by Corbin (above n 1, 532) where the funds for an advance were provided by someone other than the mortgagee, the contract would have been enforceable by the mortgagee because it was he who had accepted the obligation in law that the advance would be made and, by so doing, had provided consideration.

[48] *Metcalfe v London, Brighton & South Coast Railway* (1858) 4 CBNS 307.

[49] *Lockett v Charles* [1938] 4 All ER 170 (KBD).

[50] *Olley v Marlborough Court Ltd* [1949] 1 KB 532 (HL).

[51] *Voulis v Kozary* (1975) 50 ALJR 59 (High Court of Australia).

[52] [1900] AC 577 (PC).

[53] *New Zealand Shipping Co Ltd v AM Sattherwaite & Co* [1975] AC 154 (PC), 180; [1974] 1 NZLR 505 at 522.

[54] [1915] AC 847 (HL).

that the customer's instructions to his agent were to pay the Bank £1,000 in return for the honouring of the customer's cheques. The manager was told, too, that that sum would be paid accordingly if the manager required it. In these circumstances it would seem not unreasonable to have deduced that, had any contract at all been concluded with the customer, it would have been a contract consistent with his instructions to his agent. If that were once allowed, the deposit of the store warrant would have been a matter not of formation but of substituted performance. Equally, if the contract were to be construed as unilateral rather than bilateral, the act required would have been the customer's paying £1,000. The Bank would have accepted the deposit of the warrant as a substitute performance of that required act. If such a solution ultimately eluded their Lordships, at least they seem to have been feeling their way towards it.[56]

It is submitted that both Dr Treitel's argument from the nature of joint obligation and Mr Dawson's argument from the retiring partner cases can be met in a similar way. It would be surprising if, in any of the cases which support the requirement that all joint promisees join in any action on the promise, it were found (in the case of synallagmatic contracts not being by deed) that the promisees had not themselves all been under obligation to the promisor. Certainly Dr Treitel has not cited any such case, nor did any of the judges in *Coulls v Bagot's Executor and Trustee Co Ltd*.[57] Equally, one would not expect to find cases where a joint promisee had failed because he had not been joined by a third person who, while also a promisee, had not accepted any obligation under the contract. After all, the reason for the requirement that all joint promisees be joined in the action is the prevention of double liability rather than the creation of a liability which could not otherwise exist. Its effect is procedural, not substantive.

As to the retiring partner cases, they would support the joint promisee doctrine only if it could be shown that the retiring partner was released despite his having neither performed nor undertaken any obligations to the creditor. Since 1890, these cases have of course been governed by s 17(3) of the Partnership Act, which does not in terms stipulate for any consideration moving from the retiring partner to the creditor. But in the early cases from which the section evolved it is by no means clear that the retiring partner gave no consideration. In some cases, for example, his part in the arrangement would have been the surrender of his share in the partnership assets.[58] For the present purposes,

[55] [1900] AC 577 (PC), 586.

[56] ibid, 586–7. A similar explanation can be given for the rights of a mortgagee to recover directly from an insurance company, notwithstanding that the premiums have been paid by the mortgagor. The mortgagee is a party to the insurance, either directly or through the agency of the mortgagor, to the extent of his insurable interest, and as such is under obligation to the insurer (*cf Johnson v Ocean Accident and Guarantee Corporation Ltd* (1915) 34 NZLR 358; *Vandepitte v Preferred Accident Insurance Corporation of New York* [1933] AC 70 (PC); *Green v Russell* [1959] 2 QB 226 (CA)).

[57] (1967) 119 CLR 460 (High Court of Australia), 479, 486 and 493.

[58] *Attwood v Banks* (1839) 2 Beav 192.

though, the most important cases are a trilogy which began with *Kirwan v Kirwan*.[59] In the latter, during the course of the argument for the plaintiff, Parke B[60] said in effect that the withdrawal by a joint debtor from the debtor–creditor relationship could itself constitute a benefit (and hence consideration) to the creditor, in that it could improve his security. If it could be a benefit, Parke B asserted, it was not for the court to inquire whether in a particular case it had in fact proved to be a benefit. Lord Lynhurst CB appears to have agreed with this view. In two subsequent cases, *Thompson v Percival*[61] and *Lyth v Ault*,[62] the same reasoning formed part of the ratio decidendi. Whether or not it would nowadays carry conviction, this reasoning makes it difficult to suggest that the retiring partner cases represents an *intentional* departure from ordinary principles of consideration, let alone that they call in question the very existence of those principles.[63]

It will be recalled that in the course of his judgment in the *Coulls* case Windeyer J said that 'as between [the promisor] and the joint promisees it matters not how they were able to provide the price of his promise to them'.[64] It is certainly true that, in the absence of any provision to the contrary in the contract, it matters not that only one joint promisee supplied the funds to enable payment of the contract price. But what does matter in the case of a synallagmatic contract is that the joint promisees should both have accepted some initial obligation to the promisor that payment would be made.

## The 'Parties' to the Contract

The other fallacy on which the joint promisee principle is based stems from the use of the expressions 'party' and 'contract' in more than one sense. The word 'contract' can be used to express the relationship between parties legally bound by their agreement, or to cover the legal principles underpinning their relationship, or to denote the form in which the relationship is expressed, particularly when it is a document. In relation to simple contracts, the primary use of the word 'party' is to denote someone bound by a contractual relationship. By contrast it may be that a person can be named as a party to a deed even though he is not a covenantor, but only a beneficiary.[65] 'Party' might also be used to cover someone who was no more than a signatory to a contractual document. Finally, the word

59 *Kirwan v Kirwan* (1834) 2 C & M 617.

60 ibid, 623.

61 *Thompson v Percival* (1834) 5 B & Ad 925.

62 *Lyth v Ault* (1852) 7 Ex 669.

63 In *Corbin on Contracts*, above n 1, 618, it is asserted, not that the courts failed to find consideration, but that the consideration they found was a fictitious one.

64 (1967) 119 CLR 460 (High Court of Australia), 493.

65 *cf* Salmond and Williams, above n 1, 382–3.

has been said to cover all 'those persons who reach agreement',[66] 'agreement' being not necessarily synonymous with 'contract'.

In *Coulls v Bagot's Executor and Trustee Co Ltd*,[67] the plaintiff widow was a 'party' to the quarrying contract in the sense of being a signatory to the contractual document. She was also an intended beneficiary so that had the document been a deed she might have been a party in a second sense. She might also have been a party to an agreement, though she had taken no part in the negotiations which had led up to the signing of the document. But she could be a party in the sense of a party to a contractual relationship with the quarrying company only if it is possible to be a party to such a relationship without providing consideration for it. Whether that really is possible is a matter not so much of principle as of the definition of contracts at common law. And here the predominant view, it seems, is still that (contracts of record apart) a contract at common law is a species of bargain, an essential condition of which is the reciprocal exchange of consideration between the parties. Only those who provide consideration can be parties, the requirement that consideration move from the promisee being a consequence of this very fact.[68] To hold otherwise is to confuse contract, which must be a bargain, with agreement, which need not be. Nor is it at all clear that Windeyer J, at least, would have denied this. His argument was not that the plaintiff widow could be a party without providing consideration but rather (inter alia) that this requirement had been met by her husband on her behalf.[69] It has already been submitted that the source of this latter error was an understandable confusion between the provision of consideration on the one hand and its performance on the other. If all this is accepted, it is easy to agree with Taylor and Owen JJ that, provided the widow had been a party, it would have been immaterial that the quarry belonged to her husband. The reason she was not a party would have been, not that her husband had supplied the quarry, but that she herself had undertaken no obligation to the quarrying company, whether to be responsible in law for her husband's performance, or in any other way. So, too, while a majority of their Lordships in *McEvoy v Belfast Banking Co*[70] rejected the son's claim because he was not a party to any contract

[66] 9 *Halsbury's Laws of England* (4th ed) 202. By contrast, the third edition treated 'stranger to the contract' and 'stranger to the consideration' as synonymous (8 *Halsbury's Laws of England* (3rd ed) 66 and 115–16). On the evidence of the treatment of consideration on p 188 of vol 9 of the fourth edition, the change was made in order to take account of *Coulls v Bagot's Executor and Trustee Co Ltd* (1967) 119 CLR 460 (High Court of Australia).

[67] (1967) 119 CLR 460 (High Court of Australia).

[68] See citations above n 43. See also *Sutton and Shannon on Contracts* (5th ed by KW Wedderburn, London, Butterworths, 1956) 369; Waddams, above n 9, 164–5; and 8 *Halsbury's Laws of England* (3rd ed) 66 and 115–16. The contrary view is adopted in *Anson's Law of Contract*, above n 1, 97–8 and Cullity, above n 9, 532, where privity of *agreement* is equated with privity of contract. In *Chitty on Contracts*, above n 1, 516–17 and Treitel, above n 1, 420–2 it appears to be suggested that privity of *promise* constitutes privity of contract.

[69] See passage quoted in the text above at n 8.

[70] [1935] AC 24 (HL).

with the Bank, it was quite possible in law for Lord Thankerton, while concurring with the majority, to agree with Lord Atkin that had the son been a party it would have been immaterial that the father had provided all the funds for the deposit. What could have made the son a party would have been an acceptance by him of an obligation to make or join in making the deposit, or even a mere acceptance by him, through his father, of the ordinary duties of a customer to the Bank.[71]

## Joint Promisee as Promisor

It is concluded, therefore, that the joint promisee doctrine is misconceived and that in the case of a simple bilateral (or synallagmatic) contract a joint promisee can enforce a joint promise only if he is himself a promisor. It should be emphasised that this conclusion would not pose any difficulty to a joint promisee who was himself prepared to undertake obligations to the promisor. If he did so he would be able to enforce the contract even if it were not he but only his co-promisee who would or could perform. To this it might be objected that to make a promise which only his co-promisee could perform would be to promise the impossible and that a promise of the impossible cannot constitute consideration. Thus, in the *Coulls* case,[72] it might be said, the widow had no rights over her husband's quarry, so that any consideration she might have provided by joining in her husband's promises could only have been illusory.

The answer to such an objection, it is submitted, is that, once again, it confuses consideration with performance. It is true that a promise of the impossible may in some cases be illusory and hence not constitute consideration.[73] But except in cases requiring personal performance, a promise of something one cannot oneself perform is not a promise of the impossible if it can be performed by someone else.[74] Companies and corporations make such promises daily, as do private employers. In the *Coulls* case[75] the benefit to the quarrying company, if the widow had joined in her husband's promise, would have been, not her provision of the quarry, but her accountability in law should her husband have defaulted.

[71] *cf* Cullity, above n 9, 532.

[72] (1967) 119 CLR 460 (High Court of Australia).

[73] De facto impossibility of performance does not by itself make a promise illusory. Thus, there can be a valid promise to sell a tanker which, unknown to the parties, does not exist (*McRae v Commonwealth Disposals Commission* (1951) 84 CLR 377 (CA)). To be illusory on the ground of impossibility, the promise must be of something which the parties knew to be impossible, as, for example, a promise to perform on a date which had already passed when the promise was made (*Hall v Cazenove* (1804) 4 East 477).

[74] See, eg, *Arden v Tacker* (1833) 4 B & Ad 815 at 820–1; *cf St Margaret's Rochester Burial Board v Thompson* (1871) LR 6 CP 455.

[75] (1967) 119 CLR 460 (High Court of Australia).

## Unilateral Contracts

So far the argument has been confined to bilateral or synallagmatic contracts. Still to be considered is the position where the contract is unilateral. The difference here is of course that when a contract is unilateral it is no longer possible to separate formation from performance. Performance is both acceptance and consideration. Enforcement by a joint promisee would necessarily be confined to cases where he had himself performed, or procured the performance of, at least some part of the required act.

At first sight it might seem that there are at least some exceptions to this requirement. For example, a vendor's promise to pay commission to a partnership of land agents is normally enforceable by all the partners even in respect of a sale negotiated by only one of them. In such a case, however, the exception is only an apparent one. While the sale would signify completion of the act stipulated for in the promise, and would be the condition on which payment of the commission depended, performance itself would be more complex. The promise made to the partnership would have envisaged that resources belonging to the members collectively would be engaged. Negotiations for the sale would take place during time for which the partner would be accountable to the partnership, and partnership property would be involved in such things as advertising and interviews. Alternatively, the arrangements could be seen as one where the promise of commission envisaged that the partners collectively would procure performance of the required act by one of them.

Similarly, a promise of a prize to A and B if A should swim the English Channel would be enforceable by both A and B if the promise contemplated that B would be providing the boat to accompany A on his crossing. Completion of the swim by A would be the condition for payment of the reward, but the contemplated performance and acceptance would be compounded of the actions of both of them. On the other hand if, in the example just given, B were a stranger who it was contemplated would play no part whatever in the performance, or in procuring the performance, he could have no ground for enforcing the contract. The fact that he was a joint promisee could not help him, nor would it prevent A enforcing the contract by himself.

Conversely, of course, where the offer of a unilateral contract calls for acts by A and B jointly, and both join in the performance of those acts, rights of action would accrue to both even though the wherewithal to enable B to perform his part were a gift to him from A.[76]

[76] *Lockhart v Barnard* (1845) 14 M & W 674.

# Conclusion

To sum up, then, it is submitted that the joint promisee doctrine enunciated in *Coulls v Bagot's Executor and Trustee Co Ltd*[77] was based on a misapprehension of what constitutes the provision of consideration and of what constitutes a 'party' to a contract. The requirement of the common law remains that consideration move from the promisee. To that requirement joint promisees are no exception

# Addendum

A like confusion in relation to bids at auction is discussed in the following extract from a more recent article:[78]

Counsel's remaining argument in *Barry v Davies*[79] (that there was no consideration for any promise to sell to the highest bidder because the bidder had not promised to do anything, or at the most had made a discretionary promise, which would be an illusory consideration) is based on the premise that any contract to sell to the highest bidder would be bilateral. As an argument, it goes back some way, having appeared in a 1952 article by CJ Slade in the *Law Quarterly Review*.[80]

After reference to Professor Corbin's view that the mere making of a bid could be a sufficient consideration for the promise to sell without reserve, Slade commented:

> This reasoning cannot at least be accepted in English law. The mere making of a bid is no more consideration for the promise than the effort of saying or even writing the words 'I accept' is consideration to support a gratuitous offer. In reason and in justice there are no grounds for imposing any legal liability on a seller at a point of time before a corresponding liability is imposed on the other contracting party.[81]

In a reply published later in the same volume of the *Law Quarterly Review*,[82] Professor LCB Gower, like Professor Corbin, argued that consideration for a unilateral contract was to be found in the rule that an act done at the request of another, express or implied, is sufficient consideration to support a promise made by that other. What in the case of an auction the particular requested act would be, whether to attend the auction, to bid, or to be the highest bidder, might be a matter of dispute. But on the matter of principle, it is submitted that Professors Corbin and Gower were clearly right. That rule or principle is, by the

[77] (1967) 119 CLR 460 (High Court of Australia).

[78] Brian Coote, 'Sale of Goods at Auction Without Reserve' [2001] *New Zealand Law Review* 277 at 285–9

[79] *Barry v Davies* [2000] 1 WLR 1962 (CA).

[80] CJ Slade, 'Auction Sales of Goods Without Reserve' (1952) 68 *Law Quarterly Review* 238.

[81] ibid, 241.

[82] LCB Gower, 'Auction Sales of Goods Without Reserve' (1952) 68 *Law Quarterly Review* 457, 458.

way, the basis for the argument that, when the contract is a unilateral one, it is only on completion of the required act that consideration for *that* contract can exist and, hence, that a binding contract can come into existence. That in turn goes back to the underlying principle that, deeds and the occasional anomaly apart, no contract can exist at common law without consideration, the necessary consequence being that the consideration has to be present at the point of formation. That is why, for example, a promise to keep an offer of a reward open for acceptance has itself to be the subject of a second (collateral) contract to do so.[83]

But if, as is submitted, the consideration for the promise of a unilateral contract is the performance of the required act, where, it would be asked by someone with Slade's views, is the benefit or detriment in a bid that, without more, is not binding and that can be withdrawn at will at any time before the hammer falls? The answer to that as given by Sir William Anson in his book on contract is that:

> Courts of law will not make bargains for the parties to a suit, and, *if a man gets what he has contracted for*, will not inquire whether it was an equivalent to the promise which he gave in return. The consideration may be a benefit to the promisor, or to a third party, *or may be of no apparent benefit to anybody*, but merely a detriment to the promisee: in any case 'its adequacy is for the parties to consider at the time of making the agreement not for the Court when it is sought to be enforced'.[84]

In other words, if an auctioneer expressly or impliedly stipulates for the highest or any bid as the price of his promise and gets what he asked for, a contract is formed and he is bound by it. The benefit lies in his obtaining the act for which he stipulated and the detriment lies in its being done. It is irrelevant whether or not it has economic worth (provided it otherwise has legal value). Thus, for example, in *Carlill v Carbolic Smoke Ball Co*, Bowen LJ said of the plaintiff:

> It seems to me that her using the smoke ball was sufficient consideration. I cannot picture to myself the view of the law on which the contrary could be held when you have once found who are the contracting parties. If I say to a person, 'If you use such and such a medicine for a week I will give you £5', and he uses it, there is ample consideration for the promise.[85]

There was no suggestion, at least by that Lord Justice, that for there to be consideration the defendant must make a profit from the sale of the medicine. In a reply to Professor Gower's response to his own earlier article, CJ Slade posed the difficulty of finding a contract where a millionaire promised to give money to a hospital, saying to the secretary, 'If you will please sign this receipt, I will send you

[83] *cf Daulia Ltd v Four Millbank Nominees Ltd* [1978] Ch 231 (CA). Noted by C Harpum and D Lloyd Jones [1979] *Cambridge Law Journal* 31.

[84] WR Anson, *Principles of the English Law of Contract* (13th ed by ML Gwyer, Oxford, Clarendon Press, 1912) 97–8 (emphasis added).

[85] *Carlill v Carbolic Smoke Ball Co* [1893] 1 QB 256 (CA), 272.

a cheque for £10,000 tomorrow.' How could it be said that the secretary's signature would be sufficient consideration to enforce the promise?[86] Always assuming a secretary would be prepared to give a receipt for such a sum in anticipation of payment at a later date, it is submitted that the short answer to the problem posed by Slade is that there would almost always be no contract. The reason would be not want of consideration but want of an intention to contract.

If the emphasis, above, on the act itself being the consideration for the promise of a unilateral contract, whatever its economic significance, seems laboured, the reason for that emphasis is that a very different alternative view has been expressed elsewhere. The alternative view is that consideration is to be found, not in the act itself but in the consequences for the parties of the performance of the act. Thus, in the *Carlill* case, AL Smith LJ found consideration in the inconvenience suffered by the plaintiff from having to use the smoke ball for two weeks and in 'the money gain likely to accrue to the defendants by the enhanced sale of the smoke balls by reason of the plaintiff's user of them'.[87] What makes this significant is that, in *Barry v Davies*, Sir Murray Stuart-Smith also appears to belong to this second school of thought:

> As to consideration, in my judgment there is consideration both in the form of detriment to the bidder, since his bid can be accepted unless and until it is withdrawn, and benefit to the auctioneer as the bidding is driven up. Moreover, attendance at the sale is likely to be increased if it is known that there is no reserve.[88]

That he should have expressed this view in this particular case is perhaps hardly surprising, since it is also the view stated in passages from two textbooks to which he had just previously referred.[89] In *Barry* it made no difference to the result. But ascription of consideration to the consequences of performance in the case of unilateral contracts (or in the case of executory bilateral contracts, either to actual performance or to the benefits hoped for from performance) does have the potential to be seriously misleading. Thus, it was the perception that consideration consisted not in the undertaking to perform but in the hoped-for benefit to be derived from performance which led to the Court of Appeal to decide as it did in *Williams v Roffey Bros & Nicholls (Contractors) Ltd*.[90] There it was held that, contrary to all previous authority, the practical advantages that might accrue to the promisee from something the promisor was already bound to do, under an existing contract with the promisee, could be consideration for a promise of additional payment by the promisee. The same sort of reasoning led the High

[86] CJ Slade, 'Auction Sales of Goods Without Reserve' (1953) 69 *Law Quarterly Review* 21.

[87] [1893] 1 QB 256 (CA), 275.

[88] [2000] 1 WLR 1962 (CA), 1967.

[89] *Chitty on Contracts* (28th ed by HG Beale, London, Sweet & Maxwell, 1999) vol 1, 94; *Benjamin's Sale of Goods* (5th ed by AG Guest, London, Sweet & Maxwell, 1997) 107. The passage in the latter cites only the corresponding passage in *Chitty*, which in turn is in the same terms as those used in relation to the same subject matter in GH Treitel, *The Law of Contract* (10th ed, London, Sweet & Maxwell, 1999) 142.

[90] [1991] QB 1 (CA).

Court of New Zealand,[91] in reliance on that case, to suppose that it was consideration for the offer of a lessee to pay half the current rent and the arrears that, for example, it had enabled the lessor to retain the prospect of a renewed lease at the expiration of the then current term. Clearly, if mere matters of hope and aspiration (or even actual performance in the case of a *bilateral* contract[92]) were really to be accounted the consideration for the formation of a contract, there would be little point in retaining consideration (or the concept of an executory bilateral contract for consideration) as part of the common law.

That aside, Sir Murray Stuart-Smith having found the presence of consideration as he saw it, the Court felt able to follow and confirm the principles stated by Martin B in *Warlow v Harrison*[93] and to hold that, in failing to knock down the machines to the plaintiff, the auctioneer had been in breach of a unilateral contract with him to sell without reserve.

[91] *Machirus Properties Ltd v Power Sports World (1987) Ltd* (1999) 4 NZ Conv C 193,066 (High Court of New Zealand) (Heron and Gendall JJ). Discussed in Brian Coote, 'Common Forms, Consideration and Contract Doctrine' (1999) 14 *Journal of Contract Law* 116, 122ff.

[92] As suggested by Treitel, above n 45, 64–8.

[93] *Warlow v Harrison* (1858) 1 El & El 295; (1859) 1 EI & EI 309.

# 6

# The Function of Exception Clauses

## The Current Approach

THE FUNCTION OF exception clauses is a subject which has received very little attention from the courts over the years. It seems to have been taken for granted that an exception clause provides merely a shield to a claim for damages and that it does not in itself affect the obligations undertaken by the promisor.[1] On this approach it is the duty of the courts, when confronted with a contract containing exception clauses, to look at the contract apart from the exempting clauses and see what are the terms express or implied which impose an obligation on the promisor.[2] The exempting clauses will then operate, if at all, only as a defence to breaches of the obligation thus determined. Hence the common use of the expressions 'exemption' and 'exclusion' clause.

Perhaps the classic statement of this approach is the judgment of Wright J in *Istros v Dahlstroem*.[3] Clause 8 of the charterparty in that case stated 'Captain to prosecute all voyages with utmost dispatch', while cl 12 provided in effect that the owners should be responsible for delay only where such delay was the result of the personal default of themselves or their manager. It having been found on the facts that the captain had failed to prosecute the voyage with the utmost dispatch, the question was whether the owners were protected by the exception clause. Wright J held that they were. It was the default of the captain, not the owners or their manager, which had caused the delay. The judgment then proceeded:

> It is not necessary here to consider whether every possible case that may arise under clause 8 of a failure on the part of the captain to prosecute all voyages with utmost dispatch is covered by clause 12. I have not in my mind at this moment any specific type of breach of clause 8 by the act of the captain for which, notwithstanding clause 12, the owner would be responsible. There may be such cases, but it seems to me that clause 12 must receive effect where the case comes within its clear terms.

[1] See, eg, *E Clemens Horst v Norfolk & NASN Co* (1906) 11 Com Cas 141, 146; *Istros v Dahlstroem* [1931] 1 KB 247 (KBD), 252–3; *Spurling v Bradshaw* [1956] 1 WLR 461 (CA), 467; *Karsales v Wallis* [1956] 1 WLR 936 (CA), 940.

[2] *cf Karsales v Wallis*, ibid, 940 per Denning LJ.

[3] [1931] 1 KB 247 (KBD).

> If the effect is to render the owner free from any liability for loss or delay where there is a failure on the part of the captain to prosecute the voyage with the utmost dispatch, then I think that the owner is entitled to the full benefit of that clause. Clause 8, it may be said, has then no practical effect. It has a practical effect to the extent that it contains clear recognition of the duty of the captain so to act, and the effect of clause 12 is not to modify or qualify the existence of that duty, although it may operate if an action is brought against the owner for damages as a defence. In one sense, every exception clause is *pro tanto* inconsistent with the primary or express obligations which at law or by contract rest upon an owner or a master in respect of the goods entrusted to his charge and the duties arising under a charterparty, but, notwithstanding those obligations, exception clauses must receive in due course, if their language and the circumstances require it, their appropriate effect as a shield to a claim for damages.[4]

Thus, while Wright J left open the question whether cl 8 might not in some circumstances be enforceable, he took the view that even had all liability for the master's default been excluded, this would not have affected the existence of a duty to prosecute the voyage with the utmost dispatch. In these circumstances, the exception clause had the effect of a shield to a claim for damages. Implicit in this conclusion is the assumption that the duty was a legal one, failure to perform which would amount to a breach of the contract. The function of the exception clause was to bar a claim based on such breach. That this approach remains the dominant one cannot be doubted. As shown elsewhere, it has for example played a decisive part in the development of the doctrines of fundamental breach and fundamental term.[5]

But ought it to be assumed so easily that this is in fact the function of all exception clauses? It is submitted that analysis would suggest otherwise. A promise which, by the use of an exception clause, is made at all times wholly unenforceable, could give rise to contractual obligation, as ordinarily understood, only in one of two events. The first possibility is that exception clauses are purely procedural in their effect so that substantive rights and obligations are unaffected by them. The alternative is that there is, at common law, a category of legal, contractual rights which have effect as such despite the intention of the parties that they shall never be enforceable. As a first step, then, it is necessary to consider these two possibilities.

[4] ibid, cited with approval in *Renton v Palmyra* [1956] 1 QB 462 (CA), 507 per Hodson LJ.

[5] Brian Coote, *Exception Clauses: Some Aspects of the Law Relating to Exception Clauses in Contracts for the Carriage, Bailment and Sale of Goods* (London, Sweet & Maxwell, 1964) ch 8. See also ch 7 of this book.

# Are Exception Clauses Substantive or Procedural In Their Effect?

Generally speaking, what distinguishes a contractual promise from other undertakings is, on the one hand, that it involves the assumption by the promisor of legal obligations or duties and, on the other, that it confers on the promisee corresponding rights to the performance of those obligations. Thus, if I promise for consideration to paint Smith's house, I place myself under an obligation to do so, and Smith has a corresponding right to have his house painted by me. In the language of jurisprudence, these features can be expressed by saying that a valid contractual promise confers on the promisee a substantive primary right *in personam* to performance of the promise and imposes on the promisor a correlative primary duty to perform. In addition there are two other classes of rights and duties arising from a contractual promise.

In the illustration given, I am subject to the further duty to pay pecuniary compensation, upon which I must act if I wrongfully fail to paint the house. This duty is also a substantive one and it is called sanctioning. The promisee of course has a correlative sanctioning right. The third category of rights comprises those of the promisee to enforce performance of his primary and sanctioning rights. These are called procedural.

To sum up, a valid contractual promise gives rise to two classes of substantive right *in personam*, each corresponding to a correlative duty.[6] The promisee has a sanctioning right to pecuniary compensation for the violation of his other contractual rights. All his other substantive rights are called primary.[7] Thus, the promisee's right to performance of the contractual promise is primary, while his right to damages for its breach is sanctioning.[8] Distinct from both these classes of substantive right are the promisee's procedural rights of enforcement.[9]

Exception clauses, then, will be substantive if they qualify or exclude primary or sanctioning rights and duties. They will be procedural if their effect is upon procedural rights alone. It must be apparent that, if exceptions are indeed merely procedural in their effect, their scope will be particularly limited and this fact in itself would tend to dispose one against any such view.

Perhaps the leading example of the clause which governs procedural rights rather than substantive rights is the ordinary arbitration clause. It has been held that such clauses remain binding on the parties even after termination for breach.[10] They also continue to bind both parties notwithstanding a breach in the

[6] JW Salmond, *Jurisprudence* (11th ed by Glanville Williams, London, Sweet & Maxwell, 1957) 263; GW Paton, *Jurisprudence* (Oxford, Clarendon Press, 1951) 219; RWM Dias and GBJ Hughes, *Jurisprudence* (London, Butterworths, 1957) 259–60.

[7] Salmond, ibid, 124–127; Paton, ibid, 212 and 231–2; Dias and Hughes, ibid, 236–7.

[8] Salmond, ibid, 124.

[9] Paton, above n 6, 231 (fn), and 474ff; Salmond, ibid, 503ff.

[10] *Heyman v Darwins* [1942] AC 356 (HL).

nature of a deviation,[11] or breach of the warranty of seaworthiness.[12] In short, they have been held not to be subject to the same rules as exception clauses and the reason given has been that they are merely procedural.[13] Moreover, a purely procedural clause could never do any more than limit, without excluding, procedural enforcement. If procedural enforcement were to be excluded, substantive rights could subsist only if it were possible to create contractual rights at common law while making them unenforceable by agreement. This brings us to the second proposition.

## Can the Parties to a Contract Create Rights Intended by Them to be Unenforceable?

It is true, of course, that unenforceable contractual obligations, imperfect contractual rights, are not unknown to the common law.[14] Contracts barred by the operation of the Limitation Act 1939,[15] or by the Statute of Frauds,[16] and contracts with foreign sovereigns,[17] are fair examples. In all such cases, however, the procedural inability to sue has been imposed *ab extra* by force of some rule of law, or by statute. The contractual obligations concerned are unenforceable in spite of, not because of, the intentions of the parties. All are enforceable if the inability to sue is somehow removed.[18] It is because the parties intend their contract to be enforceable that the courts are able to enforce a contract with a foreign sovereign should the latter submit to the jurisdiction.[19] The same intention enables the court to give a remedy in quasi-contract to an employee whose contract of service is unenforceable under the Statute of Frauds.[20]

It is a very different matter to suggest that the parties themselves might create valid contractual rights and duties and at the same time, by their own agreement, make those rights and duties at all times and at all stages unenforceable. It would involve the proposition that primary contractual rights can exist even though, by the intention of the parties, sanctioning rights have never attached to them. In other contexts, at least, the courts have reached a different conclusion. Thus, a

[11] *Woolf v Collis* [1948] 1 KB 11 (CA).

[12] *Atlantic Shipping Co v Dreyfus* [1922] 2 AC 250 (HL), 258

[13] ibid, 258; [1942] AC 356 (HL), 373–4, 377 and 400; [1948] 1 KB 11 (CA), 15–17.

[14] Salmond, above n 6, 280–2; Paton, above n 6, 220.

[15] *Mills v Fowkes* (1839) 5 Bing NC 455; *Spears v Hartly* (1800) 3 Esp 81. In some cases, however, as in matters of title to chattels and land, lapse of time extinguishes the right (Limitation Act 1939, ss 3(2) and 16).

[16] *Leroux v Brown* (1852) 12 CB 801; *Maddison v Alderson* (1883) 8 App Cas 467 (HL).

[17] Salmond, above n 6, 280; *Duff Development Co v Government of Kelantan* [1924] AC 797 (HL); *Kahan v Pakistan Federation* [1951] 2 KB 1003 (CA).

[18] Salmond, ibid, 281–2; Paton, above n 6, 320; RWM Dias [1962] *Cambridge Law Journal* 160.

[19] *cf Dickinson v Del Solar* [1930] 1 KB 376 (KBD), 380.

[20] *Scarisbrick v Parkinson* (1869) 20 LT 175; *Scott v Pattison* [1923] 2 KB 723 (KBD); *James v Thomas H Kent & Co* [1951] 1 KB 551 (CA).

covenant not to sue, if unlimited as to time and unconditional, is construed as a release.[21] Should the covenant not be unlimited or unconditional, breach of it sounds in damages, but it cannot operate as a bar.[22] There is no intermediate category in which an agreement not to sue can operate as a (procedural) bar without operating as a (substantive) release. Again judges have said frequently over the years that where, in a contractual document, a specific, apparently contractual, undertaking is followed by a proviso that the promisor shall be under no liability for breach, the one is repugnant to the other.[23] In their view, apparently, the provision for unenforceability is taken to be inconsistent with the existence of substantive contractual content in the specific promise. As Devlin J has pointed out, it is illusory to say: 'We promise to do a thing, but we are not liable if we do not do it.'[24] That is not in law a contract at all. Again, an agreement which made genuine contractual rights unenforceable would surely be void as ousting the jurisdiction of the courts.[25] No such ouster would occur, however, if the effect of the agreement were to stop rights arising in the first place.[26]

At this stage, it might be objected that in the case of a promissory condition, even if rights to damages are excluded, the promisee may retain his rights to terminate the contract for failure to comply with the condition. To that extent it could be said that the promise remained enforceable notwithstanding the exclusion of sanctioning rights. The short answer here, it is submitted, is that such a condition would be unenforceable and therefore illusory qua promise. Such force as it would have would derive from its status as a contingency, that is, as a condition precedent not the subject of a promise. One may take advantage of a contingency. One does not in any real sense enforce it.[27]

[21] *Ford v Beech* (1848) 11 QB 852. A release, of course, substantively extinguishes the relevant rights: Salmond, above n 6, 385; Paton, above n 6, 34.

[22] *Thimbleby v Barron* (1838) 3 M & W 210, especially at 216 per Abinger CB

[23] YBT 7, H 6, 43b, 44a per Babbington CJ, and YBP 21, H 7, 23b, 24b, pl 15 (Bro Barre 52) per Fineux CJ, cited by Glanville Williams, 'The Doctrine of Repugnancy' (1944) 60 *Law Quarterly Review* 69, 70; *Furnivall v Coombes* (1843) 5 Man & G 736; *Brown v Bristol & Exeter Railway Co* (1861) 4 LT 830, 831; *Kelner v Baxter* (1866) LR 2 CP 174, 186; *Williams v Hathaway* (1877) 6 Ch D 544, 549 (CA); *Rosin and Turpentine Export v Jacobs* (1909) 14 Com Cas 247, 253 (CA); *Suzuki v Benyon* (1926) 42 TLR 269, 271 (HL); *Calico Printers v Barclays Bank* (1930) 36 Com Cas 197, 212 (CA); *The Albion* [1953] 1 WLR 1026, 1032 (CA). The alternative is that the promise is illusory: *Stevenson v Henderson*, 1873 SC 215 (affd on appeal sub nom *Henderson v Stevenson* (1875) LR 2 Sc & Div 470 (HL)), 220; *Firestone Tyre Co v Vokins* [1951] 1 Lloyd's Rep 32 (KBD), 39. For the contrary view, see the cases cited above n 1.

[24] [1951] 1 Lloyd's Rep 32 (KBD) 39; see also *Hughes v Great Western Railway Co* (1854) 14 CB 637; B Laskin, 'Limitation and Exclusion of Liability in Bailment' (1956) 11 *University of Toronto Law Journal* 202, 206.

[25] *Kelsall v Tyler* (1856) 11 Ex 513, 534 per Martin B: 'The law will not permit a person who enters into a binding contract to say in another clause that he will not be liable to be sued for a breach of it.' See also *Scott v Avery* (1856) 8 Ex 487, 499; *Elliott v Royal Exchange Assurance Co* (1867) LR 2 Ex 237, 244; *Trainor v Phoenix Fire Insurance Co* (1892) 65 LT 825, 827; Glanville Williams, above n 23, 69ff; GC Cheshire and CHS Fifoot, *Law of Contract* (5th ed, London, Butterworths, 1960) 306–8.

[26] *Rose and Frank v Crompton & Bros* [1925] AC 445 (HL); Glanville Williams, above n 23, 79–80.

[27] It might, perhaps, also be argued that an agreement negativing sanctioning rights will not, of itself, make a particular right or promise unenforceable, on the ground that rights to specific

It is possible to conclude then, with Professor Bohlen, that the unenforceable duty, the duty of imperfect obligation, is foreign to the whole spirit of the common law.[28] It is something which it is not in the power of the parties to create and which can be brought about only *ab extra*.[29]

## A Different Approach Suggested

If it is true that exception clauses are substantive rather than procedural in their effect, and that it is impossible for parties to create contractual rights if they intend them to be at all times unenforceable, the implications are fairly obvious. In the first place, the function of all exception clauses, being substantive, is to place substantive limitations upon the rights to which they apply, and, accordingly, to help delimit and define those rights.[30] In the second place, an exception clause which made purported contractual rights wholly unenforceable would not have effect merely as a shield to claims for damages. It would, in fact, prevent those rights accruing in the first place. Suppose, for example, that I sell a horse which I say is sound for jumping, but provide in the written agreement that I accept no responsibility whatever if the horse should prove unsound. What I am doing is to ensure that the purchaser has no primary contractual right to call for

performance may persist. The immediate objection to that argument, it is submitted, is that there are large categories of promises, and accordingly of rights, in respect of which specific enforcement will not be decreed in any event. Instances of this might be contracts for personal work or service (HG Hanbury, *Modern Equity* (8th ed, London, Stevens & Sons, 1962) 546), complicated contracts such as charterparties (*de Mattos v Gibson* (1859) 4 De G & J 276), and, presumably, warranties in the sense of contractual representations. According to Albert Kocourek, *Jural Relations* (2nd ed, Indianapolis, Bobbs-Merrill, 1928) 346 (fn), every frangible right (including primary contractual rights) 'is succeeded by a sanctional right'. Not unexpectedly, J Austin, *Lectures on Jurisprudence* (5th ed, revised and edited by R Campbell, London, J Murray, 1885) vol 2, 768, took the view that 'a primary right or duty is not of itself a right or duty, without the secondary right or duty by which it is sustained: and *e converso*'. More important, perhaps, is the consideration that we are here dealing with a question of contractual interpretation. At common law, the only remedy for a breach of contractual duty is an action for debt or damages (JW Salmond and J Williams, *Principles of the Law of Contracts* (2nd ed, London, Sweet & Maxwell, 1945) 577; Glanville Williams, above n 23, 72). Accordingly, when businessmen provide that particular rights shall not be enforceable by damages, it would seem somewhat fanciful to suggest that they envisage, let alone intend, that rights to specific enforcement shall continue to apply. The better view would be, it is submitted, that an exclusion of the remedy in damages would show an intention that the apparent particular right should be wholly unenforceable.

[28] FH Bohlen, *Studies in the Law of Torts* (Indianapolis, Bobbs-Merrill, 1926) 445.

[29] *cf* F Pollock, *Principles of Contract* (13th ed by PH Winfield, London, Stevens and Sons, 1950) 3 ('The agreement … must be concerned with duties and rights which can be dealt with by a court of justice'); *Leake on Contracts* (8th ed by RRA Walker, London, Stevens and Sons, 1931) 3 ('An agreement as the source of a legal contract imports that the one party shall be bound to some performance which the other shall have a legal right to enforce'); CB Morison, *Principles of Rescission* (London, Stevens & Haynes, 1916) 18 ('The contract having become unenforceable thereby ceases to be an obligation'); CF Chamberlayne, *Modern Law of Evidence* (Albany, NY, M Bender, 1911) [171], cited in WW Cook, *Logical and Legal Bases* (Cambridge, Mass, Harvard University Press, 1942) 158 ('A right without a remedy for its violation is a … *brutum fulmen*').

[30] *cf* J Unger, 'The Doctrine of the Fundamental Term' [1956] *Business Law Review* 30, 33ff.

a horse which is sound for jumping. I am not contracting that the horse is sound and giving myself a shield in a case of breach. I am simply refusing to contract on the point at all. This is not to say that I am under no duty, but my duty is a moral one binding in honour only.

Accordingly, in the *Istros v Dahlstroem* situation,[31] assuming that all responsibility for failure to comply with cl 8 had been excluded, the charterers had a moral, but no contractual, right to the prosecution of the voyage by the master with the utmost dispatch.

The point can be illustrated in another way. Suppose an undertaking to exercise care is followed by an exclusion of all liability whatever for negligence. On the view argued above, the effect of the exception clause would be to stop any contractual duty of care arising. There is an analogy here with the law of torts. It is submitted that an exclusion of liability in negligence negatives any duty of care in tort, as well as in contract.[32] There is authority that consent to an act which would otherwise be a tort,[33] or the voluntary assumption of the legal risk[34] of such an act,[35] is more than a mere defence. In such cases, the act when done is not a tort.[36] In much the same way, when an exception clause makes any apparent right wholly unenforceable, it is the promisee who takes the risk of non-performance. The act when done is not a breach of contract in any real sense of that phrase.

31 See text accompanying n 3 above.

32 *Shaw v York & North Midland Railway Co* (1849) 18 LJ (NS) QB 181, 184; *Stevenson v Henderson*, 1873 SC 215, 220; *Manchester, Sheffield, and Lincolnshire Railway v Brown* (1883) 8 App Cas 703 (HL), 720; *Grand Trunk Railway Co of Canada v Robinson* [1915] AC 740 (JC), 748; *Davies v Collins* [1945] 1 All ER 247 (CA), 249; *Grein v Imperial Airways* [1937] 1 KB 50 (CA) 87; *cf London Graving Dock v Horton* [1951] AC 737 (HL), 784 per Lord Reid; *Hood v Anchor Line* [1918] AC 837 (HL Sc), 850 per Lord Parmoor; *Coupar Transport v Smith's (Acton) Ltd* [1959] 1 Lloyd's Rep 369 (QBD), 378–9 per Winn J; Occupiers' Liability Act 1957, s 2(1).

33 *Salmond on Torts* (13th ed by RFV Heuston, London, Sweet & Maxwel, 1961) 43–4; F Pollock, *The Law of Torts* (13th ed, London, Stevens, 1929) 115; *Clerk and Lindsell on Torts* (12th ed, London, Sweet & Maxwell, 1961) 52; Glanville Williams, *Joint Torts and Contributory Negligence* (London, Stevens & Sons, 1951) 295–6; H Street, *The Law of Torts* (London, Butterworth & Co, 1955) 77; JG Fleming, *The Law of Torts* (2nd ed, Sydney, Law Book Co, 1961) 85.

34 As distinct from the physical risk: *Winfield on Torts* (6th ed by T Ellis Lewis, London, Sweet & Maxwell, 1954) 27–8.

35 Salmond, above n 33, 43–4; Fleming, ibid, 249 and 257–8; T Beven, *Negligence in Law* (4th ed by WJ Byrne and AD Gibb, London, Sweet & Maxwell, 1928) vol 1, 796; Pollock, above n 33, 168 and 172; *Thomas v Quartermaine* (1887) 18 QBD 685 (CA), 697 and 701; *Smith v Baker* [1891] AC 325 (HL), 344 and 352–3; *Dann v Hamilton* [1939] 1 KB 509 (KBD), 512; *London Graving Dock v Horton* [1951] AC 737 (HL), 784; *Insurance Commissioner v Joyce* (1948) 77 CLR 39 (High Court of Australia), 56 and 59; also the cases cited above n 32. The opinions both for and against have been collected in DJ Payne, 'Assumption of Risk and Negligence' (1957) 35 *Canadian Bar Review* 950. Mr Payne argues the view taken above.

36 Glanville Williams, above n 33, 295–6; Fleming, above n 33, 85; Salmond, above n 33, 44. That an exception clause can constitute an assumption of risk was recognised by Kitto and Taylor JJ in *Wilson v Darling Island Stevedoring Co* [1956] 1 Lloyd's Rep 346 (High Court of Australia) 365ff and 371, and by Lord Denning in *Midland Silicones v Scruttons* [1962] AC 446 (HL), 488–9. See also MP Furmston, 'Return to *Dunlop v Selfridge*?' (1960) 23 *Modern Law Review* 373, 386ff.

## A Suggested Classification of Exception Clauses

If the approach argued so far were accepted, it is submitted that all exception clauses would be found to fall within one or other of the two following classes, which it is proposed to call 'Type A' and 'Type B' respectively:

**Type A**: exception clauses the effect of which, if any, is upon the accrual of particular primary rights.

Thus, for example, where words relating to quality have been employed by a vendor of goods, an exclusion of conditions, warranties, or undertakings as to quality helps determine the extent to which those words are contractually binding, as, by the same token, would a stipulation by the vendor that he should not be required to make compensation for poor quality.

**Type B**: exception clauses which qualify primary or secondary rights without preventing the accrual of any particular primary right.

Examples would be limitations on the time within which claims might be made, and limitations as to the amount which might be recovered on a claim. By contrast, a clause which purported to take away a buyer's right to reject goods would belong to Type A.[37]

To bring it within Type A an exception may operate either directly or indirectly. The direct effect requires little elaboration. If we suppose, for example, a promise in general terms, and a series of particular exceptions from that promise, we have a case where an exception clause is directly limiting the substantive contractual content of a promise, or more technically, perhaps, is negativing any primary right to performance of those matters excluded from the promise. Thus, where a horse is sold warranted sound 'except for hunting', the purchaser will have no primary right to call for a horse sound for hunting. An exception may have the same effect indirectly, through the operation of the proposition that it is impossible to create valid contractual rights while at the same time agreeing that they shall be at all times unenforceable. A total exclusion, either of sanctioning rights or of procedural rights of enforcement, would have the effect of making the apparent primary right unenforceable. Insofar as the 'unenforceable right' would be illusory (that is, would have no existence as a contractual right), exceptions of this type would, accordingly, have the effect on primary rights of preventing their accrual. Thus, if the vendor of a horse should represent that the animal is sound, but stipulate that he shall not be required to make compensation if it should prove to be unsound, then unless he is merely contradicting himself, he is indicating thereby that his representation is a 'mere' representation and that he refuses to contract as to the horse's soundness. In other words, by excluding sanctioning rights he is indirectly preventing the

[37] That is, because it would bear upon the question whether the promises to which it related were conditions or warranties.

purchaser's acquiring any contractual primary right as to soundness. Similarly, if the vendor should exclude sanctioning rights by providing that 'this agreement shall not be justiciable in the courts of any place or in any circumstances', then either that provision is void as ousting the jurisdiction of the courts,[38] or it indicates that the agreement is an 'honour' agreement which does not give rise to contractual rights and duties and which is binding in the moral sense only.[39]

By contrast, exceptions of Type B do not affect the question of whether particular primary rights shall accrue, but merely qualify rights which *ex hypothesi* do accrue. There are three ways in which they do this. First, they may act directly on a primary right, as by placing a limit on its duration. To take again the sale of a horse 'warranted sound', a provision that unless the horse were returned within three days it would be deemed sound[40] would be an exception to this second Type. It would not prevent a valid primary right to soundness arising. Secondly, they may act directly on sanctioning rights, as by placing a limit on the amount recoverable for breach of particular primary rights. The carrier's notice limiting his liability to £5 in respect to any one package is a familiar example.[41] Again a valid primary right to performance arises despite the exception. Finally, the exception may lay down a time limit within which an action may be brought.[42] Whether time limitations act directly on sanctioning rights, or only indirectly by controlling procedural rights, the result is the same. Once the time limit has expired, the primary rights concerned become unenforceable and are extinguished or fulfilled.[43] But, until that time, they subsist as valid contractual rights. In other words, the exception does not prevent particular primary rights accruing.

It ought, perhaps, to be emphasised that both types of exception clause help define and delimit the rights to which they apply. One result of this is that rights affected by exceptions of Type B are qualified from their inception by the exception clause[44] just as much as are rights affected by clauses of Type A. What makes the distinction between the two types significant and important is that if the effect of clauses of Type A is upon whether particular primary rights shall arise from a promise, they are directly relevant to the existence or otherwise, in that promise, of substantive contractual content. Since promises are ordinarily

[38] *Thompson v Charnock* (1799) 8 Term Rep 139; *Czarnikow v Roth Schmidt* [1922] 2 KB 478 (CA). See also the text above at n 25.

[39] *Rose and Frank v Crompton & Bros* [1925] AC 445 (HL); *Jones v Vernon's Pools* [1938] 2 All ER 626; *Appleson v Littlewood* [1939] 1 All ER 464 (CA); *Lee v Shermans Pools* [1951] WN 70 (CA); Glanville Williams, above n 23, 79–80.

[40] *cf Buchanan v Parnshaw* (1788) 2 Term Rep 745; *Mesnard v Aldridge* (1801) 3 Esp 271; *Bywater v Richardson* (1834) 1 Ad & E 508.

[41] eg *Clarke v Gray* (1805) 6 East 564; *Brooke v Pickwick* (1827) 4 Bing 219; *Langley v Brown* (1828) 1 Moo & P 583; 6 LJ (OS) CP 139.

[42] eg *Rendall v Arcos* (1937) 43 Com Cas 1 (HL); *Smeaton Hanscomb v Sassoon I Setty* [1953] 2 All ER 1471 (QBD)

[43] *cf* Morison, above n 29, 18.

[44] *The Auditor* (1924) 18 Ll LR 464 (Ch) 468; *Grein v Imperial Airways* [1937] 1 KB 50 (CA), 88.

expressed in a number of words, or may have more than one aspect, the Type A exception may help to determine how many of the words used give rise to rights and duties, or in how many aspects the promise has contractual force. In the ordinary way a contractual promise may give rise to a whole complex of rights. It can be the function of an exception clause to show how many of these rights do in fact come into existence. Where the question is, 'has the promisor contracted to do this or this?' an exception of Type A will have a direct bearing on the answer.

## The Interpretation of Exception Clauses In Relation to Their Function

An aspect of the function of exception clauses which calls for further consideration is the stage at, and the context in which, exceptions fall to be interpreted and applied.

When a court is called upon to interpret a contract, it reaches its decisions in three stages:

> First, the court must discover the statements actually made by the parties. This is a question of evidence.
> Secondly, it must be determined whether the parties intended to create obligations by what they said or wrote. Did the statements become express terms of the contract? Obviously a party does not incur liability in respect of every statement that he may make in the course of the negotiations.
> Thirdly, the exact meaning to be attributed to the express terms must be determined. This is a question of interpretation.[45]

On the current approach as enjoined by Denning LJ in *Karsales v Wallis*,[46] '[t]he thing to do is to look at the contract apart from the exempting clauses to see what are the terms express or implied, which impose an obligation on the party.'

On this approach, exception clauses would be interpreted and applied at the third stage noted above, since they would have no relevance at that second stage when the intentions to contract of the parties are being considered. But, if the function of Type A exception clauses is to determine whether and what rights shall arise from the promises which they qualify, it must be at the second rather than the third stage that they should be applied. Suppose that in a contract for the sale of a specific motorcar, described as a 1948 model, there is a clause stating that 'the vendor gives no undertaking whatever, contractual or otherwise, that the car is a 1948 model and the statement that it is a 1948 model is intended to be only a mere representation not forming part of the contract'. In such case, it

[45] GC Cheshire and CHS Fifoot, *Law of Contract* (4th ed, London, Butterworths, 1956) 98–9. The passage has been altered in the fifth edition, above n 25, 99.

[46] *Karsales v Wallis* [1956] 1 WLR 936 (CA), 940.

would be absurd solemnly to find that the vendor had contracted that the car was a 1948 model, and that the exception clause was a mere defence. The absurdity would be less obvious, but it might be no less real, if the exception clause read: 'the vendor shall not be liable for any error of description whatever'.

If the exception clause were to be applied at this earlier stage, it is submitted that, amongst others, the following two advantages would result. In the first place, such application would bring home the judicial realities of the case. If the obligations of the parties are defined in isolation from the exception clauses, it is likely that the courts will, for some purposes, accord to apparent promises a substance they in no real sense possess.[47] On Denning LJ's approach, however wide the exception clause, the promisor's undertakings would be regarded as fully contractual, so that it would be possible for one party to be bound to his side of an apparent contract even though the other had successfully excluded all liability whatever. In such an extreme case, the different approach suggested in this piece would at least make it clear that the apparent contract was illusory and therefore void for want of consideration.

The more important advantage, however, is that in any case where the court might wish to limit the effect of a particular exception clause, this new approach would concentrate the forces at its disposal in a way which the current one could not. On the latter approach, the court has available the various restrictive rules which have grown up around exemption clauses, but that is all. On that now suggested, the exception clause would be regarded as bearing on the intention of the parties to undertake particular rights and duties. So regarded, it would take its place as but one of the factors relevant to intention to contract.[48] Take, for example, a contract for the sale of goods which purports to exclude 'conditions'. On the one approach, the court would have to look at the contract and all the surrounding circumstances (except of course the exception clause), and decide which provisions of the contract the parties intended to be conditions. The exception would then, presumably, operate as a defence to breaches of all such terms. On the other approach, an exclusion of conditions would be seen as an indication that the terms to which it applied were intended either to be excluded from the contract altogether, or to have a status less than that of a condition. If, therefore, having weighed all the circumstances, including the exception clause, the court should decide that, despite the presence of the exception, a particular term was intended to have effect as a condition, it would for that very reason be able to hold that the exception clause could not apply to it. The overall

[47] As, it is submitted, was in the case in *Istros v Dahlstroem* [1931] 1 KB 247 (KBD) and *E Clemens Horst v Norfolk & NASN Co* (1906) 11 Com Cas 141.

[48] *cf Hedley Bryne v Heller & Partners* [1963] 3 WLR 101 (HL), especially 155.

contractual intentions of the parties could be combined with the restrictive rules of interpretation to temper and confine the words of the exception clause.[49]

## Some Special Consequences of the Exception Form

If an exception clause is indeed definitive of the rights and duties of the parties, what are the special consequences, if any, of thus defining them negatively instead of positively? As an example, is there any difference between a shipowner carrying goods as a common carrier subject to exceptions, and a shipowner who defines positively the obligations he is prepared to undertake? There are several such differences, among them the following:

### The Nature of the Contract

One consequence of using exceptions is that the suggestion of a wider promise followed by exceptions from it may help to determine the nature or class of the contract. Thus, a carrier who contracts in a form appropriate to a common carrier, even while excluding this special insurer's liability, may for that reason still be classed as a common carrier and remain liable for failure to accept for carriage goods within his profession.[50]

### Suggestion of Residual Contractual Content

The very fact that a promisor has adopted the form of making a promise and followed it by an exception in itself suggests that the exception is narrower than the initial undertaking. Certainly, there is a presumption that words of exception are narrower than the words they qualify.[51] Where the two are repugnant, that is

[49] *cf Stuart v B & A Steam Navigation Co* (1875) 2 Asp MC 497, 501 per Pollock CB: 'you must not so construe a condition as to make it eat up the contract'. There seems to be a presumption against negativing any liability which the promisor has, prima facie, assumed under the contract: *Wallis v Pratt* [1910] 2 KB 1003 (CA), 1016.

[50] *Great Northern Railway Co v LEP Transport and Depository* [1922] 2 KB 742 (CA) 770 per Atkin LJ. Other examples of a wide construction being refused to an exception because it would alter the nature of the contract are: *Firestone Tyre Co v Vokins* [1951] 1 Lloyd's Rep 32 (KBD), 39; *Thorman v Dowgate* [1910] 1 KB 410 (KBD), 417; *Beck v Szymanowski* [1924] AC 43 (HL), 50. On the other hand, the existence of exceptions appropriate to one type of relationship will not necessarily mean that the contract is not of another type (*Ashby v Tolhurst* [1937] 2 KB 242 (CA); *Turner v Civil Service* [1926] 1 KB 50 (KBD); *Olley v Marlborough Court* [1949] 1 KB 532 (CA)); nor does an exception of liability for all except wilful misconduct imply a positive undertaking of liability for wilful misconduct (*Young v BT Commn* [1955] 2 QB 177 (QBD)).

[51] *Foreman v Federal SN Co* [1928] 2 KB 424 (KBD), 427.

to say completely irreconcilable, the exception is rejected altogether and the original undertaking is given unqualified effect.[52]

## Contra Proferentem

Because the promisor has chosen to use an exception, it appears in the contract as a clause in his favour. Because it is in his favour, it will automatically be interpreted against him in any case of doubt.[53]

## Expressum Facit Cessare Taciturn

An express provision in an instrument excludes any stipulation which would otherwise be implied with regard to the same subject matter.[54] A promisor, by spreading wide his initial undertaking and then excluding part of it, may hope to take advantage of this rule and prevent a misunderstanding of his position.

## Onus of Proof

The above differences are all of them consistent with either view of the function of exception clauses. The problem of onus of proof presents more difficulty. If the exception is part of the definition of the obligations arising from the contract, one might expect the onus to be on the promisee to prove that the act complained of came within the promise as qualified by the exception. In practice, however, the onus is often placed on the promisor to prove that the act falls within the exception,[55] and at least one distinguished writer has suggested that this must be wrong.[56]

Whether it is possible to argue from the burden of proof to the conclusion that an exception is, after all, distinct from, and forms no part of, the definition of rights and duties, is a very different matter. While onus of proof may, of course, reflect the substantive situation, it does not invariably do so. It is in contracts of bailment and carriage that the question of onus qua exception clauses arises most acutely. But in such cases all a bailor has to do in the first instance, if he goes about things in the right way, is to prove that he has not received the goods. It is then up to the bailee to excuse himself if he can, for example, by showing that the

52 *Williams v Hathaway* (1877) 6 Ch D 544 (Ch); and see the other cases cited above n 23.

53 'All the words of a deed shall be taken most strongly against him that doth speak them, and most in advantage of the other party': *Shep Touch*, 87.

54 11 *Halsbury's Laws of England* (Simonds ed, 1954) 395.

55 For example, the burden of proving that a loss falls within the excepted perils is upon a ship owner (*Taylor v Liverpool and Great Western Steam Co* (1874) LR 9 QB 546; *Smith v Bedouin SN Co* [1896] AC 70 (HL Sc)).

56 AL Corbin, *Law of Contract* (St Paul, Minn, West Publishing Co, 1951) vol 3, 901–2, [751].

non-delivery falls within a contractual, or common law, exception. This has nothing to do with matters of substance.[57] There is the further rule that, where the subject matter of a party's allegation is peculiarly within the knowledge of his opponent, it lies upon the latter to rebut such allegation.[58] The question of onus of proof was one which, incidentally, weighed heavily with the judges who laid down the common carrier's liability in the eighteenth century.[59]

The question of onus in a non-bailment type of case was considered by Lush J in *Hurst v Evans.*[60] A jeweler had taken out an insurance policy against loss or damage however caused, save by breakage, theft or dishonesty of his servants. One of the questions put to the Court was whether the onus was on the assured to show that the loss fell within the policy and outside the exceptions. The learned Judge held that it was. The alternative would have placed an unreasonable burden on the insurer. This decision was considered but not followed in what must be taken to be the leading case on questions of onus of proof qua exceptions, *Munro Brice & Co v War Risks Association.*[61] Bailhache J, after a review of the authorities, concluded that in general the question of onus depended on whether exceptions fell within one of two classes. If an exception merely excludes from a promise particular classes of case which, but for the exception, would fall within it, the onus is on the promisor to show that the promisee's case is within the excepted class.[62] The alternative would involve proof of a negative.[63] On the other hand, if an exception qualifies the whole scope of a promise, as, for example, a marine policy with particular average franchise where the promise is to pay only particular average exceeding three per cent, the onus is on the promisee.[64] Bailhache J confessed that the distinction was largely one of form. In construing a contract with exceptions, he said, it must be borne in mind that a promise with exceptions can generally be turned by an alteration of phraseology into a qualified promise.[65]

From the foregoing it may be concluded that, where a promisor chooses to define his obligations in terms of exceptions, his use of that form is a matter of significance involving important consequences. At the same time those consequences devolve from the form, not the substance, of the promise. After they have

[57] *cf* Denning LJ in [1956] 1 WLR 461 (CA), 466 (CA): 'A bailor by pleading and presenting his case properly, can always put on the bailee the burden of proof.'

[58] SL Phipson, *The Law of Evidence* (9th ed, London, Sweet & Maxwell, 1952) 41ff.

[59] eg *Coggs v Bernard* (1703) 2 Ld Raym 909, 918; *Lane v Cotton* (1701) 12 Mod 472, 481–2; *Forward v Pittard* (1785) 1 TR 27, 33–4.

[60] *Hurst v Evans* [1917] 1 KB 352 (KBD).

[61] *Munro Brice & Co v War Risks Association* [1918] 2 KB 78 (KBD) (reversed on a question of fact [1920] 3 KB 94 (CA)); *Firestone Tyre Co v Vokins* [1951] 1 Lloyd's Rep 32 (KBD), 38.

[62] ibid, 88.

[63] *cf* ibid, 85.

[64] ibid 88–9.

[65] ibid, 89.

all been taken into account it can still be asserted that it is upon the residual content of the promise that the promisor's obligations should depend.[66]

## Conclusions

If the argument so far has been accepted, it follows that the true juristic function and effect of exception clauses are quite different from those currently ascribed to them by the courts. Instead of being mere shields to claims based on breach of accrued rights, exception clauses substantively delimit the rights themselves. A large class of them prevents those rights from ever arising in the first place. As it has been put in an American publication: 'the ordinary function of an exception is to take out of the contract that which otherwise would have been included in it, or to guard against misinterpretation'.[67]

So regarded, the exception clause of Type A is seen to fulfill a function not unlike that of an exception from grant, an analogy which, incidentally, did not escape lawyers of the early nineteenth century.[68] Just as an exception from a grant operates immediately to prevent its subject passing to the grantee,[69] so an exception clause of Type A operates immediately to prevent its subject forming part of the rights and duties created by the contract.[70]

It may seem feasible that the parties should have intended a contractual duty to remain when they excluded liability for its breach, but this is in reality a juristic impossibility. A duty of sorts there may be, but it will be a duty of honour, not a contractual one.

## Addendum

The reports of the decision of the House of Lords in *Hedley Byrne v Heller & Partners*[71] appeared shortly before *Exception Clauses* was published. There was time to include the following comment at pp 142 and 143 of that work:

[66] *cf Browning v Elmslie* (1790) 7 TR 216, note (a) per Lord Kenyon CJ: 'the general mode of construing deeds to which there are exceptions, is to let the exception control the instrument as far as the words of it extend and no further; and then upon the case being taken out of the letter of the exception, the deed operates in full force'.

[67] *Corpus Juris Secundum*, 'Contracts', [343].

[68] See the reference in *Atkinson v Ritchie* (1809) 10 East 530, during the argument for the plaintiff, to 3 Com Dig 334, Faits E8.

[69] *Cooper v Stuart* (1889) 14 App Cas 289 (HL), 290 per Lord Watson: 'A valid exception operates immediately and the subject of it does not pass to the grantee'; 11 *Halsbury's Laws of England* (Simonds ed, 1954) 434: 'upon the grant of land there may be an exception of a specified part, and then is not included in the grant at all'.

[70] *cf Canada Atlantic v Eilers* (1929) 35 Com Cas 90 (KBD), 97 per Wright J: clause 'cut[s] down the warranty … otherwise implied'; Payne, above n 35.

[71] *Hedley Byrne v Heller & Partners* [1964] AC 465 (HL)

Until 1961, anyone arguing for a more realistic approach to exception clauses could have relied on at least one House of Lords decision, *Elder, Dempster v Paterson, Zochonis.*[72] The hopes which then seemed to have been dashed by *Midland Silicones v Scruttons*[73] have now been raised again by the very recent decision of the House in *Hedley Byrne v Heller & Partners.*[74] In that case, bankers who had been asked for a confidential report on one of their customers had by their negligence given a misleading reply. In the result, the party for whom the report had been obtained suffered substantial pecuniary loss. The House held that the relationship between the bankers and the party for whom the report was obtained, while not contractual, was such as would ordinarily have raised a duty of care in tort. But in the particular circumstances, the fact that the report had been expressly 'without responsibility on the part of the bank or its officials' was sufficient to free the bankers from liability. The significance of the decision for the present argument was the way in which the House reached that result, for all the judgments recognised not only that the exception freed the bankers from liability, but also that it effectively prevented the assumption of any duty in the first place. In the words of Lord Pearce, the disclaimer of responsibility was

> ... part of the material from which one deduces whether a duty of care and a liability for negligence was assumed. If both parties say expressly (in a case where neither is deliberately taking advantage of the other) that there shall be no liability, I do not find it possible to say that a liability was assumed.[75]

That passage so clearly expresses the main thesis of this book that it is perhaps a little saddening to have to concede that in this respect the House seemed to draw a distinction between contract and tort. The difference was expressed by Lord Devlin when he said:

> A man cannot be said voluntarily to be undertaking a responsibility if at the very moment when he is said to be accepting it he declares that in fact he is not. The problem of reconciling words of exemption with the existence of a duty arises only when a party is claiming exemption from a responsibility he has already undertaken or which he is contracting to undertake.[76]

With respect, it is submitted that the distinction thus drawn is especially difficult to justify having regard to the circumstances in which it was made. The question before the House, of whether a banker had undertaken responsibility for a report, was so close to a contractual one that it was only because of such technical requirements as consideration and privity that the claim had to be considered in the context of tort at all. Liability, it was held, depended on the voluntary acceptance of responsibility. In the words of Lord Devlin himself, the relationship

72 *Elder, Dempster v Paterson, Zochonis* [1924] AC 522 (HL).
73 *Midland Silicones v Scruttons* [1962] AC 446 (HL).
74 See above n 71.
75 ibid, 540.
76 ibid, 533.

resulting was 'equivalent to contract'.[77] The processes involved in entering into such a relationship are so obviously analogous to those involved in entering into a genuine contract, that it is not easy to see where the difference lies which would justify the distinction suggested by the House. To say that in the case of a genuine contract a party by the use of exception clauses is claiming exemption from a responsibility he has already undertaken or which he is contracting to undertake is to beg the very question to which the exception clause is directed.

Because chapter six of this book has been included primarily for its bearing on the theme of the collection, no attempt has been made to take account of the effect on exception clauses of the subsequent legislation in some, though by no means all, common law jurisdictions.

[77] ibid, 530.

# 7

# The Second Rise and Fall of Fundamental Breach

SOON AFTER THE decision of the House of Lords in the *Suisse Atlantique* case,[1] and of the High Court of Australia in *The Council of the City of Sydney v West*,[2] I wrote a paper for the 1966 AULSA (Australasian Universities Law Schools Association) Conference under the title of 'The Rise and Fall of Fundamental Breach'.[3] In the light of what followed, that title came to appear at least a little premature! *Suisse Atlantique* did come as an end, but as the end, as it turned out, merely of an episode in a continuing story. The decision of the House of Lords in *Photo Production Ltd v Securicor (Transport) Ltd*,[4] similarly marks an end, but whether of just another episode of the story as a whole is still uncertain. Accordingly, the title of this chapter is more a concession to symmetry than an attempt to prophesy.

For me, the *Securicor* case draws its meaning and significance from what led up to it. That is why the first half of the chapter deals with the background of the case, even though this involves some repetition of what I have written before.[5] Then follows a discussion of the main points of the decision as they relate to fundamental breach. Finally, some thoughts are offered about the significance of the decision for the future.

[1] *Suisse Atlantique Société d'Armement Maritime SA v NV Rotterdamsche Kolen Centrale* [1967] 1 AC 361 (HL) (hereinafter '*Suisse Atlantique*').

[2] *The Council of the City of Sydney v West* (1965) 114 CLR 481 (High Court of Australia).

[3] Published subsequently at (1967) 40 *Australian Law Journal* 336.

[4] *Photo Production Ltd v Securicor (Transport) Ltd* [1980] AC 827 (HL).

[5] Brian Coote, *Exception Clauses: Some Aspects of the Law Relating to Exception Clauses in Contracts for the Carriage, Bailment and Sale of Goods* (London, Sweet & Maxwell, 1964), especially chs 5 ('Breach of Conditions'), 6 ('Deviation') and 8 ('Fundamental Terms and Fundamental Breaches'); 'The Rise and Fall of Fundamental Breach' (1967) 40 *Australian Law Journal* 336; 'The Effect of Discharge by Breach on Exception Clauses' [1970] *Cambridge Law Journal* 221; 'Discharge for Breach and Exception Clauses Since *Harbutt's "Plasticine"*' (1977) 40 *Modern Law Review* 31.

## Discharge for Breach and Deviation Distinguished[6]

One of the principal difficulties with the concept of fundamental breach has been a tendency to confuse it with both discharge for breach and deviation. As a first step, therefore, it would seem desirable to show briefly how the three differ from each other.

### Discharge for Breach

In the sense in which it will be used in this chapter, discharge for breach is concerned with the position of one party to a contract where the other has so broken his promises that, in a significant way, the injured party is denied the performance for which he bargained. The concern is not so much with the right of that party to damages, but with whether he must complete his own performance as a condition of suing the party in breach. Two hundred years ago, if the promises were classified as dependent, neither party could sue the other unless he had first performed his own side of the bargain. This meant that a party in significant breach was unable to enforce the contract against the injured party, for the simple reason that he was not qualified to do so. In this sense, therefore, the breach of the one party automatically meant the release of the other from the need to continue performing. The history of discharge for breach since then has been of a series of explanations for this phenomenon, each of which tended to take on a life of its own. Several of them involved the idea of 'condition' in one form or another, doubtless because, originally, the rights of a party to sue were conditioned on his own prior performance.

Thus developed eventually the Sale of Goods Act division of contract terms into so-called 'conditions' and 'warranties'. The idea became current that the release of the injured party involved the 'rescission' of the contract and that the right to 'rescind' arose on the breach of a condition. In *Hirji Mulji v Cheong Yue Steamship Co Ltd*,[7] Lord Sumner, for the Privy Council, likened discharge for breach to frustration and ascribed it to the failure of a condition subsequent. Then, in *Hain Steamship Co Ltd v Tate & Lyle Ltd*,[8] the House of Lords saw discharge for breach as having the same incidents as deviation. By contrast, a few years after that in *Heyman v Darwins Ltd*[9] the House assimilated discharge for breach to anticipatory breach. The breach by the wrongdoer was a repudiation

[6] A fuller treatment appears in Coote, 'The Effect of Discharge by Breach on Exception Clauses', ibid.

[7] *Mulji v Cheong Yue Steamship Co Ltd* [1926] AC 497 (PC).

[8] *Hain Steamship Co Ltd v Tate & Lyle Ltd* [1936] 2 All ER 597 (HL).

[9] *Heyman v Darwins Ltd* [1942] AC 356 (HL).

which gave the injured party the option of discharging the contract. But that discharge was not a literal rescission. The contract as a whole remained in being for the purpose of assessing damages.[10]

More recently, the House of Lords, in *Moschi v LEP Air Services Ltd*,[11] produced yet another analysis. On a discharge for breach, the contract does terminate, in the sense that primary obligations to perform are replaced by secondary obligations to pay damages. But those obligations are to be measured by reference to the contract as a whole.

## Deviation[12]

The characteristic feature of deviation in contracts for the carriage of goods by sea is that, from the moment the ship departs from the contract route, it automatically loses the protection, not only of its exception clauses, but also of the common law exceptions of the act of God and the actions of the Queen's enemies.[13] The ship becomes absolutely liable for any loss of, or damage to, the goods carried, the only defence being that that loss or damage would have occurred anyway.[14] Similar incidents occur throughout bailment where they bear the label of 'quasi-deviation', *Lilley v Doubleday*[15] being a well-known illustration.

As already mentioned, the House of Lords tried, in *Hain Steamship Co Ltd v Tate & Lyle Ltd*,[16] to explain these incidents as being the result of a discharge for breach. That meant, they thought, that a discharge for breach automatically rescinded the contract, at least in futuro, unless it were affirmed. That analysis is, of course, quite inconsistent with the version given in *Heyman v Darwins Ltd*. Under that version, there would be no literal rescission, nor would there be any discharge unless the injured party so elected. Even then, the contract as a whole would continue to govern the remedies available to the injured party.

Several explanations have been given for the phenomena associated with deviation. One has been that they derived from marine insurance and refer back to the difficulties of communication in the days of sailing ships.[17] Another, given

[10] There is further discussion in *Exception Clauses*, above n 5, ch 5, and in Coote, 'The Effect of Discharge by Breach on Exception Clauses', above n 5.

[11] *Moschi v LEP Air Services Ltd* [1973] AC 331 (HL); applied in *Hyundai Heavy Industries Co Ltd v Papadopoulos* [1980] 1 WLR 1129 (HL).

[12] Discussed in *Exception Clauses*, above n 5, ch 6, and Coote, 'The Effect of Discharge by Breach on Exception Clauses', above n 5, 234ff. See also Brian Coote, 'Deviation and the Ordinary Law' in FD Rose (ed), *Lex Mercatoria: Essays in International Commercial Law in Honour of Francis Reynolds* (London, LLP, 2000) 13.

[13] *Ellis v Turner* (1800) 5 TR 531; 101 ER 1529; *Davis v Garrett* (1830) 6 Bing 716; 130 ER 1456; *Lilley v Doubleday* (1881) LR 7 QBD 510 (QBD) (quasi-deviation).

[14] Loss from inherent vice would seem to be about the only possibility.

[15] (1881) LR 7 QBD 510 (QBD).

[16] [1936] 2 All ER 597 (HL).

[17] GC Cheshire and CHS Fifoot, *The Law of Contract* (9th ed by MP Furmston, London, Butterworths, 1976) 165; D Yates, *Exclusion Clauses* (London, Sweet & Maxwell, 1978) 135. The

by Lord Wright in *A/S Rendal v Arcos Ltd*,[18] was that the exception clauses have reference only to the risks to be encountered along the contract route and, hence, have no reference to the altered risks of the deviation.[19] The true explanation, it is submitted, lies in the nature of a bailment relationship. Though such relationships tend to be seen as imposing burdens, they are equally a form of protection to the bailee, but the protection lasts only so long as the bailee holds the bailed goods within any limits the bailor has placed on his right to possession. If he steps outside those limits he holds, not as a bailee, but as a mere detainor, and as such becomes absolutely liable for loss or damage to the goods so detained.[20] Neither the construction nor the bailment explanation presupposes any termination of the contract.[21]

For present purposes, though, the important point is that if the incidents of deviation and quasi-deviation are taken to be the result of a rescission of the contract, they cannot be explained as flowing from a discharge for breach as it was analysed in *Heyman v Darwins Ltd*. On the other hand, in the light of House of Lords decisions like *United States Shipping Board v Bunge & Born Ltd, Buenos Aires*,[22] and *Hain Steamship Co Ltd v Tate & Lyle Ltd* itself, it seems too late to suppose that deviation can be seen by the courts to turn on anything but a rescission. In the face of such conflict, therefore, deviation and quasi-deviation would seem to be best regarded as sui generis.

## Fundamental Breach[23]

The doctrine of fundamental breach, as it developed before *Suisse Atlantique*, was a substantive rule of law. It asserted that there were categories of breach and types of contractual term so fundamental that no exception clause, however drawn, could exclude liability for them. It originated in a series of three judgments by Devlin J, in *Chandris v Isbrandtsen-Moller Co Inc*,[24] *Alexander v Railway Executive*[25] and *Smeaton Hanscomb & Co Ltd v Sassoon I Setty, Son & Co*.[26] The first

incidents of deviation were applied to bailment generally at least as early as *Coggs v Bernard* (1703) 2 Ld Raym 909; 92 ER 107. AW Knauth, *Ocean Bills of Lading* (4th ed, Baltimore, American Maritime Cases Inc, 1953) 248–9 places their appearance in charterparty disputes at about 1795.

[18] *A/S Rendal v Arcos Ltd* (1937) 43 Comm Cas 1 (HL), 15.

[19] Accordingly, affirmation would not by itself make the exceptions re-apply. The contract would need to be varied to make the exceptions cover the risks of the new route.

[20] This explanation is discussed more fully in *Exception Clauses*, above n 5, 89–93. It accounts for the fact that the liability of the deviator is absolute, and not that of a bailee.

[21] Thus, even the deviating shipowners' right to freight on a timeous delivery, long recognised by the commercial community, can be explained as arising under the contract, either as on a substantial performance, or under the equivalent of a 'warranty ex post facto'.

[22] *United States Shipping Board v Bunge & Born Ltd, Buenos Aires* (1925) 42 TLR 174 (HL); *Exception Clauses*, above n 5, 82 (fn 15) and 93 (fn 86).

[23] For a fuller treatment see Coote, 'The Rise and Fall of Fundamental Breach', above n 5.

[24] *Chandris v Isbrandtsen-Moller Co Inc* [1951] 1 KB 240 (CA).

[25] *Alexander v Railway Executive* [1951] 2 KB 882 (KBD).

[26] *Smeaton Hanscomb & Co Ltd v Sassoon I Setty, Son & Co* [1953] 1 WLR 1468 (QBD).

two of these cases were contracts for the carriage and bailment of goods, respectively, and the breaches involved were of the 'deviation' type. Devlin J referred to such breaches as 'fundamental', which was a word used of them by the House of Lords in *Hain Steamship Co Ltd v Tate & Lyle Ltd.*[27] So far there was no novelty.[28] The real departure came with the *Smeaton Hanscomb* case, where timber sold by description did not comply with specification so that there was a breach of the condition implied by s 13 of the Sale of Goods Act 1893. But the buyer had failed to take action within a contractual 14-day time limit on claims. Devlin J attempted to generalise a new principle of wider application in words well worth repeating for the light they shed on its incidents and purposes:

> It is no doubt a principle of construction that exceptions are to be construed as not being applicable for the protection of those for whose benefit they are inserted if the beneficiary has committed a breach of a fundamental term of the contract, and that a clause requiring the claim to be brought within a specified period is to be regarded as an exception for this purpose: see *Atlantic Shipping & Trading Co Ltd v Louis Dreyfus & Co.*[29] In that case, the fundamental term was the implied condition of seaworthiness, which is treated, as Lord Sumner said,[30] as 'underlying the whole contract of affreightment'. The same principle has been applied in cases of deviation and other fundamental terms. I do not think that what is a fundamental term has ever been clearly defined. It must be something I think, narrower than a condition of the contract, for it would be limiting the exceptions too much to say that they applied only to breaches of warranty. It is I think something which underlies the whole contract so that, if it is not complied with, the performance becomes something totally different from that which the contract contemplates. If, for example, instead of delivering mahogany logs the sellers delivered pine logs and the buyers inadvertently omitted to have them examined for fourteen days, it might well be that the sellers could not rely on the time clause. Roche J, in *Pinnock v Lewis & Peat Ltd,*[31] dealt with the same point in relation to another clause in the same contract which sought to exclude the right of rejection, and in relation to that he said '… the delivery in this case could not properly be described as copra cake at all'.[32]

Devlin J went on to hold that, since the logs delivered were 'round mahogany logs', the limitation clause did apply. The learned judge spoke expressly of the principle as one of 'construction'. It was Denning LJ who subsequently restated it as a substantive rule of law, in the course of his judgment in *Karsales (Harrow) Ltd v Wallis.*[33] Again it is well worth quoting the actual words he used:

27 [1936] 2 All ER 597 (HL).

28 In *The Albion* [1953] 1 WLR 1026 (CA), the Court of Appeal confirmed that the expressions 'fundamental term' and 'fundamental breach' had no special significance outside deviation.

29 *Atlantic Shipping & Trading Co Ltd v Louis Dreyfus & Co* [1922] 2 AC 250 (HL)

30 ibid, 260.

31 *Pinnock v Lewis & Peat Ltd* [1923] 1 KB 690 (KBD).

32 [1953] 1 WLR 1468 (QBD), 1470.

33 [1956] 1 WLR 936 (CA), 940. See also his judgment in *J Spurling Ltd v Bradshaw* [1956] 1 WLR 461 (CA), 469.

> Notwithstanding earlier cases which might suggest the contrary it is now settled that exempting clauses of this kind, no matter how widely they are expressed, only avail the party when he is carrying out the contract in its essential respects. He is not allowed to use them as cover for misconduct or indifference or to enable him to turn a blind eye to his obligations. They do not avail him when he is guilty of a breach which goes to the root of the contract. It is necessary to look at the contract apart from the exempting clauses to see what are the terms express or implied which impose an obligation on the party. If he has been guilty of a breach of these obligations in a respect which goes to the very root of the contract he cannot rely on the exempting clauses … The principle is sometimes said to be that a party cannot rely on an exempting clause when he delivers something 'different in kind' from that contracted for, or has broken a 'fundamental term' or a 'fundamental contractual obligation'. However, I think they are all comprehended by the general principle that a breach which goes to the root of the contract disentitles the party from relying on the exempting clause.

There are two important points to note about these passages. The first is that, since on past authority 'conditions' of the contract could be excluded, the breach of a fundamental term had to be something more fundamental than the breach of a condition, as Devlin J acknowledged and his decision illustrated. The second is that before the *Hong Kong Fir* case[34] many, if not most, lawyers thought that every discharge for breach was the breach of a condition.[35] In the 1950s, therefore, it followed that a fundamental breach had to be worse than a merely discharging breach. It also meant that for every fundamental breach there ought to be a corresponding fundamental term. That is why commentators in due course subsequently coupled the 'main objects' of the contract[36] and the condition as to title under the Sale of Goods Act,[37] as fundamental terms, with total failure of consideration[38] as a fundamental breach. Similarly, the 'core of the contract'[39] was matched with 'difference in kind'.[40] After the *Hong Kong Fir* case had shown that discharge for breach did not have to be the breach of a condition, but could depend on the scale of the breach, and of its consequences, a similar change occurred in relation to fundamental terms and fundamental breaches.

[34] *Hong Kong Fir Shipping Co Ltd v Kawasaki Kisen Kaisha Ltd* [1962] 2 QB 26 (CA) (hereinafter '*Hong Kong Fir*').

[35] This was, incidentally, reflected in the title of ch 5 of *Exception Clauses*, above n 5. The book was based on a dissertation written in the late 1950s.

[36] KW Wedderburn [1957] *Cambridge Law Journal* 17; PS Atiyah, *Sale of Goods* (London, Pitman, 1957) 81–4.

[37] GC Cheshire and CHS Fifoot, *The Law of Contract* (4th ed, London, Butterworths, 1956) 133 and 136.

[38] Cheshire and Fifoot, ibid, 133; *Sutton and Shannon on Contracts* (5th ed by KW Wedderburn, London, Butterworths, 1956) 306–7.

[39] LW Melville, 'The Core of a Contract' (1956) 19 *Modern Law Review* 26.

[40] As to 'difference in kind', see *Exception Clauses*, above n 5, ch 3 ('Exception Clauses and a Physical Subject-Matter'); Brian Coote, 'Correspondence with Description in the Law of Sale of Goods' (1976) 50 *Australian Law Journal* 17.

Instead of being regarded as two sides of the same coin, they too came to be seen as two different things, depending on the importance of the term and the scale of the breach.[41]

The basic weaknesses of the substantive doctrine of fundamental breach were that as a rule of law it lacked any previous warrant and that it was conceived as a unified principle, whereas the threads of authority on which it was based were all really quite distinct.[42] Thus, the courts had long been reluctant to construe general words of exception as excluding the warranty of seaworthiness, but the same was true of important terms generally and even of negligence. Moreover, it was clear on earlier authority that, like promissory conditions, the warranty of seaworthiness could be excluded where the words used were apt to do so. The idea that the condition as to title was unexcludable was not only inconsistent with the *emptio spei* but was hard to reconcile with the fact that the implied condition as to title was itself only a relatively modern development.[43] The very concept of an unexcludable core of obligation was inconsistent with *Rose and Frank Co v JR Crompton and Bros Ltd*[44] in which the House of Lords accepted that, even in a commercial agreement, all obligation whatever could be excluded by the use of an 'honour clause'. Moreover, it was difficult to conceive of a term more fundamental than a condition when a condition was a term so vital that any breach justified a discharge of the contract.[45] Again, to apply to a sale of goods contract, on a fundamental breach, the consequences of a deviation would be to deprive the proferens of the protection of his exceptions even in respect of those breaches which were not fundamental.

What gave the new concepts credibility was the view taken by their proponents of the function of exception clauses.

## The Function of Exception Clauses

The fundamental breach principle turned on the idea, expressed by Denning LJ in *Karsales (Harrow) Ltd v Wallis*,[46] that in construing a contract containing exception clauses it was 'necessary to look at the contract apart from the exempting clauses to see what are the terms express or implied which impose an

[41] AG Guest (1963) 26 *Modern Law Review* 301; JL Montrose, 'Some Problems about Fundamental Terms' [1964] *Cambridge Law Journal* 60, 254; GH Treitel, *The Law of Contract* (London, Stevens & Sons, 1962) 148.

[42] These matters are discussed in greater detail in Coote, 'The Rise and Fall of Fundamental Breach', above n 5, 337–41.

[43] As late as *Morley v Attenborough* (1849) 3 Ex 500; 154 ER 943, there was held to be no implied warranty of title in sales of goods.

[44] *Rose and Frank Co v JR Crompton and Bros Ltd* [1925] AC 445 (HL).

[45] See, eg, *Wallis, Son & Walls v Pratt & Haynes* [1911] AC 394 (HL), where the House of Lords adopted the dissenting judgment of Fletcher Moulton LJ in the Court of Appeal [1910] 2 KB 1003 (CA).

[46] [1956] 1 WLR 936 (CA), 940.

obligation on the party'. It was not the condition or fundamental term which was excluded from the contract. It was liability for its breach which was excused, the exception clause operating as a defence, at the point of adjudication, to accrued rights of action. That, incidentally, helps to explain the early emphasis on fundamental *breach* and the *breach* of a fundamental term.

In my book[47] and elsewhere I have argued that exception clauses qualify the promises to which they relate, and hence take effect at the formation of the contract rather than as mere defences at the point of adjudication. A party to a contract is subject to primary obligations to perform his undertakings and to corresponding sanctioning or secondary obligations to pay compensation if he commits a breach. At common law the two are inseparable, in the sense that no primary obligation arises unless the party concerned has also accepted the sanctioning obligations that go with it. Exception clauses affect the accrual of these obligations, at the time the contract is formed, either by modifying them or by preventing their arising at all. This they can do in three ways. The first involves excluding the primary obligation directly. So, if I sell a horse warranted sound except for hunting, I accept no primary obligation as to its soundness for hunting. Under the second method the primary obligation is excluded because the secondary obligation which would otherwise attach to it has been excluded. Thus, if I say I will not be liable for loss or damage from my servant's negligence, I not only refuse to pay damages, I accept no primary obligation that my servants will be careful. Under the third, sanctioning obligations are limited, without that fact preventing the initial existence of the primary obligations to which they attach. Accordingly, if I limit my potential liability to \$2,600, I accept a primary obligation to perform, but if I commit a breach, no secondary obligation accrues beyond that to pay \$2,600 in damages.

The significance of this view of exception clauses in relation to fundamental breach is not just that it means that exception clauses take effect at the formation of the contract, but also that it leaves no need for the concept of fundamental breach itself. This is because, once he exception clauses have taken effect at the formation of the contract, every breach thereafter of the residual contractual content of the agreement will be actionable.

The first appearance of this kind of analysis, of the relationship of exception clauses to primary and secondary obligations, in a reported case, seems to have been in *Hardwick Game Farm v Suffolk Agricultural & Poultry Producers Association*.[48] The judge was Diplock LJ. He said much the same thing again in the *Heron II*[49] later the same year. In due course he was to bring the analysis into *Moschi v LEP Air Services Ltd*[50] and ultimately into the *Securicor* case itself.[51]

[47] *Exception Clauses*, above n 5, ch 1 (now forming ch 6 of this book).

[48] *Hardwick Game Farm v Suffolk Agricultural & Poultry Producers Association* [1966] 1 WLR 287 (CA), 341–3.

[49] *C Czarnikow Ltd v Koufos* [1966] 2 QB 695 (CA), 730–1.

[50] [1973] AC 331 (HL).

## The *Suisse Atlantique* Case

The weaknesses of fundamental breach as a substantive rule of law did not go unnoticed. A series of dicta from 1964 onwards, by Pearson LJ[52] and Diplock LJ[53] in England, and Barwick CJ and Taylor, Kitto and Windeyer JJ in the High Court of Australia,[54] all tended towards the view that there was no rule of law but at most only a rule of construction, and it was against this background that the question came before the House of Lords in the *Suisse Atlantique* case.

### Fundamental Breach as a Rule of Law

Since the *Suisse Atlantique* was perhaps the best known and most discussed contract decision of its time, it would be tedious here to subject it to yet another analysis. For present purposes, though, a few points need to be recalled. The first was, of course, that the House unanimously denied the existence of a substantive rule of fundamental breach. Nevertheless, they left the way open to a resurgence of the doctrine in a number of ways.

[51] The idea that exception clauses could have a substantive effect seems to have originated with Professor JC Montrose who applied it to the sale of goods by description in 'Operation of Description in a Contract of Sale of Goods' (1937) 15 *Canadian Bar Review* 760, as did Professor J Unger subsequently in 'The Doctrine of the Fundamental Term' [1957] *Business Law Review* 30. *Exception Clauses*, above n 5, applied the idea to exception clauses generally. Dicta or decisions since 1964 accepting the idea in whole of in part include:
In England: *Hardwick Game Farm v Suffolk Agricultural and Poultry Producers Association* [1966] 1 WLR 287 (CA), 309 per Sellers LJ, 339ff per Diplock LJ; *Gillette Industries Ltd v WH Martin Ltd* [1966] 1 Lloyd's Rep 57 (CA), 68 per Winn LJ; *C Czanikow Ltd v Koufos* [1966] 2 QB 695 (CA), 730–1 per Diplock LJ; *Suisse Atlantique* [1967] 1 AC 361 (HL), 431 per Lord Wilberforce; *Kenyon, Son & Craven Ltd v Baxter Hoare & Co Ltd* [1971] 1 WLR 519 (QBD), 522 per Donaldson J; *Trade and Transport Inc v Iino Kaiun Kaisha Ltd (The Angelia)* [1973] 2 All ER 144 (QBD), 161–3 per Kerr J; and now, of course, those of McKenna J and Lord Diplock in *Photo Production Ltd v Securicor (Transport) Ltd* [1980] AC 827 (HL); *cf* also *Torquay Hotel Co Ltd v Cousins* [1969] 2 Ch 106 (CA), 137 per Lord Denning MR ('prepared to assume').
In Australia: *The Council of the City of Sydney v West* (1965) 114 CLR 481 (High Court of Australia), 495–6 per Kitto J, 500 per Windeyer J; *Thomas National Transport (Melbourne) Pty Ltd v May & Baker (Australia) Pty Ltd* (1966) 115 CLR 353 (High Court of Australia), 385–6 per Windeyer J; *State Government Insurance Office Queensland v Brisbane Stevedoring Pty Ltd* (1969) 43 ALJR 456 (High Court of Australia), 461 per Barwick CJ; *George Wimpey & Co Ltd v Territory Enterprises Pty Ltd* (1970) 45 ALJR 38 (High Court of Australia); *McRobertson Miller Airline Services v Commissioner of State Taxation (Western Australia)* (1975) 133 CLR 125 (High Court of Australia), 132–3 per Barwick CJ, 148 per Jacobs J.
In Canada: *Arrow Transfer Co Ltd v Royal Bank of Canada* (1971) 19 DLR (3d) 420, 432, affd (1972) 27 DLR (3d) 420, 432, affd (1972) 27 DLR (3d) 81 (rather ambiguously); *Bata v City Parking Canada Ltd* (1974) 13 DLR (3d) 190; *BC Linton Construction Ltd v Canadian National Railway Co* (1974) 49 DLR (3d) 548, 552 per Laskin CJC.

[52] *UGS Finance v National Mortgage Bank of Greece & National Bank of Greece SA* [1964] 1 Lloyd's Rep 446 (CA), 543.

[53] *Hardwick Game Farm v Suffolk Agricultural and Poultry Producers' Association* [1966] 1 WLR 287 (CA), 341–3.

[54] *The Council of the City of Sydney v West* (1965) 114 CLR 481 (High Court of Australia), 488.

The first was that none of the earlier cases was expressly overruled. Instead, they were said to be explicable on the basis of construction. That left open the possibility of a continuing 'rule of construction'. The second was that their Lordships described the incidents of fundamental breach and fundamental terms in words reserved historically for discharge for breach and conditions. At the time, this gave some ground for thinking that the House had accepted that no separate concept of a fundamental breach or a fundamental term could be justified.[55]

Nevertheless, their Lordships retained the terminology of fundamental breach. That suggested to readers of the reports that the special concepts not only survived but had continuing relevance to exception clauses. The third respect in which the House left a way open to the resurgence of the doctrine was that they confused and conflated fundamental breach, discharge for breach and deviation. It was this which was to lead before long to *Harbutt's 'Plasticine'*.[56] Conversely, it even led to the conclusion that a condition had to have the incidents of a fundamental term. That is what happened in *Ashington Piggeries Ltd v Christopher Hill Ltd*[57] where the House of Lords concluded that before there could be a discharging breach of the condition implied by s 13 of the Sale of Goods Act 1893, the goods had to be 'different in kind'. One can contrast that case with *Smeaton Hanscomb & Co Ltd v Sassoon I Setty Son & Co.*[58] Finally, Lord Wilberforce made several statements which were to be misunderstood and to which it is proposed to return later.[59]

## Three Other Aspects of the *Suisse Atlantique* Case

Three other aspects of the case were to be important for the future. In the *Suisse Atlantique* case there had been no discharge, the contract having been affirmed. This appeared to leave open the argument that their Lordships' statements about construction were limited to affirmed contracts and had no application on a discharge for breach.[60] Secondly, Lord Wilberforce acknowledged that the effect of an exception clause might be to limit or qualify the promise to which it attached and hence that such clauses could, in appropriate cases, serve to prevent

[55] I thought so in 1966. But by 1970 it had become apparent that the concept had survived. Hence my return, in 'The Effect of Discharge by Breach on Exception Clauses', above n 5, to a plea that 'fundamental breach' and discharge for breach be recognised as different things. On the other hand, it was already clear in 1966 that discharge for breach and deviation had been confused.

[56] *Harbutt's 'Plasticine' Ltd v Wayne Tank and Pump Co Ltd* [1970] 1 QB 447 (CA).

[57] *Ashington Piggeries Ltd v Christopher Hill Ltd* [1972] AC 441 (HL). I discussed the point in Coote, above n 40.

[58] [1953] 1 WLR 1468 (QBD).

[59] See text below corresponding to nn 88–91.

[60] *cf* Treitel, *The Law of Contract* (3rd ed, London, Stevens & Sons, 1970) 196; *Cheshire & Fifoot's Law of Contract*, above n 17, 165.

what would otherwise be a breach being a breach at all.[61] It was this idea which was eventually to enable McKenna J to find for Securicor on the claim against it by Photo Production Ltd. Lastly, in the closing passages of his judgment,[62] Lord Reid, in calling for statutory reform, pointed to the arbitrariness of fundamental breach, in that it failed to differentiate between consumer and commercial contracts, between fair exception clauses and those which were unconscionable, and between negotiated contracts and those in common form. This dictum subsequently influenced courts and judges in England,[63] Australia[64] and New Zealand[65] to take account of such distinctions when construing contracts containing exception clauses.

## The Second Version of Fundamental Breach[66]

### *Harbutt's 'Plasticine'*

For the reasons already given, it was open to the courts in the years following *Suisse Atlantique* to continue applying fundamental breach to exception clauses much as before, under the umbrella of 'construction'. In the case at least of deviation from bailment contracts, 'construction' might have been unnecessary even as an umbrella. Even so, there were relatively few reported cases in England on the subject before 1970.[67] In that year, and in a non-bailment case, the Court of Appeal eschewed even the semblance of 'construction' when it held in *Harbutt's 'Plasticine' Ltd v Wayne Tank and Pump Co Ltd*[68] that, even when the words did, on a proper construction, cover the events which had occurred, a limitation clause could not protect the proferens once the contract had been

[61] [1967] 1 AC 361 (HL), 431.

[62] ibid, 405–6.

[63] *Kenyon, Son & Craven Ltd v Baxter Hoare & Co Ltd* [1971] 1 WLR 519 (QBD); *Gallaher Ltd v British Road Services Ltd* [1974] 2 Lloyd's Rep 440 (QBD); *AN Satterthwaite & Co Ltd v NZ Shipping Co Ltd (The Eurymedon)* [1975] AC 154 (PC); *cf RW Green Ltd v Cade Bros Farms* [1978] 1 Lloyd's Rep 602 (QBD); *British Crane Hire Contractors Ltd v Ipswich Plant Hire Ltd* [1975] 1 QB 303 (CA), 313; *Arthur White (Contractor) Ltd v Tarmac Civil Engineering Ltd* [1967] 1 WLR 1508 (HL).

[64] *H & B Van Der Sterren v Cibernetics (Holdings) Pty Ltd* (1970) 44 ALJR 157 (High Court of Australia), 158; *Thomas National Transport (Melbourne) Pty Ltd v May & Baker (Australia) Pty Ltd* (1966) 115 CLR 353 (High Court of Australia), 373; *cf Davis v Commissioner for Main Roads* (1968) 41 ALJR 322 (High Court of Australia).

[65] *Hawkes Bay & East Coast Aero Club Inc v McLeod* [1972] NZLR 289, 295 and 300.

[66] Discussed in greater detail in Coote, 'The Effect of Discharge by Breach on Exception Clauses', above n 5, and especially in Coote 'Discharge for Breach and Exception Clauses since *Harbutts "Plasticine"*', above n 5.

[67] *Garnham, Harris & Elton Ltd v Alfred W Ellis (Transport) Ltd* [1967] 1 WLR 940 (QBD); *Anglo-Continental Holidays Ltd v Typaldos Lines (London) Ltd* [1967] 2 Lloyd's Rep 61 (CA); *BG Transport Service Ltd v Marston Motor Co Ltd* [1970] 1 Lloyd's Rep 371 (QBD), 379; *Mendelssohn v Normand Ltd* [1970] 1 QB 177 (CA).

[68] [1970] 1 QB 447 (CA).

discharged for breach. Though the decision came as a surprise, and its reasoning was almost universally condemned by the commentators,[69] it was logical enough, given its premises, both stated and unstated. The first, stated, premise was that on a discharge for breach the contract was rescinded, so that the exception clauses ceased to have effect. This appeared to be consistent not only with *Hain Steamship Co Ltd v Tate & Lyle Ltd*[70] but also with dicta in the *Suisse Atlantique* case itself.[71] And though it deprived a proferens of his exceptions by a rule of law, it was a different rule of law from that which had been condemned by the House of Lords. Moreover, counsel for the defendant had conceded that, if the contract had been discharged, his clients would have lost the protection of their limitation clauses.[72] The other, unstated, premise was that exception clauses take effect, if at all, only as defences at the point of adjudication. Only if this were so could they be denied effect by a rescission of the contract in futuro. If their true effect were to limit the obligations of the promisor, that would have occurred at the time of formation, and no rescission in futuro could affect them.[73] It follows that, whatever its surface attractions, the reasoning in *Harbutt's 'Plasticine'* was vulnerable on two counts. It would collapse if the effect of discharge for breach were not, after all, a literal rescission of the contract. It would suffer the same fate if exception clauses were recognised as being not mere defences, but qualifications of obligation.

During the decade which followed, the application of *Harbutt's 'Plasticine'* became increasingly extreme. In *Wathes (Western) Ltd v Austins (Menswear) Ltd*[74] the Court of Appeal held that the principle applied, not only where the contract had been discharged for breach, but also where it had been affirmed by the injured party. The Court purported to follow *Charterhouse Credit Co Ltd v Tolly*[75] on the basis, which was correct, that it had not been expressly overruled in the

[69] eg Coote, 'The Effect of Discharge by Breach on Exception Clauses', above n 5; T Weir [1970] *Cambridge Law Journal* 189; JH Baker (1970) 33 *Modern Law Review* 441; PN Leigh-Jones and MA Pickering, '*Harbutt's "Plasticine" Ltd v Wayne Tank and Pump Co Ltd*: Fundamental Breach and Exemption Clauses, Damages and Interest' (1970) 86 *Law Quarterly Review* 513; PN Leigh-Jones and MA Pickering, 'Fundamental Breach: The Aftermath of *Harbutt's "Plasticine"*' (1971) 87 *Law Quarterly Review* 515; JF Wilson, 'Fundamental Breach: The Plot Thickens' (1971) 4 *New Zealand Universities Law Review* 254; AM Shea, 'Discharge from Performance of Contracts by Failure of Condition' (1979) 42 *Modern Law Review* 623. The leading contract textbooks also all expressed reservations about it. For an attempt to support it, see F Dawson, 'Fundamental Breach of Contract' (1975) 91 *Law Quarterly Review* 380.

[70] [1936] 2 All ER 597 (HL).

[71] [1967] 1 AC 361 (HL), 398 per Lord Reid, 419 per Lord Upjohn.

[72] [1970] 1 QB 447 (CA), 455 and 470.

[73] In (1971) 87 *Law Quarterly Review* 515 at 520, Leigh-Jones and Pickering, while characterising such an approach as 'unrealistic', acknowledged that, if it were accepted, the result in *Harbutt's 'Plasticine'* would be 'altogether short-circuited'.

[74] *Wathes (Western) Ltd v Austins (Menswear) Ltd* [1976] 1 Lloyd's Rep 14 (CA).

[75] *Charterhouse Credit Co Ltd v Tolly* [1963] 2 QB 683 (CA).

*Suisse Atlantique* case.[76] While reference was made to 'construction' in the *Wathes* case, there was no analysis of the words used. It appeared to be assumed that the result of the case would turn, not on the wording of the contract, but on whether a fundamental breach had occurred. The significance of this was not lost on Lord Denning MR. In *Levison v Patent Steam Carpet Cleaning Co Ltd*[77] and in the *Securicor* case itself,[78] he reverted to the terminology of the pre-*Suisse Atlantique* period.

## Contrary Trends

As against these developments two other streams of authority emerged which pointed in the opposite direction. The premise that discharge for breach involves a literal rescission, depriving the contract of any future effect, became difficult to reconcile with *The Mihalis Angelos*[79] in which the Court of Appeal held that, for the purpose of assessing damages, regard had to be given to a clause in favour of the 'wrongdoer' which would not have been operative until after the contract had been discharged. Again, in *Moschi v LEP Air Services Ltd*[80] the House of Lords appeared to accept the view that, while on a discharge for breach any primary obligations ceased and were replaced by secondary obligations to pay damages, those damages were to be assessed on the basis of the contract as a whole and not just of selected parts of it.

The premise that exception clauses were mere defences also came in question. In *Kenyon Son & Craven Ltd v Baxter Hoare & Co Ltd*[81] Donaldson J distinguished three kinds of exception clause, depending on whether they excluded obligation, excluded liability, or merely limited liability. In respect of at least the first of these, he denied that the court could discover the obligations of the proferens without taking into account any exceptions of those obligations.[82] Soon afterwards, in *The Angelia*,[83] Kerr J expressed the view that an event covered by an exception of 'liability' was not and could never be a breach at all, let alone a fundamental breach. The difference between an exclusion of liability and an exclusion of obligation was merely 'semantic'. This meant that, of Donaldson J's three categories of exception clause, it could be said only of limitation clauses that they operated as mere defences. It was to the category of limitation clause

[76] In (1966) 29 *Modern Law Review* 546 at 550, Professor Treitel argued the need for the overruling of the decision by the House of Lords. On the other hand, the actual result could easily have been reached as a matter of construction; see *Exception Clauses*, above n 5, 116 (fn 89).

[77] *Levison v Patent Steam Carpet Cleaning Co Ltd* [1978] QB 68 (CA), 81.

[78] [1978] 1 WLR 856 (HL), 863.

[79] *The Mihalis Angelos* [1971] 1 QB 164 (CA).

[80] [1973] AC 331 (HL).

[81] [1971] 1 WLR 519 (QBD), 522.

[82] ibid, 532.

[83] *Trade and Transport Inc v Iino Kaiun Kaisha Ltd (The Angelia)* [1973] 1 WLR 210 (QBD), 228–31. For a contrary reading of this passage, see Barendt [1973] *Annual Survey of Commonwealth Law*, 293–4.

that the exception in *Harbutt's 'Plasticine'* belonged. But even in respect of this class, Barwick CJ[84] and, significantly, Diplock LJ[85] were already on record as saying that limitation clauses, too, qualified the obligations to which they referred, though this was not a view shared by some of the commentators.[86]

## The Revival of the Original Version of Fundamental Breach

The decision in *Wathes (Western) Ltd v Austins (Menswear) Ltd*,[87] although it purported to follow *Harbutt's 'Plasticine'*, could be interpreted as a return to the pre-*Suisse Atlantique* rule of law. But in addition there were two further factors tending in the same direction, the first of them being the dicta of Lord Wilberforce of which mention has already been made and which appeared in his judgment in the *Suisse Atlantique*.[88] There were three. First, he distinguished two meanings which had been given to the expression 'fundamental breach'. The one he saw as covering fundamental breach in the meaning given it in this chapter. The other covered discharge for breach as it is defined in this chapter.[89] His second dictum was to the effect that an exception clause could not be allowed to empty a contract of all content. To this extent, there was a rule of law.[90] The point he was making related to the formation of the contract and depended on the idea he had expressed elsewhere in his judgment that exception clauses could have the effect that what would otherwise be a breach would not be a breach at all. Third, he gave deviation, quasi-deviation and 'difference in kind' as examples of construction, as being cases where the parties 'could hardly have been supposed to contemplate such a misperformance'.[91] These passages were taken by Fenton Atkinson LJ in *Farnworth Finance Facilities Ltd v Attryde*,[92] and particularly by

[84] *State Government Insurance Office Queensland v Brisbane Stevedoring Pty Ltd* (1969) 43 ALJR 456, 461.

[85] *C Czarnikow v Koufos* [1966] 2 QB 695 (CA), 730–1; *cf Hardwick Game Farm v Suffolk Agricultural & Poultry Producers' Association* [1966] 1 WLR 287 (CA), 341–3.

[86] *Cheshire and Fifoot's Law of Contract*, above n 17, 146–7; Leigh-Jones and Pickering, 'Fundamental Breach: The Aftermath of *Harbutt's "Plasticine"*', above n 69, 520; Dawson, above n 69, 396 and 402; GH Treitel, *The Law of Contract* (5th ed, London, Stevens & Sons, 1979) 171–2.

[87] [1976] 1 Lloyd's Rep 14 (CA).

[88] [1967] 1 AC 361 (HL).

[89] ibid, 431.

[90] ibid, 432. See also Laskin CJC in *BG Linton Construction Ltd v Canadian National Railway Co* (1974) 49 DLR (3d) 548, 552; *Aita v Silverstone Towers Ltd* (1978) 86 DLR (3d) 439 (whether a right arbitrarily to withdraw from agreement); *Metrotex Pty Ltd v Freight Investments Pty Ltd* [1969] VR 9, 19. Conversely, if the agreement were not intended to be a contract, or were intended as a unilateral rather than a bilateral contract, this constraint would not apply: *Rose & Frank Co v JR Crompton & Bros Ltd* [1925] AC 445 (HL); *MacRobertson Miller Airline Services v Commissioner of State Taxation (Western Australia)* (1975) 133 CLR 125 (High Court Australia).

[91] ibid, 433.

[92] *Farnworth Finance Facilities Ltd v Attryde* [1970] 1 WLR 1053 (CA), 1060.

Donaldson J in *Kenyon, Son & Craven Ltd v Baxter Hoare & Co Ltd*,[93] to mean that fundamental breach in the narrower sense in which it has been defined in this chapter, had survived the *Suisse Atlantique* as a rule of law.

Much more important, though, was the second factor. This was that even where the courts purported to apply a rule of construction, they were in fact using the presence or absence of fundamental breach as the determinant of whether the exception clause applied, and hence were applying it as though it were a rule of law.[94] That was true of *Wathes (Western) Ltd v Austins (Menswear) Ltd*.[95] It was also very vividly illustrated in the unreported case of *Prince v Brown Bros and Merseyside & North Wales Electricity Board*,[96] which concerned an indemnity given by an employer to the Electricity Board, which failed to turn off the power to a transformer which the employer's workmen were to paint. When one of their number was electrocuted, the remainder not unnaturally refused for a time to continue, though in due course they went back to work. It was held that since work had been resumed and completed, no 'fundamental breach' had occurred. Accordingly, the Electricity Board were protected by their indemnity. Had the question asked been not 'was the breach "fundamental"?' but 'was it serious?' the whole inquiry would have been transformed. The act of the Board in putting the lives of the workmen in jeopardy was not only appallingly serious in its possible consequences, it was also probably a breach of the duty of common humanity as well.[97] To hold that the indemnity protected the Board was to hold, not just that an insurance risk had been allocated between commercial parties, but that an employer had bargained away the legal responsibility of the party whose role it was to ensure that the lives of the workmen were not endangered. Whether that truly was the intention expressed or implied in the contract could not, on the approach followed, be even considered.

Some reaction against these developments seems to have at least begun before the *Securicor* case. In 1977, Griffiths J in *RW Green Ltd v Cade Bros Farms*[98] showed that he believed something was wrong when he said:

> Nor do I find much help in approaching the question of construction by applying the label 'fundamental' to the breach or to the term breached. The Court has to look at the facts that constitute the breach and the circumstances surrounding it and ask itself

[93] [1971] 1 WLR 519 (QBD), 531–2; *cf Heffron v Imperial Parking Co* (1974) 46 DLR (3d) 642, 650–1; *Chomedy Aluminium Co Ltd v Belcourt Construction (Ottawa) Ltd* (1979) 97 DLR (3d) 170; *Cheshire and Fifoot's Law of Contract*, above n 17, 165.

[94] *cf* Capper [1976] *Annual Survey of Commonwealth Law* 526; SM Waddams, 'Unconscionability in Contracts' (1976) 39 *Modern Law Review* 369, 378.

[95] [1976] 1 Lloyd's Rep 14 (CA).

[96] Unreported, but noted at (1977) 40 *Modern Law Review* 31, 45–6.

[97] I have argued in 'Exception Clauses and Common Humanity' (1975) 125 *New Law Journal* 752, not only that this duty is not confined to occupier's liability, but also that it would be open to the courts to hold it unexcludable on grounds of public policy.

[98] *RW Green Ltd v Cade Bros Farms* [1978] 1 Lloyd's Rep 607 (QBD), 609.

> whether the clause could have been intended by the parties to apply to such a situation and the nature of the breach must loom large in such consideration.[99]

However, while it was a step forward that the seriousness of the breach, or the importance of the term, should have been seen as more relevant than its belonging to a particular technical category, it has to be noted that the facts and surrounding circumstances to which the learned judge referred were those of the breach instead of, as construction would normally require, those attending the formation of the contract.[100]

Outside England and Wales, the revival of the substantive doctrine of fundamental breach seems to have been more than matched in Canada. But from the reported cases, it appears to have had much less impact in Scotland, Australia and New Zealand.[101]

[99] From the date of his judgment (October 1977) it may be that Griffiths J had in mind *Prince v Brown Brothers & Merseyside & North Wales Electricity Board*, above n 96.

[100] Other English cases on fundamental breach during this period included *Guarantee Trust of Jersey Ltd v Gardner* (1973) 117 SJ 564 (CA); *United Fresh Meat Co Ltd v Charterhouse Cold Storage Ltd* [1974] 2 Lloyd's Rep 286 (QBD); *Gallaher Ltd v British Road Services Ltd* [1974] 2 Lloyd's Rep 440 (QBD); *J Evans & Son (Portsmouth) Ltd v Andrea Merzario Ltd* [1976] 1 WLR 1078 (CA), 1084; *Rasbora Ltd v JC Marine Ltd* [1977] 1 Lloyd's Rep 645 (QBD).

[101] Scottish cases include *Alexander Stephen (Forth) Ltd v JJ Riley (UK) Ltd*, 1976 SLT 269 (where *Harbutt's 'Plasticine'* was not agreed with); *WL Tinney & Co Ltd v John C Dougall Ltd* 1977 SLT (Notes) 58. In Australia, the High Court accepted the *Suisse Atlantique* approach in *Thomas National Transport (Melbourne) Pty Ltd v May & Baker (Australia) Pty Ltd* (1967) 115 CLR 353 , as might have been expected in view of their own approach in *The Council of the City of Sydney v West* (1965) 114 CLR 481. Thereafter, the doctrine seems to have retained very little impact; see *VL Boots Pty Ltd v Booth (ERF) Pty Ltd* [1968] 3 NSWR 519; *Hall v Queensland Truck Centre* [1970] Qd R 231. In New Zealand, the doctrine was applied in one unreported case, *Auckland Gas Co v Farnsworth Galvanisers* (1970) noted in [1972] *New Zealand Law Journal* 32, and apparently at first instance in *Devonport Borough Council v Robins* [1979] 1 NZLR 1, 16. In Canada, the Supreme Court accepted the *Suisse Atlantique* approach in *BG Linton Construction v Canadian National Railway Co* ((1974) 49 DLR (3d) 543. But that did nothing to stem what had become a profusion of cases in which the doctrine was applied, effectively as a rule of law. These were collected in SM Waddams, *The Law of Contracts* (Toronto, Canada Law Book, 1977) 285–6 (fnn 80 and 85). Later decisions include *Davidson v Three Spruces Realty Ltd* (1977) 79 DLR (3d) 481; *McKinnon v Acadian Lines Ltd* (1977) 81 DLR (3d) 480; *Evans Products Ltd v Crest Warehousing Ltd* (1979) 95 DLR (3d) 631; *Murray v Sperry Rand Corporation* (1979) 96 DLR (3d) 113; *Captain v Far Eastern Steamship Co* (1978) 97 DLR (3d) 250; *Woollatt Fuel & Lumber (London) Ltd v Matthews Group Ltd* (1978) 83 DLR (3d) 137. Two cases which illustrate the confusions attendant on a failure to distinguish between discharge for breach, deviation and fundamental breach are *Van Dorne v North American Van Lines (Canada) Ltd* (1979) 95 DLR (3d) 358 and *Whittaker v Ford Motor Co of Canada Ltd* (1979) 98 DLR (3d) 162.

# The *Securicor* Case

## The Case at First Instance

*Photo Production Ltd v Securicor (Transport) Ltd*[102] involved a 1968 agreement Caseunder which Securicor was to provide a patrol service to Photo Production's premises at a charge which worked out about 26 pence per visit.[103] The agreement included Standard Conditions of which Condition 1 provided that 'under no circumstances [should] the Company be responsible for any injurious act or default by any employee of the Company unless such act or default could have been foreseen and avoided by the exercise of due diligence on the party of the Company as his employer'. Condition 2 allowed for limitations of liability should any liability on the part of the company arise 'notwithstanding the foregoing provision'. While on an inspection of the premises, one of Securicor's employees deliberately started a fire which resulted in loss totaling £615,000. The employee in due course was convicted of arson and sentenced to three years' imprisonment. In the meantime Photo Production Ltd re-engaged Securicor under a new contract.[104]

Photo Production's claim in the High Court was for damages in contract or tort, or both. They alleged that the contract contained two implied terms, one that the patrolmen would exercise all reasonable diligence, skill and care, and the other that Securicor would itself exercise all proper care in the selection, training, supervision, employment and use of their patrolmen. The trial judge, McKenna J, rejected the first of these implied terms as being inconsistent with Condition 1 of the Standard Conditions. As to the second, he held that there had been no want of care or diligence on the part of Securicor as employers. But for Condition 1, Securicor would also have been vicariously liable in tort for their servant's criminal act,[105] but since that act was not one Securicor could have foreseen and avoided, their responsibility for this too had been excluded. The provision was a reasonable one and there was no cause for the Court to put a strained meaning on its language. Photo Production had also argued that Securicor had committed a fundamental breach which prevented their relying on Condition 1. As to this, McKenna J held that if a contract provided that one of the parties to it should not be 'responsible' if a particular event occurred, the occurrence of that event could not be treated as being a breach of contract by that party. If it could not be

[102] [1980] AC 827 (HL).

[103] The amount of the defendant's charge was not stated in the reports of the case in the Court of Appeal ([1978] 1 WLR 856 (CA); [1978] 3 All ER 146 (CA)).

[104] This interesting, though strictly irrelevant, fact appears in the case for the appellant, for a copy of which I am indebted to Professor David Yates. I have used the same source to fill out the accounts of the case at first instance given in the *Weekly Law Reports* and the *All England Law Reports.*

[105] *Morris v CW Martin & Sons Ltd* [1966] 1 QB 716 (CA). Contrast *Keppel Bus Co Ltd v Sa'ad bin Ahman* [1974] 1 WLR 1082 (JC). See also G Samuel (1979) 95 *Law Quarterly Review* 25, 26.

treated as a breach, it could not be treated as a fundamental breach, however serious its consequences. He referred to the judgment of Kerr J in *The Angelia*.[106]

Of the two grounds upon which the reasoning in *Harbutt's 'Plasticine'* could be challenged, from the nature of discharge for breach and from the function of the exception clauses, McKenna J had chosen the latter. Though his decision apparently caused 'astonishment' in some quarters,[107] he had in large measure foreshadowed it in the earlier case of *Mayfair Photographic Supplies v Baxter Hoare*.[108]

## The Case in the Court of Appeal

But if the judgment at first instance came as a surprise, that could hardly be said of the reaction of the Court of Appeal (Lord Denning MR, Shaw and Waller LJJ) in unanimously allowing the appeal.[109] In his judgment, Lord Denning accepted that, taken in their natural and ordinary meaning, Conditions 1 and 2 either exempted or limited Securicor's liability but held, nevertheless, that on three grounds the company were not entitled to rely upon those clauses. His first ground was based on *Harbutt's 'Plasticine'*, but restated in terms reminiscent of the pre-*Suisse Atlantique* substantive doctrine. 'The Court itself', he said, 'deprives the party of the benefit of an exemption or limitation clause if he has been guilty of a breach of a fundamental term or of a fundamental breach of one of the terms of the contract.'[110] His second ground was that the courts were entitled to construe a contract in the light of the presumed intentions of the parties as reasonable persons, and could say in the present case that they would not have intended the Conditions to apply in the events which had occurred. His final ground was that the courts would not allow a party to rely on an exemption or limitation clause where it would not be fair or reasonable for the party to do so. The other members of the Court both held that, by reason of their fundamental breach, Securicor had lost the protection of their exception clauses but that, in any event, on their proper construction, the Conditions did not apply in the events which had occurred.

## The Case in the House of Lords

Before the House of Lords, the two basic issues were whether, on their proper construction, Conditions 1 and 2 could apply and, if so, whether Securicor were prevented from relying upon them because of fundamental breach or on any

[106] [1973] 1 WLR 210 (QBD), 230–1.

[107] See Samuel, above n 105, who is critical of the approach followed by McKenna J.

[108] *Mayfair Photographic Supplies (London) Ltd v Baxter Hoare & Co Ltd* [1972] 1 Lloyd's Rep 410 (QBD).

[109] [1978] 1 WLR 856 (CA).

[110] ibid, 863.

other ground. As to the construction point, their Lordships were unanimous that the words used in Condition 1 were apt to protect Securicor. On the second issue, they unanimously denied the existence of any substantive doctrine of fundamental breach with the reservation, in the case of Lord Diplock, that the agreement must still exhibit 'the legal characteristics of a contract'.[111] *Harbutt's 'Plasticine'* and *Wathes (Western) Ltd v Austins (Menswear) Ltd*[112] were both overruled, as was *Charterhouse Credit Co Ltd v Tolly*,[113] the decision relied on in the *Wathes* case. Nor did Lord Denning's alternative grounds of 'presumed intention' and his test of reasonableness find favour. The House reaffirmed that, within the limits of legality, the parties were free to contract on terms of their own choice, and to agree beforehand what the consequences of breach should be.

## The Rejection of *Harbutt's 'Plasticine'*

The reaffirmation of what had been decided in *Suisse Atlantique* no doubt disposed of the more recent developments, so far as they were a direct revival of the former substantive doctrine, and also of the *Harbutt's 'Plasticine'* principle in the form in which it had recently been expressed. But it did not necessarily dispose of the reasoning on which *Harbutt's 'Plasticine'* itself was based. As we have seen, there were two grounds on which that could be attacked. Of their Lordships, all except Lord Diplock chose the route of discharge for breach. This made it necessary to distinguish the deviation cases and to hold that discharge for breach did not mean a rescission of the contract. In his leading judgment, Lord Wilberforce accepted the *Heyman v Darwins Ltd*[114] analysis. Upon a discharge for breach the contract remained in being for the purposes of assessing damages, and this included any provisions of the contract which dealt with damages, whether they liquidated, limited or excluded them.[115] In a sense, the choice of the *Heyman v Darwins Ltd* analysis was an arbitrary one. It was put forward in my book and earlier articles because it was at that time the most recent. But since then the House of Lords has produced a new analysis in the *LEP Air Services* case.[116] Since it is the more recent analysis it ought arguably to have been the one to follow. A possible reason why this did not happen will be suggested in due course.[117] As to the deviation cases, Lord Wilberforce recalled that in the *Suisse Atlantique* he had said it was a matter of the parties' intentions whether, and to what extent, clauses

[111] The fact that the point presupposes that exception clauses can prevent the accrual of obligation may explain why it was taken by Lord Wilberforce in *Suisse Atlantique*, and by Lord Diplock but not by Lord Wilberforce in *Securicor*. See text below corresponding to the footnotes between nn 149 and 154.

[112] [1976] 1 Lloyd's Rep 14 (CA).

[113] [1963] 2 QB 683 (CA).

[114] [1942] AC 356 (HL).

[115] [1980] AC 827 (HL), 844.

[116] [1973] AC 331 (HL).

[117] See text below corresponding to the footnotes between nn 149 and 154.

in shipping contracts could be applied after a deviation. He allowed that it might be preferable to consider them 'as a body of authority sui generis with special rules derived from historical and commercial reasons'.[118] But on either view, what they could not do was to lay down different rules, as to contracts generally, from those stated by the House in *Heyman v Darwins Ltd*.

Because of his part in formulating the rather different analysis in *Moschi v LEP Air Services Ltd*,[119] it was not so easy for Lord Diplock to dispose of *Harbutt's 'Plasticine'* by a simple reliance on *Heyman v Darwins Ltd*. Under the *LEP Air Services* case, the contract determined on a discharge for breach, in that primary obligations were replaced by secondary ones. That would suggest that clauses irrelevant until adjudication would come too late to take effect. Lord Diplock was able to overrule *Harbutt's 'Plasticine'* by following the second route, that of the function of exception clauses. Both primary and secondary obligations were the product of the contract as a whole, including any exception or limitation clause and came into existence as modified by them.[120] This also meant that he was able to conclude, with McKenna J below, that Securicor's primary obligation to procure visits by persons who would exercise skill and care was not absolute but had been modified by Condition 1. It was limited to the exercise of due diligence by Securicor, in their capacity as employer, to procure that those persons would exercise reasonable skill and care.[121]

## Construction of the Exception Clause

The other major issue discussed by their Lordships was that of construction. None had any doubt that in its natural and ordinary meaning Condition 1 covered the events which had occurred. The question was, rather, whether there was any reason why the natural and ordinary meaning should not be applied. Though regard had to be had to the contra proferentem rule,[122] this was a commercial contract[123] 'negotiated between businessmen capable of looking after their own interests and of deciding how risks inherent in performance … [could] be most economically borne (generally by insurance)'.[124] The risk concerned was a 'misfortune risk' of the kind that the reasonable diligence of neither party could prevent.[125] The fee charged by Securicor was modest[126] and would probably have

[118] [1980] 2 WLR 283, 291; *cf Cheshire and Fifoot's Law of Contract*, above n 17, 165; Yates, above n 17, 155.

[119] [1973] AC 331 (HL).

[120] [1980] AC 827 (HL), 848–9. See also his earlier dicta on the subject in *Hardwick Game Farm v Suffolk Agricultural & Poultry Producers Association* [1966] WLR 287 (CA), 341–3; *C Czarnikow v Koufos* [1966] 2 QB 695 (CA), 730–1; *R v Ward Ltd v Bignall* [1967] 1 QB 534 (CA), 548.

[121] [1980] AC 827 (HL), 851.

[122] ibid, 846 and 850.

[123] ibid, 843, 850, 851 and 852.

[124] ibid, 850, and 851.

[125] ibid, 851.

been less than the reduction in premiums Photo Production might have enjoyed as a result of obtaining their services.[127] The allocation of risk in the contract was fair,[128] reasonable[129] and probably the most economical.[130] A businessman entering the contract could have had no doubt as to the real meaning of Condition 1 and would have made his insurance arrangements accordingly.[131] In these circumstances it would be wrong to place a strained construction upon the words used when they were clear, and fairly susceptible of only one meaning.[132]

In treating these factors as relevant to the question of construction their Lordships were applying established principles. As we have seen, it has been accepted since the judgment of Lord Reid in the *Suisse Atlantique* that the construction of a contract can vary depending on whether it is a commercial or a consumer one, or negotiated as distinct from being a contract of adhesion.[133] While the reasonableness or otherwise of a provision is not at common law a ground for modifying it once a true construction has been arrived at,[134] such considerations are certainly relevant to the process of arriving at a true construction in the first place, provided the words used are properly capable of more than one meaning.[135] It is also an established test that the words used should be clear to the class of persons to whom they are addressed.[136]

## The Significance of *Securicor* for the Future

### Fundamental Breach

In the course of his judgment in *Securicor*, Lord Wilberforce gave some prominence to his view that the passing of the Unfair Contract Terms Act 1977 had made the doctrine of fundamental breach superfluous.[137] That was true, he thought, not only of contracts falling within the Act but also of those outside it.

[126] ibid, 846 and 852.

[127] ibid, 852.

[128] ibid.

[129] ibid, 846.

[130] ibid, 851–2.

[131] ibid, 852.

[132] ibid, 850–1.

[133] See the cases in nn 63–5 above.

[134] *Anson's Law of Contract* (25th ed by AG Guest, Oxford, Clarendon Press, 1979) 185–6; Treitel, above n 86, 179.

[135] eg *Wickman Machine Tool Sales Ltd v L Schuler AG* [1974] AC 235 (HL), 251–2, 255–6 and 272; *In re Gulbenkian's Settlements* [1970] AC 508 (HL), 517 and 524; *Bremer Handels G mbH v Vanden-Avennelzegem PVBA* [1978] 2 Lloyd's Rep 109 (HL), 113.

[136] *Hollier v Rambler Motors (AMC) Ltd* [1972] 2 QB 71 (CA); *Gallaher Ltd v British Road Services Ltd* [1974] 1 Lloyd's Rep 440 (QBD), 448; *RW Green Ltd v Cade Bros Farms* [1978] 1 Lloyd's Rep 602 (QBD), 608 ('any farmer who read it'). The earlier cases were cited in Coote, 'The Effect of Discharge by Breach on Exception Clauses', above n 5, 240.

[137] [1980] AC 827 (HL), 843.

The very fact that the Act had not been made to apply to commercial contracts otherwise than on one party's standard form confirmed that the parties to such contracts were intended by the legislature to be left free to make their own arrangements.

Moreover, while he acknowledged that, despite its imperfections and doubtful parentage, fundamental breach had served a useful purpose, Lord Wilberforce was otherwise dismissive of it. His references to 'a legal complex so uncertain as the doctrine of fundamental breach must be' and to 'analysis, which becomes progressively more refined, of decisions in other cases leading to inevitable appeals' suggest that he would be content to see it disappear altogether.[138] It is far from certain, however, that that is what will happen.

A first point is that not all the contracts excluded from the Unfair Contract Terms Act are commercial. Contracts not on one party's standard terms, where neither deals in the course of business, also fall outside it.[139] Even in respect of contracts within it, the Act says nothing about the initial construction and interpretation of the clauses concerned and, since fundamental breach has until now been seen as relevant to those questions, it would require a major change in attitudes to make it irrelevant hereafter.[140] For similar reasons fundamental breach is likely to be seen as relevant to the statutory requirement of reasonableness and, possibly, to the reasonable expectation postulated by s 3(2)(b)(i). As for common law countries with no equivalent to the Unfair Contract Terms Act, the pressures to retain a fundamental breach principle will remain unchanged.

Conceivably, in countries without equivalent legislation, and in England itself in respect of non-business contracts outside the Act, there might be a temptation to distinguish *Securicor*, so far as it denies the existence of a rule of law, on the ground that it applies only to contracts in respect of which the new Act has made fundamental breach unnecessary.[141] But that would be a travesty of legal reasoning, since the contract in *Securicor* antedated the Act and had therefore to be decided on ordinary common law principles, as Lords Diplock and Salmon were careful to emphasise.[142] Almost as bad would be an attempt to distinguish the case on the grounds that it was confined to reasonable, negotiated, arrangements for the allocation of insurance risks between commercial parties. Of course those factors were relevant, but only to the issue of construction. On the substantive points covered in the judgments, the reasoning of the House of Lords applies just as strongly to all types of contract.

[138] ibid, 843.

[139] Sections 11(3) and 3(1).

[140] Discussed in Brian Coote, 'Unfair Contract Terms Act 1977' (1978) 41 *Modern Law Review* 312, 323. *Howard Marine & Dredging Co Ltd v A Ogden & Sons (Excavating) Ltd* [1978] 1 QB 574 (CA) illustrates the point.

[141] *cf Levison v Patent Steam Carpet Cleaning Co Ltd* [1978] 1 QB 69 (CA), 81 per Lord Denning MR.

[142] [1980] AC 827 (HL), 847 and 852.

When it comes to questions of construction there would, despite Lord Wilberforce's strictures, seem to be sufficient material available to enable any country to retain fundamental breach should it wish to do so. Initially the concept would be retained as a guide to construction. But the pressures towards treating it once more as a rule of law could be expected to build quite rapidly. This point is that, apart from negativing the *Harbutt's 'Plasticine'* version of fundamental breach, the *Securicor* decision has left things fairly much as they were after *Suisse Atlantique*. In the first place, no pre-*Suisse Atlantique* case other than *Charterhouse Credit Co Ltd v Tolly*[143] has actually been overruled. Second, the terminology of fundamental breach has in substance been retained, in all its ambiguity.[144] Accordingly, and this is a third factor, there is little in *Securicor* to prevent lawyers, so-minded, concluding that a rule of 'construction' remains, to the effect that exception clauses do not apply to fundamental breaches. On past experience, that will almost certainly mean that the inquiry will be directed not to the words used, but to the presence or absence of fundamental breach, as the determinant. In consequence the test will in reality be applied as one of law.[145] Fourth, the fact that *Hain Steamship Co Ltd v Tate & Lyle Ltd*[146] has been distinguished in no way affects its application to deviation and quasi-deviation. Those breaches will continue to deny the proferens the protection of his exception clauses. The temptation to generalise from these breaches to others outside bailment will remain, if only because the concept of deviation is not very clearly understood. Finally, there remain those dicta of Lord Wilberforce in the *Suisse Atlantique* case which misled Fenton Atkinson LJ and Donaldson J.[147] His Lordship was prepared neither to qualify nor to explain them in *Securicor*. Moreover, his dictum about there being a rule of law which would not allow an exception clause to empty a contract of all content has now been echoed by Lord Diplock. Of course the

143 [1963] 2 QB 683 (CA).

144 Lord Diplock would reserve the word 'fundamental' for a discharge for breach based on the scale of the breach, or of its consequences, as in the *Hong Kong Fir* case; see [1980] 2 WLR 283 [HL], 294.

145 The Supreme Court of Canada has in effect now done this in *Beaufort Realties (1964) Inc & Belcourt Construction (Ottawa) Ltd v Chomedey Aluminium Co Ltd* (1980) 116 DLR (3d) 193, dismissing an appeal from the Ontario Court of Appeal (1979) 97 DLR (3d) 170. The case concerned a building sub-contract which included, inter alia, a clause waiving statutory lien rights. The judgment contained no analysis of the clause or of the contract. The Court simply asserted that, like the Court below, it was satisfied that, in the context of the contract as a whole, the true construction to be placed on the waiver clause was that it ceased to bind once the contract had been terminated for failure to make progress payments, a breach which the Court characterised as 'fundamental'. As Professor SM Waddams has commented in a note in (1981) 15 *University British Columbia Law Review* 189, 194: 'Can it really be thought that the parties genuinely intended that the lien waiver should be effective except in the one case where a lien is likely to be claimed, where the sub-contractor was unpaid?' The Ontario Court of Appeal appears to have accepted (at 177–8) that the waiver clause was clear and unambiguous, and also that it was fair and reasonable at the time the contract was entered into. Rather, the 'construction' test (so-called) which it applied was: 'Is it fair and reasonable in the context of this fundamental breach that the waiver of lien continue to bind the appellant?'

146 [1936] 2 All ER 597 (HL).

147 See text accompanying nn 89–91 above.

reference of both dicta was to the formation of the contract, and presupposed that exception clauses define obligation, but in a world of lawyers who see exception clauses as mere defences, that qualification seems no more likely now to be appreciated than it was after *Suisse Atlantique.*

If construction was what *Suisse Atlantique* and *Securicor* were really about, two changes in approach ought to occur. The inquiry of the courts ought in the first place to be directed to finding the meaning of the words used, in the light of the contract as a whole, and of the surrounding circumstances at the time the contract was formed. Of course it would be relevant to that inquiry that the acts or events claimed to be covered by the exceptions were of a serious nature. The more serious they were, the clearer the words used should be, but it would be the degree of seriousness which would count, not whether they were 'fundamental' in any technical sense. Second, a return might be expected to the principles which have heretofore governed the construction of exception clauses. I have attempted to list some of these elsewhere.[148] Nevertheless, so much water has passed under the bridge since the *Smeaton Hanscomb* case in 1953 that it may be asking too much to expect either change to occur, at least in England and Canada, where fundamental breach has had its greatest influence.

## The Function of Exception Clauses

Since Lord Diplock concurred in overruling *Harbutt's 'Plasticine'*, he can be taken to have affirmed his earlier expressed view that even limitation clauses qualify the (secondary) obligations to which they relate. To that extent, the gap left after *The Angelia*[149] has been closed.

On the other hand, Lord Wilberforce did not advert to the function of exception clauses at all. More than that, he chose to overrule *Harbutt's 'Plasticine'* by applying the *Heyman v Darwins Ltd* analysis of discharge for breach rather than by adopting the more recent analysis in the *LEP Air Services* case. To adopt the latter could have involved his accepting Lord Diplock's view of the function of exception clauses. This may tend to suggest that he has changed his mind since his dictum in *Suisse Atlantique.* What is perhaps at least as likely is that, in a case which he could decide without having to advert to the point, Lord Wilberforce simply preferred to 'leave well alone'. That, certainly, is what he did earlier when he was in a similar position in *The Eurymedon.*[150] The difficulty is that if the House of Lords were to decide, definitively, that exception clauses are more than mere defences, the repercussions would not be confined to discharge for breach,

[148] Coote, 'The Effect of Discharge by Breach on Exception Clauses', above n 5.

[149] [1973] 1 WLR 210 (QBD).

[150] [1975] AC 154 (PC), 168; and see also *Port Jackson Stevedoring Pty Ltd v Salmond & Spraggon (Australia) Pty Ltd* (1980) 54 ALJR 552 (PC).

or to exception clauses intended to benefit third parties,[151] but would extend across the whole spectrum. In particular such a finding could have radical consequences for the Unfair Contract Terms Act 1977, which was drafted throughout on the premise that exceptions are mere defences. It could be rendered in some respects largely ineffective if a different approach were to be followed.[152]

The fact that Lord Diplock has now based a judgment on the 'qualification' view of exception clauses at House of Lords level adds that much force to what he has said previously on the topic.[153] But it is scarcely likely that, on that account, an idea which has been mooted now for over 40 years will overnight win general acceptance.[154]

## Rescission

One other point that might be made concerns rescission ab initio. Before the case of *Johnson v Agnew*[155] English Chancery lawyers appeared to believe that the only remedy for a party to a sale of land who had suffered a serious breach and wished to terminate his obligations was to rescind ab initio, with a restitution in integrum, but without damages. Now that the House of Lords has, in *Johnson v Agnew*, agreed with the courts of Australia and New Zealand in holding that the common law remedy of discharge for breach with damages is available, the pendulum seems to be swinging to the opposite extreme, and it is being said that rescission ab initio without damages is not an option open to the injured party.[156]

Past authority has supported the existence of both remedies, as well as of a third remedy of rescission followed by a claim for a quantum meruit.[157] At the least, it is submitted that neither *Securicor* nor *Heyman v Darwins Ltd* is inconsistent with there being such a choice, where the appropriate conditions of the remedy can be met. That in turn would depend inter alia on the terms of the contract, including any exception clauses. But if the three remedies do co-exist, it

[151] In *The Eurymedon*, ibid 182, Lord Simon of Glaisdale (dissenting) made the point that to accept the argument based on the 'qualification' view would mean that *Midland Silicones Ltd v Scruttons Ltd* [1962] AC 446 (HL) 'should have been decided the other way'.

[152] Coote, above n 140; JN Adams, 'An Optimistic Look at the Contract Provisions of Unfair Contract Terms Act 1977' (1978) 41 *Modern Law Review* 703; L Sealy [1978] *Cambridge Law Journal* 15.

[153] See the cases cited above n 85.

[154] See above n 51.

[155] *Johnson v Agnew* [1980] AC 367 (HL).

[156] M Albery, 'Mr Cyprian Williams' Great Heresy' (1975) 91 *Law Quarterly Review* 337; G Woodman (1979) 42 *Modern Law Review* 696; AJ Oakley [1980] *Cambridge Law Journal* 58; M Hetherington, 'Keeping the Plaintiff Out of his Contractual Remedies: The Heresies that Survive *Johnson v Agnew*' (1980) 96 *Law Quarterly Review* 403.

[157] F Dawson (1976) 39 *Modern Law Review* 214, 215, 216 and 219; A Shea, 'Discharge from Performance of Contracts by Failure of Condition' (1979) 42 *Modern Law Review* 623, 627–9.

is possible to foresee the emergence of yet another substantive version of fundamental breach amongst those who see exception clauses as mere defences. It would involve rescission of the contract ab initio followed by a claim in tort or quasi-contract.[158]

## Developments Since *Securicor*

It has been suggested above that fundamental breach could survive the *Securicor* decision in one form or another in any country which wished to retain it.[159] Early published comment on the *Securicor* case[160] has been varied enough to suggest that uncertainty exists as to its meaning and effect. That in itself may help to keep the concept alive. On the other hand, two subsequent cases at the highest level have tended, if anything, to point in the other direction.

In *Hyundai Heavy Industries Co Ltd v Papadopoulos*,[161] the House of Lords has adopted and applied the *LEP Air Services* analysis of the effect of discharge for breach. It seems that *Heyman v Darwins Ltd* and the *LEP Air Services* case must now be read as two different ways of saying the same thing. That in turn would seem to lend weight to Lord Diplock's judgment in *Securicor*. More recently, in *Port Jackson Stevedoring Pty Ltd v Salmond & Spraggon (Australia) Pty Ltd*,[162] the Privy Council reaffirmed its decision in *The Eurymedon* and insisted that the principle in that case should not be whittled away by 'fine distinctions'.[163] This means that two courts of final resort have now shown distaste for devices which would defeat the allocation of insurance risks between commercial parties.[164] In the course of delivering the judgment of the Privy Council, Lord Wilberforce restated the effect of Lord Diplock's analysis in the *Securicor* case. (Like Lord Wilberforce and Lord Scarman, Lord Diplock sat in both cases.) It was, he said, a matter of the construction of the contract whether the secondary obligations which arose on a discharge for breach had 'been modified by agreement'.[165] In its context there is some doubt whether Lord Wilberforce's restatement meant that the analysis itself had been accepted by the Privy Council. At the least, though, it

[158] *cf United States v Zara Contracting Co*, 146 F 2d 606 (1944, US Circuit Court of Appeals, 2nd Cir). For this reference I am indebted to GF Dawson.

[159] It seems that this has now happened in Canada; see above n 145.

[160] A Guest (1980) 96 *Law Quarterly Review* 324; NC Seddon (1980) 54 *Australian Law Journal* 289; A Nichol and R Rawlings (1980) 43 *Modern Law Review* 567; ML Melville, 'The Nature of Fundamental Breach' (1980) 130 *New Law Journal* 307; ML Melville, 'Breach of Contract and Exclusion Clauses' (1980) 130 *New Law Journal* 646; McDonald, 'Exclusion Clauses Severed', 1980 SLT 141; editorial comment [1980] *Journal of Business Law* 153; Harper (1980) 130 *New Law Journal* 203; L Sealy [1980] *Cambridge Law Journal* 252; JS Ziegel, 'The House of Lords Overrules *Harbutt's Plasticine*' (1980) 30 *University of Toronto Law Journal* 421.

[161] *Hyundai Heavy Industries Co Ltd v Papadopoulos* [1980] 1 WLR 1129 (HL).

[162] *Port Jackson Stevedoring Pty Ltd v Salmond & Spraggon (Australia) Pty Ltd* (1980) 54 ALJR 552.

[163] ibid, 555.

[164] Compare, too, *A/S Awilco v Fulvia spA di Navigazione; The Chikuma* [1981] 1 All ER 652, 658–9 per Lord Bridge.

[165] [1980] 5 ALJR 552, 515.

does confirm that, on Lord Diplock's analysis, exception and limitation clauses modify the obligations arising from a contract and are, therefore, more than mere defences.

## Conclusion

By reaffirming *Suisse Atlantique* and overruling *Harbutt's 'Plasticine'*, the House of Lords has done what it can to remove two obvious distortions from the law, but neither action, by itself, can solve the continuing problem of unacceptable contractual terms generally. Neither 'construction' nor a third revival of fundamental breach can provide a fully satisfactory answer. The better approach, it is submitted, would be the development of an overall control based on some such test as reasonableness or, much more narrowly, on unconscionability. Nor, in logic, should such a control be restricted to only one form of contract term.

It may be that in a country like Canada, where the approach to law appears to be rather more functional than it is in, say, England, Australia or New Zealand, such a control could be evolved by the courts themselves.[166] But in countries where the approach is more determinist, it would seem far too late, now, to expect any such development to be possible. For such countries, the need is surely for statutory intervention, as Lord Reid indicated in *Suisse Atlantique*.[167]

[166] *cf* Ziegel, above n 160.
[167] [1967] 1 AC 361 (HL), 406.

# 8

# Contract Damages, *Ruxley*, and the Performance Interest

THE STORY IS told of FE Smith, the future Lord Birkenhead LC, that he and a friend were once walking along a narrow residential street when they came upon a couple of men arguing with each other from the upper floors of houses on opposite sides of the street. 'They will never agree', Smith is supposed to have said, 'they're arguing from different premises!'

Arguments from different premises are not altogether unknown in the field of contract damages at common law, especially where an injured party has sought to recover the damages-equivalent of performance. There, typically the question is whether the award should cover the cost of cure, or only difference in value. Claims for consequential loss or damage, such as loss of profits or income, or physical injury or damage (which of course can be cumulative on cost of cure[1]), have been relatively uncontroversial because covered by such established authorities as *Hadley v Baxendale*[2] and *The Heron II*.[3] Claims of the former kind, though, have been affected by the existence of rather different perceptions, not least of the role and function of contract damages and also, by implication, of the very nature of contractual obligation itself.

Some of these differences surfaced in the recent case of *Ruxley Electronics and Construction Ltd v Forsyth*[4] where the claim was for the cost of demolishing and

[1] eg *Harbutt's 'Plasticine' v Wayne Tank and Pump Ltd* [1970] 1 QB 447 (CA). The difference between performance damages and consequential loss was adverted to by Lord Griffiths in *Linden Gardens Trust Ltd v Lenesta Sludge Disposals Ltd* [1994] 1 AC 85 (HL), 97. Claims against professionals for failure to exercise skill and care will normally be in respect of consequential loss, so that difference in value can be an appropriate measure (GH Treitel, *The Law of Contract* (9th ed, London, Sweet & Maxwell, 1995) 852), though not necessarily so (*Auburn Municipal Council v Arc Engineering* [1973] 1 NSWLR 513; *Bevan Investments Ltd v Blackhall & Struthers* [1978] 2 NZLR 97).

[2] *Hadley v Baxendale* (1854) 9 Exch 341; 156 ER 145. The two categories have not always been distinguished, eg, *Surrey County Council v Bredero Homes Ltd* [1993] 1 WLR 1361 (CA), 1365.

[3] *Koufos v C Czarnikow Ltd* [1969] 1 AC 350 (HL).

[4] *Ruxley Electronics and Construction Ltd v Forsyth* [1994] 1 WLR 650 (CA); [1996] 1 AC 344 (HL). Noted: (CA) H Beale (1995) 111 *Law Quarterly Review* 54; DC Price (1995) 69 *Australian Law Journal* 32; R Halson [1995] *Lloyd's Maritime and Commercial Law Quarterly* 27; F Dawson, 'Reflections on Certain Aspects of the Law of Damages for Breach of Contract' (1995) 9 *Journal of Contract Law* 125, 146ff; (HL) J Poole (1996) 59 *Modern Law Review* 272; J O'Sullivan [1995]

rebuilding a swimming pool to make it comply with contract specifications. In his judgment in the House of Lords, Lord Lloyd of Berwick[5] told how Mann LJ, below,[6] had described the question at issue as a simple one but one which went to the foundation of the measure of damages for breach of contract. Lord Lloyd commented that he, himself, was surprised and perhaps disconcerted that, at this stage in the development of the law of damages, such a simple question should have caused such a wide diversity of judicial opinion. It is the purpose of this chapter to explore the underlying reasons for this diversity and to consider how far greater coherence in the law might be achieved.

## The *Ruxley* case

In *Ruxley*, a homeowner, Forsyth, had contracted with a company, Ruxley, for the construction of a swimming pool and with a related company for a building to enclose it. The pool was to have been 7 feet 6 inches deep six or seven feet out from the deep end, this being the crucial point for someone diving from that end. As constructed, though, it was a mere 6 feet deep at that point. That was, nevertheless, still a safe depth and one which, it was held, did not affect the sale value of the pool. On the other hand, to make it conform to the contract, the pool would have had to be demolished and rebuilt, at an estimated cost of £21,500.

At first instance, the contractor was awarded the balance of his contract price and a counter-claim for the cost of rebuilding the pool was dismissed. However, general damages in the sum of £2,500 were awarded to Forsyth for 'loss of amenity'. The Court of Appeal, by contrast, while accepting that the shallower depth had made no difference to the value of the pool, awarded Forsyth the cost of demolishing and rebuilding it. That award, in turn, was reversed by the House of Lords on the ground that to demolish and rebuild would be unreasonable because the cost of so doing would be out of all proportion to any benefit that would be obtained. Their Lordships did, though, affirm the award of general damages, as to the quantum of which there had been no dispute.

It is useful to an understanding of that result to note a couple of the more detailed aspects of the facts. One concerned the behaviour of the respective parties. The depth of the pool as first specified was only 6 feet 6 inches at the deep end. Ruxley agreed subsequently to increase that depth at no extra charge (though no point was later made of the apparent absence of consideration). As first constructed by a subcontractor, the pool had a defective bottom. Ruxley

*Cambridge Law Journal* 496; G McMeel [1995] *Lloyd's Maritime and Commercial Law Quarterly* 456; A Bruce (1995) 145 *New Law Journal* 1088; AFH Loke, 'Cost of Cure or Difference in Market Value? Towards a Sound Choice in the Basis for Quantifying Expectation Damages' (1996) 10 *Journal of Contract Law* 189; A Phang, 'Subjectivity, Objectivity and Policy—Contractual Damages in the House of Lords' [1996] *Journal of Business Law* 362.

[5] [1996] 1 AC 344 (HL), 361.

[6] [1994] 1 WLR 650 (CA), 660.

arranged for the whole pool to be demolished and rebuilt, again without additional charge. When Forsyth subsequently objected to paying the contract price because of the disturbance the rebuilding had caused, Ruxley agreed, in compensation, to a reduction of £10,000. Despite this gesture, Forsyth still failed to pay for either the pool or the building enclosing it. When Ruxley sued for its price, Forsyth raised a number of defects by way of defence and counter-claim. But it was not until the hearing that, having dismissed his legal advisers, he claimed for the first time the cost of rebuilding the pool in order to give it a depth of 7 feet 6 inches. Taking all in all, it would be difficult for a court not to feel some sympathy for Ruxley, the contractor.

The other aspect of the facts concerned the significance of the prescribed depth of 7 feet 6 inches. Forsyth wanted that depth in order to allow plenty of room for someone diving from the pool-side. At no stage did he suggest that he might want a diving board installed. At first instance, it was held that, at 6 feet deep, the pool was perfectly safe for diving without a board, even by someone who was inexperienced. At that depth, however, it was not suitable for a diving board, though had it been of the specified depth, a low-level board could have been installed. That being so, it seems strange that the learned judge should have held that the depth had made no difference at all to the value of the pool. The reason he gave, that Forsyth had not wanted to install a board, suggests that the pool was being valued by its subjective worth to Forsyth, the putative vendor, rather than by its objective value to a potential purchaser.[7] And if indeed there were no difference in subjective value to Forsyth, it might be questioned whether he should at the same time have been awarded damages for (subjective) loss of amenity.[8] However, that question apart, the judge at first instance and the House of Lords were obviously sceptical of the bona fides of Forsyth's stated intention to rebuild if awarded damages. Given the use he could in fact be expected to make of the pool, he would have had next to nothing to gain from so doing.[9] And that raised the spectre of double compensation in the sense of his ending up with both the pool and a 'windfall' payout of more than £21,000 in damages.

In these circumstances, it is scarcely surprising that the House of Lords should have allowed the appeal on the ground that, in the circumstances, to rebuild the pool would be unreasonable, despite the fact that the decision of the Court of Appeal below had been well enough received by such textbooks as *Hudson's Building and Engineering Contracts*[10] and *Treitel on Contract.*[11]

[7] While subjective factors are relevant to general damages (*cf Scholtz v Thompson*, 1996 (2) SA 409, 417), the issue here was one of market worth.

[8] *cf* D Harris, A Ogus and J Phillips, 'Contract Remedies and the Consumer Surplus' (1979) 95 *Law Quarterly Review* 581, 582, for whom the 'consumer surplus' (value to a consumer beyond market value) is subjective.

[9] [1996] 1 AC 344 (HL), 354, 357, 358, 362 and 372–3.

[10] *Hudson's Building and Engineering Contracts* (11th ed by IND Wallace, London, Sweet & Maxwell, 1995) 1058. See also Price, above n 4.

[11] Above n 1, 853.

## A Basic Ambiguity in Contract Damages

The very different conclusions of the Court of Appeal and the House of Lords in *Ruxley* help to illustrate a basic ambiguity in the classic statements of the function of damages for breach of contract at common law. The most famous such statement is that of Parke B in *Robinson v Harman*:

> The next question is: what damages is the plaintiff entitled to recover? The rule of the common law is, that where a party sustains a loss by reason of a breach of contract, he is, so far as money can do it, to be placed in the same situation with respect to damages, as if the contract had been performed.[12]

Behind that apparently simple formulation lies the question whether the purpose of contract damages includes to secure performance on the one hand or is confined to securing the economic end-result of performance on the other, which may well be less. To put it another way, do the interests to be protected include performance itself, or should damages be confined to compensating for the loss of the economic benefits of performance? *Hadley v Baxendale*[13] can be read as similarly ambiguous, though it dealt more with remoteness than with the purpose of damages. If the question is whether the consequence of the breach of a contract 'could have been fairly and reasonably contemplated by both the parties when they made the contract',[14] the answer could equally cover performance itself or just the economic consequences of non-performance.

In situations where the damages-equivalent of performance is being claimed, Parke B himself seems to have favoured performance.[15] But his dictum has also been cited for the opposite view, an early example being the 1880s case of *Wigsell Corporation v School for the Indigent Blind.*[16] While Kelly CB in the Exchequer Division was clear that the plaintiff was entitled to recover the cost of performance (in that case, erecting a wall), the Queen's Bench Divisional Court was equally clear, citing *Robinson v Harman*, that damages in contract were to be confined to the economic loss caused by the non-performance (in that case, the difference in value of the land on which the wall was to have been erected).

## Damages as Protection of the Performance Interest

This uncertainty as to the purpose of contract damages in turn reflects a similar uncertainty about the nature and purpose of contract itself.

12 *Robinson v Harman* (1848) 1 Exch 850, 855; 154 ER 363, 365.
13 (1854) 9 Exch 341; 156 ER 145.
14 ibid, 356.
15 *Pell v Shearman* (1855) 10 Ex 766, 769 and 770; 156 ER 650, 651 and 652.
16 *Wigsell Corporation v School for the Indigent Blind* (1880) 43 LT 218 (Exch D); (1882) 8 QBD 357 (QBD). A more recent example is *Surrey County Council v Bredero Homes Ltd* [1993] 1 WLR 1361 (CA).

Elsewhere,[17] I have argued that in essence a contract is a promise or undertaking in respect of which legal contractual obligation, and the liability that goes with it, has been assumed by a means which the law recognises to be effective for that purpose. On this view, contract is a facility by which the state enables promisors to take upon themselves a particular (ie, contractual) kind of legal obligation, usually because they seek to obtain reciprocal benefits by doing so. The contractual obligation thus assumed is, of course, not just to perform. Nor is it merely a generalised 'legal' obligation, indistinguishable from obligation in the criminal law or under the law of torts. It is a specifically contractual obligation as defined and delimited by the whole of the law of contract. It therefore includes such potential incidents as responsibility for warranties of past and present fact and (within the rules of remoteness and mitigation applying in contract cases) responsibility for consequential loss, always subject to the qualifications the law imports.[18]

One consequence of the view that contract is a facility to enable the assumption of contractual obligation is that remedies for enforcement are provided by law, not as punishments for non-compliance, nor even merely to ensure compensation, but because without them, the obligations undertaken could not be legal contractual ones. In other words, the extent to which the law lends enforcement determines the greatest extent to which it is possible to assume an effective contractual obligation.[19] Thus, if I contract with a builder for the construction of a folly which will cost much more than its economic worth, and on breach the damages recoverable could be based only on that economic worth (ie, the difference in value of the land with the folly on it), it would mean that the binding obligation the builder was able to undertake would not be to build the folly but merely to compensate me for any economic loss I would suffer from its not being built. Conversely, if the obligation undertaken by the builder is to perform and the performance is defective, damages ought at least prima facie to include providing the promisee with the wherewithal to obtain alternative performance or the cost of cure[20] unless the contract had been made on some other basis such as obtaining merely a particular economic end-result.[21]

In what follows, the interest of a promisee in obtaining performance will be referred to as the 'performance interest'[22] to distinguish it from the wider

[17] See ch 2 of this book; *cf* eg *Kleinwort Benson Ltd v Glasgow City Council* [1996] QB 678 (CA).

[18] *cf* [1966] 2 QB 695 (CA), 722–30 per Diplock LJ.

[19] In the course of an interesting discussion, Dawson, above n 4, 125–6, elaborates the same point from a slightly different angle.

[20] *cf* [1996] 1 AC 344 (HL), 358 and 370–1 (though contrast ibid, 361); *cf James v Hutton and Cook Ltd* [1950] 1 KB 9 (CA), 17.

[21] *cf Ruxley*, ibid, 360; *The Rozel* [1994] 2 Lloyd's Rep 161 (QBD), 166–7. The purpose of a negative covenant like a restraint of trade might well be confined to protecting an economic asset.

[22] D Friedmann, 'The Performance Interest in Damages' (1995) 111 *Law Quarterly Review* 628. For ease of exposition the two notions of performance interest and compensation for economic loss are treated as distinct, but, of course, recovery in respect of the performance interest need not prevent

'expectation interest'[23] which covers consequential loss as well. The notion that the function of contract damages does include protection of the performance interest has much more than merely a priori reasoning to support it, as witness, for example, the wide acceptance of the phrase '*pacta sunt servanda*'. Were it otherwise, the suggestion by OW Holmes Jr that contracts were undertakings in the alternative, to perform or to pay damages,[24] would have been more influential than it has been.

## Other Protections of the Performance Interest

Theory and argument apart, the law is not short of examples of the protection and enforcement of the performance interest. The most obvious are the availability of specific performance and injunctions in equity and debt at common law. But there are others as well.

On non-delivery of fungible and other non-unique goods, damages are measured by the cost of obtaining alternative supplies in the market.[25] That measure has even been applied to the non-supply of land in cases where, for the purposes of the particular contract, the land was not to be regarded as unique.[26] Then there is the attitude of the law to repair and reinstatement. As their Lordships acknowledged in *Ruxley*, and as it is proposed to demonstrate, the ordinary rule in building cases is that damages should cover the cost of putting right defects or omissions.[27] And this is so even when the cost of so doing exceeds the economic loss the defects or omissions might have caused the building owner.[28]

A similar rule, it will be shown, applies at common law to covenants requiring lessees to deliver up possession of premises in good repair at the expiration of a lease. That was established a century ago in *Joyner v Weeks*.[29] In England, the

recovery for consequential loss under other heads of liability. Similarly, compensation may be measured, at least in part, by the cost of cure or substituted performance.

23 LL Fuller and WR Perdue, 'The Reliance Interest in Damages' (1936) 46 *Yale Law Journal* 52, 373.

24 OW Holmes, *The Common Law* (Boston, Macmillan, 1881) 300ff; 'The Path of the Law' (1896) 10 *Harvard Law Review* 457.

25 *Benjamin's Sale of Goods* (4th ed by AG Guest, London, Sweet & Maxwell, 1992) 833–4. A more complete protection of the performance interest would also take account of transaction costs. The law can be similarly blind to the costs of litigation.

26 See *Semelhago v Paramadeven* (1996) 136 DLR (4th) 1. Torts cases to similar effect were *Mummelly v Calcon Ltd* [1978] IR 387 and *Pantalone v Alouie* (1989) 18 NSWLR 119. Contrast *Parramatta CC v Lutz* (1988) 12 NSWLR 293.

27 [1996] 1 AC 344 (HL), 355–6, 360 and 366–9. See also *East Ham Corporation v Bernard Sunley & Sons Ltd* [1966] AC 406 (HL), 434–5 and 445; *Linden Gardens Trust Ltd v Lenesta Sludge Disposals Ltd* [1994] 1 AC 85 (HL), 96; *Darlington BC v Wiltshier Northern Ltd* [1995] 1 WLR 68 (CA), 79.

28 [1996] 1 AC 344 (HL), 358, 360, 366 and 371. And see text accompanying nn 126–7 below.

29 *Joyner v Weeks* [1891] 2 QB 31 (CA).

effect of that case was subsequently negated by statute.[30] In New Zealand it has been held by the Court of Appeal in *Maori Trustee v Rogross Farms Ltd*[31] to have the status of a prima facie rule. Either way, it is still excellent evidence of what at common law has been seen to be the purpose of contract damages.

The performance interest is also protected collaterally by the right to reject for the breach of an essential term[32] and, in the case of entire contracts, to refuse to pay anything for less than substantial performance.[33] There is further evidence, too, in the date at which damages are to be calculated where the cost of making good has increased since the breach complained of. There, depending on the justice of a case, damages may be assessed either at the date of judgment or, if earlier, at the date the plaintiff ought to have taken action or to have had the work done himself.[34] And it can be argued that the tort of inducing breach of contract further supports the *pacta sunt servanda* principle.[35] So, too, can the *res inter alios acta* rule, an example being the refusal in Canada[36] and New Zealand[37] to apply the *Gourley*[38] ruling to contract cases, with the result that damages for an employee's loss of income are not to be reduced by reference to taxation considerations (though it has to be admitted that a contrary conclusion has been reached in England and possibly Australia[39]). Finally, the protection of the performance interest means that where a special service has been contracted for and something inferior has been done, the injured party will not have to pay more than the inferior work was worth, even if he has not suffered any financial loss by reason of the inferiority.[40]

## Extending the Potential Inclusiveness of Performance Protection

If, on the basis of both the theory and the practice of the law of contract, it were concluded that a primary purpose of damages, as of other means of enforcement, is to give substance to the performance interest, it would follow that a result like that reached by the Court of Appeal in *Ruxley* would at least be consistent. But

30 See text below before n 110.

31 *Maori Trustee v Rogross Farms Ltd* [1994] 3 NZLR 410.

32 *Bunge Corporation v Tradax* [1981] 1 WLR 711 (HL).

33 *H Dakin & Co Ltd v Lee* [1916] 1 KB 566 (CA).

34 *Johnson v Agnew* [1980] AC 367 (HL); *Radford v De Froberville* [1977] 1 WLR 1262 (Ch); *East Ham Corporation v Bernard Sunley & Sons Ltd* [1966] AC 406 (HL).

35 Friedmann, above n 22, 631–2.

36 *R (in Right of the Province of Ontario) v Jennings* (1966) 57 DLR (2d) 644.

37 *NZ Wholesale Groceries v Hewin* [1982] 2 NZLR 176; *Horsburgh v NZ Meat Processors Union* [1988] 1 NZLR 698.

38 *British Transport Commission v Gourley* [1956] AC 185 (HL).

39 See text accompanying nn 66 and 67 below.

40 *cf White Arrow Express Ltd v Lamey's Distributors Ltd* (CA, 21 July 1995), noted by H Beale (1996) 112 *Law Quarterly Review* 205.

even a decision like that of the House of Lords to disallow the cost of rebuilding might also, in many situations, be accommodated to the performance principle by recourse to the construction of the contract.

If, in a case like *Ruxley*, a pool had not been constructed to the depth specified and to the knowledge of the contractor the purpose of building it had been to enable a diver to prepare for the Olympics, so that the minimum specified depth were crucial, it seems most unlikely that the cost of rebuilding would be refused. On the other hand, if the depth specified were greatly in excess of what were needed, it could well be possible to read the contract as requiring the depth as stated 'be the same a little more or less'.[41] In the same way, the specification of a component might be read to encompass an alternative of similar quality. After all, the House of Lords in *Ashington Piggeries Ltd v Christopher Hill Ltd*[42] felt able to hold that the correspondence with description requirements of the Sale of Goods Act could be satisfied by the delivery of goods merely of the same genus as those specified. Other possibilities would be to characterise any difference as de minimis, or to construe the contract on the assumption that the parties would have intended a reasonable result, the latter being a principle of construction articulated and applied, for example, by the House of Lords in *Photo Production Ltd v Securicor Ltd*.[43]

A problem, though, with these sorts of solution is that on facts like those in *Ruxley* they would presumably have prevented the award of general damages. And it would be difficult to dismiss a defect which attracted £2,500 in damages in respect of a £20,000 contract as being de minimis or as just 'a little more or less'.[44]

## The Compensation Principle

Strong though the support for it may be, the perception that the object of contract damages is in the first instance to protect the performance interest is not the only one currently held. As already indicated, the competing view is that their proper object (as with consequential loss) is to compensate for the loss of the economic benefits of performance. It is a perception not without support in the cases. A leading example is a dictum by Lord Blackburn in *Livingstone v Rawyards Coal Co*, who described the appropriate measure of damages as 'that sum of

[41] This, and the de minimis principle, would answer any objection that to give cost of cure in a case like *Ruxley* would entail the absurdity of having to do so even if the discrepancy had been only one inch.

[42] *Ashington Piggeries Ltd v Christopher Hill Ltd* [1972] AC 441 (HL).

[43] *Photo Production Ltd v Securicor Ltd* [1980] AC 827 (HL).

[44] Lord Lloyd did, though, suggest that the award had been too large: [1996] 1 AC 344, 374.

money which will put the party who has been injured … in the same position as he would have been if he had not sustained the wrong for which he is now getting his compensation'.[45]

That was a tort case, but the dictum or statements to similar effect have since appeared in many leading contract cases. A well-known example was the statement of Viscount Haldane LC in *British Westinghouse v Underground Electric Railways* that the 'fundamental basis [for contract damages] is thus compensation for pecuniary loss naturally flowing from the breach'.[46]

Those formulations are unexceptionable as applied to loss from the results of breach (consequential loss). But they and their like have also been taken to mean that even where the cost of alternative performance has been in issue, difference in value is the primary measure.[47]

It can be no coincidence that Lord Blackburn's dictum should have come from a tort case. The assertion is from time to time made that there is no difference in principle between damages in contract and tort in that the object of both, it is said, is compensation from loss flowing from a wrongful act.[48] Just as the use of damages to protect the performance interest corresponds to a particular view of the nature of contractual obligation, so too, it is suggested, does the compensation approach. At the least, it draws support from the common perception that legal contractual obligation is not something parties to contracts take, and therefore impose, upon themselves (contract being a facility enabling them effectively to do so) but rather, as in the law of torts, is something imposed by the courts *ab extra* on those who fail to keep their promises.[49]

At first sight, this perception may seem inconsistent with the also common acceptance that assumption of obligation is a distinguishing feature of contract. But it is fairly clear that what is thought to be being assumed is not contractual obligation as such but a promissory obligation of some other kind, perhaps

[45] *Livingstone v Rawyards Coal Co* (1880) 5 App Cas 25 (HL), 39.

[46] *British Westinghouse v Underground Electric Railways* [1912] AC 673 (HL), 689.

[47] eg *Cunningham v Insinger* [1924] 2 DLR 433, 439; *McGarry v Richards, Ackroyd & Gall Ltd* [1954] 2 DLR 367, 389; *James v Hutton and Cooke* [1950] 1 KB 9 (CA); *Chitty on Contracts* (27th ed by AG Guest, London, Sweet & Maxwell, 1994) vol 1, 1204; H McGregor, *McGregor on Damages* (15th ed, London, Sweet & Maxwell, 1988) 26. Phang, above n 4, 370–1, characterises cost of cure as 'exceptional'.

[48] *cf* AS Burrows, *Remedies for Torts and Breach of Contract* (2nd ed, Oxford, Oxford University Press, 1994) 16.

[49] This seems to be a basic premise of most theories of contract. See, eg, C Fried, *Contract as Promise: A Theory of Contractual Obligation* (Cambridge Mass, Harvard University Press, 1981) and P Benson, 'The Idea of a Public Basis of Justification for Contract' (1995) 33 *Osgoode Hall Law Journal* 273. See also Burrows, ibid, 20; J Evans, 'The Concept of Legal Power' (1984) 11 *New Zealand Universities Law Review* 149, 163 (the parties define the acts in respect of which the law imposes a duty to perform); *South Australia Asset Management Corporation v York Montague Ltd* [1977] AC 191 (HL), 211 per Lord Hoffmann (though contrast *ibid*, 212). The point is discussed in Brian Coote, 'The Essence of Contract' (1988) 1 *Journal of Contract Law* 183, 194–5, 196 (see ch 2 of this book at text accompanying nn 228–32).

moral[50] or social. Thus, Professor Atiyah is able within a few pages of his *Essays on Contract*[51] to affirm both that the parties to contracts assume obligation and that contractual obligation is imposed by law.[52] In the same way, the assumption of responsibility referred to in *Hedley Byrne & Co Ltd v Heller & Partners Ltd*[53] must *ex hypothesi* have been something other than contractual responsibility, notwithstanding suggestions by Lord Devlin that, but for the absence of consideration, the relationship between the parties would have been 'equivalent to contract'.[54] The *legal* obligation lay in tort. This question is discussed in greater detail in chapter eleven below.

## Factors Supporting the Compensation Approach

To those who believe that contractual obligation is imposed rather than assumed, the analogy with liability in tort must appear very close. From that perspective, the purpose of contract damages can very easily be perceived, just as in tort, simply to be compensation for the economic loss flowing from a wrongful act. As it happens, in the case of torts causing damage to buildings, compensation was believed, until relatively recent times, to require that damages be fixed by reference exclusively to difference in value.[55] Nowadays, there has been increasing reference in torts cases to the cost of cure.[56] But the undiscriminating recourse, in contract cases, to torts cases decided in former times could easily have reinforced the perception that difference in value was as much the appropriate measure in contract as in tort.[57]

Another factor favouring the compensation view of contract damages might be the high proportion of commercial cases amongst those which reach the appellate courts.[58] It can be argued that commercial parties are more likely than private consumers to have bargained for an economic end-result rather than for performance as such. Wherever that was the case, compensation would actually

[50] eg J Gava and P Kincaid, 'Contract and Conventionalism' (1966) 10 *Journal of Contract Law* 141, 142, 143 and 145; Burrows, above n 49; N Enonchong, 'Contract Damages for Injury to Reputation' (1996) 59 *Modern Law Review* 592, 599.

[51] PS Atiyah, *Essays on Contract* (Oxford, Clarendon Press, 1986) 280, 282–3.

[52] See also his *An Introduction to the Law of Contract* (5th ed, Oxford, Clarendon Press, 1985) 41.

[53] *Hedley Byrne & Co Ltd v Heller & Partners Ltd* [1964] AC 465 (HL).

[54] ibid, 529 per Lord Devlin.

[55] In *Hollebone v Midhurst & Fernhurst Builders Ltd* [1968] 1 Lloyd's Rep 38, (QBD), 40, the then contemporary editions of *Salmond on Torts, Mayne and McGregor on Damages,* and *Street on Damages* are cited to this effect. See also *Woollongong CC v Fregnan* [1982] 1 NSWLR 244; *Carosella v Ginos* (1981) 46 LGRA 51. Because the result is not guaranteed, awards against professionals for want of care, even in contract, will normally be based on difference in value. *Perry v Sidney Phillips & Son* [1982] 1 WLR 1297 (CA).

[56] eg [1968] 1 Lloyd's Rep 38; *Evans v Balog* [1976] 1 NSWLR 36; *Dodd Property (Kent) Ltd v Canterbury CC* [1980] 1 WLR 433 (CA); *Paramatta CC v Lutz* (1988) 12 NSWLR 293.

[57] This might explain the failure of counsel to ask for cost of cure in the contract cases cited at nn 129 and 130 below.

[58] *cf* [1996] 1 AC 344 (HL), 353 per Lord Bridge.

be a protection of the performance interest. On the other hand, it is not difficult to envisage situations where a commercial party would be just as concerned as a private consumer to secure actual performance. For that matter, there might also be situations where a private individual's interest could be purely in the economic results of performance. Yet another factor conducive to the subordination of performance to compensation may simply have been a failure in some cases to differentiate between claims for performance on the one hand and claims for the loss consequent on failure of performance (consequential loss) on the other.

## The Application of the Compensation Approach

One of the most obvious applications of the compensation approach has been to contracts for the benefit of third parties, as in *Beswick v Beswick*.[59] There, although the estate of the husband promisor obtained specific performance of a contract to benefit the widow, it was assumed it could not have recovered damages. The reasoning was that only the widow beneficiary had suffered any loss. Then there are the cases where intended legacies have failed through the neglect of the testator's legal advisers. At all stages, from *Ross v Caunters*[60] before Megarry V-C to *White v Jones*[61] before the House of Lords and *Hill v Van Erp*[62] before the High Court of Australia, it seems to have been taken absolutely for granted that the testator's estate could have no substantial claim in contract because it had suffered no loss.[63]

Another application occurred in *Surrey County Council v Bredero Homes Ltd*,[64] where defendants had built 77 houses in breach of a covenant allowing them only 72. The Court of Appeal refused a remedy on the ground that the plaintiff Councils had suffered no financial loss. Similar reasoning led the Queensland Court of Appeal to conclude in *Hadoplane Pty Ltd v Edward Rushton Pty Ltd*[65] that the wrongful repudiation of a contract for a company to provide services had not caused that company any compensatable loss since, because of the repudiation, it had not had to pay its employees for performing those services.

59 *Beswick v Beswick* [1968] AC 58 at 81, 83 and 102. See also *Woodar Investment Development Ltd v Wimpey Construction UK Ltd* [1980] 1 WLR 277 (HL). The position is different in respect of loss suffered by the promisee other than the loss of performance as such: *Coulls v Bagots Executor and Trustee Co Ltd* (1967) 119 CLR 460 (High Court of Australia), 501–2.

60 *Ross v Caunters* [1980] Ch 297 (Ch).

61 *White v Jones* [1995] 2 AC 207(HL).

62 *Hill v Van Erp* (1997) 71 ALJR 487 (High Court of Australia). In New Zealand, the equivalent case is *Gartside v Sheffield, Young & Ellis* [1983] NZLR 37 (CA).

63 The one exception seems to have been Nicholls V-C in the Court of Appeal in *White v Jones* [1995] 2 AC 207 (HL), 223–4.

64 [1993] 1 WLR 1361 (CA).

65 *Hadoplane Pty Ltd v Edward Rushton Pty Ltd* [1996] 1 Qd R 156.

A further example is the application in England[66] and possibly Australia[67] of the *Gourley* principle to contract cases, the justification being that to the extent that income would have been taxable, the plaintiff would have suffered no loss and so would obtain a windfall if he could recover the equivalent of his gross income. Until *Gourley*, the tax liability had been characterised as *res inter alios acta*.[68] *Gourley*, therefore, was a case in which the compensation approach was used to limit the scope of the *res inter alios* principle. As will be seen,[69] a similar use of the compensation approach has on occasion been employed in respect of claims for repairs and reinstatement in leases.

The compensation view has also provided a basis for criticising some forms of performance protection which the law does allow. Thus, the Law Commission of Ontario has objected to the rule that a buyer of goods who obtains substitutes at a favourable price is still able to recover the value of the goods promised.[70] There has similarly been objection to the rule that a seller who has resold at a profit is allowed to retain that profit.[71] Again, one of the main arguments against the award of exemplary damages in contract is that the purpose of contract damages is merely to compensate.

A factor common to these examples of the compensation approach is concern to prevent the plaintiff getting a 'windfall'. It is a selective concern because the common law has been quite prepared to allow a degree of actual or apparent over-compensation in other contexts. There are, for example, the already-mentioned[72] rejections in Canada and New Zealand of the *Gourley* principle, the result of which is that a plaintiff can end up with more than he could have retained from his income had he earned it. And under the law relating to entire contracts, a building owner can end up with both the price (because he does not have to pay it) and the partially completed works, at least if he is content to leave those works in their unfinished state.[73]

There is an element of windfall, too, in the fact that damages for loss of wages are not reduced by the work not having been done[74] or by the expenses which

[66] *Beach v Reed Corrugated Cases Ltd* [1956] 1 WLR 807 (QBD); *Re Houghton Main Colliery Ltd* [1956] 1 WLR 1219 (Ch); *Parsons v BNM Laboratories Ltd* [1964] 1 QB 95 (CA).

[67] JW Carter and DJ Harland, *Contract Law in Australia* (3rd ed, Sydney, Butterworths, 1996) 813.

[68] *Fairholme v Firth & Brown Ltd* (1933) 149 LT 332, 332–5; *Blackwood v Andre* 1947 SC 333, 333–4.

[69] See text below following n 100.

[70] SM Waddams, *The Law of Damages* (2nd ed, Toronto, Canada Law Book, 1995) 1–2.

[71] ibid.

[72] See text accompanying nn 36 and 37 above.

[73] *H Dakin & Co Ltd v Lee* [1916] 1 KB 566 (CA). In New Zealand, completion by the building owner could be classed as 'cancellation' and enable relief under the Contractual Remedies Act 1979, s 9.

[74] This was accepted in *British Transport Commission v Gourley* [1956] AC 185 (HL).

have not been incurred.[75] So, too, where damages have been given for reinstatement of buildings without reduction for betterment.[76] And a seller of shares, on the buyer's breach, is entitled to the difference in market price notwithstanding resale at a higher price.[77] Then, at least in Canada and New Zealand, punitive damages have been awarded for breach of contract.[78] Outside the field of damages, illegality of contracts can provide yet another example of tolerated potential windfalls, through the operation of the *in pari delicto* principle.

In the case of entire contracts, the 'windfall' results from their being conditional and there are similarly special reasons for punitive damages and for the consequences of illegality. The rest, as Professor Waddams has suggested, are probably to be justified on grounds of simplicity and convenience.[79] They are hardly consistent with a strict compensation approach.[80] But all except illegality are consistent with protection of the performance interest in the sense that they actually increase the legal incentives to perform.

To return, though, to the examples of the compensation approach, a much more important consideration is that the perception of a windfall has for the most part arisen because of a failure to ascribe value to performance as such, or to the right to performance, whether directly or through the *res inter alios acta* principle not being applied. It is worth noting that the departure in *Gourley* from *res inter alios acta* has not made it easier to explain and distinguish the continued application of that principle in other contexts.[81] The fact that Canada and New Zealand on the one hand and England and Australia on the other have taken opposing views on *Gourley* is a reflection of the underlying tensions. And in what follows, it is hoped to show, starting with contracts for the benefit of third parties, that there is very real support in the cases for the proposition that performance, and the right to performance, do in fact have intrinsic economic worth.

## Promises for the Benefit of Third Parties

Professor Waddams[82] has proposed that one way of solving the problem of damages for the promisee in third-party-beneficiary cases would be to allow him to recover what the promisor would have been prepared to pay in order to be

[75] *The Maratha Envoy* [1978] AC 1 (HL), 12–13.

[76] eg *Harbutt's 'Plasticine' Ltd v Wayne Tank and Pump Co Ltd* [1970] 1 QB 447 (CA); though contrast *Cooke v Rowe* [1950] NZLR 410; *Ryons v Thomas* [1986] IR 666.

[77] AKAS *Jamal v Moolla Dawood Sons & Co* [1916] 1 AC 175 (PC).

[78] eg *Ribeiro v Canadian Imperial Bank of Commerce* (1989) 67 OR (2d) 385; *Tak & Co Inc v AEL Corporation Ltd* (1995) NZBLC 103,887.

[79] SM Waddams, 'The General Principles of the Law of Damages', in Law Society of Upper Canada, *Law of Remedies: Principles and Proofs* (Scarborough, Ont, Carswell, 1995) 15, 17.

[80] See, eg, Burrows, above n 48, 124–8; MJ Tilbury, *Civil Remedies* (Sydney, Butterworths, 1993) vol 2, [13051]–[13054].

[81] *cf* [1956] AC 185 (HL), 199 per Earl Jowitt LC.

[82] Above n 70, [553]. See also Beale, above n 4.

released from his obligation to perform. He has conceded, though, that the amount could be very small except in cases where specific performance would lie. That sort of solution was rejected by Megarry VC in *Tito v Waddell (No 2)*[83] and also by the Court of Appeal in *Surrey County Council v Bredero Homes Ltd.*[84]

The real problem, it is submitted, lies in the way in which, in some contexts, the courts have ascribed value to the benefits which flow from performance rather than to performance itself, or to contractual rights to performance. What that reflects, it is believed, is a not uncharacteristic confusion between bargained-for contractual rights (benefits in law) on the one hand and enjoyment of the fruits of performance (benefits in fact) on the other. It is the sort of confusion which led the Court of Appeal in *Williams v Roffey Bros & Nicholls (Contractors) Ltd*[85] to suppose that the fruits of an already-contracted-for performance (benefit in fact) could, against all previous authority, be the consideration (benefit in law) for the variation of a contract. In a reverse way, it also led the House of Lords in *Midland Silicones Ltd v Scruttons Ltd*[86] to conclude that a stevedore could not enjoy the benefit of an absolution of its liability in tort (for which no contract is needed) because the absolution was in a document recording a contract to which it was not a party.

Suppose, say, that a father wished to give his daughter a new refrigerator and arranged with the retailer that it be delivered direct to his daughter's address. If the refrigerator were defective, could it be suggested that the father would have no right to damages for the defect because it was not he but his daughter who had suffered the loss? True, the value of the refrigerator would be less than it should have been and she would have lost some of her use and enjoyment of it. But so far as the contract was concerned, those losses would be only accidental, and of benefits in fact. The relevant contractual loss would be of the father's right to have a refrigerator without defects delivered to his daughter, that being his benefit in law. Quite clearly, a proper solution would involve according value to this benefit in law and, it is submitted, just as clearly the proper measure of that value would be the cost of cure or of alternative performance. In a proposal which came fairly close to this, Lord Scarman suggested in *Woodar Investment*

83 *Tito v Waddell (No 2)* [1977] Ch 106 (Ch).

84 (1993) 1 WLR 1361 (CA). See W Goodhart, 'Restitutionary Damages for Breach of Contract' [1995] *Restitution Law Review* 3 for a contrary argument. Third-party beneficiaries have been given a statutory right of enforcement in New Zealand (Contracts (Privity) Act 1982), Western Australia (Property Law Act 1969, s 11(2)), Queensland (Property Law Act 1974, s 55), and England and Wales (Contracts (Rights of Third Parties) Act 1999). As to the last-mentioned piece of legislation, see ch 10 of this book.

85 *Williams v Roffey Bros & Nicholls (Contractors) Ltd* [1991] 1 QB 1 (CA). See also ch 3 of this book.

86 *Midland Silicones Ltd v Scruttons Ltd* [1962] AC 446 (HL). Compare how in discussion of *Appleby v Meyers* (1867) LR 2 CP 651, 'benefit' is ascribed to enjoyment of the use of the machinery rather than to the legal rights which passed when it was affixed to the premises: *Cheshire, Fifoot and Furmston's Law of Contract* (12th ed by MP Furmston, London, Butterworths, 1991) 589; *cf BP v Hunt (No 2)* [1979] 1 WLR 783 (QBD), 801 per Robert Gough J.

*Development Ltd v Wimpey Construction Ltd*[87] that the measure of the promisee's loss should be the benefit intended for the third party but not received. That proposal, though, seems still to be conceived of in terms of the recipient's benefit in fact.

That the promisee's damages should be valued by the cost of alternative performance has now been proposed by Lord Griffiths in *Linden Garden Trust Ltd v Lenesta Sludge Disposals Ltd.*[88] There, the issue was whether a promisee might receive damages for defective work by the promisor on land which had been assigned to a third party before the contract had been performed. Citing Lord Blackburn's dictum in *Livingstone v Rawyards Coal Co*[89] the defendant argued that since the land no longer belonged to the promisee company it had suffered no loss and therefore could not recover more than nominal damages. Lord Griffiths rejected this argument and gave the example of a husband contracting with a builder for repairs to a house which was in his wife's name. He continued:

> The builder fails to replace the roof properly and the husband has to call in and pay another builder to complete the work. Is it to be said that the husband has suffered no damage because he does not own the property? Such a result would in my view be absurd and the answer is that the husband has suffered loss because he did not receive the bargain for which he had contracted with the first builder and the measure of damages is the cost of securing the performance of that bargain by completing the roof repairs properly by the second builder.[90]

In the event, the case was decided on other grounds but Lords Keith, Bridge and Browne-Wilkinson all expressed sympathy with Lord Griffiths' view[91] as, subsequently, did Steyn LJ in *Darlington Borough Council v Wiltshier Northern Ltd.*[92]

Professor Beale[93] has suggested that Lord Griffiths' approach would not give the promisee any right, whether on his own behalf or on behalf of the beneficiary, to recover damages for consequential losses suffered by the intended beneficiary. If this were so, it would mean not only that the suggested solution was only partial but also that the contractual obligation the promisor could assume would be one which was limited to performance only. Any recovery for consequential

[87] [1980] 1 WLR 277 at 300–1 (HL). Compare *Coulls v Bagots Executor and Trustee Co Ltd* (1967) 119 CLR 460 (High Court of Australia), 501–2.

[88] [1994] 1 AC 85 (HL). More strictly, he was addressing himself to *St Martin's Property Corporation v Sir Robert McAlpine Ltd*, heard and decided at the same time, but the case seems likely to be remembered by the name in the text.

[89] (1880) 5 App Cas 25 (HL), 39.

[90] [1994] 1 AC 85 (HL), 96–7.

[91] ibid, 95, 96 and 111–12, respectively.

[92] [1995] 1 WLR 68 (CA), 80. See also [1996] 1 AC 344 (HL), 360 ('value of the promise to the promisee').

[93] H Beale, 'Privity of Contract: Judicial and Legislative Reform' (1995) 9 *Journal of Contract Law* 103, 107.

loss would have to be by the beneficiary herself in tort, or by the promisor on behalf of the beneficiary under a trust[94] or by some extension of the rule in *Dunlop v Lambert.*[95]

On the other hand, it may be that an answer could be found if, as has been suggested above, the problem were to be seen in terms of contracted benefits in law rather than 'accidental' benefits in fact. What were the rights the husband acquired and what were the obligations assumed by Lord Griffiths' builder? Would the parties objectively have intended his responsibility to have been limited strictly to performance, or to have been fully contractual, so as to have included consequential loss? In his Lordship's words, what was the bargain for which the husband had contracted? If it did include responsibility for consequential loss to the wife-beneficiary, that loss would be the husband's in exactly the same sense as the cost of securing completion of the roof repairs by a second builder. It would be no more a windfall for the husband than the cost of repairs would be, and it would be just as much a legal benefit for which the husband had 'paid' by providing consideration for the contract.

Enabling the husband in that way to recover damages for his wife's consequential loss could, of course, raise the possibility of double jeopardy for the builder. The latter might well find himself, in respect of the same actions, liable both to the husband in contract and to the wife in tort. Ordinarily, that sort of consequence would be neither objectionable nor unusual.[96] But it could be regarded as much less acceptable in relation to a type of loss which, though notionally in law suffered by the husband, was as a matter of practical fact endured by the wife. Statutory modification of the privity rule apart,[97] the answer would be to treat the husband as holding the damages for consequential loss in trust for the wife. For that sort of development, analogies exist at the highest level both in bailment[98] and in tort.[99] A similar solution could also be applied to the loss of a legal benefit in the frustrated legacy cases. There, while perfomance-equivalent damages would be confined to the costs of drawing a will, the consequential loss would be another matter. The estate, having been deprived of the ability and wherewithal to give effect to the testator's intentions, ought to be able to recover an equivalent amount in damages for breach of contract. If that is

[94] [1995] 1 WLR 68 (CA).

[95] *Dunlop v Lambert* (l839) 6 Cl & F 600; 7 ER 824; *The Albazero* [1977] AC 744 (HL), 847; *Linden Gardens Trust Ltd v Lenestra Sludge Disposals Ltd* [1994] 1 AC 85 (HL); *Darlington BC v Wiltshire Northern Ltd* [1995] 1 WLR 68 (CA).

[96] *Henderson v Merrett Syndicates Ltd* [1995] 2 AC 145 (HL), 195. But see A Burrows, 'Legislative Reform of Remedies for Breach of Contract: The English Perspective' (1997) 1 *Edinburgh Law Review* 155, 173.

[97] See n 81 above.

[98] (1839) 6 Cl & F 600; 7 ER 824 and *The Albazero* [1977] AC 744 (HL). It was the *justification* for the promisee's claim in *The Albazero* ('transferred loss') which Lord Goff held did not apply to the situation in *White v Jones* [1995] 2 AC 207 (HL), 266–7.

[99] *Hunt v Severs* [1994] 2 AC 350 (HL), 363.

allowed, it should not be too difficult to see the executors as trustees of those damages, not for the residuary beneficiaries, but for the intended legatee.[100]

## Reinstatement and Repair: Leases

That there are already established contexts in which the courts will award damages for the lost 'legal benefits' of performance above and beyond the economic losses to the promisee consequent on breach is amply demonstrated by the way questions of reinstatement and repair have been treated in cases involving leases and building contracts. At the same time, those cases have also reflected the tensions between the opposing views of the purpose of the contract damages and of the scope of the *res inter alios acta* principle.

Mention has already been made of *Joyner v Weeks*,[101] the leading case on covenants to render up premises in good repair at the expiration of a lease. What had caused the difficulty in that case was that damages were being sought for repairs for which the new lessee would have had no use, and part of which would have been demolished anyway. In the Divisional Court, Wills and Wright JJ held that the lessor was entitled only to compensation for the diminution in value caused by the failure to repair, but they did insist that those damages were not to be reduced by reference to any arrangements the lessor might have made with the incoming lessee or by what the new lessee proposed to do with the premises.[102] These they clearly regarded, so far as the lessee was concerned, as *res inter alios acta*. In the Court of Appeal, Lord Esher MR and Fry LJ agreed that those matters were not the concern of the lessee.[103] Where they differed from the judges below was in concluding that damages were to be assessed by reference not to difference in value but to the cost of repairs. A line of decided cases was cited in support.[104] The significance of that decision is that damages were being valued by reference to the obligation to perform rather than to the economic end-result of the failure to perform.

A few years later, the question of what damages should be paid for non-repair during the currency rather than at the end of a lease came before the Court of Appeal in *Conquest v Ebbetts*.[105] The defendant was an under-lessee whose term had about four years to run. The under-lessor had a reversion of 10 days and an obligation to yield up the premises in reasonable repair as, in his turn, had the head lessee to the head lessor. The under-lessee objected to having to pay damages for non-repair on the ground that the condition of the premises was so bad that they ought to be demolished and redeveloped at the end of the term.

100 *cf* [1995] 2 AC 207 (HL), 233–4 per Nicholls V-C.
101 [1891] 2 QB 31 (CA).
102 ibid, 39.
103 ibid, 45 and 47–8. See also *Inderwick v Leech* (1885) 1 TLR 484.
104 ibid, 45.
105 *Conquest v Ebbetts* [1895] 2 Ch 377 (CA).

The official referee, below, had held that damages were to be based on the difference between the value of the head lessor's reversion with the covenant to repair performed, and the value with the covenant unperformed. Since the head lessee was himself required to deliver up the premises in reasonable repair, that value was to be calculated on the basis of the cost of repair (£1,500) less a discount (£195) in respect of the unexpired portion of the under-lessee's term. The reason for that discount had been explained half a century before in *Doe & Worcester School Trustees v Rowlands.*[106] It was that the landlord (here, the under-lessor) had no obligation to the tenant (here the under-lessee) to spend the damages on doing the actual repairs so that there was therefore no guarantee of their being of any benefit to the under-lessee during the currency of the tenancy. The Court of Appeal in *Conquest v Ebbetts* (Lindley, Lopes and Rigby LJJ) affirmed, first, that in respect of the covenant to deliver up the premises in good repair, the head lessor would be entitled to the cost of that repair and, secondly, that in respect of the covenant to keep in repair during the term of the under-lease, damages were to be based on the diminution in the value of the reversion. The official referee had been right to assess that value by reference to the discounted cost of the repair.

In the House of Lords, the decision of the Court of Appeal was affirmed.[107] Delivering the main judgment, Lord Herschell indicated that for non-repair during the course of a term, the extent to which the cost of repair was recoverable in damages would depend on how much of the term had still to run.[108] He also confirmed that what the head lessor in the instant case might do with the premises at the end of the term was of no concern to the under-lessee.[109]

Doubtless, it would be possible to interpret *Conquest v Ebbetts*, with its references to diminution in value of the reversion, as an expression of the compensation approach to contract damages and therefore as inconsistent with *Joyner v Weeks.* If so, it would have been an inconsistency of which the Court of Appeal and House of Lords would have been unaware, since the damages actually awarded were entirely consistent with those in the earlier case.

## Reaction to *Joyner v Weeks*

However, if there were any uncertainty as to which view of contract damages was reflected in *Conquest v Ebbetts*, there could be no doubt which view motivated the effective reversal of *Joyner v Weeks* by s 18(1) of the Landlord and Tenant Act 1927, which stated:

[106] *Doe & Worcester School Trustees v Rowlands* (1841) 9 C & P 734, 739; 173 ER 1030, 1033 per Coleridge J.

[107] [1896] AC 490 (HL).

[108] ibid, 494.

[109] ibid, 494–5.

> Damages for a breach of a covenant or agreement to keep or put the premises in repair during the currency of the lease, or to put premises in repair at the termination of a lease, whether such covenant or agreement is expressed or implied, and whether general or specific, shall in no case exceed the amount (if any) by which the value of the reversion (whether immediate or not) of the premises is diminished owing to the breach of such covenant or agreement as aforesaid: and in particular no damage shall be recovered for a breach of any such covenant or agreement to leave or put premises in repair at the termination of a lease, if it is shown that the premises, in whatever state of repair they might be, would at or shortly after the termination of the tenancy have been or be pulled down, or such structural alterations made therein as would render valueless the repairs covered by the covenant or agreement.

It has since been held that under this Act recourse may still be had to the cost of repairs in appropriate cases but only as a measure of the diminution in value of the reversion.[110] By similar reasoning, the cost of repairs is the maximum recoverable in cases where that cost is actually less than the diminution of value.

Legislation to similar effect has been passed in New South Wales and in Queensland.[111] In New Zealand, the Law Commission[112] in 1991 recommended that *Joyner v Weeks* be reversed by statute, expressly because it was seen to be inconsistent with what the Commission saw as the basic principles of contract damages.[113] A bill to that effect was submitted to Parliament but was withdrawn after the decision of the Court of Appeal in *Maori Trustee v Rogross Farms Ltd*.[114] That was a case where Greig J at first instance assessed the cost of cure at $19,500 but held that damages should be confined to diminution in value. Since no such diminution had been proved, only nominal damages were awarded. Tipping J, who delivered the judgment of the Court in which he referred to the Law Commission report, was clearly aware of the tension between the performance interest and the compensation principle, stating:

> Damages in contract are designed to represent the monetary equivalent of the promised benefit which has not been provided. … That sum of money will ordinarily equate to the cost to the lessor of having the covenant performed.[115]

He went on to say that while there was a strong case for holding that the *Joyner v Weeks* rule was not absolute, there was also a strong case for retaining the rule on a prima facie basis, 'if only because people who have agreed to do something should prima facie, at least, be required to do it'.[116] On that basis, the cost of repairs was awarded since it had not, as a matter of evidence, been shown to have been inapplicable.

[110] R Megarry and HWR Wade, *Law of Real Property* (5th ed, London, Stevens & Sons, 1984) 720.
[111] Conveyancing Act 1919, s 133A (NSW); Property Law Act 1974, s 112 (Qd).
[112] New Zealand Law Commission, *Aspects of Damages: The Rules in* Bain v Fothergill *and* Joyner v Weeks (NZLC R19, 1991).
[113] ibid, 18 and 28.
[114] [1994] 3 NZLR 410 (CA).
[115] ibid, 418–19.
[116] ibid, 420.

The *Maori Trustee* solution is a compromise between the competing views but it is not entirely clear quite how far it will affect the law in New Zealand. *Joyner v Weeks* is to be the prima facie rule to be applied

> ... unless [the defendant] can show by sufficiently cogent evidence that in both the short and the long term [the defendant] will definitely suffer no loss or will suffer a loss which can definitely be assessed at less than the prima facie measure.[117]

While there is a sense in which loss always has to be established as a matter of evidence, the prior question is what the law should count as a loss. The Court of Appeal has emphasised that cost of cure is very much the norm while not attempting to canvass the considerations of reasonableness of cure which occupied the courts in cases like *Ruxley*, beyond saying that intention to cure 'may' be relevant to the rebuttal of that norm.[118] Nor has it discussed either the situations in which value should be accorded to performance (or to the right to performance) per se, or the question of damages for loss of amenity.

## Reinstatement and Repair: Building Contracts

Reinstatement and repair issues can arise just as sharply in building cases as they do in respect of leases. This can be especially true in cases where the builder has sued to recover the price and some of the work done is incomplete or defective, so that an appropriate deduction needs to be made. An early statement of how such a deduction ought to be quantified was made in *Thornton v Place*[119] by Parke J who said:

> What the plaintiff is entitled to recover is the price agreed upon in the specification, subject to a deduction; and the measure of that deduction is the sum which it would take to alter the work, so as to make it correspond with the specification.[120]

That statement was subsequently approved in the Divisional Court and the Court of Appeal in the leading case of *H Dakin & Co Ltd v Lee*.[121] There, concrete had been laid to a depth of to 2 feet instead of the 4 feet called for in the contract. It was held that the owner was entitled to deduct the cost of making good the deficiency notwithstanding that both parties thought that the work done was sufficient for its purpose.

A similar position was taken by the Manitoba Court of Appeal in *Pearson-Burleigh Ltd v Pioneer Grain Co Ltd*,[122] another case dealing with foundations

[117] ibid.
[118] ibid, 119.
[119] *Thornton v Place* (1832) 1 Moo & R 218; 174 ER 74.
[120] ibid, 219.
[121] *H Dakin & Co Ltd v Lee* [1916] 1 KB 566 (CA). See also *Miller v Advanced Farming* (1969) 5 DLR (3d) 369.
[122] *Pearson-Burleigh Ltd v Pioneer Grain Co Ltd* [1933] 1 WWR 179.

which were not as specified. The question there was whether the owner was entitled to have the cost of complying with the contract, or merely of enough repairs to make the defective foundations sufficient for their purpose. Trueman JA, delivering a judgment with which all the members of the Court agreed, rejected the notion that the measure of damages could be reduced to the cost of a remedy which did not really give to the owner what he had contracted for. He cited an earlier case to which it had been said: 'The owner of the building is, therefore, entitled to recover such damages … as will put him in a position to have just the building he contracted for.'[123]

In a third case dealing with defective foundations, this time in Australia, the High Court held in *Bellgrove v Eldridge*[124] that the measure of damages was not the difference in value of the building but the cost (less any part of the contract price still unpaid) of 'reasonable and necessary' work to make it conform to the contract.

These and other cases confirm that the normal rule in building cases is that damages are to be assessed by reference to the cost of cure and are not limited to diminution in value.[125] In other words, they protect the performance interest and go beyond mere compensation for the economic consequences of breach. Nor is this a matter of the cost of cure being simply a measure of difference in value. As was held, for example, by the New South Wales Court of Appeal in *Evans v Balog*,[126] the costs of remedial work can be awarded even when they would substantially exceed any diminution in value. That is consistent, too, with cases where it has been held that no allowance has to be made for betterment. The best-known example is probably *Harbutt's 'Plasticine' Ltd v Wayne Tank and Pump Co Ltd*,[127] where the cost of building an entirely new factory was awarded.

## Difference in Value in Building Cases

Though the cost of cure is clearly the normal measure of damages in building contract cases, the reference in *Bellgrove v Eldridge* to the works having to be 'reasonable and necessary' shows that that is not the full story. Another line of cases, culminating in *Ruxley*, shows that there are still some situations where, potentially, damages for defective performance may be limited to diminution in value or, where such diminution is absent, may be denied altogether.

123 ibid, 183.

124 *Bellgrove v Eldridge* (1954) 90 CLR 613 (High Court of Australia).

125 See also *Hudson's Building and Engineering Contracts*, above n 10, 1036–7; *Thornton v Place* (1832) 1 Moo & R 218; 174 ER 74.

126 *Evans v Balog* [1976] 1 NSWLR 36. See also *Mertens v Home Freeholds Co* [1921] 2 KB 526 (CA); *Paramatta CC v Lutz* (1988) 12 NSWLR 293.

127 [1970] 1 QB 447 (CA). And see *Hollebone v Midhurst and Fernhurst Builders Ltd* [1968] Lloyd's Rep 38 (QBD).

Yet, while there have been dicta from time to time stating that it must be reasonable to repair or reinstate if damages are to be calculated by the cost of doing so,[128] the number of reported building contract cases where damages have in fact been confined to difference in value seems to have been quite small. Of those few, two[129] were based on concessions by counsel for which no reasons were given, and in a third the possibility that the cost of cure might be the proper measure seems never to have been raised.[130] And in the eleventh edition of *Hudson's Building and Engineering Contracts*, of 25 contract and torts cases summarised,[131] in only one other contract case were damages given simply for difference in value. That case was *GW Atkins Ltd v Scott*,[132] which involved a claim for the cost of removing and replacing defective tiling work at a cost of between £1,229 and £1,500. The contract price for the job had been less than £500. At first instance, the learned judge seems to have decided that the defects were unimportant and that it would be unreasonable for anyone to go to the expense of stripping and replacing the tiles. He awarded, instead, £250 for 'bad workmanship' and that award was upheld by the Court of Appeal.

In the course of his dissenting judgment in the *Ruxley* case,[133] Dillon LJ referred to *Cotton v Wallis*[134] as another case where it had been held that a building owner was not entitled to the cost of bringing works up to specification. But that was a claim for negligence against an architect and the question at issue was whether in giving a certificate he could reasonably have been satisfied with the work that had been done. A majority of the Court of Appeal (Denning LJ dissenting) thought the defects so slight (presumably de minimis) that the architect could not be said to have been negligent. Accordingly, it is not really a case where the performance measure was displaced.

For the most part, therefore, before the decision of the House of Lords in *Ruxley*, authority for the application of the compensation measure to breaches of building contracts has depended on dicta in cases where damages were in fact awarded for the cost of cure. In general, these dicta have been expressed in terms of potential limitations upon an acknowledged prima facie right to that cost of cure. Moreover, it would seem that in practice cost of cure has only rarely been denied. The main significance of the *Ruxley* case is that it has confirmed at the

128 eg *East Ham Corporation v Bernard Sunley & Sons Ltd* [1996] AC 406 (HL); *Radford v De Froberville*, [1977] 1 WLR 1262 (Ch); *Evans v Balog* [1976] 1 NSWLR 36; *McGarry v Richards* [1954] 2 DLR 367; *Nu West Homes Ltd v Thunderbird Petroleums Ltd* (1975) 59 DLR (3d) 292; *Strata v Winkler* (1987) 45 DLR (4th) 741.

129 *Newton Abbot Development Ltd v Stockman Bros* (1931) 47 TLR 616; *Perry v Sidney Phillips & Son* [1982] 1 WLR 1287 (CA).

130 *Applegate v Moss* [1971] 1 QB 406 (CA). The cost of reinstatement was refused by May J as unreasonable in *CR Taylor (Wholesale) Ltd v Hepworths* [1997] 1 WLR 659 (QBD), but that was a torts case.

131 *Hudson's Building and Engineering Contracts*, above n 10, 1038–46.

132 *GW Atkins Ltd v Scott* (1980) 7 *Construction Law Journal* 125 (CA).

133 [1994] 1 WLR 650 (CA), 662.

134 *Cotton v Wallis* [1955] 1 WLR 1168 (CA).

highest level, and as part of the ratio, that while damages for the cost of cure are the norm in building contract cases, they will not be recoverable if it would be unreasonable to effect such a cure.

## Three Questions

The *Ruxley* decision on reasonableness (which, incidentally, had the support of all their Lordships) raises at least three questions. When will it be unreasonable to cure the defective performance? Must the relevant works be intended and done? And is the reasonableness test the only appropriate answer?

### When Will Cure Be Unreasonable?

The reasonableness test applied in this context is clearly an objective one,[135] there being no suggestion that the plaintiff himself should be the arbiter.[136] On the other hand, the hypothetical reasonable person required by the test would be one who, like the plaintiff, had bargained for the defendant's promises[137] and who also had the plaintiff's tastes and needs.[138] And both in principle and on authority the degree of unreasonableness required to deny the plaintiff the cost of cure would not be slight. After all, *pacta sunt servanda.* It can rarely be wholly unreasonable for a contracting party to want what he has bargained and (under the common law system) therefore paid for, even if it be the construction of a folly having no market value whatever.[139] Similarly, a cure is not unreasonable just because it will cost more than the end-result will be worth.[140] Nor will a court be over-critical of the potential cost of cure, given that the need for cure has been occasioned by the other party's default.[141]

In the famous New York case of *Jacob & Youngs v Kent*,[142] Cardozo J said that a building owner was entitled to the money which would permit him to complete, 'unless the cost of completion is grossly and unfairly out of proportion to the good to be attained'. In *Ruxley*, Lord Lloyd of Berwick cited that judgment for the principle that the cost of cure would be inappropriate if the expenditure were 'out of all proportion' to the good to be obtained.[143] Lord Mustill used the phrase 'wholly disproportionate'[144] and Lord Bridge spoke of a cost of reinstatement

135 Phang, above n 4, suggests that although the test is objective, it ought to be subjective.
136 [1996] 1 AC 344 (HL) 358–9.
137 ibid, 358, 360 and 370–1.
138 ibid, 353, 358, 360 and 370–1.
139 ibid, 358, 360, 361 and 370–1.
140 See text accompanying nn 125 and 126 above.
141 *Nu West Homes Ltd v Thunderbird Petroleums Ltd* (1975) 59 DLR (3d) 292.
142 *Jacob & Youngs v Kent* 129 NE 889, 891 (1921).
143 [1996] 1 AC 344 (HL), 367 and 369. And see [1995] 1 WLR 68 (CA), 79 per Steyn LJ.
144 ibid, 361. And see [1977] Ch 106 (Ch), 328.

'however unreasonable'.[145] The degree of disproportion, then, has to be a fairly high one, but disproportion alone cannot be the determinant if the interests of those who build follies or who have special or idiosyncratic needs are to be respected. There must be some further factor present if the cost of cure is to be denied. It is here that the second question becomes relevant.

## Must the Works Be Intended and Done?

On the evidence of the reports, what, it is believed, is the real motivation of the courts in the cases on cost of cure is not a desire for reasonableness for its own sake[146] but a concern lest plaintiffs reap a windfall by recovering compensation for losses they are not perceived to have suffered.[147] Reasonableness has, instead, been a device to stop that happening.

One obvious context in which this fear has arisen is contracts for the benefit of third parties. As has already been pointed out,[148] it has been a concern fed by the rather strange notion that performance of an obligation, as distinct from the results of performance, is of no economic value to the person who paid for it. A second context involves cases such as *Tito v Waddell (No 2)*[149] where the plaintiff is no longer in a position to spend his damages on actually effecting the cure as, for example, where the thing to be cured has passed out of the plaintiff's ownership or possession. In the *Tito* case, the contract breakers, having promised the people of Ocean Island that they would replant once guano had been extracted, had instead transported the injured parties 1,600 miles across the Pacific to another island. In confining them to the diminution in market value of their land, Megarry V-C plainly expected that any damages he awarded would therefore not be devoted to replanting.[150]

But the concern to avoid windfalls is perhaps easiest to understand and to justify in cases like *Ruxley* where the cost of cure is a substantial proportion of the contract price and where performance has nearly been completed and cannot be 'returned' to the defendant. Here the risk is not just of the damages being spent otherwise than on cure, but of double compensation in the sense that the plaintiff

[145] ibid, 354.

[146] Where a choice is possible, a reasonable interpretation of a contract will be preferred, and reasonableness is relevant also to mitigation. But in general there is no requirement at common law that either contracts, or the parties, be reasonable.

[147] See, eg: [1996] 1 AC 344 (HL), 357 and 358; [1950] 1 KB 9 (CA), 15; [1972] 1 WLR 659 (QBD), 670; [1977] 1 WLR 1262 (Ch), 1270; *Henderson v Thorn* [1893] 2 QB 164 (QB), 167; *Strata Corp v Winkler* (1987) 45 DLR (4th) 741, 750; *Tito v Waddell (No 2)* [1977] Ch 106 (Ch), 332; *Moon Trustee v Bolton* [1971] NZLR 226; Harris, Ogus and Phillips, above note 8, 586 and 593–4. And see New Zealand Law Commission, above n 112, 27.

[148] See text above from n 82ff.

[149] [1977] Ch 106. Other examples are *Wigsell v School for Indigent Blind* (1882) 8 QBD 357 (QBD); *Smiley v Townshend* [1950] 2 KB 311 (CA), 322–3; *McGarry v Richards, Akroyd & Gall* [1954] 2 DLR 367.

[150] [1977] Ch 106 (Ch), 332.

might well end up with both the benefits of an effectively sufficient performance and a sum by way of damages which no reasonable person would spend on cure.[151]

Almost certainly, it is the concern over such windfalls which accounts for the suggestions to be found in the cases and in texts that, before awarding damages for the cost of cure, the courts should be satisfied that they will in fact be so spent. An early example of the way damages might be spent being treated as relevant was *Wigsell v Schools for the Indigent Blind.*[152] There, the Queen's Bench Divisional Court, in refusing to award the cost of cure (the erection of a boundary wall), pointed out that the plaintiffs 'most probably would never think for a moment of any such expenditure which to us, at least, would seem a simple waste of money'.[153]

Two more recent examples were the judgments of Megarry V-C and Oliver J in *Tito v Waddell (No 2)*[154] and *Radford v De Froberville*[155] respectively. In the former, the Vice-Chancellor said:

> [I]f the plaintiff has suffered little or no monetary loss in the reduction in value of his land, and he has no intention of applying any damages towards carrying out the work contracted for, or its equivalent, I cannot see why he should recover the cost of doing work which will never be done.[156]

In the latter, Oliver J regarded it as important that the plaintiff did genuinely intend to build the wall which the defendant had failed to provide.[157]

This sort of concern with what a plaintiff might do with his damages is, of course, quite foreign to the usual approach of the law. No one suggests, for example, that damages for non-delivery of goods have to be spent actually going into the market to purchase substitutes.[158] It also runs counter to the *res inter alios acta* principle. So, it is not surprising that there should also exist a line of cases to the effect that what a plaintiff might do with his cost-of-cure damages is no concern of the defendant. An early example was *Joyner v Weeks*[159] where, it will be recalled, an under-lessee was held liable for the cost of repairs, notwithstanding that part of the premises would be demolished. In a 1950 case, *James v Hutton and Cook Ltd,*[160] where the cost of the restoration of a shop front at the end of a lease was being sought, Lord Goddard accepted that, provided the

[151] *cf Carosella v Ginas* (1981) 46 LGRA 51.
[152] (1882) 8 QBD 357 (QBD).
[153] [1977] Ch 106 (Ch), 364.
[154] [1977] Ch 106 (Ch).
[155] [1977] 1 WLR 1262 (Ch).
[156] [1977] Ch 106 (Ch), 332.
[157] [1977] 1 WLR 1262 (Ch), 1283–4. See also *Jones v Stroud District Council* [1986] 1 WLR 1141 (CA), 1150. For other examples, see n 143 above and *Imodco Ltd v Wimpey Major Projects Ltd* (1987) 40 BLR 1 (CA), 19; *Linden Gardens Trust Ltd v Lenesta Sludge Disposals Ltd* [1994] AC 85 (HL).
[158] *Shearson v Lehmann* [1980] 1 Lloyd's Rep 441, 443.
[159] [1891] 2 QB 31.
[160] *James v Hutton and Cook Ltd* [1950] 1 KB 9 (CA), 15.

plaintiff was entitled to the cost of restoration, it would be no concern of the defendant how those damages might subsequently be spent. The High Court of Australia expressed a similar view in *Bellgrove v Eldridge*[161] in 1954 and in very recent times there have been further dicta along the same lines from Steyn,[162] Kerr[163] and Staughton LJJ (in the latter's case, in the course of *Ruxley* itself).[164]

In the House of Lords in *Ruxley*, Lord Jauncey sought to reconcile the two lines of authority by saying:

> Intention or lack of it, to reinstate can have relevance only to reasonableness and hence to the extent of the loss which has been sustained. Once that loss has been established intention as to the subsequent use of the damages ceases to be relevant.[165]

In practical terms, though, the apparent reconciliation, in the way in which Lord Jauncey stated it, is really only an affirmation of the intention requirement. That the actual expenditure might not thereafter be questioned would in no way diminish the need to show that the intention to rebuild did in fact exist at the time of trial. Moreover, the award of damages would still turn on evidence that is necessary in no other context. And even though, once judgment were obtained, the plaintiff were free to do what he wanted with the proceeds, the fact that the cure was not affected might well put in issue the genuineness of his state of mind at the time he gave evidence. A second problem arises from the fact that while the test of reasonableness itself is objective, the intention requirement is treated as subjective. So long as that remains the case, its effect will be to reinstate the plaintiff as an arbiter.[166]

With respect, it is submitted that in this context, as in others, the normal rule should apply and that, in words also used by Lord Jauncey in *Ruxley*,[167] the courts should have 'no concern with the use to which [the] plaintiff puts an award of damages for a loss which has been established'. That purpose could be achieved, and at the same time the concern about windfalls could be met, if the objective reasonableness test were to be enlarged to include the question whether, and to what extent, a reasonable person in the position of the plaintiff, having his tastes and needs, would spend the damages award in effecting the cure.[168]

[161] (1954) 90 CLR 613 (High Court of Australia). Followed in *De Cesare v Deluxe Motors Pty Ltd* (1996) 67 SASR 28 (FCSA).

[162] [1995] 1 WLR 68 (CA), 80. And see ibid, 75–6 per Dillon LJ. See also *Sealace Shipping Co Ltd v Oceanvoice Ltd (The Alecos M)* [1990] 1 Lloyd's Rep 82 (QBD), 85 per Steyn J (rev'd on other grounds [1991] 1 Lloyd's Rep 120 (CA)).

[163] *Dean v Ainley* [1987] 1 WLR 1729 (CA), 1737–8.

[164] [1994] 1 WLR 650 (CA), 657. There is an analogy, too, with claims in restitution for the recovery of overpaid tax: eg *Commissioner of State Revenue (Victoria) v Royal Insurance Australia Ltd* (1994) 182 CLR 51 (High Court of Australia), 78–9.

[165] [1996] 1 AC 344 (HL), 359. Lord Lloyd, ibid, 372–3, also thought the relevance of intention was to reasonableness and to the extent of the loss.

[166] ibid, 359.

[167] ibid, 369.

[168] *cf Darlington BC v Wiltshier Northern Ltd* [1995] 1 WLR 68 (CA), 80–1 per Steyn LJ.

## Is Reasonableness the Only Answer?

Even if the intention requirement were to become part of a single objective test of reasonableness, there might still be some unease amongst those who, like the present writer, believe that primary and secondary obligations in contract are interrelated. It is one thing for a legislature to decree that exception clauses, say, should be enforced only to the extent that they are reasonable.[169] That involves only a relatively narrow limit on the ability to contract. But the common law being what it is, a finding that the performance interest in contract is to be protected only to the extent that it is reasonable for the promisee to want performance could easily be enlarged to form a general rule that independently of the intention of the parties contracts generally should be enforceable only to the extent that they are reasonable. On the other hand, that concern would be met if, as Francis Dawson has suggested,[170] the starting point were the situation of the parties at the time they entered into the contract. Would the promisee have been entitled at that time to infer that the promisor was accepting contractual responsibility for a cure which it would be unreasonable to effect? Alternatively, would an unreasonable cure have been within the reasonable contemplation of the parties?

The question that next arises is whether there exist other ways by which the judicial concern to avoid windfalls could be met.

## Disgorging of Profits or Savings?

One possibility, suggested for example by *Hudson's Building and Engineering Contracts*,[171] would be to require the defaulting contractor to disgorge any savings he might have made through his breach. This seems to have been done only once in a reported Commonwealth case, by Macarthur J in *Samson & Samson Ltd v Proctor*,[172] but his brief judgment contains no discussion of the point. Remembering that a penny saved is a penny gained, this way of approaching the matter would be just a particular application of a more general requirement that contract breakers be made to forfeit the profits of their breach. There have, indeed, been arguments advanced for the existence of such a principle[173] but as recently as 1993 it was rejected by the English Court of Appeal in *Surrey*

[169] eg Unfair Contract Terms Act 1977 (UK).

[170] Above n 4, 152; *cf South Australia Asset Management Corporation v York Montague Ltd* [1997] AC 191 (HL), 211 ('a duty in respect of the kind of loss which he has suffered').

[171] Above n 10, 1046–7 and 1057–8.

[172] *Samson & Samson Ltd v Proctor* [1975] 1 NZLR 655. Contrast, though, *Honeybun v Harris* [1995] 1 NZLR 64, 74 and 75; *Tito v Waddell (No 2)* [1977] Ch 106 (Ch), 332.

[173] eg DW Greig and JLR Davis, *The Law of Contract* (Sydney, Law Book Company, 1987) 1362–3; JLR Davis, 'Damages', in PD Finn (ed), *Essays on Contract* (Sydney, Law Book Company, 1987) 200, 203ff.

*County Council v Bredero Homes.*[174] On the other hand, in the different legal climate, say, of New Zealand, it would presumably not be too difficult to obtain the desired result by recourse to constructive trusts on the analogy, for example, of the law relating to bribes and secret commissions.[175] Such a solution, though, would not have helped the plaintiff in a case like *Ruxley* where, far from making a profit from its breach, the contractor seems to have incurred extensive losses.

## The Avoidance of Waste?

A second possibility, suggested by Harris, Ogus and Phillips,[176] would be to give the plaintiff the cost of cure unless, and to the extent that, to cure would be wasteful. By that is meant that the cost of the cure would exceed its utility for the plaintiff. Waste as such, though, has not in the past been a concern of the common law of contract, as witness the decision of the House of Lords in *White & Carter (Councils) v McGregor.*[177] As an objective of damages, the avoidance of waste was rejected by the High Court of Australia in *Bellgrove v Eldridge*[178] in a passage which was cited by Lord Lloyd in the *Ruxley* case,[179] apparently with approval.

## General Damages as an Alternative?

A third possibility would be to calculate the plaintiff's economic loss by reference to the compensation principle but to give him, in addition, general damages for loss of amenity, enjoyment or disappointed expectation on the analogy of cases like *Jarvis v Swans Tours.*[180] This, of course, is what was done in the *Ruxley* case and it was obviously a matter of some relief to Lords Bridge, Mustill and Lloyd especially, to be able to make at least that gesture towards protection of the performance interest.[181] The problem with this as a solution is that it is no more than a gesture. Once again, as in the case of third-party contracts, it treats performance (or the right to performance) as having no worth in itself and values it by reference only to its results, or the enjoyment of its results. And, at least on English and Australian reasoning,[182] it may be restricted to cases where the enjoyment or amenity to be achieved by the performance was itself something for which the plaintiff had contracted, either expressly or by implication.

[174] [1993] 1 WLR 1361 (CA).
[175] *Attorney-General of Hong Kong v Reid* [1994] 1 NZLR 1; [1994] 1 AC 324 (PC).
[176] Above n 8, 586.
[177] *White & Carter (Councils) v McGregor* [1962] AC 413 (HL).
[178] (1954) 90 CLR 613 (High Court of Australia), 618–9.
[179] [1996] 1 AC 344 (HL), 367.
[180] *Jarvis v Swans Tours* [1973] QB 233 (CA).
[181] [1996] 1 AC 344 (HL), 354, 361 and 374.
[182] ibid, 374; *Baltic Shipping Co v Dillon* (1993) 176 CLR 344. It is assumed the word 'amenity' in *Ruxley* carries its dictionary connotations of pleasantness.

## Apportionment of Windfalls: The Consumer Surplus

A fourth possibility, again suggested by Harris, Ogus and Phillips,[183] is that any 'windfall' be apportioned between the parties. They point out that prevention of the injured party's recovering a windfall can have the result that, in consequence, the windfall accrues to the wrongdoer. They cite *Tito v Waddell (No 2)*[184] where the defendants' successful removal of the plaintiffs from their homeland had freed the defendants from what would otherwise have been a very expensive obligation indeed (and, one might add, one for which the indigenous inhabitants had paid dearly). They argue that it ought to be possible in such a case to award the plaintiffs a sum somewhere between the two extremes. They had in mind an allowance made for the islanders' 'consumer surplus',[185] meaning thereby a subjective value beyond the market price which performance might have had for them. That is something which might nowadays be possible under the *Ruxley* ruling, at least in some cases.[186]

Yet again, though, the consumer surplus is a solution which treats performance (or the right to performance) as having no worth in itself. It would be one thing to have the monetary equivalent of performance plus damages for loss of an additionally covenanted subjective benefit as, for example, in the lost holiday cases.[187] It would be quite another to treat the latter as a sufficient substitute for the former.

## Narrowing the Gap

For those who favour the performance principle, the challenge is to find a way, so far as possible, of ensuring its universality while making allowance for the desire to prevent those windfalls which really do offend against 'common sense'.[188]

The task of so doing would be lightened and the law would be made much more certain and predictable if the courts were prepared to allow:

(a) that, at common law, performance itself (or the right to performance), as distinct from the benefits that flow from performance, has a value to a promisee equivalent to the cost of cure whether those benefits stand to be enjoyed by the promisee or by some third person;
(b) that whether it would be reasonable to cure is to be determined objectively;
(c) that, in consequence, how a plaintiff chooses to spend his damages is no concern of the defendant; and

183 Above n 8, 593–4.
184 [1977] Ch 106 (Ch).
185 Above n 8, 592–4. And see EA Farnsworth, 'Legal Remedies for Breach of Contract' (1970) 70 *Columbia Law Review* 1145, 1160–75.
186 *cf* [1996] 1 AC 344 (HL), 353 and 360–1.
187 eg [1973] QB 233 (CA); *Jackson v Horizon Holidays Ltd* [1975] 1 WLR 1468 (CA).
188 [1996] 1 AC 344 (HL), 354 per Lord Bridge.

(d) that to dealings plaintiffs may have with third parties independently of the contract, the principle *res inter alios acta* would normally apply.

Support in principle or authority, or both, can be found for all of these conditions. If they were to be accepted, the concept of a windfall could be confined to 'double-dipping', that is, to cases where a plaintiff who had been awarded the cost of cure would stand to benefit from both an original albeit imperfect performance, which an objectively reasonable person would retain, and also damages for a cure which in practical terms would not be effected by any similarly reasonable person in the plaintiff's position. In those cases, damages for defects in performance would be restricted to difference in value, if any, plus, where applicable, damages for loss of amenity.

## Application of the Suggested Approach

This kind of approach would prevent recovery of the cost of cure in cases like *Ruxley* and *GW Atkins Ltd v Scott*,[189] the latter being a case where trivial defects in tiling would have cost a large amount to repair and had been lived with by the plaintiff for four and a half years. On the other hand, the approach could make possible recovery of the cost of performance in third-party beneficiary cases and also in cases like *Tito v Waddell (No 2)*[190] and *Wigsell v School for the Indigent Blind*[191] where there had effectively been no performance by the defendants.

If it were objected that in the *Tito* case damages based on the cost of reinstatement would still be disproportionate, one would have to ask, disproportionate to what? To the obligation undertaken or only to the economic end-result? If the covenant to reinstate had been intended just to ensure either that the Ocean Islanders could obtain substitute land for reinvestment or that their resettlement elsewhere in the Pacific should be facilitated, the performance interest would have been met by an award of not much more than difference in value. But the likelihood that an indigenous Polynesian people would have entertained those sorts of purposes for their homeland seems less than compelling.

However, in not every case would an absence of 'double-dipping' mean that the cost of repairs was appropriate, as is illustrated, for example, by *Attica Sea Carriers Corp v Ferrostaal*[192] and *Sealace Shipping Co v Oceanvoice Ltd.*[193] In the former, the repairs required under a charterparty would have cost £2 million and the vessel would then have been worth only half that amount. In the words of Lord Denning MR, it would have been economic nonsense to have done them. In

[189] (1980) 7 *Construction Law Journal* 215 (CA).
[190] [1977] Ch 106 (Ch).
[191] (1882) 8 QBD 357 (QBD).
[192] *Attica Sea Carriers Corp v Ferrostaal* [1976] 1 Lloyd's Rep 250 (CA).
[193] *Sealace Shipping Co v Oceanvoice Ltd (The Alecos M)* [1991] 1 Lloyd's Rep 120 (CA).

the form in which the matter came before them, the Court of Appeal was not concerned with what damages should be awarded. But the case was a commercial one and it does not appear that the ship was unique. Assuming that to be so, the performance interest, itself, could have been met by giving the owners the difference between the value of the ship as it stood and the cost of a comparable second-hand replacement in good repair.

In the *Sealace* case, the sellers of a ship had failed to supply a spare propeller as specified in the contract. Damages were awarded only for the scrap value a second propeller would have had. The evidence was that spare propellers have no longer any commercial use, from which it would seem to follow that the propeller mentioned in the contract would have been included in the sale as being of scrap value only.

Another exceptional type of case is exemplified by *Surrey County Council v Bredero Homes Ltd*[194] where the defendants had built 77 houses on land sold to them by the plaintiff councils, in breach of covenants permitting only 72. That case illustrates the problem of relating breach of undertakings *not* to act to the compensatory approach to damages. But another approach could be to recognise that a refraining from acting can itself be the performance of a negative covenant. On that basis, and in appropriate cases, the performance interest of the covenantee might well justify an award of the costs of reinstatement. The sole contractual purpose of the council was to ensure that the defendants would have to apply to and pay them for a relaxation of the covenants if they wished to build more than the agreed number.[195] The Court of Appeal held that the councils had therefore suffered no loss at all. The claim might have appeared differently had it been approached instead, under the *Hadley v Baxendale*[196] formula, as turning on the consequences flowing from the breach, as was done, for example, by the Court of Appeal in *Anglia Television Ltd v Reed*.[197]

## The Place of General Damages

A final point concerns the situations in which general damages of the kind sanctioned in *Ruxley* ought to be awarded. That will depend in part on whether such damages are to be a mere *solatium*, a minimal protection of the performance interest, confined to those cases where, in the absence of any difference in value, the plaintiff would otherwise get nothing. In principle, it is submitted they ought not to be so confined. As *Ruxley* demonstrated, the enjoyment of an amenity has a quantifiable value quite separate from the cost of performance and from the economic losses caused by a breach. Even if the cost of cure is awarded,

194 [1993] 1 WLR 1361 (CA).
195 ibid, 1364.
196 (1854) 9 Ex 341; 156 ER 145.
197 *Anglia Television Ltd v Reed* [1972] 1 QB 60 (CA).

there could still be loss of amenity until such time as the cure could reasonably be completed. And where a difference in value amounting to less than the cost of cure has been awarded, the loss of amenity will be permanent and general damages ought therefore to be no less than they would have been in a case like *Ruxley* where there was no difference in value at all.

## Summary and Conclusions

There can be little doubt that a primary purpose of contractual remedies is to protect the parties' rights to performance of their contracts, whether directly or indirectly. That there should have been confusion about this can be ascribed to a number of factors.

Those factors include a difference of opinion about whether contractual obligation is assumed or imposed and about the role of remedies and their relation to contractual obligation. There has also been a failure to distinguish between lost performance on the one hand and loss or damage consequent on defective performance on the other. There has been a particular concern in some contexts, though not in others, to prevent over-compensation or 'windfalls', a concern to which the principle *res inter alios acta* has occasionally been a casualty. In large measure, the concern about over-compensation has stemmed from a failure in some contexts (though, again, not in others) to ascribe value to performance itself or to the right to performance and the resulting restriction of the concept of loss to the consequences of defective performance. In some of these cases, the result can even be that no remedy at all can be obtained against a defaulting promisor.

The obvious solution would be to value performance or the right to performance by the cost of cure, or of alternative performance, and there is clear authority for this in such contexts as leases and building contracts. In the recent case of *Linden Gardens Trust Ltd v Lenesta Sludge Disposals Ltd*,[198] Lord Griffiths has grasped the nettle and suggested that the cost of alternative performance be awarded to the promisee even where the enjoyment of performance is intended to be by third parties.

Recognition that performance and the right to performance have a value equivalent to the cost of cure or of alternative performance, if it were coupled with a reinstatement of the *res inter alios acta* principle, would remove most of the present concern about over-compensation. There would, though, remain cases like *Ruxley* where the risk would be of 'double-dipping', of putting the plaintiff in the position of having both a performance which would be retained and the costs of a cure which would in practice never be effected. The answer in *Ruxley* was to ask whether, in the objective sense, it would be reasonable to

[198] [1994] 1 AC 85 (HL).

embark on a cure, and to add the requirement that the plaintiff should subjectively intend to do so. That requirement runs counter to the ordinary principles of damages but it could easily be brought into line by making intention part of a single objective test.

The conclusions to which all this has been tending are:

(1) That protection of the performance interest be accepted as a primary object of damages in contract, irrespective of who stands to enjoy the fruits of performance, what dealings the promisee may intend to make with third parties, and how he actually intends that his damages be spent.

(2) To that end, that:
   (a) The principle of *res inter alios acta* be restored to its historic position.
   (b) The question of intention to effect a cure be part of a single objective test of reasonableness which would give the hypothetical reasonable person the needs and tastes of the actual promisee.
   (c) That the reasonableness test be confined to cases of 'double-dipping' as defined.

For all these proposals, support exists in principle, authority or both. Their adoption would make the law much more consistent and, therefore, potentially more predictable. Perhaps more importantly, it is believed that it would also bring the law rather closer to the normal expectations of those who enter into contracts.

## Addendum: Two Recent Cases

A not uncommon view is that, in contract, obligation and liability are conceptually distinct, as witness the perception that exclusions of liability are mere defences to accrued rights of action. It is a view which can also effect questions of remoteness. Take (say) a valuer who in breach of contract submits a negligently prepared valuation, and, relying on it, his client lends money and suffers loss when the market falls. Whether or not the valuer is liable may well be taken to depend on whether such loss was the foreseeable consequence of his breach. By contrast, if it is accepted that obligation and liability are interrelated and are both assumed, responsibility is seen to depend, not on foreseeability alone but, initially, on whether liability for it had been undertaken by the valuer. It is this latter approach which, arguably, draws support from what was said in *Transfield Shipping Inc v Mercator Shipping Inc*,[199] particularly by Lord Hoffmann and Lord Hope of Craighead.

[199] *Transfield Shipping Inc v Mercator Shipping Inc (The Achilleas)* [2009] 1 AC 61 (HL). See also *South Australia Asset Managements Corporation v Yorke Montague Ltd* [1997] AC 191 (HL) per Lord Hoffmann.

In that case, charterers had failed to redeliver the chartered vessel on the due date. The owners had previously arranged a follow-on charter with another company at a favourable rate, but on the condition that the company could cancel should there be delay in redelivery. In the meantime, market rates had fallen and, in order to prevent cancellation, the shipowner had to agree with the company to a corresponding reduction in hire. The main question before the House of Lords was whether the damages for delay recoverable from the original charterers should cover the profits lost over the whole of the follow-on, or be restricted to the difference between the market and the charter rates of hire during the period of the overrun. It was the general understanding in the shipping market that a charterer who returned a vessel late was liable only for damages in respect of the overrun. Nevertheless, both the arbitrators (by a majority) and the courts below decided that the charterer was liable for the larger amount, on an application of the ordinary rules laid down in such cases as *Hadley v Baxendale*[200] and *The Heron II.*[201] It was said that the charterer should have realised at the time the contract was made that a loss of the greater amount would be 'not unlikely' to result from a late redelivery. Nevertheless, the House of Lords (Lord Hoffmann, Lord Hope, Lord Rodger of Earlsferry, and Lord Walker of Gestingthorpe, Baroness Hale of Richmond dubitante) allowed the charterer's appeal, holding that it was liable only for the lower amount.

What makes the case of particular interest in the present context is that both Lord Hoffmann and Lord Hope based their speeches on the premise that the damages recoverable for the late redelivery should depend on the extent of the contractual liability undertaken by the charterers. In particular, were the losses for which recovery was being sought of a type or kind for which the appellant charterer could be treated as having assumed responsibility? According to Lord Hoffmann, in determining the limits of liability for damages, the charterparty should be interpreted to 'reflect the liabilities the parties may reasonably be expected to have assumed and paid for'. Thus, a party might not be liable for foreseeable losses because they were not of the type or kind for which he could be treated as having assumed responsibility. In the instant case, the losses arising in respect of the follow-on charter were not of a kind for which the original charterer had assumed responsibility, particularly having regard to market expectations.

Lord Hope also spoke in terms of an assumption of responsibility for loss caused by the delay. He agreed with the dissenting arbitrator, who had pointed out that a party cannot be expected to assume responsibility for something he cannot control and cannot quantify. Where his Lordship differed from Lord Hoffmann was that he saw the matter as one of presumed intention, whereas Lord Hoffmann had seen it as depending on an application of the ordinary rules

200 (1854) 9 Exch 341.

201 *Koufos v C Czarnikow Ltd* [1969] 1 AC 350 (HL).

governing the interpretation of commercial documents. For his part, Lord Rodger found it unnecessary to consider what he called 'the issues concerning assumption of responsibility'. On the other hand, Lord Walker spoke of the second limb of *Hadley v Baxendale* as itself involving 'a notion of assumption of responsibility'. For him, the question, 'what was the common basis on which the parties were contracting?', was 'essential to the rule in *Hadley v Baxendale* as a whole'. Baroness Hale, in her speech, interpreted the question put by Lord Hoffmann and Lord Hope as being 'is the charterer to be taken to have undertaken legal responsibility for this type of loss?' She was, she said, not immediately attracted to this incorporation of an idea derived from tort into the law of contract. It could introduce much room for argument in other contractual contexts. With some hesitation, she agreed that the appeal should be allowed, but on other grounds.

It may be that the reservations expressed by Baroness Hale will ultimately prevail. But as to her concern at the introduction of a tort idea into the law of contract, a possible response might be that, on the contrary, adoption of the notion of assumption of responsibility in *Hedley Byrne v Heller & Partners*[202] was, in fact and advisedly, the introduction of a contract idea into the law of torts! After all, it was on the basis that the situation of the parties in *Hedley Byrne* was equivalent to contract, lacking only consideration, that the assumption of responsibility test was justified, especially by Lord Devlin.

Whatever residual doubts may have been left by *Transfield Shipping Inc v Mercator Shipping Inc*, there can be few about the unanimous judgment of the High Court of Australia in *Tabcorp Holdings Ltd v Bowen Investments Pty Ltd.*[203] In respect of damages, it is an emphatic endorsement of the performance interest in general and of liability for alternative performance and the cost of cure in particular. And, as had the High Court previously in *Zhu v Treasurer (NSW)*,[204] it also unequivocally rejected the Holmes theory that a contract is an option at will to perform or pay damages, and its modern equivalent of 'efficient breach'.

Office premises had been leased for a term of 10 years from 1 February 1997 with a right of renewal for a further five years from 1 February 2006 (which was exercised), and an additional option to renew for the five years to 2017. By cl 2.13, the tenant covenanted:

> Not without the written approval of the Landlord first obtained (which consent shall not be unreasonably withheld or delayed) to make or permit to be made any substantial alteration or addition to the Demised Premises.

[202] [1964] AC 465 (HL).

[203] *Tabcorp Holdings Ltd v Bowen Investments Pty Ltd* (2009) 236 CLR 272 (High Court of Australia).

[204] *Zhu v Treasurer (NSW)* (2004) 218 CLR 530 (High Court of Australia), 574–5.

The tenant also covenanted, by cl 2.10, to keep the premises in repair; by cl 2.11, to yield up the premises on the determination of the lease in good repair; and, by cl 2.12.4, to make good any breakage or damage.

On 14 July 1997 one of the directors of the landlord was shocked, on arrival at the building, to find that the recently installed foyer, over the design and decoration of which she had lavished much care, was being destroyed by the tenant with a view to replacing it. Despite her protests, the tenant continued with the destruction and replacement for the next six weeks. The trial judge's description of this conduct as being in 'contumelious disregard' of the landlord's rights was, the High Court said, 'not hyperbolic'.

From its conduct, and the arguments its counsel addressed to the Court, it is a fair deduction that the tenant had relied on a notion of efficient breach and had been confident that its destruction and replacement of the foyer would cause little, if any, diminution in the value of the building. Accordingly, it would have expected that any damages by way of compensation would be only minor. At first instance, this sort of argument won the day, the damages awarded being only $34,820. The Full Court of the Federal Court of Australia took a different view and increased this sum to $1.38 million, made up of $580,000 being the cost of restoring the foyer to its original condition and $800,000 for loss of rent while restoration was taking place. It was from this judgment that the tenant appealed. In dismissing the appeal, the High Court relied primarily on what it called 'one short ground in which the Full Court's orders [were] plainly to be supported' and which had explicitly been raised at the hearing by members of the High Court bench. The landlord had a legitimate interest in preserving the physical character of the premises leased. Clause 2.13 was an express negative covenant which could have been enforced by a negative injunction had the tenant's clandestine conduct not removed that possibility. Its argument that it should be liable only for diminution in value of the reversion was based on a misunderstanding of the ruling principle stated by Parke B in *Robinson v Harman*:

> The rule of the common law is, that where a party sustains a loss by reason of a breach of contract, he is, so far as money can do it, to be placed in the same situation, with respect to damages, as if the contract had been performed.[205]

According to their Honours, Oliver J was correct to say in *Radford v De Froberville*[206] that the words 'the same situation, with respect to damages, as if the contract had been performed' do not mean 'as good a *financial* position as if the contract had been performed'.[207] They pointed out that, in some circumstances, putting the innocent party into 'the same situation … as if the contract had been performed' could coincide with placing the party into the same financial situation. Thus, in the case of the supply of defective goods, the prima facie measure

[205] (1848) 1 Exch 850 at 855.
[206] [1977] 1 WLR 1262 (Ch).
[207] ibid, 1273 (emphasis added).

of damages is the difference in value between the contract goods and the goods supplied. In the case of fungible goods, that measure did in fact place the buyer in the 'same [financial] situation … as if the contract had been performed'. But the measure of damages would be very different if the goods were not marketable.

The trial judge had found that the landlord had erected and leased the building for commercial purposes and as an investment property. It was the tenant's contention that its actions had not affected the value of the building as an investment. But the High Court preferred the view which Oliver J had also expressed in *Radford v De Froberville*,[208] that although others might consider performance not to be to a plaintiff's financial advantage, that was for the plaintiff to judge. *Pacta sunt servanda*. This was subject to the proviso that he was not merely using a technical breach to secure an uncovenanted profit. In *Bellgrove v Eldridge*,[209] the High Court had required that to undertake restoration must be 'a reasonable course to adopt'. It gave as an example a contract for the erection of a building with cement-rendered external walls of secondhand bricks. If the builder had instead used new bricks of first quality, the owner would not be entitled to the cost of replacement. There remained, of course, the decision of the House of Lords in the *Ruxley* case[210] (reversing the Court of Appeal) not to allow the replacement cost of the swimming pool. Their Honours considered that while 'on one view' that decision was inconsistent with principle, it was sufficient to say that the facts of *Ruxley*, 'which their Lordships evidently saw as quite exceptional', were plainly distinguishable from those of the present appeal.

Their Honours also held that, because of the way the appeal had been argued, they did not have to consider the question whether damages should be reduced for betterment. Nor did they have to consider as at what date damages should be calculated, the effect of any legislative reversal of *Joyner v Weeks*,[211] or how far it was relevant whether the landlord in fact intended to reinstate.

In the current chapter it was submitted that the real concern of the courts, in refusing reinstatement damages in cases where they would otherwise be awarded, was to prevent 'double-dipping', meaning an unwarranted windfall. The latter part of the chapter was devoted to a rather elaborate attempt to confine, to cases of that sort, the reasonableness exception affirmed by the House of Lords in *Ruxley*. For its part, the High Court confined it to circumstances which, it said, were 'fairly' or 'quite' exceptional. But from the examples given in the judgment, it would seem that for their Honours, too, the prevention of unwarranted windfalls was the underlying concern.

208 ibid, 1270.
209 (1954) 90 CLR 613 (High Court of Australia), 617
210 [1996] AC 344 (HL).
211 [1891] 2 QB 31 (CA).

# 9

# The Performance Interest, *Panatown*, and the Problem of Loss

IT IS A well-established principle of contract that while a party can always recover at least nominal damages for breach, he can recover substantial damages only in respect of his own loss. As a corollary, it is commonly supposed that if A as promisor contracts with B as promisee to confer a benefit on C, neither B nor C can recover substantial damages. The 'black hole'[1] thus created is said to result from B's having suffered no loss and C's want of privity.

The problem thus created was directly in issue before the House of Lords in *Alfred McAlpine Construction Ltd v Panatown Ltd.*[2] Although they divided three to two on the means, their Lordships all agreed that, in one way or another, a solution to the 'black hole' could in principle be found. It was only on the particular facts that, in the view of the majority, the promisee in the case before them was left, effectively, with no substantial rights of recourse.

The case arose out of a contract between McAlpine as contractors and Panatown as employers to design and build an office block and multi-storey car park on a site in Cambridge. Panatown alleged that the building as completed was seriously defective and might even have to be demolished, thus raising the possibility of a £40-million claim arising from breach of a £10-million contract. However, at no stage had Panatown owned the construction site, which at all times belonged to their associated company Unex Investment Properties Ltd ('UIPL') who were the actual developers. On the day the construction contract was signed, McAlpine entered into a separate Duty of Care Deed ('the DCD') with UIPL under which limited liability for negligence was accepted.

[1] So characterised by Lord Keith of Kinkel in *J Dykes Ltd v Littlewoods Mail Order Stores Ltd*, 1982 SC (HL) 157, 177.

[2] *Alfred McAlpine Construction Ltd v Panatown Ltd* [2000] 3 WLR 946 (HL).

## The Arguments

The matter came before the courts on an issue of law under the interim award of an arbitrator. The question for decision, as defined by Evans LJ in the Court of Appeal,[3] was 'are Panatown debarred from recovering substantial as opposed to nominal damages by reason of the fact that they were not and are not owners of the land?' Before the House of Lords, the argument for Panatown was based essentially on two grounds. One, referred to as the 'narrow' ground, sought to apply the rule in *Dunlop v Lambert.*[4] There, the House of Lords held that, where goods had been lost at sea, a consignor could recover substantial damages even though ownership of the goods, by the time of the loss, had passed to the consignee. Since then, it has generally been accepted that the same result follows even though the consignor has neither title, the burden of risk, nor an immediate right to possession of the goods. It has also been assumed that the consignor holds the damages for the benefit of the true owner as the party who suffered the loss.[5] In modem times, the rule has been confirmed by the House of Lords in *The Albazero,*[6] with the modification that it does not apply to contracts which contemplate that the carrier will enter into separate contracts (such as bills of lading) with the eventual owner. Both the rule and the modification were later applied to building contracts by the House of Lords in *St Martins Property Corporation Ltd v Sir Robert McAlpine Ltd (sub nom Linden Gardens Trust Ltd v Lenesta Sludge Disposals Ltd),*[7] and by the Court of Appeal in *Darlington Borough Council v Wiltshier Northern Ltd.*[8]

This so-called narrow ground, therefore, is directed to situations where it is the third party who has suffered the loss or damage in respect of which the promisee claims substantial damages. By contrast, under what was referred to in argument and in the speeches as the 'broad' ground, the loss alleged is that of the promisee himself. Here, Panatown relied on the speech of Lord Griffiths in the *St Martins* case and in particular on a passage in which an analogy was drawn with a husband who contracts with a builder to replace the roof of his wife's house.[9] Should the job be done badly, his Lordship said, it would be 'absurd' to suggest that the husband suffered no loss just because the house was not his. The loss he

[3] (1998) 14 *Construction Law Journal* 267 (CA), 269. Discussed by GH Treitel, 'Damages in Respect of a Third Party's Loss' (1998) 114 *Law Quarterly Review* 527; IND Wallace, 'Third Party Damage: No Legal Black Hole?' (1999) 115 *Law Quarterly Review* 394; and H Unberath, 'Third Party Losses and Black Holes: Another View' (1999) 115 *Law Quarterly Review* 535. A further discussion of the *Panatown* case, prompted by the decision of the Court of Appeal, appears in Brian Coote, 'Dunlop v Lambert: The Search for a Rationale' (1998) 13 *Journal of Contract Law* 91.

[4] *Dunlop v Lambert* (1839) 6 Cl & F 600.

[5] *Joseph v Knox* (1813) 3 Camp 320.

[6] *The Albazero* [1977] AC 774 (HL).

[7] *St Martins Property Corporation Ltd v Sir Robert McAlpine Ltd (sub nom Linden Gardens Trust Ltd v Lenesta Sludge Disposals Ltd)* [1994] 1 AC 85 (HL).

[8] *Darlington Borough Council v Wiltshier Northern Ltd* [1995] 1 WLR 68 (CA).

[9] ibid, 96.

suffered was that he did not receive the bargain for which he had contracted and the measure of damages was the cost of securing the performance of that bargain by getting the work done properly by another builder.

On one view, that passage expresses and applies the notion of a 'performance' interest in contract.[10] According to this notion, at least as I understand it,[11] what distinguishes an effective contractual promise from any other is that it is intended to, and does in fact, confer on the promisee an enforceable legal right to have the promise performed. In contract, primary and secondary rights are so closely related that, so far as the law allows, it is each which gives contractual content to the other. Accordingly, except where the promise is of something less (or other) than actual performance (as, for example, merely of an improvement in the promisee's overall financial position) performance of the action promised is what the promisee ought to be entitled to receive. And if specific performance should be unavailable, the promisee ought, in lieu, to obtain on breach by way of damages at least the cost of obtaining an equivalent performance by someone else. Moreover, should the covenanted benefits include the avoidance of consequential loss, whether to the promisee or to a third party, that too should be recoverable as part of the bargain for which the promisee had contracted, though in the latter case questions of accountability would arise. Of course, there are some qualifications to these rights, as *Ruxley Electronics and Construction Ltd v Forsyth*[12] demonstrates, but there has been plenty of authority for recognition of the performance interest as between contracting parties. It has been the failure, rightly or wrongly, to recognise such an interest in third-party cases which effectively has created the promisee's black hole.

Of the five Lords of Appeal who heard the *Panatown* appeal, Lord Clyde, Lord Jauncey of Tullichettle and Lord Browne-Wilkinson held that the rule in *Dunlop v Lambert* applied but that Panatown's claim failed on the facts because of the rights of action given UIPL under the DCD. Lord Goff of Chieveley and Lord Millett, on the other hand, held for Panatown on the basis of the 'performance interest' broad ground. As to that, while Lord Clyde found some difficulty in adopting it,[13] Lord Jauncey[14] and Lord Browne-Wilkinson[15] were of the view that, even on the assumption that Panatown could in principle rely on a performance interest, such rights as it might have had were negatived by the existence of the DCD.

[10] The expression was given currency by Professor D Friedmann in 'The Performance Interest in Contract Damages' (1995) 111 *Law Quarterly Review* 628.

[11] See ch 8 of this book.

[12] *Ruxley Electronics and Construction Ltd v Forsyth* [1996] 1 AC 344 (HL).

[13] [2000] 3 WLR 946 (HL), 959–61.

[14] ibid, 998.

[15] ibid, 1002.

## The Problem of Characterisation

It will already be apparent that the approach their Lordships would take to Panatown's claim was likely to be influenced in large measure by how they characterised the question before them. Was it whether Panatown could recover substantial damages for a loss suffered by UIPL? Or was it whether Panatown could recover substantial damages for its own loss? Could it even be a combination of those questions? If it were the first, and it were assumed that the loss had been suffered by UIPL, the problem would in effect be one of privity because of UIPL's inability to sue on a contract to which it was not a party. That could, inter alia, suggest that, having regard to the recently enacted Contracts (Rights of Third Parties) Act 1999 and the report of the Law Commission on which it was based,[16] the courts ought not to interfere in an area so recently considered by the legislature. On the other hand, if the loss were Panatown's, the issue would be simply one of damages and the legislation would be irrelevant. More importantly, however, an assumption that the loss was UIPL's had the potential to colour the reasoning of both court and counsel in at least three ways. First, the *Dunlop v Lambert* rule is directed specifically to situations where the loss is that of a third party. To apply that rule would therefore be the obvious choice. Secondly, if the loss were indeed that of UIPL, it would in logic be very difficult to conclude that it could at the same time have been suffered by Panatown, which is what the broad view would then have required. Thirdly, the same assumption as to loss would have made it inevitable that, should Panatown recover substantial damages, it would have to account for them to UIPL. As Lord Millett observed:

> Compensation for a third party's loss is a contradiction in terms. It is impossible on any logical basis to justify the recovery of compensatory damages by a person who has not suffered the loss in respect of which they are awarded unless he is accountable for them to the person who has.[17]

As will be seen, most of the discussion in the majority speeches does in fact assume that the promisee (Panatown) is suing to recover a loss suffered by a third party (UIPL). That is hardly surprising since a good deal of the discourse in this area, in both textbooks and legal journals, has been conducted in those terms and on that assumption. Whether and how far the assumption is correctly made in a building construction case like *Panatown* is a question which will need to be considered at a later point.

[16] *Report on Privity of Contract; Contracts for the Benefit of Third Parties* (Law Com No 242, 1996).
[17] [2000] 3 WLR 946 (HL), 1005.

## The Narrow Ground

All five of their Lordships were agreed that the rule in *Dunlop v Lambert* was a rule of law having its origins in a misunderstanding of what that case had been about.[18] There was much less agreement as to the extent to which its modern revival in *The Albazero*[19] had been limited by the speech of Lord Diplock in that case where his Lordship had extended the rule from contracts of carriage to commercial contracts concerning goods generally. But he had also seemed to confine it to situations where the contracting parties contemplated that ownership of the goods would be transferred at a later date. He also stated that the rule could not be extended to contracts for the carriage of goods which contemplated that the carrier would in due course enter into separate contracts of carriage with the new owners. Such a case was a charterparty which provided for the issue of bills of lading to cover goods shipped on the chartered vessel, which bills would have the effect of contracts once ownership had passed. In such cases the shipowner could not have been intended to accept concurrent liabilities to be sued for the same loss of or damage to the same goods under the two contracts.

Where their Lordships disagreed was on whether the rule as thus expounded by Lord Diplock could properly be applied to a building contract and, if so, whether the separate rights of action given UIPL under the DCD defeated Panatown's claim. In the *St Martins* case,[20] Lord Griffiths had distinguished between a claim, as in *The Albazero*, for loss of or damage to goods and a claim under a building contract where what was in issue was the non-performance of a bargain. In *Panatown*, Lord Goff also regarded the invocation of the rule in *Dunlop v Lambert* as 'inapposite' in such cases.[21] He saw that rule as a response to the problem that only the party who had suffered a loss could recover damages for it, which was not the problem here. It was not that UIPL had no enforceable rights under the building contract. On the contrary, it had been given its own, albeit different, rights under a separate contract, the DCD. Moreover, there was no question here of the contracting party's property being transferred to a third party after the contract had been entered into. Yet such a transfer was regarded by Lord Diplock as essential and had been present in the *St Martins* case. What was at issue in the instant case was the effectiveness of the rights conferred on Panatown under the building contract. Lord Millett drew similar distinctions between a contract of carriage where the loss was suffered by the person who owned the property at the date of breach and a contract for the supply of services.[22] The rationale of *Dunlop v Lambert* was lacking, there being no need to

18 See in particular the speech of Lord Clyde, ibid, 949–54, for a detailed discussion of the background to the case.

19 [1977] AC 774 (HL), 847–8.

20 [1994] 1 AC 85 (HL), 97.

21 [2000] 3 WLR 946 (HL), 970ff.

22 ibid, 1009.

treat a building employer with no title to the land as contracting on behalf of a building owner who, unlike succeeding owners, was already identifiable and perfectly capable of contracting on his own behalf. To extend the benefit of the rule beyond the successors in title of the original contracting party to anyone with an interest in the property was to go too far and would come near to repealing the rule as to compensatory damages.

For the most part, the three Lords of Appeal in the majority found it unnecessary to consider these sorts of objections. All of them saw the basic question as being whether a promisee could recover damages for a loss suffered by a third party and, on ordinary compensatory principles, that patently was not possible.[23] However, the rule ascribed to *Dunlop v Lambert*, as restated in *The Albazero*, created an exception which had been extended to building contracts by the House itself in the *St Martins* case. Its justification was that it supplied a remedy where no other would be available and which any rational legal system ought to provide.[24] That justification ceased if some other remedy were available to the injured third party. Their Lordships were agreed that the rights of action given UIPL under the DCD were sufficient to exclude any application of the rule.[25] In addition, both Lord Clyde[26] and Lord Browne-Wilkinson[27] thought that the recent legislation made judicial development of the rights of third parties inappropriate, at least on the facts of the present case.

## The *Albazero* Exception

Under the DCD which, it will be recalled, was entered into on the same day as the building contract itself, McAlpine undertook to UIPL that

> … in respect of all matters that lie within the scope of his responsibilities under the building contract, (a) he has exercised and will continue to exercise all reasonable skill, care and attention; (b) he shall owe a duty of care to the building owner in respect of such matters; (c) the building owner shall be entitled to rely upon the contractor's professional skill and judgment in respect of such matters as defined in the terms of the building contract.

Since the obligations undertaken under a building contract go beyond the mere exercise of reasonable skill and care, the DCD and the building contract with Panatown could not be said to cover the same ground. Nevertheless, Lord Clyde saw the deed as a reflection of the parties' deliberate intention that the third party

[23] [2000] 3 WLR 946 (HL), 954–5 per Lord Clyde; 992 per Lord Jauncey; 999, 1000 and 1002 per Lord Browne-Wilkinson.

[24] ibid, 955 per Lord Clyde; 992 per Lord Jauncey; 1001 per Lord Browne-Wilkinson; see also [1977] AC 774 (HL), 847; [1994] 1 AC 85 (HL), 114.

[25] ibid, 957 per Lord Clyde; 993 per Lord Jauncey; 1001 per Lord Browne-Wilkinson.

[26] ibid, 960.

[27] ibid, 1002–3.

have a direct cause of action to the exclusion of any substantial claim by the employer. For him, the difference between a strict contractual basis of claim and a basis of reasonable care made the DCD all the more clearly a substitution which invoked the operation of the *Dunlop v Lambert* exception.[28] Lord Jauncey took a similar view. What was important, as he saw it, was that the third party should have been given the right to recover substantial damages for breach of its own contract even if they were not identical to those which would have been recovered under the main contract.[29] For his part, Lord Browne-Wilkinson, in a passage to which it will be necessary to return, saw the building contract and the DCD as forming a contractual matrix which envisaged 'that McAlpine's obligations under the building contract were to be enforceable against McAlpine *not only by Panatown* but also to a very substantial extent by UIPL'.[30] With the existence of a direct remedy for the third party, 'the whole rationale of the rule' disappeared.

Lord Goff and Lord Millett took a very different view. The former thought it 'a strange conclusion indeed' that the effect of providing a subsidiary remedy for the third party on restricted terms should prevent enforcement by the principal party, who had provided the consideration, of the elaborate and specially adapted provisions of the main contract.[31] He cited the passages from the speech of Lord Diplock in *The Albazero*[32] from which that result was said to follow, and to which reference has already been made. In Lord Goff's view, those passages showed that the exception to *Dunlop v Lambert* was confined to claims for loss of or damage to goods where it had been contemplated that a third person who had acquired an interest in the goods would himself enter into a separate contract of carriage with the same carrier. He was impressed by the suggestion[33] that the real purpose of the DCD had been to provide a remedy in negligence (to fill the gap left by *Murphy v Brentwood District Council*[34]) for the benefit of subsequent owners, to whom the DCD expressly contemplated assignment. It was because of the need to have something to assign that the rights created by the deed had first to vest in UIPL. This explanation was also accepted by Lord Millett who thought it could not have been contemplated that UIPL would itself have relied on the DCD. The parties would have supposed that a much better cause of action would have been

[28] ibid, 957.
[29] ibid, 993.
[30] ibid, 1001 (emphasis added).
[31] ibid, 982.
[32] [1977] AC 774 (HL), 847–8.
[33] D Lewis, 'Investigating the JCT Standard Forms of Agreement for Collateral Warranty' (1997) 13 *Construction Law Journal* 305.
[34] *Murphy v Brentwood District Council* [1991] AC 398 (HL).

available under the building contract itself.[35] As it happens, Lord Browne-Wilkinson, in the passage quoted above,[36] seems to concede that the parties would have at least envisaged enforcement of the building contract by Panatown.

Had the contrary been the case, it might be asked why the claim had not been brought directly by UIPL under the DCD, since they and Panatown were so closely connected. While the precise reasons can only be a matter of speculation, one or two possible explanations do occur. As was pointed out by Evans LJ in the Court of Appeal,[37] there was not just the difference between absolute and negligence liability. The building contract contained an arbitration clause (under which the present litigation had been commenced) and provisions relating to liquidated damages and extensions of time. Moreover, McAlpine's parent company guaranteed its performance of the building contract but not of its liability under the DCD. Perhaps an even stronger reason, both for proceeding under the building contract rather than the DCD and for intending that it rather than the DCD be the principal contract, would have been a desire, identified by Mr Duncan Wallace QC,[38] to preserve budgetary certainty and to avoid the 'limitless defences' and 'best endeavours' arguments made possible by a claim in negligence.

The fact that the building contract and the DCD were in such different terms raises the further question of how great the difference can be before the *Albazero* exception would cease to apply. In the *St Martins* case, Lord Browne-Wilkinson had said:

> If, pursuant to the terms of the original building contract, the contractors *have undertaken liability to the ultimate purchasers to remedy defects* appearing after they acquired the property, it is manifest the case will not fall within the rationale of *Dunlop v Lambert.* If the ultimate purchaser is given a direct cause of action against the contractor (as is the consignee or endorsee under a bill of lading) the case falls outside the loss suffered by others *who can themselves sue for such loss.*[39]

In *Panatown,* however, McAlpine's undertaking was not to remedy defects generally but only those caused by want of care and, as we have seen, Lord Clyde thought the difference between a direct contractual basis and one of reasonable care made the express remedy given by the DCD all the more clearly a substitution which involved the operation of the exception.[40] Nor, it now seems, is the exception to be confined to loss for which the third party could itself sue. It appears to have been accepted by the majority judges that Panatown's rights of

[35] [2000] 3 WLR 946 (HL), 1018.

[36] Above n 30.

[37] (1998) 14 *Construction Law Journal* 267 (CA), 277–9.

[38] D Wallace, 'Defects and Third Parties: No Peace for the Wicked?' (1999) 15 *Construction Law Journal* 245, 254.

[39] [1994] 1 AC 85 (HL), 115 (emphasis added).

[40] [2000] 3 WLR 946 (HL), 957.

action under the *Dunlop v Lambert* rule had been displaced altogether, even in respect of loss which, because not due to want of care, would not have been recoverable by UIPL under the DCD.

Another problem with the solution reached by the majority, it is submitted with respect, is its artificiality, a result which it is believed is not necessarily inherent in the *Albazero* exception. It will be recalled that Lord Diplock referred in particular to a charterparty where it was envisaged that bills of lading would be issued for the particular goods to be shipped in the chartered vessel, which would in turn become the shipowner's contracts of carriage with subsequent owners of the goods. An essential point, here, was that there would, in such a case, be

> ... no sensible business reason for inferring that the shipowner in entering into the charterparty intended to accept concurrent liabilities to be sued for the same loss or damage by the charterer and by the consignee or indorsee of the bill of lading.[41]

What the exception required, therefore, was that the contracts subsequently entered into should have been envisaged and intended to *supersede* and *replace* the carrier's obligations to the charterer in respect of the same loss or damage.

In the *Panatown* case, by contrast, the DCD, far from constituting a subsequent replacement for the building contract, was a contemporary part of a single contractual matrix. Moreover, the land and, hence, potentially, anything built upon it, belonged to UIPL from the start. Accordingly, on the 'narrow' view of the majority, at no point could Panatown have suffered a loss recoverable in damages or had a claim in respect of breach of the building contract (unless for nominal damages) either at common law or under the *Dunlop v Lambert* rule. Nor is it likely they could have relied instead on specific performance, since large and complex building contracts have not so far been treated as specifically enforceable.[42] They doubtless could have withheld payments, but that would also have been true of an agreement binding in honour only. So far as McAlpine's *obligations* were concerned, the building contract would, for any practical purposes, have operated merely as a sort of schedule to the DCD by reference to which its duties of care could be measured. On the other hand, since the DCD appears not to have contained any reciprocal undertakings by either Panatown or UIPL (whence the recourse to a deed), McAlpine would have had to look for its *rights* to the building contract, presumably as modified by reference to the DCD. So its obligations ended up being defined by a contract with one party and its rights by quite a different contract with another. Could there really have been no sensible business reason for inferring that the parties intended any other result?

[41] [1977] AC 774 (HL), 848.

[42] Specific performance has been granted of a covenant to repair in a lease (*Price v Strange* [1978] 1 Ch 337). But with large and complex building contracts, the problem of supervision would presumably remain.

Or being, in Lord Millett's words, 'businessmen and more sensible than lawyers',[43] would they have envisaged something rather more orthodox? If so, would there not be good grounds for seeking, if possible, a 'sensible solution on a principled basis'[44] rather closer to the expectations of laypersons? It is this, of course, which Lord Goff and Lord Millett sought to find in Lord Griffiths' broader ground and in the concept of a performance interest.

## The Broad Ground

It is not proposed here to canvass fully the arguments their Lordships advanced in support of the wider ground. Their speeches did, however, contain large areas of agreement. Both concluded the contractual loss was that of Panatown and that the issue raised was accordingly one of damages and not of privity.[45] For that reason, the Contracts (Rights of Third Parties) Act 1999 and the report on which it was based ought not to prevent judicial development of the rights of a promisee. Earlier cases such as *Woodar Investment Development Ltd v Wimpey Construction UK Ltd*,[46] *Jackson v Horizon Holidays Ltd*,[47] *Radford v De Froberville*[48] and *Ruxley Electronics and Construction Ltd v Forsyth*[49] had tended towards the recognition of a performance interest, and academic comment on Lord Griffiths' wider ground had been numerous and generally favourable. (More than a dozen textbooks and articles were referred to.) Unless Panatown were able to recover substantial damages, it would effectively have been without a remedy should McAlpine repudiate the building contract.[50] Both thought damages for delay should be recoverable by a promisee as being part of the bargain for which consideration had been given.[51] They also seemed to agree that, the loss being that of the promisee, he would not without more be accountable to the third party for the damages recovered.[52] However, an intention to devote the proceeds to the provision of alternative performance could be relevant as going to reasonableness, that is, to whether damages should be recoverable in the first place.[53] For various reasons, neither saw any serious risk of double recovery, and certainly not in the case before them.[54]

[43] [2000] 3 WLR 946 (HL), 1017.
[44] ibid, 978 per Lord Goff.
[45] ibid, 971 and 983 per Lord Goff, and 1011 and 1016 per Lord Millett.
[46] *Woodar Investment Development Ltd v Wimpey Construction UK Ltd* [1980] 1 WLR 277 (HL).
[47] *Jackson v Horizon Holidays Ltd* [1975] 1 WLR 1468 (CA).
[48] *Radford v De Froberville* [1977] 1 WLR 1262 (Ch).
[49] [1996] AC 344 (HL).
[50] [2000] 3 WLR 946 (HL), 971 per Lord Goff, and 1016 per Lord Millett.
[51] ibid, 980 per Lord Goff, and 1015 per Lord Millett.
[52] ibid, 1016 per Lord Millett; *cf* ibid, 984–5 per Lord Goff, and 959 per Lord Clyde.
[53] ibid, 1016 per Lord Millett; *cf* ibid, 975–6 per Lord Goff.
[54] ibid, 985–6 per Lord Goff, and 1019 per Lord Millett.

Lord Millett drew an analogy with a contract between A and B under which A undertook to sell goods to B and deliver them to a non-party, C.[55] Clearly, B could recover substantial damages for breach, despite the intention to benefit C. To award only nominal damages because the contract was for the supply of services rather than goods would produce an artificial distinction and would be 'indefensible'. His Lordship was inclined 'for the present' to restrict the broad ground to contracts for the supply of work and materials. Lord Goff thought that full recognition of the performance interest would open the way to a principled solution of 'other well-known problems in the law of contract'. He gave, as an example, package holidays booked by one person for members of his family.[56]

Of the three judges of the majority, Lord Clyde and Lord Jauncey preferred to confine Lord Griffiths' dicta to situations where the promisee had himself paid for alternative performance or would account to the third party for any damages awarded. Otherwise, the promisee would have suffered no loss.[57] Lord Jauncey distinguished the *Radford* case on the ground that, there, the works were to be performed for the benefit of the promisee's own property.[58] He also considered that Panatown's having been supplied with the contract moneys from elsewhere in the group was a further reason for saying it had suffered no loss.[59] Towards the end of his speech, he commented that he agreed with Lord Goff that the third party's ownership of the land did not prevent recovery by the promisee, but such recovery would have to depend on whether he had made good the effects of the breach or intended to do so.[60] Lord Browne-Wilkinson's view was that, even assuming that the wider view prevailed (and he acknowledged that examination by academic writers had disclosed no serious difficulties, though there was some division of opinion on accountability), the fact that the DCD gave UIPL 'the right to enforce the contract' meant that the instant case was not an appropriate one 'for developing the rights of third parties'.[61]

As mentioned, Lord Clyde agreed with Lord Griffiths' broad ground to the extent that it depended upon the promisee paying to obtain alternative performance.[62] But to any suggestion that the wider ground properly could go beyond that, he was unconvinced. In the first place, he saw the proper measure of damages to be applied as being not the cost of repair but the difference in value. (It is, of course, this approach to damages in some, though not all, situations which caused the problem of the black hole in the first place.) Secondly, consequential loss might not be recoverable. Thirdly, since the claim would be for damages, there would be no obligation to account to the party who had actually

[55] ibid, 1013.
[56] ibid, 977.
[57] ibid, 958–9 per Lord Clyde, and 998 per Lord Jauncey.
[58] ibid, 996.
[59] ibid, 998.
[60] ibid.
[61] ibid, 1003.
[62] ibid, 958–9.

suffered the loss, thereby raising the risk of 'double' jeopardy. If the promisee did have to account to the third party, the result would anyway approximate to the *Albazero* principle. Fourthly, the 'loss' caused by a breach of contract, in the absence of damage, has historically sounded in nominal damages only. A breach of contract is not itself a loss, though it may cause a loss. In the third-party cases, the promisee suffers only a 'theoretical loss'.

## Who Suffered the Loss?

It was suggested earlier that the ascription of loss was likely to influence the way in which their Lordships would view the *Panatown* case. In the event, the three judges in the majority did appear to have assumed that it was UIPL, as building owner, which had suffered the loss. Accordingly, it would hardly have been consistent to treat the loss as having instead been suffered by Panatown. It followed that the solution to the black hole would have to be found in *Dunlop v Lambert*, which was specifically directed to cases of third-party loss or damage, rather than in a wider ground which placed the loss where *ex hypothesi* it was not. Hence, too, the need to limit Lord Griffiths' wider ground to cases where the promisee had paid for alternative performance or was otherwise accountable to the third party for any damages suffered. By the same token, placing the loss with UIPL meant that, while a claim for damages arose, the problem was at root one of privity and the rights of third parties. In these and other ways, therefore, the question of who suffered the loss was of central importance. Yet it was not expressly discussed by the majority. And though Lord Goff and Lord Millett argued affirmatively and at length that the loss was that of the promisee, neither devoted as much argument to the negative proposition, that UIPL had not suffered the loss. However, Lord Millett did say:

> It is to my mind far from axiomatic that the loss arising from the defective or incomplete performance is suffered exclusively by the building owner and not, or not also, by the building employer who ordered and promised to pay for the works to be carried out.[63]

It is submitted, again with respect, that Lord Millett was right and that the assumption that the loss was UIPL's is indeed far from axiomatic. It has to be remembered that whatever the commercial relations amongst the three parties might have been outside the building contract, UIPL was in respect of *that* contract a volunteer and stood to receive, by way of improvements to its land, benefits for which it had provided no consideration and for which it had not contracted.[64] In lay terms, therefore, UIPL would, so far as the building contract

[63] ibid, 1008.

[64] According to Lord Goff (ibid, 962), it was common ground that Panatown entered into the building contract as principal and not as UIPL's agent, for reasons to do with the incidence of VAT.

was concerned, have received the improvements as a benefit akin to a gift. It then has to be asked how far one can be said to have suffered loss or damage just because a gift one has received is defective. In the course of his speech in the *Murphy* case,[65] Lord Oliver of Aylmerton gave the example of a builder who had built a house with inadequate foundations and had presented it to his son and daughter-in-law as a wedding present. In his view, it would be 'manifestly absurd, if the son spends money on rectifying the defect, … to hold him entitled to recover the expenditure from the father because the gift turns out to be less advantageous than he at first supposed'. Earlier in the same speech,[66] his Lordship gave the further example of an owner-occupier who had inherited a defective property, of whom he commented: 'He suffers, in fact, no loss save that the property for which he paid nothing is less valuable to him by the amount which it will cost him to repair it if he wishes to continue to live in it.' Lord Oliver was, of course, speaking in the context of a tort action but the illustrations are nonetheless apt. The fact that a gift is less or other than what was hoped for by the recipient does not by itself constitute loss or damage in the legal sense of those words. Even expenditure on repairing the defect is merely by way of augmentation or improvement of the benefit as received. It is true that if the works are so defective that they have to be demolished and removed, a non-party owner of the land can suffer loss or damage if the land was his to begin with. The measure of that loss or damage would be the cost of demolition and removal and might well be recoverable in tort. Again, since by accession any improvements automatically become the property of the owner from the moment of installation, actions which damaged works already done could create a loss, the measure of which would be the cost of repairing that damage. Loss and damage of those kinds could well be substantial but that is not primarily what the *Panatown* claim was about.

What Panatown was claiming and what UIPL was supposed to have 'lost' was performance, as specified, of the building contract. And that 'loss' could have involved not just the demolition of the new structure but its complete replacement. Arguably, therefore, we have the somewhat ironic result that the expectation by someone not a party to a contract that it would be performed is by some fiction of the law accounted a loss to the non-party but only a 'theoretical' or nominal loss to a promisee who was not only a party to the contract but also provided the consideration for it. In other words, the performance interest of a non-party is being recognised at the same time as the performance interest of an actual party is being denied! The fact that UIPL could have had a claim under the DCD is not the point. It is clear that, on the view of the majority, had there been no DCD, any recovery of substantial damages by Panatown under *Dunlop v*

Nor, presumably for similar reasons, is there any statement that UIPL contracted with Panatown, as principal, for the erection of the building by McAlpine (*cf* ibid, 1017 per Lord Millett).

65 [1991] AC 398 (HL), 490.

66 ibid, 488.

*Lambert* would have been in respect of UIPL's assumed loss and Panatown would have been accountable to UIPL for them.

## The Position Where Both Have Suffered Loss

One of the objections raised to reliance on the performance interest has been that it does not answer the problem of consequential loss actually suffered by the third party.[67] It is submitted, however, that solutions ought to be available. One would be to recognise that the performance interest extends to performance of the contractual promise in its entirety and that this could include the promisor's obligation not to cause consequential loss to third parties where such loss is within the contemplation of the contracting parties.[68] In that case, the promisee could in practice be accountable to the third party as a trustee for the damages recovered in respect of such loss, or perhaps on the basis of its being something which went to reasonableness.[69] A more direct route to a similar result would be to allow a claim by the promisee to operate at two levels, under the ordinary common law rules in respect of his performance interest, and under *Dunlop v Lambert* for losses actually suffered by the third party, with consequent accountability for the latter proportion of the damages recovered. If the thought of separately based claims appears slightly inelegant, it is submitted that it would be no more so than the solution proposed by Lord Clyde at the end of his speech when he said:

> It seems to me a more realistic and practical solution is to permit the contracting party to recover damages for the loss which he and a third party has suffered, being duly accountable to them in respect of their actual loss ...[70]

Read out of context, that proposition has an appealing simplicity. In fact, though, it comes after a passage in which his Lordship had, in effect, rejected the notion of a performance interest. Based on the *Dunlop v Lambert* rule,[71] it assumes that in a building contract case like *Panatown* the loss from defective performance is that of the third party. Unless what Lord Clyde had in mind was a claim for nominal damages, the promisee, if he were to recover anything for himself, would have to rely on some cause of action at common law other than a breach of the building contract. *Ex hypothesi,* he could not rely on *Dunlop v Lambert.* The result would be a two-tier claim, in part under the ordinary law and in part under the special rule. In respect of any claims under the building contract, he would necessarily be accountable to the third party for all substantial damages recovered. He would,

[67] See, eg, [2000] 3 WLR 946 (HL), 959 per Lord Clyde.

[68] *cf* ibid, 980 per Lord Goff.

[69] See above n 52.

[70] [2000] 3 WLR 946 (HL), 960.

[71] Lord Clyde had earlier (ibid, 956) envisaged that a *Dunlop v Lambert* decision could include consequential loss by the third party.

therefore, have no control over their application. For a promisee who had accepted the contractual risks and provided the consideration, that might well be thought rather unattractive.

## Conclusion

The *Panatown* case raised questions fundamental to the nature of contractual obligation and to the role of contract damages. They include questions about which differing views have long been held and it would be asking too much to hope that they could have been resolved in a single case, no matter how exalted the forum. It would therefore be a great pity if the decision in *Panatown* were taken to be the last word, whether on *Dunlop v Lambert* and its exception, or on the nature of the performance interest.

In the meantime, those who accepted the invitation in *St Martins* to write about Lord Griffiths' broad ground can be grateful that their contributions have been taken into account (and duly acknowledged).

# 10

# Contract not Trust: Some Questions about the Contracts (Rights of Third Parties) Act from another Perspective

ALTHOUGH THE DIFFERENT drafting might suggest otherwise, the Contracts (Rights of Third Parties) Act 1999 of England and Wales (hereinafter 'the C3PA')[1] is, in important respects, similar to the New Zealand Contracts (Privity) Act 1982 (hereinafter 'the (Privity) Act') and, as perusal of the Law Commission's Consultation Paper[2] and Report[3] confirms, was clearly influenced by it. When it appeared, the (Privity) Act attracted relatively little adverse comment, no doubt in part because of the limited size of the local legal academic community. So far as I can recall, the main criticism came from an Australian law teacher, Peter Kincaid, who at a conference in Wellington questioned the justification for any such reform on grounds substantially those he has since elaborated in a series of articles.[4]

Given the much greater corps of potential commentators, it was inevitable that the C3PA should attract a wider range of comment,[5] some of which has been collected into two substantial books.[6] The two pieces of legislation being basically similar, several of the questions raised have been potentially relevant to both. The

[1] The abbreviation used by Professor Chee Ho Tham, 'Trust, not Contract: Restoring Trust in the Contracts (Rights of Third Parties) Act' (2005) 21 *Journal of Contract Law* 108, which I gratefully adopt.

[2] *Privity of Contract: Contracts for the Benefit of Third Parties* (L Com No 121, 1991).

[3] *Privity of Contract: Contracts for the Benefit of Third Parties* (L Com No 242, Cm 3329, 1996).

[4] P Kincaid, 'Third Parties: Rationalising a Right to Sue' [1989] *Journal of Contract Law* 243; 'Privity and the Essence of Contract' (1989) 12 *University of New South Wales Law Journal* 59; 'The UK Law Commission's Privity Proposals and Contract Theory' (1994) 8 *Journal of Contract Law* 51; 'Privity and Private Justice in Contract' (1997) 12 *Journal of Contract Law* 47; and 'Privity Reform in England: The Contracts (Rights of Third Parties) Act 1999' (2000) 116 *Law Quarterly Review* 43.

[5] See, eg, the list provided by Professor Phang in 'On Justification and Method in Law Reform The Contracts (Rights of Third Parties) Act 1999' (2002) 18 *Journal of Contract Law* 32, 33–4 (fn 7). See also R Stevens, 'The Contracts (Rights of Third Parties) Act 1999' (2004) 120 *Law Quarterly Review* 292.

[6] R Merkin (ed), *Privity of Contract: The Impact of the Contracts (Right of Third Parties) Act 1999* (London, LLP, 2000); P Kincaid (ed), *Privity: Private Justice or Public Regulation* (Aldershot, Ashgate, 2001).

New Zealand Act derived from a Report and Draft Bill[7] prepared by the local Contracts and Commercial Law Reform Committee (hereinafter 'the CCLRC') of which I was a member. What I have found most interesting about the published comment on the C3PA and its preceding Consultation Paper and Report has been the ingenuity with which grounds have been found on which to criticise or question both the provisions and the purposes of the reform. The recent article by Professor Chee Ho Tham[8] is the latest in this line. The present chapter can be seen as an admittedly rather subjective reaction to some of the points made in that article, from one who was involved (with the other members of the CCLRC) in drawing up the New Zealand Report and Draft Bill.

If I have understood them correctly, Professor Chee's chief concerns are threefold.[9] First, he says, the cause of action created by s 1 of the C3PA is obscure and, arguably, cannot be interpreted in a manner consistent with the view that its underlying basis is contractual. Secondly, because the third party (in the (Privity) Act called 'the beneficiary') is a volunteer vis-à-vis the head contract, he may well be debarred by that fact from access to equitable remedies. Thirdly, if the right of action under s 1 were contractual, double liability could well result where, the price having been paid in advance, the beneficiary recovers damages for non-performance if the promisee, at the same time, is able to pursue a claim in restitution for the amount prepaid. The solution offered by Professor Chee to these perceived problems is to treat claims made under s 1 as being based on a relaxation of the requirements for the existence of a trust rather than as a weakening of the common law requirements of privity and consideration in the formation of a contractual cause of action.[10] It is proposed to discuss these questions in the order followed by the Professor.

## Contract or Not?

The s 1 cause of action is, of course, a creature of statute, as is its equivalent under the (Privity) Act. The question at issue is whether what the two Acts have created is a statutory form of contract. Alternatively, are the legal obligations created in favour of the third party contractual in nature so that breach attracts, effectively, the same consequences as a breach of contract? Put another way, is the legal relationship between promisor and third-party beneficiary determined 'as if' they had been parties to a contract between them? The provisions most directly relevant to those questions are, in the case of the C3PA:

7 CCLRC, *Privity of Contract* (Wellington, Dept of Justice, 1981).
8 Above n 1.
9 ibid, 110.
10 ibid, 110–11 and 117ff.

**1. Right of third party to enforce contractual term**

(1) Subject to the provisions of this Act, a person who is not a party to a contract (a 'third party') may in his own right enforce a term of the contract if—

(a) the contract expressly provides that he may, or

(b) subject to subsection (2), the term purports to confer a benefit on him.

(2) Subsection (1)(b) does not apply if on a proper construction of the contract it appears that the parties did not intend the term to be enforceable by the third party.

...

(5) For the purpose of exercising his right to enforce a term of the contract, there shall be available to the third party any remedy that would have been available to him in an action for breach of contract if he had been a party to the contract (and the rules relating to damages, injunctions, specific performance and other relief shall apply accordingly).

**7. Supplementary provisions relating to third party**

...

(3) In sections 5 and 8 of the Limitation Act 1980 the references to an action founded on a simple contract and an action upon a specialty shall respectively include references to an action brought in reliance on section 1 relating to a simple contract and an action brought in reliance on that section relating to a specialty.

The equivalent provisions of the (Privity) Act are:

**4. Deeds or contracts for the benefit of third parties—**

Where a promise contained in a deed or contract confers, or purports to confer, a benefit on a person, designated by name, description or reference to a class, who is not a party to the deed or contract (whether or not the person is in existence at the time when the deed or contract is made), the promisor shall be under an obligation, enforceable at the suit of that person, to perform that promise:

Provided that this section shall not apply to a promise which, on the proper construction of the deed or contract, is not intended to create, in respect of the benefit, an obligation enforceable at the suit of that person.

**8. Enforcement by beneficiary—**

The obligation imposed on a promisor by section 4 of this Act may be enforced at the suit of the beneficiary as if he were a party to the deed or contract, and relief in respect of the promise, including relief by way of damages, specific performance, or injunction, shall not be refused on the ground that the beneficiary is not a party to the deed or contract in which the promise is contained or that, as against the promisor, the beneficiary is a volunteer.

In the (Privity) Act, there is no express reference to the limitation of actions but that matter would presumably be covered by s 7, which accords to the promisor the defences which would have been available had the beneficiary been a party to the deed or contract in which the provision was contained.

Although in the end it may make very little difference which answer is correct, it can certainly be argued that both Acts have either created new statutory forms of contract or, alternatively, while not actually deeming promisor and beneficiary to be parties to a contract between them or with the promisee, in effect dictate that for practical purposes they be treated as though they were.

## A New Form of Contract?

Whether the two Acts can be said to have created new, if limited, forms of contract depends, like most important questions of contract, on the first principles from which argument proceeds. In this instance, the answer depends, essentially, on what a contract is conceived to be. Clearly, if contracts are thought of exclusively as bargains which require offer and acceptance, consideration, and agreement between the parties as essential to their existence, the relationship between promisor and third-party beneficiary cannot possibly constitute a contract. As Professor Chee himself says, to suggest otherwise may even be thought by some to threaten the very foundations of the law of contract.[11] It is submitted, however, that this is to adopt much too narrow a definition. The requirement for consideration, for example, is exclusive to the common law system and has no conceptual equivalent in the civil law. Even within the common law system itself, there are simple contracts like letters of credit and compositions with creditors which require no consideration. And within Commonwealth countries, the consideration requirement has been modified, at least to some degree, by appellate courts in England,[12] Australia,[13] Canada[14] and New Zealand.[15] It is also possible at common law for a promisor, by the use of a deed, to assume a binding legal obligation to a beneficiary who has provided no consideration—a facility which has its equivalents in civil law countries. Such deeds can properly be regarded as a type of contract, even in the absence of a bargain, the mark of which is not consideration but the use of a form, and could themselves nowadays be said to be the creatures of statute where their form is prescribed by legislation.[16] In the light of all this, the possibility that a legislature might have provided a new additional facility by which contractual obligations could be assumed ought to appear rather less improbable.

[11] ibid, 109, citing in particular the writings of Kincaid, above n 4. So much for the adage that the exception proves the rule!

[12] *Williams v Roffey Bros & Nicholls (Contractors) Ltd* [1991] 1 QB 1 (CA) (see ch 3 of this book); and see also *Homburg Hout Import BV v Agrosin Private Ltd* [2004] 1 AC 715 (HL), 744, 749 and 801 (hereinafter '*The Starsin*').

[13] *Trident General Co Ltd v McNiece Bros Pty Ltd* (1988) 165 CLR 107 (High Court of Australia).

[14] *London Drugs Ltd v Kuehne Nagel International Ltd* [1992] 3 SCR 299 (SCC).

[15] *Antons Trawling Co Ltd v Smith* [2003] 2 NZLR 23 (CA) (see ch 4 of this book).

[16] eg s 9 of the Property Law Act 2007 (NZ).

In the first volume of the *Journal of Contract Law*,[17] I argued that, in essence, a contract is a promise by which legal contractual obligation has effectively been assumed and that the institution of contract is a facility provided by society and the state in order to make such an assumption possible. Naturally enough, whether such an assumption was intended and has occurred has to be determined objectively. A bilateral contract is brought into existence by the mutual exchange of these assumptions of contractual obligation; and the exchange is also, in the case of simple contracts for consideration at common law, the exchange of the considerations which each provides for the other. But it does not follow that these need be the only ways in which contractual obligation can be assumed. From this viewpoint, the provisions of the two privity Acts could very plausibly be regarded as having created a new form of contract, albeit of only limited application. The indicia are there: a promise made with an intention, express, implied or imputed, to assume legal obligation which is to be enforceable in substantially the same manner as more conventional contracts; and the provision by law of a facility enabling such assumptions to be made, within the limits prescribed. Even consideration is present, albeit supplied by a third party. If it is asked why society and the state should have intervened to provide such a facility, the answer would be the same as for conventional contracts: that in general they serve the classic governance objectives of peace, order and good government[18] and, in addition, that the new facility helps to plug a gap identified as such by a succession of practitioners, judges and legal academics.[19]

However, if that view of what constitutes a contract is too radical, there remains the alternative that promisor and third-party beneficiary are required by the respective Acts to be treated 'as if' they had been parties to a contract either between themselves or with the promisee. Thus, under s 1(5) of the C3PA, the remedies available to the third party are all expressed to be the same as would have been available to him for breach of contract had he been a party to the head contract. The same result would follow under s 8 of the (Privity) Act. There may be a possible analogy here with the effect of art III r 8 of the Hague Rules which, according to Lord Millett in the House of Lords,[20] is that an owner or demise charterer can become a party to a contract of carriage without having met the ordinary requirement that it undertake an obligation to carry. But whichever approach to the Acts is adopted, it is submitted that there is nothing, thus far, in either of them to compel the view that what they are intended to provide is a facility for creating a new form of trust. Certainly, as one of those who helped to

[17] See ch 2 of this book, especially at p 42ff.

[18] This expression appears in s 4 of the Colonial Laws Validity Act 1865 (Imp) and is not directed exclusively to the quelling of riots in the streets!

[19] This was a stated objective of the Law Commission. See the Report, above n 3, 41, and the discussion of the various grounds for criticism of the privity rule, 39–52.

[20] *The Starsin* [2004] 1 AC 715 (HL), 801.

draw up the Draft Bill on which the (Privity) Act was based, I doubt that such a result of the reform would have occurred to any of us.

## The Availability of Equitable Remedies

Professor Chee's argument that equitable remedies, in particular specific performance, would not be available to the third-party beneficiary (since, *ex hypothesi*, he would be a volunteer, at least so far as the promise of benefit was concerned) seems at first blush not implausible, although it would necessarily apply only to claims made under the C3PA. This is because s 8 of the (Privity) Act states expressly that relief under that Act shall not be refused on the ground that the beneficiary is a volunteer. In the case of the C3PA, however, if the head contract between promisor and promisee had been a simple contract for consideration, the short answer to the problem would be that to treat the third party for the purpose of remedy as if he were a party to the head contract, as s 1(5) requires, necessarily must mean treating him as though he had been a party to the consideration on which the existence of that contract depends. This is because, at least on my own view (which I see is shared by, amongst others, Peter Kincaid[21]), one cannot ordinarily be a party to a simple bilateral contract at common law without providing consideration for it. No doubt, the decision in *Coulls v Bagot's Executor & Trustee Co Ltd*[22] has been read the other way but, on the other hand, what Windeyer J had to say on the point is instructive.[23] To the argument that no consideration had moved from the plaintiff joint promisee in that case, he replied that consideration could include 'consideration given on behalf of [the joint promisees] and therefore *moving from* all of them'.[24] If consideration in that context can be treated in law as having moved from someone who has not himself provided it, why not in the present context also?

But the real answer must be that, in practice, no court would conceivably allow the obvious intention of the reform to be defeated by a technical argument of this kind. To treat the third party as a volunteer would set at naught the express provision in s 1(5) which makes available to him the equitable remedies of injunction and specific performance. It is no wonder that, in addressing a comparable provision of a local statute, a Western Australia court, in a case mentioned by Professor Chee,[25] should by a majority have accepted that sort of argument.[26] And while s 1 does not refer specifically to deeds, it would have to follow that the same conclusion must be true of deeds made for consideration.

21 See, eg, his 'Privity and Private Justice in Contract', above n 4, 56; *cf The Starsin* [2004] 1 AC 715 (HL), 801 per Lord Millett.

22 *Coulls v Bagot's Executor & Trustee Co Ltd* (1967) 119 CLR 460 (High Court of Australia).

23 ibid, 495. See ch 5 of this book.

24 ibid (emphasis added).

25 *Westralian Farmers Co-operative Ltd v Southern Meat Packers Ltd* [1981] WAR 241.

26 ibid, 245.

That does, however, leave unresolved the case of a deed made otherwise than for consideration, in respect of which different arguments would have to be found.

Once again, the question does not arise under the (Privity) Act, since s 4 contains an express reference to deeds, with the result that the absence of consideration could not be used by the promisor as a defence. It might perhaps be argued that the word 'contract' in s 1 of the C3PA could be read to include deeds generally, depending on whether a broad or a narrow definition of contract were adopted. If the former, the argument might be made that even voluntary deeds were covered. They are, after all, enforceable at common law, if not in equity. On the other hand, it could no longer be said that to deny the availability of specific performance and injunctions would defeat one of the purposes of the reform, since their availability in respect of contracts (and deeds) for consideration is enough to give adequate content to s 1(4). Another, perhaps despairing, argument might be based on the fact, noted by Fry J in *Gale v Gale*,[27] that there have been exceptions made in the past to the rule that deeds cannot be enforced by volunteers. According to Lord Hardwick,[28] those exceptions have been based on the proposition that the relevant provisions were 'reasonable, prudent and natural'. To invent a new exception in order to further the perceived general intent of the C3PA, on the ground that the results of so doing would be reasonable, prudent and natural, would be heroic but it would not be totally without precedent! The other possible course is simply to accept that s 1 was never intended to apply to voluntary deeds, in which case, while the third party would lose the benefit of the Act, he would, at least, still be able to pursue his remedies at common law.

## Failure of Consideration

As mentioned earlier, one of Professor Chee's main concerns is that, if the right of action under s 1 were contractual, double liability might be imposed on the promisor. The example he cites is of A promising B that he, A, will wash C's car if B pays him £20.[29] After receiving payment, A refuses to perform. Assuming C qualifies as a third party under the C3PA, he can then claim in damages the cost of getting someone else to wash the car for him (say £30). The Professor's argument is that even if A pays such damages to C, B has still suffered a total failure of consideration if C chooses to use the damages for some other purpose. The reason given is that B has obtained nothing of that for which he has contracted. There has been no performance of his contract with A either because the car remains unwashed or, if washed, because it has been washed by someone other than A.

[27] *Gale v Gale* (1877) 6 Ch D 144 (Ch), 150.
[28] *Jthell v Beane* (1749) 1 Ves Sen 215, 216.
[29] Above n 1, 126.

It has to be remembered that while both the C3PA and the (Privity) Act purport to create rights of enforcement for the third party, neither purports to take from the promisee whatever rights he might have apart from the legislation. Accordingly, if C, himself, fails to bring an action against A, B ought to be able to recover his £20 from A under the ordinary law. The perceived difficulty arises if C does in fact bring an action. If he recovers judgment and the damages are actually paid, it is submitted with respect that again no real difficulty should arise. Even if C fails to spend the damages on having the car washed, he has at least received the cost of alternative performance which means that B has received what Mason CJ has characterised as the equivalent in law of performance.[30] In other words, B's performance interest has been satisfied and there can be no failure of consideration. What might appear more problematic would be a situation where C has recovered judgment but A fails to pay and the amount owing proves to be irrecoverable. In that case, whatever the answer might be in theory, there would be little point in B's lodging a claim in restitution to recover his £20.

The other possibility is that B has recovered £20 from A but C subsequently and at long last himself claims to recover £30 from A in damages. Section 5 of the C3PA, which is headed 'Protection of promisor from double liability', arguably would not help since it applies only where the promisee has recovered from the promisor a claim in respect of (a) the third party's loss in respect of the term, or (b) the expense to the promisor of making good to the third party the default of the promisor. However, A should be entitled under either Act to the defence he would have had if C had been B, the promisee, which is that B had already recovered £20 from A in restitution.[31] Given the universal antipathy of the courts to double recovery, there can be no realistic prospect that in such a case C could recover from A judgment for more than £10. Professor Chee argues that to achieve such a result it is necessary to treat the C3PA cause of action as based on a species of trust.[32] With the greatest respect it is submitted that, as the foregoing demonstrates, no such recourse is required.

## Defences Available to the Promisee

As it happens, Professor Chee is not the only commentator to have identified a situation where the different drafting of the C3PA has created a problem which the New Zealand legislation has largely avoided. Referring to the C3PA, Robert Stevens writes:

[30] *Baltic Shipping Co v Dillon (The Mikhail Lermontov)* (1993) 176 CLR 344 (CA), 359 and 380 per Deane and Dawson JJ. See also *Stocznia Gdanska SA v Latvian Shipping Co* [1998] 1 WLR 574 (CA), 588. These passages are cited by Professor Chee.

[31] See C3PA, s 3(2); the (Privity) Act, s 9(2).

[32] Above n 1, 129.

> The Act entitles the promisor to invoke against the third party some of the defences that would have been available to him against the promisee. It does not, however, either entitle or require him to invoke any defence against the third party which would have been available to the promisee against the third party. This can lead to the frustration of the promisee's intentions. This problem is most serious where the third party has induced the promisee to enter into a contract for his benefit through a misrepresentation, duress or undue influence. Once the third party's right has become irrevocable there is no mechanism whereby the promisor is either required or able to invoke against the third party the defences which would have been available to the promisee. An assignment procured by the misrepresentation, duress or undue influence of the assignee could be set aside by the assignor. There is no similar redress available to the promisee under the Act.[33]

The contrast arises because of the different ways in which the two Acts have treated the rights of the promisor and promisee to vary or discharge the head contract. Under s 7 of the (Privity) Act, the court may, on the application of either party, order the variation or discharge of the relevant promise or obligation or both, on such terms as it thinks fit, notwithstanding that variation or discharge by the parties themselves would otherwise have been precluded, unless the third-party beneficiary has already obtained judgment. This means, of course, that a promisee can raise his concerns independently, without having to rely on the cooperation of the promisor. Nor does the jurisdiction of the court depend on the third party's attitude to the requested variation or discharge. It is sufficient that the change sought by the promisee has otherwise been precluded. Once that is established, the jurisdiction of the court to do justice as it sees fit is effectively unfettered.

By contrast, it seems that under s 2 of the C3PA, application to the court must be made by both parties for a variation or discharge to which they both agree. The function of the court is then to dispense with the consent of the third party, which would otherwise also be needed. This it may do on terms if it sees fit, but only if the whereabouts of the third party cannot reasonably be ascertained, or if he is mentally incapable of consenting, or if it cannot reasonably be ascertained whether he has in fact already relied on the relevant contractual term. Accordingly, in case of misrepresentation, duress or undue influence, a promisee might not in every circumstance be without remedy, but he would have to rely on the cooperation of the promisor and, for that matter of the third party as well, unless the latter's consent could be dispensed with by the court in the very limited circumstances stated.

[33] Above n 5, 294.

## Conclusion

From the foregoing, it is submitted that, as one conclusion, there is no need to treat either Act as creating a trust. Any perception that there is a need to do so may well, at least in part, derive from either a particular view of what constitutes a contract or a reluctance to accept that it is possible by statute to create a new set of rights and obligations taking effect as if created by contract.

It is interesting that, in support of his argument, Professor Chee suggests that a New Zealand textbook on contract law has expressed the view that variations of trusts of promises cannot now be achieved without the consent of the third-party beneficiary having first been obtained under the (Privity) Act equivalent of s 2 of the C3PA.[34] From this he concludes that, in New Zealand, it is apparently accepted that the (Privity) Act has modified the ordinary law of trusts. With the greatest respect, however, it is submitted that the relevant textbook passage does in fact say just the opposite, once it is remembered that s 14(1) of the (Privity) Act provides that nothing in the Act 'limits or affects' rights or remedies existing or available apart from it. The textbook passage reads:

> [T]he reform achieved by the Contracts (Privity) Act means that any pressing need to make resort to the law of trusts in order to give a remedy to a third party has now been removed. However, in cases where it is clear that a trust *has* been created it is not limited or affected by the Act. In particular this means that the arrangement cannot be varied without the consent of the beneficiary, pursuant to ss 5, 6 and 7 of the Act.[35]

In other words, as with s 7(1) of the C3PA, the legislative intention has been to leave unaffected existing exceptions to the third-party rule, including the law of trusts.

The other conclusion which might perhaps be drawn from some of the questions discussed in this chapter is that they illustrate a truism: that 'improving' on an existing model may result in the creation of a whole new set of problems. That, of course, is not to deny that such improvements have their own validity, or to suggest that they ought not to have been made!

[34] JF Burrows, J Finn and SMD Todd, *Law of Contract in New Zealand* (2nd ed, Wellington, LexisNexis, 2002).

[35] ibid, 506.

# 11

# Assumption of Responsibility and Pure Economic Loss in New Zealand

IN RECENT YEARS, the New Zealand Court of Appeal has been taken to task for not adopting a single test for the tort of negligent misstatement.[1] The perceived choice for such a test has been on the one hand between assumption of responsibility and *Hedley Byrne & Co Ltd v Heller & Partners Ltd*[2] (hereinafter '*Hedley Byrne*') and, on the other, the New Zealand version of the two-stage test propounded by Lord Wilberforce in *Anns v Merton London Borough Council*[3] (hereinafter '*Anns*'). Preference has been expressed for assumption of responsibility, although that preference has not been unanimous.[4] While the commentators have been concerned with just the one manifestation of the *Hedley Byrne* tort, the principles of that case have, of course, been extended from words to include services, acts and omissions,[5] with an inevitable intermingling of authority, so that the potential relevance of the assumption-of-responsibility approach within New Zealand is not confined solely to negligent misstatement.

As it happens, by the time the first of the comments was published, the Court of Appeal had, arguably, already come down on the side of treating assumption of responsibility as just one of the factors to be taken into account, albeit a central

[1] A Barker, 'Divining an Approach to the Duty of Care: The New Zealand Court of Appeal and Claims for Negligent Misstatement' (2001) 10 *Otago Law Review* 91; J Taylor, 'The Conceptual Basis of the Tort of Negligent Misstatement' (2003) 9 *New Zealand Business Law Quarterly* 177; A Beever, 'All at Sea in the Law of Negligent Misrepresentation' (2003) 9 *New Zealand Business Law Quarterly* 101; N Price, 'The Approach of New Zealand Courts to Negligent Misstatement' (2003) 9 *Auckland Universities Law Review* 1267.

[2] *Hedley Byrne & Co Ltd v Heller & Partners Ltd* [1964] AC 465 (HL).

[3] *Anns v Merton London Borough Council* [1978] AC 728 (HL), 751–2. The New Zealand version of the *Anns* test, as summarised by Thomas J in *Connell v Odlum* [1993] 2 NZLR 257, 265, includes 'all the relevant factors', among them forseeability, proximity, policy, and fairness and justice, and would therefore seem in practice to comprehend all the elements of the English threefold test enunciated in such cases as *Caparo Industries plc v Dickman* [1990] 2 AC 605 (HL) (which include questions of policy: *Spring v Guardian Assurance plc* [1995] 2 AC 296 (HL), 308).

[4] Barker, above n 1, for example, expressly declined to state a preference.

[5] *Henderson v Merrett Syndicates Ltd* [1995] 2 AC 145 (HL), 181; and see *White v Jones* [1995] 2 AC 207 (HL), 268–9 and 288; *Brownie Wills v Shrimpton* [1998] 2 NZLR 320, 325. The expression 'novel situations' has also been used; see, eg, *Connell v Odlum* [1993] 2 NZLR 257, 264.

one, within the two-stage *Anns* approach. The evidence for this includes *RM Turton & Co Ltd v Kerslake & Partners*[6]—a case concerning an auditor's report—where, although *Hedley Byrne* criteria were employed, the tests the majority applied also included fairness, reasonableness and justice. They also remarked that there were no broad questions of policy needing to be considered. Subsequently, in *Attorney-General v Carter*,[7] the Court of Appeal, in a judgment delivered by Tipping J, affirmed that in New Zealand the two-stage test prevails in situations not covered by authority and that, in such cases, the relevance of assumption of responsibility is to the proximity required by it. The latter point has most recently been reaffirmed, obiter, by the Court of Appeal in *Rolls-Royce NZ Ltd v Carter Holt Harvey Ltd*,[8] where judgment was delivered by Glazebrook J. She also stated that the enquiry into proximity includes consideration of the degree of analogy with cases in which duties have already been established, that 'courts should only move gradually into new areas of liability', and that 'the examination of factors that have influenced earlier decisions ensures that any development of the law occurs in a principled and cohesive manner'.[9] Decision by reference to principle alone, it would seem, can no longer be considered sufficient.

Nevertheless, it is clear that the concept of assumption of responsibility, and the learning associated with it, still remain relevant to New Zealand law. As Tipping J observed in *Attorney-General v Carter*,[10] the way judgments are expressed (and therefore, presumably, their general approach and content) can be influenced by the way in which a case has been argued. On the evidence of the *Rolls-Royce* judgment, among others, the issues to be considered under the New Zealand two-stage test are potentially extremely wide-ranging.[11] Accordingly, if counsel can bring his case within *Hedley Byrne* criteria, there could be obvious advantages. As was pointed out by the majority in *RM Turton & Co Ltd v Kerslake & Partners*,[12] to do so would 'usefully' focus the enquiry. Moreover, as Tipping J also observed in *Attorney-General v Carter*[13] (echoing, in this, dicta by Lord Goff of Chieveley and Lord Steyn in the House of Lords[14]), if a defendant has, or is

6 *RM Turton & Co Ltd v Kerslake & Partners* [2000] 3 NZLR 406.

7 *Attorney-General v Carter* [2003] 2 NZLR 160 (CA), 168, [22], and 170, [31].

8 *Rolls-Royce NZ Ltd v Carter Holt Harvey Ltd* CA 259/02, 23 June 2004, [97].

9 ibid, [59].

10 [2003] 2 NZLR 160 (CA), [31] and [32].

11 In *Rolls-Royce*, the judgment lists some 18 factors as being relevant to proximity alone. Jane Stapleton, 'Duty of Care Factors' in P Cane and J Stapleton (eds), *The Law of Obligations: Essays in Celebration of John Fleming* (Oxford, Clarendon Press, 1998) 59, 92–5, lists 29 factors as relevant to the recognition of a duty, and a further 21 that she considers unconvincing.

12 [2000] 3 NZLR 406; and see *Attorney-General v Carter* [2003] 2 NZLR 160 (CA), 170, [32]. On the other hand, the judgment in *Rolls-Royce*, above n 8, [124], does suggest, obiter, that a *Hedley Byrne* claim would be subject to the same or a similar analysis to that accorded the more general negligence claim in that case.

13 [2003] 2 NZLR 160 (CA), [24].

14 *Henderson v Merrett Syndicates Ltd* [1995] 2 AC 145 (HL), 181 per Lord Goff of Chieveley; *Williams v Natural Life Health Foods Ltd* [1998] 1 WLR 830 (HL), 834 per Lord Steyn.

deemed to have, assumed responsibility, it will usually, subject to policy considerations, be fair, just and reasonable to hold him liable for want of care. And where the latter criteria are met, there are unlikely to be general policy considerations militating against the existence of the duty.[15]

Admittedly, to seek to focus enquiry by shaping one's case around assumption of responsibility would not be without its own hazards. The case law and literature are vast, not least because the words 'assumption of responsibility' can bear more than one meaning. Not only has this ambiguity been a potential source of uncertainty, it may also have tended to obscure the possibility that the phrase does in fact cover more than one concept. What this chapter attempts to do is isolate three major variants and to suggest that each of them has its own incidents and criteria that, in turn, can draw at least collateral support from quite disparate lines of authority.

## Assumption of Legal Liability in Tort

In its strongest variant, assumption of responsibility arguably means taking upon oneself legal obligations and liabilities in the tort of negligence, rather as it is possible to assume legal contractual obligations and liabilities by entering into a deed or simple contract, or, in the case of equitable legal obligations and liabilities, by a declaration of trust. The common understanding is that, while contractual liabilities can be assumed, obligations in tort can only be imposed *ab extra*, independently of consent.[16] Thus, for example, a motorist who drives along the highway incurs but does not assume potential obligations and liabilities in tort for his negligence.[17] It may have been his choice whether or not to drive, but his potential liability arises independently of his will. Accordingly, any suggestion that obligations in tort can be assumed in the way that contract obligations can be may well appear counter-intuitive and to involve a departure from the ordinary law. Of course, the problem would largely disappear if contractual liability, while being taken by the parties upon themselves, were also, at the same time, being imposed upon them by law *ab extra*, as some would have it.[18] Assumption of legal liability in tort would then no longer be inconsistent with ordinary understandings. But that, it is submitted, would be to treat assumption as though it were passive rather than active. When parties enter into a contract, they incur contractual obligations and liabilities, with all the consequences that those imply, not because they have been imposed but rather because, within the constraints the law prescribes, the parties have actively, for their own reasons,

15 *Edgeworth Constructions Ltd v ND Lea & Associates Ltd* (1993) 107 DLR (4th) 169 (SCC), 176.

16 See, eg, [2003] 2 NZLR 160 (CA), [23] per Tipping J.

17 It is clear from the context that in his apparently contrary statement in *Harris v Wyre Forest District Council* [1988] 1 QB 835 (CA), 853, Kerr LJ by 'assume' meant 'incur'. A dictum by Lord Nolan in *White v Jones* [1995] 2 AC 207 (HL), 293 is not so easy to explain.

18 eg PS Atiyah, *Essays on Contract* (Oxford, Oxford University Press, 1986) 280 and 282–3.

taken them upon themselves.[19] In the institution of contract, the law has provided a facility, the first purpose of which is to enable them to do so. To take the view that legal liability in tort, if it can be assumed, cannot at the same time be imposed, no doubt is to court difficulty. But that was a difficulty that the chief progenitor of assumption of legal liability in the tort of negligent misstatement was prepared to face. As we shall see, in *Hedley Byrne* Lord Devlin stated clearly that, on his understanding, legal responsibility for negligent misrepresentation was assumed and was not imposed by law.[20] And it is submitted that, for several reasons, that view is not really quite as radical a departure as might be supposed.

## The Conceptual Background

To begin with, it has long been established that at common law there are a number of ways in which the incidents and application of the law of tort can be altered by reference to the individual will, both with and without recourse to contract. An obvious example is the rule of volenti non fit injuria, under which an assumption of physical risks operates also as an assumption of the attendant legal risks. Similarly, and not always by contract, exception and limitation clauses can, as the case may be, prevent an act being a tort, or exclude or limit liability that would otherwise arise or be incurred.[21] Then, too, a person who takes part in a boxing match is absolved from liability for what otherwise would be a series of batteries. By his consent, he stops his opponent's blows being tortious as long as they are delivered within the rules of the contest.[22] In much the same way, permission can prevent an entry being a trespass; or the taking of goods, a conversion. A tortfeasor can also, by his admission, assume legal responsibility for an act already committed, and both principals and employers can accept legal responsibility for tortious acts that their agents or employees have yet to commit.[23]

Of course, none of these examples is strictly analogous, since none of them involves a situation where the will of the actor makes tortious, acts of his own for which he would not otherwise be legally responsible. However, the perception that legal liability can derive from a non-contractual assumption of obligation or duty was not entirely new in 1963. For example, in 1883, in *Heaven v Pender*,[24] Brett MR said of an occupier's liability that 'if you permit a person to enter [premises] you impose on yourself a duty not to lay a trap for him'.[25] Five years

[19] Argued at length in ch 2 of this book.

[20] See text below accompanying nn 37–43.

[21] This was, for example, the effect of the disclaimer clause in *Hedley Byrne*.

[22] A very recent example is *Blake v Galloway* [2004] 1 WLR 2844 (CA) (horseplay among 15-year-old members of a jazz quintet).

[23] For example, by the use of indemnities and guarantees. Compare, too, the 'insurer's' liability of innkeepers and common carriers, and the negligence liability of bailees.

[24] *Heaven v Pender* (1883) 11 QBD 503 (CA).

[25] ibid, 509.

later, in *Cann v Willson*,[26] Chitty J said of that case that 'it was held that the dock-owner had undertaken an obligation towards the [third-party] plaintiff'.[27] In 1910, in *Bank of Montreal v Stuart*,[28] the Privy Council spoke of a solicitor 'undertaking a duty' to the wife of his client.[29] In 1914, in *Nocton v Lord Ashburton*,[30] Viscount Haldane LC referred to 'people [who] can be held to have assumed such a special duty' (to exercise care).[31] And in the 1942 case of *Gold v Essex County Council*,[32] which involved the liability of a public hospital for gratuitous care, Lord Greene MR referred to the 'liability undertaken' in such a case and said that 'the first task was to discover the extent of the obligation assumed by the person who it is sought to make liable'.[33] He was clear that it could not make any difference whether the 'obligation' was 'assumed' gratuitously or for profit. This last point is perhaps reminiscent of the treatment of claims based on a warranty, which depend on the vendor's having warranted the accuracy of what he has said about the subject matter of a sale. There was a time in the later part of the eighteenth century and the earlier part of the nineteenth century when it was possible to sue on such a warranty in either assumpsit or case.[34] Under the former, it would have been treated as a contractual undertaking and, hence, as literally an assumption of contractual legal responsibility as to its truth. Logically, when it was made, a warranty could have been no less an intended assumption of legal liability just because the claim had been brought in case, even if the legal liability thus assumed would have to have been treated as having been in tort rather than in contract.

Thirdly, it should be remembered that a principal point at issue in *Hedley Byrne* was whether damages could be recovered in tort for pure economic loss. Until that case, it had been thought that damages of that sort, and the notion of expectation loss, lay primarily, if not exclusively, within the province of contract.[35] So it ought not to seem strange that when Lord Devlin, in particular,

26 *Cann v Willson* (1888) 39 Ch D 39.
27 ibid, 42.
28 *Bank of Montreal v Stuart* [1911] AC 120 (PC).
29 ibid, 139.
30 *Nocton v Lord Ashburton* [1914] AC 932 (HL).
31 ibid, 948.
32 *Gold v Essex County Council* [1942] 2 KB 293 (CA).
33 ibid, 300 and 301.
34 eg *Stuart v Wilkins* (1778) 1 Doug 18; *Power v Wells* (1778) 2 Cowp 818 (assumpsit); *Williamson v Allison* (1802) 2 East 446; *Jones v Bright* (1829) 5 Bing 533 (tort).
35 eg D Howarth, 'Economic Loss in England: The Search for Coherence' in EK Banakas (ed), *Civil Liability for Pure Economic Loss* (The Hague, Kluwer, 1996) 27 and 29; Lord Cooke of Thorndon, 'The Template of Elegance Resisted' in RB Cooke, *Turning Points of the Common Law* (London, Sweet & Maxwell, 1997) 53–4; J Murphy, 'Expectation Losses, Negligent Omissions and the Tortious Duty of Care' (1996) 55 *Cambridge Law Journal* 43; *Seale v Perry* [1982] VR 193, 201 and 220; *Hill v Van Erp* (1997) 188 CLR 159 at 232.

sought to expand the law of tort to cover pure economic loss, he should have drawn on the concept of a relationship 'equivalent' to contract, wanting only the presence of consideration.[36]

Ultimately, if the law of contract and the law of trusts can be a guide, whether legal liability in tort can be assumed must depend on whether the legal system has provided a facility that the courts recognise as being effective for that purpose. If in *Hedley Byrne* the existence of such a facility was indeed either recognised or confirmed, it might well have appeared to be an innovation, but no more so than was the recognition, in that case, of the right to recover damages in tort for pure economic loss.

## *Hedley Byrne*

One of the problems involved in analysing *Hedley Byrne* is the wide range of views expressed by their Lordships, not all of which are consistent with one another. However, as for Lord Devlin, there are, as already suggested, good grounds for concluding that the dominant meaning of 'assumption of responsibility' was the assumption (in the sense of 'taking upon oneself') of legal liability in tort. There was, for example, his characterisation of the problem before him as a by-product of the doctrine of consideration.[37] He saw the case as one where the relationship of the parties was '"equivalent to contract", that is, where there is an assumption of responsibility in circumstances in which, but for the absence of consideration, there would be a contract'.[38] If that analogy is to be taken seriously, it strongly implies the presence of an intention on the part of the tortfeasor to accept legal responsibility. He went on to say: 'I do not understand any of your Lordships to hold that it is a responsibility imposed by law … It is a responsibility that is voluntarily accepted or undertaken.'[39] Two pages later, he referred to acceptance of responsibility as the 'essence' of the matter and, in the same paragraph, to the defendant's 'assuming a legal responsibility'.[40] His treatment at the end of his speech of the effect of disclaimer and words of exemption also carries the inference that the responsibility being qualified is a legal one.[41] And, although in its context it should not be given too much significance, Lord Pearce in his speech did also refer to 'liability for negligence' being 'assumed'.[42]

*Hedley Byrne* was concerned with negligent misrepresentation, but there is no reason to suppose that Lord Devlin intended what he said about 'equivalent to contract' to apply only to cases of that sort. On the contrary, he said that he did

36 See text below accompanying nn 37–43.
37 [1964] AC 465 (HL), 525.
38 ibid, 529.
39 ibid.
40 ibid, 531.
41 ibid, 533.
42 ibid, 540.

not think it possible 'to formulate with exactitude all the conditions under which the law will in a specific case imply a voluntary undertaking any more than it is possible to formulate those in which the law will imply a contract'.[43]

At the least, 'equivalence to contract' would seem to require something akin to an offer and acceptance, together creating a relationship between the parties. Even an express undertaking of legal liability by a potential tortfeasor would need to be confirmed by his having embarked upon performance, since, in the absence of consideration, the executory promise would not be binding. From the plaintiff, there would presumably need to have been either a request or a reasonable acting in reliance. The latter would also usually be needed in order to show consequential economic loss. It was largely because he considered equivalence to contract required mutuality that Lord Mustill dissented in *White v Jones*.[44]

## Since *Hedley Byrne*

Since *Hedley Byrne*, the notion that assumption of responsibility can mean assumption of legal liability has expressly been accepted by such judges as Kitto J in the High Court of Australia,[45] Purchas LJ in the English Court of Appeal,[46] and Lords Jauncey,[47] Mustill[48] and Nolan[49] in the House of Lords. Again, while in *Smith v Eric S Bush*[50] Lord Griffiths did not think voluntary assumption of responsibility was a helpful or realistic test for liability, he allowed that, if an advisor expressly assumes responsibility, a duty of care would arise, although he thought it extremely unlikely in the ordinary course of events. What would have made it so unlikely, it is perhaps fair to suggest, is that what he envisaged being expressly assumed was more than a merely moral or social liability. That the notion of the assumption being of legal obligation has been widespread was also acknowledged by Lord Browne-Wilkinson in *White v Jones*.[51] There, he sought to replace it with the idea that the assumption meant no more than undertaking (in the sense of embarking upon) a task. Since then, the House of Lords in *Williams v Natural Life Health Foods Ltd*[52] has reaffirmed the notion of an assumption of 'personal liability' and, relying on dicta by La Forest J in the Supreme Court of Canada, has accepted, as a test of liability, whether the plaintiff had reasonably

[43] ibid, 529–30.
[44] *White v Jones* [1995] 2 AC 207 (HL), 283 and 287.
[45] *Mutual Life & Citizens' Assurance Co Ltd v Evatt* (1968) 122 CLR 556 (High Court of Australia), 582, 583, 584 and 586.
[46] *Pacific Associates Inc v Baxter* [1990] 1 QB 993 (CA), 1009, 1010 and 1022 (accept liability for pecuniary loss).
[47] *Smith v Eric S Bush* [1990] 1 AC 831 (HL), 871.
[48] *White v Jones* [1995] 2 AC 207 (HL), 289.
[49] ibid, 294.
[50] [1990] 1 AC 831 (HL).
[51] [1995] 2 AC 207 (HL), 274.
[52] *Williams v Natural Life Health Foods Ltd* [1998] 1 WLR 830 (HL), 836.

relied on the defendant's 'pocket book' or on an 'indemnification' from him.[53] Those analogies, which have also been endorsed extra-judicially by Lord Cooke of Thorndon,[54] indicate that at least the appearance of an acceptance of legal responsibility is required. And that inference is strengthened by the House having also accepted the view of La Forest J that what was involved was an acceptance of 'risk' by the tortfeasor.[55] In the context of pure economic loss, the risk referred to could only have been of legal liability. To take another example, this time from the field of public health, in *McFarlane v Tayside Health Board*[56] Lord Slynn accepted that the alternative to applying a general test for negligence in that case would be to ask whether the doctor or the Health Board had assumed responsibility for 'the economic interest' of a claimant who was being treated gratuitously under the National Health Service. (The claim had been in respect of inaccurate advice given after a vasectomy.) Then again, some additional collateral support might be drawn from references, since *Hedley Byrne*, to 'equivalence to contract' by such judges as Lord Templeman,[57] Lord Goff of Chieveley,[58] Lord Woolf of Maltravers[59] and Peter Gibson LJ.[60] To that list can now be added the following dictum from *Rolls-Royce*:

> Assumption of responsibility for a statement or a task does not usually entail a voluntary assumption of legal responsibility to a plaintiff, except in cases where the defendant is found to have undertaken to exercise reasonable care in circumstances which are analogous to, but short of, contract, and it is foreseeable that the plaintiff will rely on that undertaking. If that is the case then, subject to any countervailing policy factors, a duty of care will arise.[61]

While it may not be easy to envisage actual situations where someone who is not being paid to do so expressly assumes legal liability, Lord Devlin himself gave the example of a defendant who said 'Let me do this for you; do not waste your money in employing a professional, I will do it for nothing and you can rely on me'.[62] More likely, though, are cases where one of the parties to a contract makes a statement or performs an act that is intended to influence the conduct of a third party in ways affecting his economic interests. In the New Zealand case of *Allied*

[53] *Edgeworth Constructions Ltd v ND Lea & Associates Ltd* (1993) 107 DLR (4th) 169, 171; *London Drugs Ltd v Kuehne & Nigel International Ltd* (1992) 97 DLR (4th) 261, 315–16. To similar effect, see: *Mutual Life & Citizens' Assurance Co Ltd v Evatt* (1968) 122 CLR 556 (High Court of Australia), 582 per Kitto J; *McFarlane v Tayside Health Board* [2000] 2 AC 59 (HL), 76 per Lord Slynn and 105 per Lord Clyde; *Harris v Wyre Forest District Council* [1988] 1 QB 835 (CA) 844 per Nourse LJ.

[54] *Turning Points of the Common Law*, above n 35, 19–21.

[55] [1998] 1 WLR 830 (HL), 835 and 837.

[56] [2000] 2 AC 59 (HL), 76.

[57] [1990] 1 AC 831 (HL), 846.

[58] *Spring v Guardian Assurance plc* [1995] 2 AC 296 (HL) 324.

[59] ibid, 344–5. See also *Standard Chartered Bank v Pakistan Shipping Corp* [2003] 1 AC 959 (HL), [21] per Lord Hoffmann.

[60] *Reeman v Department of Transport* [1997] 2 Lloyd's Rep 648 (CA), 684.

[61] CA 259/02, 23 June 2004, [99].

[62] [1964] AC 465 (HL) 531.

*Finance & Investments Ltd v Haddow & Co*,[63] a firm of solicitors gave an unqualified certificate intending that, in reliance on it, a third party would advance $25,000 to the solicitors' client. There was held to have been no contract between the solicitors and the third party. At the least, a solicitor who gives an unqualified certificate or other undertaking subjects himself to the discipline of the court that may, in its discretion, compel performance or order payment of compensation, as in equity.[64] But it might confidently be hoped that someone belonging to a profession that depends upon the integrity of its members implicitly also accepts full legal responsibility at common law, whether in contract or tort. In the event, the Court of Appeal held the solicitors liable in negligence, relying, inter alia, on *Hedley Byrne*.

That decision raises the prospect of using the *Hedley Byrne* type of tort to fill gaps left by legislation relating to privity of contract. But it also raises the further question whether a solicitor's unqualified certificate really warrants only his care in making it, and not also its accuracy. Might not the next step in such cases conceivably be to recognise that the liability in tort assumed by the giver was not confined to care but was absolute, a possible precedent being the recovery for breach of warranty, brought in case as distinct from assumpsit, which obtained until the earlier years of the nineteenth century?[65] And if that were eventually to happen, might not the way then be opened for the development of what would in effect, if not in theory, be a new type of reliance-based contract (with resulting expectation interest) to add to those contracts without consideration, such as deeds, that already exist? As the New Zealand Court of Appeal showed recently in *Antons Trawling Co Ltd v Smith*,[66] there can be situations where it is prepared to accept, even in relation to simple contracts, that consideration may not always be necessary.

Accordingly, while absence of remuneration may for the present make express assumptions of legal liability in tort generally uncommon, they may be found more often where remuneration does exist but is provided under a contract to which the plaintiff was not a party. A certificate intended to be binding on the giver might be one example where the assumption could be at least implicit.

## Implied Assumption of Legal Liability in Tort

Assuming, as it is submitted we can, that one way in which a *Hedley Byrne* tort can arise is through an assumption of tort liability, it has to be accepted that, at

[63] *Allied Finance & Investments Ltd v Haddow & Co* [1983] NZLR 22.

[64] *Udall v Capri Lighting Ltd* [1988] QB 907 (CA); *John Fox (a Firm) v Bannister, King & Rigbeys (Note)* [1988] QB 925 (CA); Rule 607, *Rules of Professional Conduct for Barristers and Solicitors*, New Zealand Law Society (7th ed, 2004) 52–4.

[65] See text above at n 34.

[66] *Antons Trawling Co Ltd v Smith* [2003] 2 NZLR 23 (CA), noted (2004) 120 *Law Quarterly Review* 19; [2003] *New Zealand Law Journal* 54. See also ch 4 of this book.

least in the absence of remuneration, express assumptions are likely to be relatively infrequent. On the other hand, implied assumptions of tort liability may more easily be found to occur.

On the authorities, as well as on the analogy of a contract, the test to be applied would be an 'objective' one.[67] In other words, whether there were held to be an implied assumption would depend not on the subjective intention of the defendant but rather on the inferences that a reasonable person in the position of the plaintiff would draw, having regard to the words and actions of the defendant, seen in the light of the surrounding circumstances, so far as they were known to both parties. Once again, there would need to be an embarking on performance by the tortfeasor either specifically or in the general sense of having taken over management of some aspect of the plaintiff's affairs.[68] Under the test approved in *Williams v Natural Life Health Foods Ltd*,[69] it would need to have been reasonable for the plaintiff not just to have relied on the defendant[70] but also to have relied on him as a potential indemnifier or 'pocket book'. The relevant surrounding circumstances would no doubt include: the known skills or knowledge of the defendant; the particular context, business or social, in which the implied assumption was alleged to have occurred;[71] and whether the defendant was acting under a contract with,[72] or on the apparent behalf of,[73] a third party or pursuant to a statutory duty.[74] In the latter case, the purpose for which the duty had been imposed would obviously be crucial.

Clearly, the burden on the defendant to show it could reasonably have been inferred that an obligation in tort was being assumed (a burden that Lord Steyn described in *Williams v Natural Life Health Foods Ltd*[75] as evidential) would not be light. The implied assumption approach might, therefore, even be used as a means by which the application of the tort was limited.[76] Even so, there are at least some situations in which it could be envisaged that an assumption of tort liability might be implied. One would be the type of case where, in order to obtain an advance, the plaintiff paid for a third party to do a valuation, required by the lender as a condition of the advance, but where all parties were aware that the plaintiff would himself also be relying on it.[77] The same could be true where

[67] eg [1995] 2 AC 145 (HL),181 per Lord Goff of Chieveley. A recent account of what is meant by an objective approach is given by the High Court of Australia in *Toll (FGCT) Pty Ltd v Alphapharm Pty Ltd* (2004) 219 CLR 165.

[68] *cf White v Jones* [1995] 2 AC 207 (HL), 274 per Lord Browne-Wilkinson; *Henderson v Merrett Syndicates Ltd* [1995] 2 AC 145 (HL).

[69] [1998] 1 WLR 830 (HL).

[70] *cf Hedley Byrne* [1964] AC 465, 486 per Lord Reid, 503 per Lord Morris, 514 per Lord Hodson.

[71] eg ibid, 482–3 per Lord Reid.

[72] [1990] 1 AC 831 (HL).

[73] [1998] 1 WLR 830 (HL).

[74] *Price Waterhouse v Kwan* [2000] 3 NZLR 39.

[75] [1998] 1 WLR 830 (HL), 837.

[76] ibid.

[77] [1990] 1 AC 831 (HL).

a service was provided by a public body in the knowledge that it would be relied on by the recipient, where it was acting under a statute intended to serve private as well as public interests.[78] On the other hand, the plaintiff could not expect to succeed (except in unusual circumstances) in a claim for a large amount, brought against an employee who, at the relevant time, was ostensibly acting merely as the agent of his employer.[79] Similarly, a claim against a body having limited functions would also be unlikely to succeed if it fell outside those limits.

## Imputed Assumption of Legal Responsibility in Tort

The third possibility is an assumption of obligation in tort imputed by the court. Since it would be necessary only if the conditions for an express or implied assumption were absent, any resulting imputation would necessarily be fictional. The question then raised would be as to the alternative criteria to be applied if the imputation were not to be purely arbitrary. The answer, it is suggested, is that imputation will occur when a court wishes as a matter of policy (as, for example, in order to fill a lacuna in the law) to find for the plaintiff where one or more of the factors ordinarily needed for an implied assumption are absent. A classic example of that approach, on at least one view, was *White v Jones*.[80] The question there was whether a solicitor could be liable to an intended beneficiary when he had negligently failed to obtain execution of a will before the testator died. One of the issues raised was whether the failure of an intended beneficiary to receive a gift, to which he had never in law become entitled, could be classed as a recoverable economic loss.[81]

All but one of their Lordships took the robust approach of merely asserting that there had been a loss, as had Megarry V-C in the earlier case of *Ross v Caunters*.[82] Only Lord Goff of Chieveley acknowledged that a problem did exist. His solution was that an imputed assumption of responsibility by the solicitors created an enforceable expectation right.[83] That would undoubtedly have been the case had the imputation been of an assumption of obligation in tort, recognised by law as effective for that purpose, on the analogy of an expectation interest created by contract. In *White v Jones*, the imputed assumption also had the advantage of making good the absence of both a request and reliance on the part of the plaintiff.

78 [2000] 3 NZLR 39.
79 [1998] 1 WLR 830 (HL).
80 [1995] 2 AC 207 (HL).
81 ibid, 255, 257, 261 and 267 per Lord Goff of Chieveley; *Seale v Perry* [1982] VR 193, 210.
82 [1980] Ch 297 (Ch). See also *Hill v Van Erp* (1997) 188 CLR 159.
83 [1995] 2 AC 207 (HL), 269.

## Assumption of Legal Liability Disclaimed

If it is possible to assume legal liability in tort, it must also be possible for a party to indicate that no such assumption is being made. As Lord Devlin stated in *Hedley Byrne*: 'A man cannot be said voluntarily to be undertaking a responsibility if at the very moment when he is said to be accepting it he declares that in fact he is not.'[84] That would certainly be true if the alleged assumption were express or implied. If it were not also true of an imputed assumption, that would be another indication of the fictional nature of the assumption.

It has sometimes been suggested that disclaimers of assumption can anyway be largely ignored, reliance being placed on dicta by members of the House of Lords in *Smith v Eric S Bush*.[85] But to read those dicta in that way is to reckon without the particular problem the House was addressing, which was whether a disclaimer could prevent the application of the Unfair Contract Terms Act 1977 (UK), so far as it disqualified notices or terms purporting to exclude liability in tort, if they were unreasonable. The argument accepted in the Courts below had been that, by reason of the disclaimer, there never had been any liability to be excluded.[86] The short answer to that problem was s 13(1) of the Act, which stated:

> To the extent that this part of this Act prevents the exclusion … of any liability it also prevents … excluding or restricting liability by reference to terms and notices which exclude or restrict the relevant obligation or duty.

That this was the correct explanation was subsequently confirmed by Lord Bridge and Lord Roskill in *Caparo*.[87]

Disclaimers are, of course, not the only way in which an intention to assume legal liability can be negatived. Subject to any relevant legislation, there could be no finding against a defendant of an express or implied assumption of such liability if, on the documents and the evidence, the relevant legal risks had been allocated to the plaintiff or to a third person. That might be effected by, for example, the use of exception clauses or the application to the plaintiff of the principle of volenti non fit injuria.

[84] [1964] AC 465 (HL).

[85] [1990] 1 AC 831 (HL).

[86] This according to Lord Templeman, ibid, 848, although the report of the Court of Appeal decision ([1988] QB 743) does tend to suggest otherwise.

[87] *Caparo Industries plc v Dickman* [1990] 2 AC 605 (HL), 620 and 629; although, for a different view, see ibid, 639 and 641 per Lord Oliver of Aylmerton. The contra proferentem rule applies; *cf Yianni v Edwin Evans & Sons* [1982] QB 438 (QBD) (did not 'warrant' had no application to negligence).

## Summary

To summarise to this point, it is submitted that there exist sufficient grounds for the proposition that *legal* liability in tort can, after all, be assumed by a potential tortfeasor. To the extent that that is so (and by analogy with contract), it can extend, to the province of tort, clear doctrinal justification for the existence of expectation interests and for the recovery of damages for pure economic loss. On the one hand, because it will not always be easy to show on the evidence that an assumption of legal obligation occurred expressly or by implication, that very fact might be used by a court, so-minded, as an exclusionary device. But, on the other hand, recourse to the imputation of such an assumption could equally be used as a means of extending the application of the *Hedley Byrne* tort more widely.

In the longer term, and more speculatively, assumption of an absolute legal liability in tort might in time become a means of reducing the disadvantages of the privity doctrine more fully than could a mere duty of care. And if that were to happen, it might even lead to the eventual development of what, in effect if not in theory, would be a new form of contract for which consideration was unnecessary.

# Assumption of Non-Tort Obligation

A second type of assumption of responsibility would cover situations of two kinds. One would be where the assumption is of social, moral, religious, professional, commercial or other such non-legal obligations, and might also include ineffective purported assumptions of tort responsibility. The other would cover situations where the legal obligation assumed is exclusively other than in contract or tort. In both cases, if a tort is held to exist it can undoubtedly be said that there have been both an assumption of responsibility and an imposition of tort obligation or liability.

## Non-Legal Obligation

In practice, there has been little discussion or identification of the precise nature of the non-legal obligations being assumed in any particular case. One exception was *Mutual Life & Citizens' Assurance Co Ltd v Evatt*[88] where, in their joint dissenting opinion in the Privy Council, Lord Keith and Lord Morris of Borth-y-Gest spoke of a person who gave advice as 'putting himself under a moral obligation to take some care'.[89] On the other hand, in *Seale v Perry*,[90] Lush J

[88] *Mutual Life & Citizens' Assurance Co Ltd v Evatt* [1971] AC 793 (PC).
[89] ibid, 812.
[90] *Seale v Perry* [1982] VR 193, 198.

questioned whether the existence of a moral obligation could even be relevant, while in *Lowns v Woods*,[91] Mahoney J insisted that, moral obligations not being legal obligations, the defendant in that case could not be liable in law just because he had had a moral or professional obligation to act. In *Brownie Wills v Shrimpton*,[92] Tipping J also spoke of a strong moral duty as not being a duty for breach of which the defendant could be liable in tort. The express or implied acceptance of a non-legal responsibility would, no doubt, always be relevant as having helped to create a relationship between the parties, but it could not by itself justify the imposition of legal liability.

Clearly, additional factors would have to be present before liability could be imposed and, so far as negligent misrepresentations are concerned, indications of what they might be were given in *Hedley Byrne* itself. Setting to one side Lord Devlin's views, the speeches of others of their Lordships summarised the requirements in very similar terms. Lord Reid, for example, stated the position thus:

> I can see no logical stopping place short of all those relationships where it is plain that the party seeking information or advice was trusting the other to exercise such a degree of care as the circumstances required, where it was reasonable for him to do that, and where the other gave the information or advice when he knew or ought to have known that the inquirer was relying on him. I say 'ought to have known' because in questions of negligence we now apply the objective standard of what the reasonable man would have done.[93]

Lord Morris's version, repeated in almost identical terms by Lord Hodson,[94] was:

> [I]f in a sphere in which a person is so placed that others could reasonably rely upon his judgment or his skill or upon his ability to make careful inquiry, a person takes it upon himself to give information or advice to, or allows his information or advice to be passed on to, another person who, as he knows or should know, will place reliance upon it, then a duty of care will arise.[95]

Similarly, according to Lord Pearce:

> [I]f persons holding themselves out in a calling or situation or profession take on a task within that calling or situation or profession, they have a duty of skill and care. In terms of proximity one might say that they are in particularly close proximity to those who, as they know, are relying on their skill and care although the proximity is not contractual.[96]

While both the second and the third of these formulae refer to the acceptance of a task, in none of the three is assumption of responsibility in the wider sense said to be an essential component of the tort. Elsewhere in his speech, Lord Reid did

[91] *Lowns v Woods* (1996) Aust Torts Reports 81–376, 63,165.
[92] *Brownie Wills v Shrimpton* [1998] 2 NZLR 320, 327.
[93] [1964] AC 465 (HL), 486.
[94] ibid, 514.
[95] ibid, 503.
[96] ibid, 538.

refer to an undertaking to assume a duty as being something to be inferred from the defendant's having chosen to answer.[97] Lord Pearce, too, spoke of materials from which one deduced whether a duty of care was assumed.[98] For Lord Morris, the relevant undertakings of the defendant were to give deliberate advice, to apply skill, to give information and, more generally, to do something.[99] None of them could be relevant in the absence of consideration, unless the defendant had actually at least embarked upon them. The conclusion to be drawn, it is submitted, is that on the version of the *Hedley Byrne* tort contained in the three formulae, the cause of action arises not from any assumption of a less-than-legal responsibility as such, whether express or implied, but rather from the establishment of facts that meet the listed criteria. That would be consistent with Lord Griffiths' statement in *Smith v Eric S Bush*[100] that he did not think that voluntary assumption of responsibility was a helpful or realistic test for liability. In the absence of an express assumption, he thought the phrase could only have real meaning if it were understood as referring to the circumstances in which the law would deem the assumption to have been made. To adapt what Lord Clyde said in *Phelps v Hillingdon London Borough Council*,[101] it might be concluded that the expression 'voluntary assumption of responsibility', if the responsibility were other than a legal one, should be read as 'descriptive' rather than 'definitive'.

That an assumption of non-legal obligation is not a necessary condition of liability when the criteria stated in the three formulae are applied could be said to draw at least some collateral support from the one-time principle that representations be made good. According to an early nineteenth century account by Lord Eldon LC:

> [I]t is a very old head of equity, that if a representation is made to another person, going to deal in a matter of interest upon the faith of that representation, the former shall make that representation good, if he knows it to be false ...[102]

That jurisdiction, he said, also existed concurrently at common law. His dictum was applied a few years later by Sir William Grant MR[103] in a case where a trustee had misrepresented to a third party the entitlement of a beneficiary, knowing that the former would be taking an assignment in reliance on what he was being told. The trustee's defence was that he had forgotten that the entitlement had earlier been reduced by the sum of £10. The Master of the Rolls described the misrepresentation as grossly negligent and ordered that, if the beneficiary failed to make up the deficiency, the trustee himself must do so. The principle was

97 ibid, 486.

98 ibid, 540.

99 ibid, 499 and 502–4.

100 [1990] 1 AC 831 (HL), 862. See also *Phelps v Hillingdon London Borough Council* [2001] 2 AC 619 (HL), 654; *Ministry of Housing v Sharp* [1970] 2 QB 223 (CA), 268 per Lord Denning MR.

101 [2001] 2 AC 619 (HL), 670.

102 *Evans v Bicknell* (1801) 6 Ves Jun 174, 183; 31 ER 998, 1002.

103 *Burrowes v Lock* (1805) 10 Ves Jun 470; 32 ER 927.

further refined by Lord Campbell LC, sitting in the Court of Appeal in the 1860 Chancery case of *Slim v Croucher*.[104] There, a lessor had assured a potential creditor of the lessee that a long-term lease would be granted, forgetting that he had already leased the property to someone else. At first instance, the defendant lessor was ordered to indemnify the creditor for the loss occasioned by his having taken the security of a worthless lease. Dismissing the appeal, the Lord Chancellor thought the situation at common law was quite clear:

> Here was a misrepresentation made by the Defendant of a fact which ought to have been within his knowledge, it was made with the intention of being acted upon, it was acted upon and thereby a loss accrued to the Plaintiff, and there is no doubt in my mind that an action would lie and that it would be for a jury to assess the damages.[105]

The same rule, he said, applied in equity, except that Courts of Equity had superior powers to do justice in minute detail. The principle did not depend upon there being a fiduciary duty. Nor did there have to be moral fraud. Concurring, Knight Bruce LJ felt strongly enough to state: 'A country whose administration of justice did not afford redress in a case of the present description would not be in a state of civilization.'[106]

Subsequently the Court of Appeal in *Peek v Derry*[107] relied upon the same principle, only to have the House of Lords put a stop to its development in *Derry v Peek*,[108] at least for a time. The stage that development had reached to that point was later summarised by Lindley LJ in *Low v Bouverie*,[109] when he said of *Derry v Peek*:

> [U]ntil that case was decided, it was generally supposed to be settled in Equity that liability was incurred by a person who carelessly, although honestly, made a false representation to another about to deal in a matter of business upon the faith of such representation.[110]

All this is not to say that where a non-legal responsibility has been, or appears to have in fact been, assumed it serves no purpose at all. It could, as already suggested, help to explain how the defendant came to act in the particular circumstances and it would also help to provide a context, including a relationship, within which the plaintiff came to act in reliance, or to repose his trust in the defendant.[111] By the same token, a disclaimer of any intention to assume a

[104] *Slim v Croucher* (1860) 1 De GF & J 518; 45 ER 462. It was on these cases that, in *Peek v Gurney* (1871) 13 LR Eq 79, 97, Sir Roundell Palmer QC based his influential statement about such representations being equivalent to a contract.

[105] ibid, 523. See also *Brownlie v Campbell* (1880) 5 App Cas 925, 930 per Lord Selbourne LC.

[106] ibid, 527.

[107] *Peek v Derry* (1887) 37 Ch D 541 (CA), 568, 578 and 585.

[108] *Derry v Peek* (1889) 14 App Cas 337 (HL).

[109] *Low v Bouverie* (1891) 3 Ch 82. Compare the argument of Gardiner QC in *Hedley Byrne* [1964] AC 465 (HL), 471 and 473.

[110] ibid, 100.

[111] eg *Kondis v State Transport Authority* (1984) 154 CLR 672 (High Court of Australia), 687 per Mason J.

non-legal obligation could hardly be conclusive of liability, but it might well go to the reasonableness of the plaintiff's reliance. The main reason why the concept of an assumption of non-legal responsibility has retained its hold may well be the perception that, as Lord Steyn expressed it in *McFarlane v Tayside Health Board*[112] (echoing words used in his earlier speech in *Williams v Natural Life Health Foods Ltd*),[113] assumption of responsibility is simply 'the rationalisation and technique adopted by English law to provide a remedy for the recovery of damages in respect of economic loss caused by the negligent performance of services'.[114]

In sum, it is submitted that under this particular version of the *Hedley Byrne* tort, the reality is that the law imposes liability not because the defendant expressly or impliedly assumed a moral or other non-legal responsibility, but rather because, in the case of a misstatement, it was made when he knew or ought to have known that he was being trusted to be careful, and that what he said would reasonably be relied on by the plaintiff to his potential economic disadvantage. Whether reliance in this sense was 'reasonable' would obviously depend on such factors as the purpose for which, and the context in which, the statement was made, and any relevant statutory background. It would also depend on whether expressly or by necessary implication it was made clear to the plaintiff, at the time, that he must act on his own responsibility and should not look to the defendant for redress.

By the same token, it is submitted that where the act complained of is not a statement or advice, but is some other act or service, an assumption of non-legal liability can to no greater extent be the determinant of whether liability will be imposed. In some such cases, it may well be that a better alternative would be to look not to assumption of liability as such, but rather to the assumption of a task.

## Legal Obligations Other Than In Tort

Included here are obligations such as those arising in trust, under statute or under the disciplinary powers of the court. Unless they were also accompanied by an express, implied or implicit additional assumption of liability in tort, it would have to follow that the conditions under which tort liability would be imposed would be similar to those applying to the assumption of non-legal obligations. One potential difference could be that, where some other form of legal liability has been assumed, it may be that much easier to infer a parallel assumption of liability in tort.[115] On the other hand, in the case of some forms of statutory liability, the 'assumption' may in reality be no more than the assumption of a task.[116]

112 [2000] 2 AC 59 (HL), 83–4.
113 [1998] 1 WLR 830 (HL).
114 ibid, 834.
115 As might be the case, for example, of a solicitor's unqualified undertaking.
116 As, for example, where a hospital is obliged by statute to accept a patient.

## Assumption of a Task

In his speech in *White v Jones*,[117] Lord Browne-Wilkinson identified two categories of case where a special relationship between the parties gave rise to a duty of care to avoid pure economic loss. A fiduciary relationship was one, and the other was where the defendant had 'voluntarily answered a question or tendered skilled advice … in circumstances where he knows or ought to know that an identified plaintiff will rely on his answers or advice'.[118] In both of these categories, he said, 'the special relationship is created by the defendant voluntarily assuming to act in the matter by involving himself in the plaintiff's affairs or by choosing to speak'.[119] He also referred to the defendant's assumption of responsibility for a task. In doing so, he was responding to criticism of the concept of assumption of responsibility voiced, for example by Lord Griffiths in *Smith v Eric S Bush*[120] and Lord Roskill in *Caparo*.[121]

It would seem, therefore, that for Lord Browne-Wilkinson the relevant assumption was of a task assumed, undertaken and embarked upon in much the same sense as a stage actor assumes, undertakes or embarks upon a role in a play. By assumption of responsibility for the task, he appears to have meant an actual taking over of the conduct of, or an acting in, another person's affairs, despite an absence of consideration.[122] The act of the defendant in so doing establishes a relationship for which (on the facts of *White v Jones*) mutuality is not required. Nor is the intended beneficiary's knowledge or reliance, unless reliance is needed in order to show economic loss.[123] Even skill or special knowledge on the defendant's part would seem not to be necessary, so long as reliance and loss by the plaintiff are reasonably foreseeable.[124] What is important is that the defendant knows or ought to know that the other party's economic wellbeing depends on the actor's careful conduct of the other's affairs, or of the performance of his task.[125]

The idea that a volunteer can become bound by embarking upon a task and causing loss has a long history. In *Hedley Byrne* itself, Lord Devlin referred to a number of examples, including *Coggs v Bernard*[126] and a dictum by Lord Finlay

[117] [1995] 2 AC 207 (HL).

[118] ibid, 274.

[119] ibid.

[120] [1990] 1 AC 831 (HL), 862.

[121] [1990] 2 AC 605 (HL), 628.

[122] [1995] 2 AC 207 (HL), 274. This, presumably, is the sort of assumption required for liability for omissions: *Brownie Wills v Shrimpton* [1998] 2 NZLR 320, 329 per Tipping J. See also, eg, *Reid v Rush & Tompkins Group plc* [1990] 1 WLR 212 (CA), 229 per Ralph Gibson LJ; *Ramsay v Larsen* (1964) 111 CLR 16, 28 per Kitto J; *Cornish v Midland Bank* [1985] 3 All ER 513 (CA), 516, 520 and 521.

[123] ibid, 272 and 275.

[124] ibid, 272; *cf Mutual Life & Citizens' Assurance Co Ltd v Evatt* [1971] AC 793 (PC), 812.

[125] ibid, 275.

[126] *Coggs v Bernard* (1703) 2 Ld Raym 909; 92 ER 107. See also, eg, *Wilkinson v Coverdale* (1873) 1 Esp 75; 170 ER 284.

LC in *Banbury v Bank of Montreal*[127] (also referred to by Lord Browne-Wilkinson in *White v Jones*[128]), in which it was said that if a person undertakes to perform a voluntary act he is liable if he performs it improperly, but not if he neglects to perform it at all. Again, in the judgment of the majority of the Privy Council in *Mutual Life & Citizens' Assurance Co Ltd v Evatt*[129] reference was made to the 'ancient' principle that it is the duty of every artificer to exercise his art right and truly as he ought.[130] This principle, it was said, applies to anyone who gratuitously does an act that calls for the exercise of some special skill and competence that he has held himself out as possessing. Lord Browne-Wilkinson's version of the *Hedley Byrne* tort can also be said to gain some support from the references to taking on a task and to the actual giving of advice or information contained in the already-quoted formulae propounded respectively by Lords Reid, Morris and Hodson in *Hedley Byrne.*[131]

Where Lord Browne-Wilkinson's version of assumption differs most from the other two treated in this chapter is that, having dispensed with the need for any assumption of obligation, mutuality or reliance, it has, by making the requirements for the tort fewer and less specific, also made the application of the tort potentially more general. However, in what was an obvious reflection of Lord Bridge's threefold test in *Caparo,*[132] his Lordship went on to consider whether it should be fair, just and reasonable to impose liability on the defendant. And that, in a sense, brings us back full circle, to the New Zealand version of the twofold *Anns* test for liability in negligence.

## Conclusion

When negligence causing pure economic loss is in issue in New Zealand, the courts now apply the local version of the *Anns* two-stage approach if the situation is not already covered by authority or is otherwise 'novel'. What those two expressions mean in practice could itself be the subject of a study. But when they do apply, the local approach can potentially require consideration of an extremely wide range of factors. That being so, anything that focuses the enquiry and narrows its range should have its advantages. That function, it seems, can be served by the 'assumption of responsibility' associated with the *Hedley Byrne* tort and its derivatives.

In practice, though, 'assumption of responsibility' has proved to have more than one meaning. What this chapter has tried to do is identify and explore three

[127] *Banbury v Bank of Montreal* [1918] AC 626 (HL), 654.

[128] [1995] 2 AC 207 (HL) 273. Another analogy is with voluntary bailment: *East West Corp v DKBS A/S* [2003] QB 1509 (CA), 1529 per Mance LJ.

[129] [1971] AC 793 (PC).

[130] ibid, 803.

[131] See text above at nn 93–6.

[132] [1990] AC 605 (HL).

of those meanings. The concept of the assumption of a legal obligation in tort may have limited application at present, even when it is implied or imputed. Rather, its significance may lie in its potential eventually to develop into what in effect, if not in theory, would be a new form of contract without consideration, based perhaps on reliance, at least in part. The other two identified kinds of assumption could, potentially, be rather simpler of application than may generally have been supposed.

While, under the local two-stage test, assumption of responsibility is to be treated as relevant only to questions of proximity and relationship, there are good indications that, once an assumption is held to be present, questions of fairness and justice are unlikely to arise. By the same token, so too would be questions of policy telling against the existence of a tort. If so, the law in such cases ought to be that much more certain, and its ascertainment and application that much more focused, to the potential advantage of clients, counsel and the courts alike.

# Index

Introductory Note
References such as '178–9' indicate (not necessarily continuous) discussion of a topic across a range of pages. Wherever possible in the case of topics with many references, these have either been divided into sub-topics or only the most significant discussions of the topic are listed. Because the entire volume is about 'contract' and 'assumption', the use of these terms (and certain others which occur constantly throughout the book) as entry points has been minimised. Information will be found under the corresponding detailed topics.


acceptance, 7, 16–17, 21, 29, 32, 74–5, 196–8
actual performance, 26, 56–7, 59, 70, 78–9, 137, 167
additional payment, 54–5, 78
advice, 203–4, 207–9
agents, 67, 69, 71, 194, 201
agreement and definitions of contract, 11–12
*Alhazero case*, 142, 166, 169–74
alternative performance, 47, 131, 135, 140–1, 158, 161, 174–6
  cost of, 47, 135, 141, 158, 188
amenity, loss of, 128–9, 146, 154, 156–8
Ames, JB, 2, 25, 27, 39–40, 54, 59
*assumpsit*, 18, 22, 26, 41, 45, 195, 199
assumptions:
  *see also Introductory Note*
  of non-tort obligation
    legal obligations, 207
    non-legal obligations, 203–7
  of obligation, 1, 3, 44–5, 135, 201, 209
  purported, 3, 44
  reciprocal, 39, 58
  of responsibility, 4, 48, 160–1, 191–210
    assumption of non-tort obligation, 203–7
    assumption of tasks, 208–9
    conclusion, 209–10
    implied, 199–202
    imputed, 201–2
    New Zealand, 191–210
    tort, 193–203
    voluntary, 197, 205
  of tasks, 208–9
Atiyah, PS, 7–10, 18–19, 21–3, 25–6, 32–6, 40–1, 66–8
auctioneers, 77–9
auctions, 23, 76
Australia, 4, 10, 107, 109, 114, 124–5, 138–9
avoidance of waste, 154

bailees, 93–4, 102, 194
bailment, 93, 101–3, 121, 142
bargain, 12, 15, 27–8, 44, 141–2, 167
  theory, 12, 17–18, 29, 37
Barnett, RE, 13, 37, 41
benefit and consideration, 53–60
bilateral contracts, 10, 24–5, 27–8, 38–9, 44–5, 78–9
  and consideration, 57–8
  executory, 2–4, 10, 24, 28, 38–9, 57, 78–9
black holes, 165, 167, 175–6
breach:
  discharge for, 100–1
  fundamental *see* fundamental breach
Bronaugh, RN, 22, 24–5
builders, 131, 141–2, 146, 163, 166–7, 177
building cases/contracts, 143, 158, 166, 169–74, 176–8
  and difference in value, 147–9
  reinstatement and repair, 146–7
building owners, 53, 132, 138, 148–9, 170, 176
burden of proof *see* onus of proof
Burrows, AS, 13, 19–21, 43, 48–9, 135–6, 139, 142

Canada, 21, 66, 107, 114, 122, 124–5, 138–9
care, duty of, 87, 96, 115, 118, 170–3, 197–9, 203–5
carriage, 93, 103
  contracts of, 169, 171, 173, 185
ceremonies, 14, 23, 29, 41, 43
certificates, unqualified, 199
charterers, 87, 160–1, 173, 185
charterparties, 81–2, 86, 156, 160, 169, 173
Chee Ho Tham, 181–2, 184, 186–8, 190
Cheshire and Fifoot, 11–12, 20, 59, 66–7, 69, 104, 112–13
Chitty, J, 11, 65, 73, 78, 135, 195
classical common law of contract, 8, 13, 50–1

# Index


classical contract law, 8, 10, 28–9, 33–4, 39, 49
co-promisees, 74
codification, 30–1
Cohen, MR, 14–16, 18–19, 22–4, 27–8, 33, 41
commercial parties, 113, 120, 124, 136–7
common humanity, 113
compensation, 1, 21, 30, 49, 88, 131–2
  principle, 134–46, 154
    application, 137–9
    factors supporting compensation approach, 136–7
    and promises for the benefit of third parties, 139–43
    and reinstatement and repair, 143–6
completion, 3, 55–6, 58, 75, 77, 138, 149
concurrent liabilities, 169, 173
conditions, 41–2, 75, 91–2, 99–100, 103–6, 108, 115–19
  promissory, 85, 105
consent, 16, 87, 161, 189–90, 193–4
consequential loss, 127, 131–2, 134–5, 137, 141–2, 167, 178
consideration:
  and benefit, 3, 53–60
  and bilateral contracts, 57–8
  failure of, 187–8
  fresh, 54–5, 59
  and joint promisees, 65–79
  and performance, 69–72
  and unilateral contracts, 58–9
  and variations, 61–4
consignees, 166, 172–3
consignors, 166
construction, 34, 102–3, 107–9, 111–14, 116, 118–22, 124–5
  rules of, 107–8, 113
  and *Securicor case*, 118–19
consumer surplus, 129, 155
*contra proferentem*, 34, 118, 202
  and exception clauses, 93
contract:
  *see also Introductory Note*
  damages see damages
  definitions, 10–13
    in terms of agreement, 11–12
    in terms of promise, 12–13
  price, 56, 70, 72, 128–9, 147–8, 150
  reaction against classical concepts, 29–37
    formalism, 29–33
    freedom of contract, 33–7
  sanctity of, 1, 43
  theories, 1, 10–11, 13–24, 50
    bargain theory, 17–18
    failure of traditional theories, 28–9
    miscellaneous, 23–4
    need for a more inclusive theory, 37–8
    promise theory, 18–20
    purposes, 14–15
    reasonable expectations theory, 20–1
    reliance theory, 21–3
    will theory, 15–17
  versus trust, 181–90
  for ulterior ends, 35–7
contracting parties, 1, 3, 27, 36, 76–7, 169–70, 178
contractors, 3, 53, 61, 64, 128–9, 140, 172
contracts:
  bilateral *see* bilateral contracts
  building, 143, 146, 148, 158, 166, 169–74, 176–8
  of carriage, 169, 171, 173, 185
  definition of, 10–12, 16, 18, 42
  equivalence to, 97, 136, 196–8
  executory, 22–3, 41
  head, 53–4, 182, 185–6, 189
  new forms of, 44, 48–9, 185, 203, 210
  simple, 18, 44, 61, 72, 183–6, 193, 199
  synallagmatic, 42, 70–2, 75
  unilateral, 3, 42, 45, 49, 57–9, 62, 75–9
Contracts (Rights of Third Parties) Act 1999 (England and Wales), 181–90
contractual liability, 1–2, 35, 40, 43, 50, 160, 193
contractual obligations, 1–3, 16, 46–7, 131, 135–6, 158, 184–5
  legal, 3–4, 14, 39–40, 42–4, 47–9, 58, 131
contractual promises, 1, 28, 39–40, 83, 90, 167, 178
contractual responsibility, 41, 50, 136, 153
  *see also* contractual liability
contractual rights, 82–6, 88–9, 140
Corbin, AL, 2, 20, 25, 32–3, 65–6, 70, 76
cost:
  of alternative performance, 47, 135, 141, 158, 188
  of cure, 127, 131–2, 134, 136, 140, 145–51, 154–8
  of demolition, 127–8
  of performance, 4, 130, 156–7
  of rebuilding, 128–9, 134
  of reinstatement, 148–9, 156
  of repairs, 142–5, 151, 156, 175
covenants, 44, 85, 132, 137, 143–5, 156–7, 173
creditors, 67, 71–2, 184, 206
cure, 127–8, 131–2, 134–6, 140, 145–56, 158–9
  cost of, 127, 131–2, 134, 136, 140, 145–51, 154–8

damages, 22–3, 46–7, 85–6, 100–2, 127–63, 166–71, 173–8
  ambiguity, 130
  and compensation principle, 134–46
  compensatory, 168, 170
  conclusions, 158–9
  cost-of-cure, 151
  exemplary/punitive, 138–9
  expectation, 48–9

# Index


expectation measure of, 35, 47
general, 128–9, 134, 154, 157–8
liquidated, 172
measure of, 47, 128, 134, 141, 147, 163, 167
nominal, 141, 145, 165–6, 173, 175–6, 178
as protection of performance interest, 130–2
recent cases, 159–63
reinstatement (and repair), 163
leases, 143–6
substantial, 165–6, 168, 171, 174–5, 177–8
unreasonableness of cure, 149–50
Dawson, F, 10, 67–8, 71, 110, 112, 123–4, 153
Dawson, JP, 14, 32
deeds, 41, 77, 95, 183–4, 186–7, 199
defective performance, 147, 149, 158, 178
defects, 53, 129, 132, 134, 140, 148, 177
defences, 16, 81–2, 91, 106, 110–11, 122–5
available to promisees, 188–9
definition of contract, 10–12, 16, 18, 42
delay, 55, 81–2, 160, 174
detriment, 22, 24–7, 38, 45, 49, 57, 77–8
deviation, 84, 99–103, 105, 108–9, 112, 114, 121
difference in kind, 104, 112
difference in value and building cases, 147–9
diligence, 115, 118
diminutions in value, 143–5, 147, 150, 162
disappointments, 20–1
discharge, 31, 99–105, 108–12, 114, 116–19, 121–4, 189
disclaimers, 96, 194, 196, 202, 206
disgorging of profits/savings, 153–4
double-dipping, 156, 158–9, 163
double liability, 71, 182, 187–8
*Dunlop v Lambert case*, 142, 166–73, 176–9
duress, 16, 34, 55, 62, 64, 189
duties, 36, 81–4, 86–7, 89–93, 95–6, 192–4, 204–5
existing, 24, 45, 54, 59–60, 63
duty of care, 87, 96, 115, 118, 170–3, 197–9, 203–5

economic benefits of performance, 130, 134
economic end-result of performance, 130–1, 136, 143, 156
economic loss, 9, 48, 130–2, 136, 196–8, 200–2, 206–8
pure *see* pure economic loss
Eisenberg, MA, 15, 21, 31, 35, 47
employees, 34, 84, 115, 133, 137, 194, 201
employers, 62, 113, 115, 118, 165, 171, 194
enforcement, 14–15, 19, 23–4, 28–9, 42–3, 49–50, 131–3
enjoyment, 140, 154, 157–8
equitable remedies, 186–7
equity, 34, 44, 48–9, 132, 182, 186–7, 205–6
equivalence to contract, 97, 136, 196–8
essence of contract, 7–51
conclusion, 50–1
consequences, 42–7
contract theories, 13–23
failure of traditional theories, 28–9
introduction, 7–10
and near-contracts, 47–50
need for a more inclusive theory, 37–8
reaction against classical concepts, 29–37
secret paradox, 24–8
suggested solution, 38–41
textbook definitions, 10–13
estoppel, 10, 13, 48–9, 61
evidence, 23, 37, 40, 145–6, 152, 192, 202–3
exception clauses, 4, 99–102, 104–13, 116–19, 121–4
classification, 88–90
conclusions, 95
consequences of exception form, 92–5
construction, 118–19
and *contra proferentem*, 93
current approach, 81–2
effect, 83–4
and *expressum facit cessare taciturn*, 93
function, 4, 81–97, 105–6, 122–3
and fundamental breach, 105–6
interpretation in relation to function, 90–2
and nature of contract, 92
and onus of proof, 93–5
and residual contractual content, 92–3
and rights intended to be unenforceable, 84–6
and *Securicor case*, 118–19, 122–3
suggested change of approach, 86–7
exchange:
equality of, 34–5
of promises, 3, 25–7, 38–9, 57, 70
exclusion of liability, 87, 95, 111
executory bilateral contracts, 2–4, 10, 24, 28, 38–9, 57, 78–9
exemplary/punitive damages, 138–9
exempting clauses, 81, 90, 104–5
exemptions, 81, 96–7, 116, 196
existing duties, 24, 45, 54, 59–60, 63
expectation damages, 48–9
expectation interests, 132, 199, 201, 203
expectation measure, 22, 35, 47
expectations, 3, 21, 26, 28, 36, 46, 49
reasonable, 13, 20–1, 23, 36–7, 120
expressum facit cessare taciturn, 93

fairness, 35, 49, 191–2, 210
fathers, 67, 74, 140, 177
formalism, 8
form, 30
internal consistency, 30–3
reaction against, 29–33
formation, 1–3, 22–4, 38–9, 44–6, 57–8, 69–71, 106
fraud, 55, 64, 84

freedom of contract, 7–9, 16–18, 28–30, 41, 43
classical controls, 34
contract for ulterior ends, 35–7
reaction against, 33–7
French law, 17, 28
fresh consideration, 54–5, 59
Fried, C, 1, 16, 18–19, 22–3, 29–30, 37, 41
fundamental breach, 99–125
conclusion, 125
contrary trends, 111–12
and deviation, 101–2
discharge for breach, 100–1
doctrine of, 102–5
and exception clauses, 105–6
*Harbutt's 'Plasticine' case*, 109–11
revival of original version, 112–14
as rule of law, 107–8
*Securicor case*, 115–24
*Suisse Atlantique case*, 107–9
fundamental terms, 82, 86, 99, 103–8, 116
Furmston, MP, 9, 11, 65, 69, 87, 101, 140

general damages, 128–9, 134
as alternative, 154
place of, 157–8
Germany, 16, 30–1
gifts, 18, 25, 75, 176–7, 201
Gilmore, G, 7, 22, 29–30, 33
good faith, 35–6, 64
good repair, in, 132, 143–4, 157, 162
*Gourley case*, 133, 138–9
Guest, AG, 16, 20, 65, 78, 105, 119, 132

*Harbutt's Plasticine case*, 99, 108–12, 114, 116–18, 121–2, 127
Harris, D, 129, 150, 154–5
head contracts, 53–4, 182, 185–6, 189
head lessees, 143–4
head lessors, 143–4
*Hedley Byrne line of cases*, 9–10, 48, 136, 161, 191–2, 194–200, 202–9
Holmes, OW, 12, 14, 23, 31, 59, 132
honour, binding in, 2, 87, 173
humanity, common, 113
husbands, 65–7, 69–70, 73–4, 137, 141–2, 166

implied assumption of legal liability in tort, 199–202
imputed assumption of legal responsibility in tort, 201–2
indemnities, 113, 194
inferences, 17, 26, 29, 196, 198, 200
injunctions, 132, 183, 186–7
intention requirement, 152–3
intentions, 15–17, 19–20, 32–4, 41, 44–5, 49–50, 151–3
presumed, 116–17, 160
interpretation, 16, 34, 86, 120, 150
*see also* construction
exception clauses, 90–2

joint promisees, 3, 46, 65–72, 74–6, 78, 186
arguments for joint promisee principle, 67–9
and consideration, 65–79
fallacies, 69–74
and 'parties' to the contract, 72–4
as promisors, 74
and unilateral contracts, 75
*Joyner and Weeks case*, 132, 144–6, 151, 163

knowledge, 94, 134, 200–1, 206

land, 84, 95, 130–2, 141, 150–1, 157, 175–7
landlords, 144, 161–3
Langdell, CC, 2, 8, 24, 26, 30–2, 40
language, 82–3, 115
leases, reinstatement and repair, 143–6
legal contractual obligations, 3–4, 14, 39–40, 42–4, 47–9, 58, 131
legal liability, 76, 193–9, 201–4, 207
legal obligations, 1, 25–7, 38–9, 44–6, 131, 184–5, 203–4
equitable, 193
reciprocal, 39
legal responsibility, 46, 113, 161, 194–6, 198–9, 201
*LEP Air Services case*, 101, 106, 111, 117–18, 122, 124
lessees, 79, 132, 143, 206
lessors, 79, 143, 145, 206
head, 143–4
liability, 22, 46–8, 89–92, 96, 159–61, 192–5, 202–9
concurrent, 169, 173
contractual, 1–2, 35, 40, 43, 50, 160, 193
double, 71, 182, 187–8
exclusion of, 87, 95, 111
legal, 76, 193–9, 201–4, 207
negligence, 172, 194
lien waiver, 121
limitation clauses, 4, 103, 109–12, 116, 118, 122, 125
liquidated damages, 172
literal rescission, 101, 110–11
Llewellyn, KN, 15, 26, 32
loss, 22, 137–8, 140–2, 146, 152–62, 165–79
of amenity, 128–9, 146, 154, 156–8
consequential, 127, 131–2, 134–5, 137, 141–2, 167, 178
economic *see* economic loss
pecuniary, 96, 135, 197

market value, 129, 149–50
measure of damages, 47, 128, 134, 141, 147, 163, 167
normal, 47, 147

# Index


misrepresentation, 16, 189, 205–6
misstatement, negligent, 191, 194
moral obligations, 3, 27, 203–4
mortgagees, 68, 70–1
mortgagors, 68, 71
mutuality, 18, 20, 32, 208–9

near-contracts, 47–50
negligence, 34–5, 87, 96, 171–2, 193, 198–9, 209
  tort of, 9, 193
negligent misstatement, 191, 194
negligent performance, 207
New Zealand, 4, 62–4, 133, 137–40, 145–6
  assumption of responsibility and pure economic loss, 191–210
nominal damages, 141, 145, 165–6, 173, 175–6, 178
non-legal obligations, 203–7
normal measure of damages, 47, 147

oaths, 14, 29, 39, 45
obligations, 3–5, 19–26, 32–41, 43–7, 70–1, 81–3, 104–6
  *ab extra*, 34, 42
  assumptions of, 1, 3, 44–5, 135, 201, 209
  contractual, 1–3, 16, 46–7, 131, 135–6, 158, 184–5
  legal, 1, 25–7, 38–9, 44–6, 131, 184–5, 203–4
  moral, 3, 27, 203–4
  non-legal, 203, 205, 207
  primary, 13, 101, 106, 111, 118
  secondary, 101, 106, 111, 118, 124, 153
  and secret paradox, 26
Ogus, A, 47, 129, 150, 154–5
omissions, 132, 191, 208
onus of proof, 93–5
over-compensation, 138, 158
  *see also* windfalls
owners, 81–2, 146–7, 157, 160, 163, 166, 169–71

*pacta sunt servanda*, 43, 132–3, 149, 163
*Panatown case*, 4, 165–79
  *Albazero* exception, 170–4
  arguments, 166–7
  characterisation problem, 168
  conclusion, 179
paradox, secret, 2, 22, 24–5, 27, 29, 38–9, 41–2
'parties' to the contract and joint promisee principle, 72–4
partners, 68, 75
  retiring, 69, 71
Paton, GW, 11, 16, 29, 83–5
pecuniary loss, 96, 135, 197
performance, 56–7, 59–61, 73–5, 130–3, 139–43, 153–8
  actual, 26, 56–7, 59, 70, 78–9, 137, 167
  alternative, 47, 131, 135, 140–1, 158, 161, 174–6
  and consideration, 69–72
  cost of alternative, 47, 135, 141, 158, 188
  defective, 147, 149, 158, 178
  economic benefits of, 130, 134
  economic end-result of, 130–1, 136, 143, 156
  interest, 4, 130–40, 144–8, 152–4, 156–62
    and damages, 130–2
    extension of potential inclusiveness, 133–4
    and loss problem, 165–79
    other protections, 132–3
    and *Panatown case*, 165–79
  personal, 70, 74
  substitute, 47, 71, 132
personal performance, 70, 74
Phillips, J, 47, 129, 150, 154–5
Pollock, F, 2–3, 8, 12, 14, 16, 24, 26–7, 40–1, 57–8, 86–7
Pound, R, 8, 12, 14–15, 19–21, 32–3
premises, 15, 29, 56, 110–11, 127, 143–5, 162
price, 35, 43, 65–6, 68–70, 129, 138–9, 146
  contract, 56, 70, 72, 128–9, 147–8, 150
primary obligations, 13, 101, 106, 111, 118
primary rights, 84, 86, 88–9
privity, 4, 7, 32–3, 66–8, 73, 181–3, 185–90
  rule, 44, 48, 63, 68, 142, 185
procedural effect:
  exception clauses, 83–4
procedural rights, 83, 89
profits, 57, 64, 77, 127, 138, 153–4, 160
promise theory, 18–20
promisees, 19–23, 45–7, 68–9, 83, 165–8, 174–8, 188–9
  defences available to, 188–9
  joint, 3, 46, 65–72, 74–6, 78, 186
promises, 7–16, 18–23, 25–7, 37–50, 53–9, 70–8, 88–95
  ceremonial, 45
  and definitions of contract, 12–13
  exchange of, 3, 25–7, 38–9, 57, 70
  joint, 68, 74
  nature of, 38–40
  and secret paradox, 25–6
  words of, 25, 38, 41
promises for the benefit of third parties:
  and compensation principle, 139–43
promisors, 19–20, 22–6, 44–7, 49, 56–9, 92–4, 182–9
  joint promisees as, 74
promissory estoppel, 49
promissory theory, 28–9, 34, 37
proof, onus of, 93–4
proximity, 191–2, 204, 210
public policy, 17, 34, 45, 113
punitive/exemplary damages, 138–9
pure economic loss, 9, 191–210
purported assumptions, 3, 44

quasi-deviation, 101–2, 112, 121

Raz, J, 19, 21, 49
reasonable expectations, 13, 23, 36–7, 120
  theory, 20–1
reasonable person, 46, 116, 151–2, 156, 200
reasonableness, 29, 36, 117, 119–20, 125, 149–50, 152–3
  *see also* unreasonableness of cure
  test, 117, 149, 152, 159
rebuilding, cost of, 128–9, 134
reciprocal assumptions, 39, 58
reinstatement, 132, 138–9, 157–8
  building cases, 146–7
  cost of, 148–9, 156
  damages, 163
  leases, 143–6
Reiter, BJ, 8, 15, 19, 21–2, 31, 33–7, 49
reliance, 20, 22–3, 37–8, 48–9, 79, 183, 204–10
  theory, 21–3, 28–9
remoteness, 47, 130–1, 159
remuneration, 199–200
  additional, 53, 55–6
repairs, 132, 138, 141–8, 156, 162, 173, 177
  *see also* reinstatement
  cost of, 142–5, 151, 156, 175
replacement, 30, 55, 162–3, 173
  cost, 163
representations, 48–9, 86, 88, 90, 205–6
*res inter alios acta*, 133, 138–9, 143, 151, 156, 158–9
rescission, 100, 102, 110, 117
  *ab initio*, 123
  literal, 101, 110–11
  and *Securicor case*, 123–4
residual contractual content:
  and exception clauses, 92–3
responsibility, 48, 96–7, 159–61
  assumption of, 4, 48, 160–1, 191–210
  non-legal, 204, 206–7
restitution, 7, 13, 29, 33, 35, 123, 188
restoration, 151–2, 162–3
retiring partners, 69, 71
reversion, 143–5, 162
Reynolds, FMB, 8–9, 31, 47
rights:
  contractual *see* contractual rights
  primary, 84, 86, 88–9
  procedural, 83, 89
  sanctioning, 83–5, 88–9
  substantive, 82–4
  of third parties, 4, 140, 168, 170, 174–6, 181
*Roffey Bros case*, 3, 53–60, 78, 140, 184
  conclusion, 60
  explanation for decision, 56–7
  facts, 53–4
  judgment, 54–6
  meaning of decision, 56
rule of law, 25, 84, 102–3, 107, 110, 112–14, 120–1
*Ruxley case*, 4, 127–34, 146–50, 152, 154, 156–8, 162–3

Salmond, JW, 11, 20–1, 26, 44, 65, 83–7, 124
sanctioning rights, 83–5, 88–9
sanctity of contract, 1, 43
seals, 11, 13, 27, 29–30, 42, 44
secondary obligations, 101, 106, 111, 118, 124, 153
secret paradox, 2, 22, 24–9
  and justification in logic, 27
  need for a different solution, 27–8
  and obligation, 26
  and promise, 25–6
  stated, 24–5
  suggested solutions, 25–7, 38–41
*Securicor case*, 99, 106–7, 109, 111, 113, 115–24
  and construction, 118–19
  in Court of Appeal, 116
  developments since, 124–5
  and exception clauses, 118–19, 122–3
  at first instance, 115–16
  and *Harbutt's 'Plasticine'*, 117–18
  in House of Lords, 116–17
  and rescission, 123–4
  significance for future, 119–22
shipowners, 92, 160, 169, 173
simple contracts, 18, 44, 61, 72, 183–6, 193, 199
solicitors, 195, 199, 201, 207
Stuart-Smith, Sir Murray, 78–9
substantial damages, 165–6, 168, 171, 174–5, 177–8
substantive effect, exception clauses, 83–4
substantive rights, 82–4
substantive rule of law *see* rule of law
substitute performance, 47, 71, 132
*Suisse Atlantique case*, 99, 102, 107–13, 117, 119, 121–2, 125
Swan, J, 15, 21–2, 31, 33, 37
synallagmatic contracts, 42, 70–2, 75

tenants, 144–5, 161–2
  *see also* lessees
terms, 10–13, 90–1, 104–5, 141–4, 183, 188–9, 202–4
  fundamental, 82, 86, 99, 103–8, 116
third parties, 166–72, 174–6, 178, 181–3, 185–90, 198–200
  promises for the benefit of, 139–43
  rights of, 4, 140, 168, 170, 174–6, 181
third-party beneficiaries, 44, 47, 182, 184–6, 189–90
tort, 9–10, 35–6, 47–8, 86–7, 133–6
  and assumption of responsibility, 193–203
    assumption of legal liability disclaimed, 202
    conceptual background, 194–6
    *Hedley Byrne case*, 196–7

implied assumption of legal liability, 199–201
imputed assumption of legal responsibility, 201
since *Hedley Byrne case*, 197–9
implied assumption of legal liability in, 199–202
imputed assumption of legal responsibility in, 201–2
liability/responsibility, 35, 193–203, 207
Treitel, GH, 11, 64–8, 71, 78–9, 105, 111–12, 127
trustees, 143, 178, 205
trusts, 44, 142, 206–7
versus contract, 181–90
law of, 190, 196

ulterior purposes, 34–7, 43
under-lessees, 143–4, 151
under-lessors, 143–4
unenforceable rights, 84–6
unilateral contracts, 3, 42, 45, 49, 62, 75–9
and consideration, 58–9
and joint promisees, 75
unitary systems, 31–2
United States, 7–8, 16, 20, 30–4, 37, 65–6, 124
unqualified certificates, 199
unreasonableness of cure, 149–50

value, 25–7, 127–31, 135–6, 140–1, 143–8, 154–8, 162–3
diminutions in, 143–5, 147, 150, 162
market, 129, 149–50
variation of contract, 3, 48, 54, 140, 189
and consideration, 60–4
voluntary assumption of responsibility, 197, 205
volunteers, 66, 176, 182–3, 186–7, 208

Waddams, SM, 13, 21, 47, 49, 66, 113–14, 138–9
warranties, 13, 86, 88, 95, 100, 103, 195
of seaworthiness, 84, 105
will theory, 15–17
Williston, S, 2, 8, 12–13, 25, 33, 66, 68
windfalls, 138–9, 142, 150–3, 158, 163
apportionment, 155–6
wives, 65, 67, 69–70, 142, 195
words of promise, 25, 38, 41
works intended and done, 150–2